D0231709

UNDERSTANDING POVERTY

Also by Pete Alcock

Poverty and State Support
Social Policy in Britain (2nd edn)
International Social Policy (editor with G. Craig)
Welfare Law and Order (with P. Harris)
The Student's Companion to Social Policy (2nd edn, edited with A. Erskine and M. May)
Welfare and Wellbeing: Richard Titmuss's Contribution to Social Policy (edited with H. Glennerster, A. Oakley and A. Sinfield)
Work and Welfare: How Men become Detached from the Labour Market (with C. Beatty, S. Fothergill, R. Macmillan and S. Yeandle)

Understanding Poverty

Third Edition

Pete Alcock

Consultant Editor: Jo Campling

LRC Stoke Park
GUILDFORD COLLEGE

palgrave
macmillan

361.6 ALC
362.5
179057

© Pete Alcock 1993, 1997, 2006

All rights reserved. No reproduction, copy or transmission of this
publication may be made without written permission.

No paragraph of this publication may be reproduced, copied or transmitted
save with written permission or in accordance with the provisions of the
Copyright, Designs and Patents Act 1988, or under the terms of any licence
permitting limited copying issued by the Copyright Licensing Agency,
90 Tottenham Court Road, London W1T 4LP.

Any person who does any unauthorised act in relation to this publication
may be liable to criminal prosecution and civil claims for damages.

The author has asserted his right to be identified as the author of this work in
accordance with the Copyright, Designs and Patents Act 1988.

First edition 1993
Second edition 1997
Third edition 2006

Published by
PALGRAVE MACMILLAN
Houndmills, Basingstoke, Hampshire RG21 6XS and
175 Fifth Avenue, New York, N.Y. 10010
Companies and representatives throughout the world

PALGRAVE MACMILLAN is the global academic imprint of the Palgrave
Macmillan division of St. Martin's Press, LLC and of Palgrave Macmillan Ltd.
Macmillan® is a registered trademark in the United States, United Kingdom
and other countries. Palgrave is a registered trademark in the European
Union and other countries.

ISBN–13: 978 1–4039–4093–3 paperback
ISBN–10: 1–4039–4093–2 paperback
ISBN–13: 978 1–4039–4092–6 hardback
ISBN–10: 1–4039–4092–4 hardback

This book is printed on paper suitable for recycling and made from fully
managed and sustained forest sources. Logging, pulping and manufacturing
processes are expected to conform to the environmental regulations of the
country of origin.

A catalogue record for this book is available from the British Library.

10   9   8   7   6   5   4   3
15   14   13   12   11   10   09

Printed in China

For Anna and Chris, Tom and Dan

Contents

Part III

Social Divisions and Poverty

Part IV

The Policy Framework

List of Figures and Tables

Figures

Tables

Preface to the First Edition

'What thoughtful rich people call the problem of poverty, thoughtful poor people call with equal justice a problem of riches' (R.H. Tawney, 1913)

I set out to write a book about poverty in Britain with Tawney's famous words echoing in my mind. I felt that in one short sentence he had summed up the main issues involved in both the political and the definitional debates on poverty in modern society. After completing the task I had not changed my view on this; and if this book achieves the goals I set for it, it will be by explaining to those who are new to these debates, or to those who wish to revisit them, why Tawney was right eighty years ago and why today we are still struggling to come to terms with the implications of his analysis.

The title of the book expresses these goals. The book is intended as a textbook, providing students of social policy, sociology and related disciplines with an analysis of the various debates that have been conducted in the UK and beyond on the problem of poverty, and of the policies that have been developed in response to these. The book therefore discusses research on poverty carried out in the UK and elsewhere; but it is not a report of research and it is not itself based on any new or original research. As we shall see, especially in Part II, both existing research and the academic and political debates that flow from it involve major contradictions and conflicts of view – most fundamentally over the very meaning of the word poverty itself.

Academics and politicians have not come to an agreement what poverty is or what should be done about it. Indeed they frequently talk at cross purposes about the size and seriousness of the problem. What all are agreed on, however, is that poverty, where it does exist, is a problem, and a problem that requires policy responses to deal with it. This book is a guide to the various ways in which the problem of poverty has been defined and measured, and to the policies that have been developed in attempts to respond to it. It assumes some knowledge of the social science context of the debate on social phenomena, but presumes no prior acquaintance with writing on or research into poverty and related issues. I hope that the understanding that it provides is accessible and self-explanatory. What it does not provide, of course, is any simple answer to the problem itself – beyond that which is implicit in Tawney's early insights.

PETE ALCOCK

Preface to the Third Edition and Acknowledgements

This third edition of *Understanding Poverty* has been substantially rewritten and extended from the second edition, which was published almost a decade ago. In that time there have been important advances in research and major developments in theoretical debate on the meaning and causes of poverty. These include increasing recognition of the importance of a dynamic under-standing of the causes and impact of poverty and a significant broadening of academic and policy interest to embrace the more expansive concept of social exclusion. At the same time the policy context has been transformed with the election to power of the Labour governments under Tony Blair since 1997. These developments, and many others, have been incorporated into this revised third edition, including a new chapter on the wide range of area-based initiatives which the government has initiated in the new century which build on and develop the local anti-poverty action discussed in Chapter 15.

When writing the second edition of this book I commented in the Preface that most of the evidence suggested a worsening of the problem of poverty in the UK during the period since the first edition. This time it is indeed uplifting to be able to report on many more positive changes, including for the first time a formal commitment by government to end child poverty. Commitments need to be translated into achievements of course, but at the beginning of the twenty-first century the policy climate on poverty in the UK is more optimistic than that which existed towards the end of the last century.

I should like to thank a few people who have supported and assisted me in the preparation of this third edition. Jo Campling encouraged me to write the first edition and was again supportive and helpful, as were the staff at Palgrave. I should also like to thank Ruth Lister, who read through the final draft for Palgrave and provided numerous helpful comments which certainly improved the final version of the text. Particular thanks are also due to Kath Pryce, who helped me during preparation for the writing to locate and sift some of the new material on poverty and who also provided comments on the final draft. As ever, of course, final responsibility for the content remains with me.

PETE ALCOCK

The author and publishers wish to thank the following who have kindly given permission to use copyright material: John Hills and Oxford University Press for Figure 2.1 from *Inequality and the State*; David Piachaud and Jo Webb, and the Joseph Rowntree Foundation, for Figure 11.2 from Chapter 4 of Glennerster *et al.*'s *One Hundred Years of Poverty and Policy*; and Markku Lindqvist and the Policy Press for Figure 4.1, which is derived from Chapter 9 of Gordon and Townsend's *Breadline Europe*. Some of Chapter 7 was also included in Alcock (2004b), published in the *Journal of Social Policy*.

Every effort has been made to trace all the copyright-holders, but if any have been inadvertently overlooked the publishers will be pleased to make the necessary arrangement at the first opportunity.

List of Abbreviations

AA	Attendance Allowance
ABI	Area-Based Initiative
AHC	After Housing Costs
ASI	Adam Smith Institute
BHC	Before Housing Costs
BHPS	British Household Panel Survey
BLS	Bureau of Labour Statistics
CAB	Citizens' Advice Bureau
CASE	Centre for Analysis of Social Exclusion
CB	Child Benefit
CDP	Community Development Project
COS	Charity Organisation Society
CPAG	Child Poverty Action Group
CTC	Child Tax Credit
DETR	Department of the Environment, Transport and the Regions
DGV	Directorate General Five
DHSS	Department of Health and Social Security
DLA	Disability Living Allowance
DOE	Department of the Environment
DPTC	Disabled Person's Tax Credit
DSS	Department of Social Security
DWA	Disability Working Allowance
DWP	Department for Work and Pensions
EAPN	European Anti-Poverty Network
EBL	European Baseline Living
EBN	European Baseline Needs
EC	European Commission
ECHP	European Community Household Panel
EFS	Expenditure and Food Survey
EPA	Educational Priority Area
ERDF	European Regional Development Fund
ESF	European Social Fund
EU	European Union
FBU	Family Budget Unit
FC	Family Credit
FEOGA	European Agricultural Guidance and Guarantee Fund
FES	Family Expenditure Survey
FIS	Family Income Supplement
GHS	General Household Survey
GIS	Geographical Information Systems
GLC	Greater London Council
HB	Housing Benefit
HBAI	Households Below Average Incomes
ID	Indices of Deprivation
IEA	Institute of Economic Affairs

IFS	Institute for Fiscal Studies
ILO	International Labour Organisation
IMD	Index of Multiple Deprivation
IMF	International Monetary Fund
IS	Income Support
LIF	Low Income Families
LIS	Luxembourg Income Study
LSE	London School of Economics
LSP	Local Strategic Partnership
LWT	London Weekend Television
MA	Mobility Allowance
MORI	Market and Opinion Research International
MUD	Moralistic and Underclass Discourse
NA	National Assistance
NAB	National Assistance Board
NACAB	National Association of Citizens' Advice Bureaux
NCC	National Consumer Council
NDC	New Deal for Communities
NHS	National Health Service
NI	National Insurance
NPI	New Policy Institute
NRF	Neighbourhood Renewal Fund
ODPM	Office of the Deputy Prime Minister
OECD	Organisation for Economic Co-operation and Development
OEO	Office of Economic Opportunity
ONS	Office of National Statistics
OPCS	Office of Population Censuses and Surveys
PSE	Poverty and Social Exclusion Survey
PSI	Policy Studies Institute
PSID	Panel Study of Income Dynamics
RCU	Regional Co-ordination Unit
RED	Redistribution and Egalitarian Discourse
SB	Supplementary Benefit
SBC	Supplementary Benefit Commission
SDA	Severe Disablement Allowance
SERPS	State Earnings Related Pensions Scheme
SEU	Social Exclusion Unit
SID	Social Integrationist Discourse
SOAs	Super Output Areas
SRB	Single Regeneration Budget
SSP	Second State Pension
TAS	Tribunal Appeals Service
TUC	Trades Union Congress
UK	United Kingdom
UN	United Nations
UNDP	United Nations Development Programme
UNICEF	United Nations Children's Fund
US	United States
WFTC	Working Families Tax Credit
WHO	World Health Organisation
WTC	Working Tax Credit

Part I

The Context of Poverty

What is Poverty?

SUMMARY OF KEY POINTS

- There are different definitions and measures of poverty. Poverty is a contested concept.
- Poverty is a problem – something must be done about it. Hence academic and political debate on poverty is generally *prescriptive*.
- Poverty is not the same as inequality. All societies are unequal to some extent.
- The history of poverty in the UK reveals how it is in part a product of changing social and economic trends but has also been shaped by the policies adopted to respond to it.
- Research on poverty, beginning at the end of the nineteenth century, has revealed how it has remained a problem in the UK, despite growing affluence and the introduction of welfare policies.
- The legacy of a distinction between the 'deserving poor' and the 'undeserving poor' remains a potent element of academic and political debate on poverty.

Why poverty is a problem

> Poverty has various manifestations, including lack of income and productive resources to ensure sustainable livelihoods; hunger and malnutrition; ill-health; limited or lack of access to education and other basic services; increased morbidity and mortality from illness; homelessness and inadequate housing; unsafe environments and social discrimination and exclusion. (*Copenhagen Declaration*, United Nations, 1995, p. 57)

> Children who grew up in poverty in the 1970s consistently did worse at school, were six times less likely to enter higher education, one and a half times more likely to be unemployed and earned ten per cent less during their lifetimes than those who did not experience poverty. (*The State of the Nation*, Paxton and Dixon, 2004, p. 9)

As these quotations reveal, poverty is recognised as a problem both nationally and internationally. It is a problem that is not just about money, but also about a wide range of dimensions of deprivation and exclusion; and it affects us not just now but potentially throughout the course of our lives – and these are issues that we will return to discuss in more depth later in this book. As we shall also see there is much debate and disagreement amongst both academics and policy-makers about how to define and to measure poverty, and hence there is no one correct, scientific, agreed definition. Poverty is inherently a contested concept.

However, academics, policy-makers and even politicians do agree about one thing, that poverty is a problem. Whatever the definition or description of poverty, whatever state of affairs the authors of these are seeking to draw our attention to, the underlying message is that poverty is not just a state of affairs, it is an *unacceptable* state of affairs – it implicitly contains the question, what are we going to do about it? Now in practice, of course, many commentators perhaps do have a clear idea of what they think should be done about poverty, and their description and definition of it is usually intended to provide a justification for this. In debates about poverty the ends and the means – and the terms – are always inextricably intertwined. Thus what commentators mean by poverty depends to some extent on what they intend or expect to do about it. Consequently academic and political debate about poverty is not merely descriptive, it is *prescriptive*. Thus in understanding poverty we need to recognise that, not only are there differences of view over the nature of the problem, but also over what should be done about it.

This can perhaps be exemplified by looking at recent political debate about poverty in the UK, although poverty is an international problem too, as we discuss in Chapter 4. That poverty is a problem requiring political action seems clearly to be recognized by the Labour government at the beginning of the twenty-first century. We will discuss the wide range of measures that they have introduced to combat what they define as poverty and social exclusion in Part IV; but most significant is the commitment that they have made to end child poverty. It was captured in the words of the Prime Minister, Tony Blair, in his Beveridge lecture in 1999, 'And I will set out our historic aim that ours is the first generation to end child poverty forever, and it will take a generation' (Blair, 1999, p. 7).

This spawned a debate about how child poverty should then be defined and measured in order to assess the government's achievements (for summaries of some of these debates see Dornan, 2004; Sutherland *et al.*, 2003; and Piachaud and Sutherland, 2002). Some argued that the government was not meeting its target because, as overall living standards rose, a measure based on families with incomes somewhere below the average would still leave many children in poverty; while others pointed out that compared to the standards existing in 1997, when the commitment was made, significant improvement had been made. Of course both of these involve rather different measures of poverty; and they prompted the government to initiate a formal consultation about how to measure child poverty, which we discuss at the end of Chapter 5. Despite a strong commitment to combating poverty by government therefore, issues of the definition and measurement poverty became central to the policy debate.

This compares interestingly with the policies of the Conservative governments under Margaret Thatcher in the 1980s. At this time the government was keen to play down the problem of poverty and argue that government policy should be focused instead upon promoting wealth more generally by encouraging overall economic growth and reducing commitments to redistribute resources from those who were rich to those who were poor. In 1985, the then Secretary of State for Social Security, John Moore famously said,

> The evidence of improving living standards over this century is dramatic, and it is incontrovertible. When the pressure groups say that one-third of the population is living in poverty, they cannot be saying that one-third of people are living below the draconian subsistence levels used by Booth and Rowntree. (Moore, 1989, p. 5)

What he meant by this was that those who argued that the relative measures of poverty which showed a third of the British population were in poverty in the 1980s ignored the fact that all of the population were better off at the end of the last century than at the beginning; and therefore that, by the measures used then by researchers such as Booth and Rowntree (to whom we shall return shortly), there were few or no people who could still be counted as poor. Here again was an implicit dispute about the values of different measures of poverty linked to a political commitment about the eradication of poverty (or in this case the lack of need to do this).

Therefore, poverty is a contested concept and debates about its meaning are inextricably bound up with debates about what, if anything, to do about it. In effect this means that an understanding of poverty requires us also to undertake an understanding of the social policies that have been developed in response to it and have thus removed, restructured or even recreated it. Indeed there are many who argue that poverty is in part a product of the social policies pursued by states which may even have forced some people into poverty, a point to which we shall return shortly. Certainly it is the case that, in Britain at the beginning of the twenty-first century, the problems of determining who is poor, how poverty is experienced and how it may or may not be escaped have been heavily influenced by past policies with a long and complex history.

Poverty, inequality and exclusion

Debates about the meaning of poverty also frequently overlap with debates about the extent of inequality within society. It is worth bearing in mind here that all societies exhibit some degree of inequality. Even if it were desirable for everyone to be equal (and this rather begs the questions of how we, or they, might measure this) there is no evidence that equality has been achieved in practice in any social order. The political, and the academic, debates about equality therefore turn in practice on attempts to determine the extent of inequality within society and desirability of seeking to reduce the gap between those at the top and the bottom of the distribution of income and wealth. And, as with poverty, academic debate about how to measure inequality is a complex and a contested one – for instance, do we just measure inequalities in incomes or should we also include holdings of wealth and other material assets such as housing? What is more, as we shall see in Chapter 6, many measures of poverty in fact are based upon data about inequalities, for instance counting as poor those with incomes less than a certain proportion of national average levels.

Certainly levels of inequality within society are, like poverty, linked to political views about the acceptability of differing levels of inequality and the desirability of pursuing policies to reduce, or expand, these differences. It is no coincidence therefore that levels of inequality increased in the UK in the 1980s at a time when the government was more concerned with the promotion of market-based economic growth than with the distribution of additional resources to those in poverty. Although, as Figure 2.2 reveals, there have been other fluctuations in inequality before and after this.

Whether increasing levels of inequality within society is a good or a bad thing is, of course, a matter of opinion, and a concern of politics. Opinions are hotly disputed about whether increasing inequality is acceptable – or rather about the extent of inequality that should be tolerated. But the dispute here is about the extent of inequality, not the existence of it. Poverty, however, is the unacceptable dimension of inequality. Those who are defined as poor are not just those at the bottom of the distribution of resources, they are those who have too few resources to live within society. Poverty means not having enough; and, as we said above, it implies that something should be done about this – usually to redistribute resources to those who are poor to raise their standard of living. Such redistribution will also reduce inequality to some extent, although how this impact is felt will depend upon where the resources given to those in poverty have come from. But the aim here is to remove poverty, not to reduce inequality.

In her recent book on poverty Lister (2004) discussed these academic and political debates about poverty and inequality in more depth. She linked them to some of the definitional and measurement issues to which we shall return in Part II, and situated them within an analysis of the different conceptual debates about poverty which underpin these. She also discussed the relationship between poverty and social exclusion, a term which is increasingly used as both an additional and an alternative problem on which to focus public policy. She showed how this concept had developed from international, and in particular EU, policy debate to come to influence current academic research and policy development in the UK.

We will return in Chapter 8 to discuss social exclusion in more detail. In simple terms, though, it is generally used to refer to circumstances of deprivation and disadvantage that extend beyond lack of material resources which are generally associated with measures of poverty, which means that people may be socially excluded even if they are not materially poor. However social exclusion, like poverty, is a prescriptive concept – it suggests an unacceptable state of affairs requiring policy action. This is also true of another relatively new concept, social polarisation, which is a broader conceptualisation of inequality implying not just differences in levels of resources but also the development of undesirable gaps between social groups.

For many commentators, such as Lister and most of the others who will be discussed in this book, it is this political and moral terrain within which the debate on poverty, exclusion and polarisation is situated that makes it so attractive for study and argument. It is because poverty is not just one aspect of inequality, but the unacceptable face of extreme inequality, that it is so important to study it; and it is because the identification of poverty requires policy action to respond to it that both academics and politicians have been concerned to identify it. It is the moral and the political thrust of poverty research that is its great attraction, and as the policy debate on poverty has developed it has attracted some of the most eminent and important academics and politicians concerned with social policy in Britain and beyond.

Creating poverty

Poverty exists within a dynamic and changing social order; and to some extent, as we have suggested, it is created by, or at least *recreated* by, the social and economic policies that have developed over time to respond to or control it. Thus the history of poverty involves an examination of the policies directed at or developed for those who are poor. As Vincent (1991) discusses in his history of poverty in Britain in the twentieth century, this interrelation between poverty and policy has consistently shaped the position of people who are poor within all aspects of the broader social structure.

It is possible to extend the history of poverty as far back as the history of society itself, but most of those writing historically about poverty in Britain trace the current development of poverty and anti-poverty policy from the period of the gradual replacement of feudalism by capitalism as the modern economy began to develop in the seventeenth and eighteenth centuries. Indeed in his book on the history of poverty in Britain, Novak (1988) argued that it was only at that point that poverty was created. This is because at that time the majority of people were separated from the land and became workers, they thus lost control over the means of producing material support and became dependent on wages from paid labour. After that those who could not work for wages could not support themselves and thus became poor.

Poverty, it is argued from this perspective, is therefore a product of capitalism, and it is sustained and recreated by capitalism in order to provide a discipline – through fear of poverty – for workers to maintain their commitment to the labour market. For Novak, therefore, poverty is caused by the logic of the capitalist wage labour market and is maintained by capitalism, as he further argued in 1995 (Novak, 1995); it will thus only be eliminated when capitalism is replaced by some other economic system.

There are, however, some serious problems with such a strict economic, or Marxist, approach to the understanding of poverty, in particular its failure to perceive or discuss poverty within other economic systems and its rejection of any attempts to ameliorate or reduce poverty within capitalism. It is also over simplistic in its assumption that modern economies such as Britain experience only a capitalist economic order. Arguably the British economy has only ever been partly capitalist. Elements of feudalism survived alongside capitalism during the early period of capital development; and more recently collective or state-owned forms of production have developed within capitalism – prompting some commentators to refer to modern Britain as a 'mixed economy' (Crosland, 1956). Consequently poverty in Britain is the product of a range of economic and other social forces, and not only of the structural exclusion of the capitalist wage labour market.

However, the link between poverty and the development and control of the wage labour market is an important, indeed a crucial one. Clearly exclusion from paid labour is likely to lead to poverty when there are no, or few, other sources of material support. At the same time the employers of wage labour will wish to maintain a ready and willing surplus of workers to undertake paid employment at the lowest possible cost. State policies to respond to the problem of poverty have always been directly influenced by such demands, and have created a legacy of policy priorities that have shaped images of the problem of poverty and the needs of those who are poor.

Thus early laws dealing with the 'landless poor', dating from 1349, branded them as vagrants and subjected them to controls to prevent unwanted competition for their labour. Through a series of later statutes, in 1530, 1536 and 1547, these controls became more extensive and also began to invoke a distinction between those who were poor and unable to work and support themselves, such as the elderly or sick, and those who were poor but were able in theory at least to support themselves. It was a distinction later represented in the categories of the *deserving* and the *undeserving* poor.

- The 'deserving poor' were those in social groups who were not felt to be able to do much to help themselves, generally the elderly, children or the sick and disabled. For them poverty was an unfortunate event and would justify state help to alleviate their plight.
- The 'undeserving poor' were those of working age (particularly men) who could, and should, expect to provide for themselves and their families through paid labour. For them poverty was assumed to be the product of idleness, indolence and possibly criminal intent and therefore justified punitive policies of control designed to encourage or force those experiencing it into employment and self-sufficiency.

During the time of Elizabeth I this approach was encapsulated in the Poor Law Act of 1601, the aims of which, according to Golding and Middleton (1982, p. 11), were work discipline, deterrence and classification. The Poor Law was the most important policy development dealing with poverty until the end of the nineteenth century; and it was a development that focused in particular on control and deterrence. This could be seen most clearly in the growth of the institution of the workhouse or bridewell. Workhouses were institutions to which poor and destitute individuals could be sent to be provided for if they could not provide for themselves. This was a form of poverty relief, but the regime within workhouses was extremely harsh and punitive so as to discourage both present and potential residents from perceiving them to be a desirable alternative to employment and self-sufficiency.

However, workhouses could not provide for all who were poor, especially in rural areas at times of low wages and high prices. Thus after 1795 the *Speenhamland* system (so called because of the parish in Berkshire where it was reputed to have been introduced) of the local payments to top up agricultural workers' wages to meet higher prices was introduced, and spread rapidly. This was an indiscriminate and costly form of support, however, and it did not include direct disciplinary measures of control or encouragement of self-support. It was one the key concerns of a major review of the Poor Law by a Royal Commission, established up in 1832, and associated with the ideas of Edwin Chadwick, the civil servant who worked on it. The Commission was followed by the Poor Law Amendment Act of 1834 in which 'outdoor relief', as Speenhamland payments were called, was ended; parish control of the Poor Law was replaced by central and uniform administration; and the workhouse test of encouragement to self-sufficiency was intended to be invoked for all.

Central to the philosophy of the 1834 Poor Law was the notion of 'less eligibility'. This was the belief that the support provided by the state should confer a lesser status than that of the lowest labourer, in order to encourage all who were poor to seek any employment rather than remain dependent upon the state. As the 1834 report put it: 'The first and most essential of all conditions ... is that his situation on the whole shall not be made really or apparently so eligible as the situation of the independent labourer of the lowest class' (quoted in Novak, 1988, p. 46).

The workhouse test was of course the epitome of the idea of less eligibility, and its inhospitable regime underlined the punitive attitude towards poverty upon which the Poor Law was based and which dominated nineteenth-century Victorian attitudes towards the problem of poverty. Indeed it was evidence of a more fundamental feature of the Victorian conception of the problem of poverty, and that was the belief that it was not poverty, but *pauperism*, that was the real problem.

Behind the notion of pauperism was the assumption was that it was not the condition of poverty that should be the concern of policy but the people who were experiencing it, the paupers. And for most paupers, certainly the 'undeserving poor', the experience of poverty was the product of the inter-action of the twin problems of indolence and vice. Therefore state policies should not aim to ameliorate the experience of poverty, but rather should seek to counteract its presumed causes in indolence and vice by encouraging self-sufficiency and penalising dependency. That this also enforced labour discipline amongst the workers by putting them in fear of losing their jobs and falling into poverty was also no coincidence. State support for the labour market through social policy, as well as through the laws of contract and combination, was part of the agenda of reform of nineteenth-century British government. Despite the protestations by some politicians therefore of adherence to the ideals of a *laissez-faire* non-interventionist politics, the nineteenth century response to the pauperism created a policy framework that resulted in definite attempts to shape and control the lives of those experiencing poverty.

This is a legacy that has continued to influence debate and policy on poverty ever since. As we shall see in Chapter 14, although the gradual replacement of the Poor Law by other forms of insurance-based social security and national assistance in the twentieth century removed some of the harshest aspects of the workhouse test, the notions of less eligibility and labour market discipline have continued to dominate state policy responses to poverty and to maintain the priorities developed in these earlier forms of state control. Modern social security benefits have by and large been maintained at low levels of payment in order to prevent any competition with low wages, and benefits for the unemployed have generally required recipients to demonstrate that whilst receiving state support they are also seeking employment. Thus state policies have continued to be predicated upon support for the labour market and an attempt to divide 'the poor' from the employed.

Research on poverty

Not surprisingly, perhaps, the draconian Poor Law policies of the nineteenth century did not in practice lead to the removal of poverty or pauperism. Despite the fact that, at the end of the century, the UK was the wealthiest and most powerful country in the world, large sections of its population were still living in poverty. This was revealed most graphically in the first modern research on poverty carried out in London in the 1880s and 1890s by Charles

Booth. Booth's research was extensive and eventually ran to seventeen volumes; but it was the first volume, *Life and Labour of the People of London*, which appeared in 1889 which made the biggest impact, demonstrating that almost a third of people living in London were poor. Booth's evidence was drawn from a large-scale survey carried out in London, and it established a tradition, now respected across the world, of basing academic and political debate about poverty on empirical evidence of the condition, and numbers, of those who are poor. It also made a major political impact, in particular, because of the imperative, discussed above, that something should be done about it.

In fact nothing was done about it, at least not straight away – although, as we discuss in Chapter 14, at the beginning of the next century the Poor Law was subject to review and new policies to combat poverty introduced. However, Booth's research set an example to others, and was followed in particular by another of the 'founding fathers' of modern poverty research, B. Seebohm Rowntree. Rowntree was the son of Joseph Rowntree, owner of the chocolate factory in York and himself a supporter of progressive policies to improve society. Seebohm Rowntree was inspired to conduct research in his home town to see if the extent of poverty in York was as great as that discovered by Booth in London. This he did by surveying over 11,000 households in York and developing a relatively sophisticated definition of poverty by which to measure the extent of the problem, which we will return to look at in a little more detail in Chapter 5. His findings were published in an extensive and fascinating book (Rowntree, 1901), which has recently been republished in full, with an introduction by Bradshaw explaining in detail how, and why, Rowntree carried out the research (Rowntree, 2000).

Rowntree's research revealed high levels of poverty in York too (28 per cent compared to Booth's 30 per cent), and Rowntree also saw the research as a call to action for government. Although, given that many of those found to be poor were in paid work on low wages, it had implications for local employers too, including presumably the Rowntree chocolate factory. Rowntree continued his commitment to research on poverty and repeated his study in York in the 1930s and the 1950s (Rowntree, 1941; Rowntree and Lavers, 1951), with these studies revealing continuing high levels of poverty in the 1930s and a significant reduction in the 1940s, at a time when new social security measures were being introduced. He also, therefore, established a tradition for longitudinal research, tracking the changing circumstances of people over time, which has only recently been taken up again in earnest by poverty researchers, as we explain in Chapter 7.

In the early part of the twentieth century further research on poverty was developed, in particular at the London School of Economics (LSE) with the support of the Ratan Tata Foundation, including the work of Bowley and Burnett-Hurst (1915) and Tawney (1913 and 1931, quoted at the beginning of this book). However, it was some time after the welfare reforms of the mid twentieth century and Rowntree's final, more optimistic, report on poverty in York that the next major development in academic and policy debate about poverty came.

As we discuss in Chapter 14, the welfare reforms of the 1940s had been intended, *inter alia*, to address the problem of poverty, or 'want' as Beveridge referred to it in his famous report on social security (Beveridge, 1942); and Rowntree's final report seemed to confirm that this had to some extent been achieved. However, a new group of LSE researchers, led by Townsend, began to undertake new research in Britain in the 1950s and 1960s to assess the extent to which poverty had, or had not, been eradicated by welfare reform. Townsend's research used new methods, in particular the analysis of statistical data collected by the government itself, and adopted a new approach to defining poverty using an explicitly relative measure, linking it to broader changes in affluence, as we discuss in Chapter 5. Townsend's early ideas were published in 1954. In the 1960s the first significant findings were published (Abel Smith and Townsend, 1965), revealing that high levels of poverty remained in modern Britain, despite the reforms of the welfare state. And in the 1960s Towsend led a major survey of poverty in the UK, the first signifi-cant such study since Rowntree, which, when it was eventually published in 1979, revealed in great detail the scale of modern poverty both statistically and in qualitative description, as we discuss in Chapter 5 (Townsend, 1979).

This revitalisation of research has sometimes been referred to as the 'rediscovery of poverty', and it provided a catalyst for further studies of the problem to be developed. Since the 1960s the scale and the breadth of research on poverty has extended significantly, with more complex definitions and measures being adopted and more sophisticated methodological approaches being used to measure and describe poverty. Poverty research since then has also extended beyond the UK. The European Union now conducts research across the (currently 25) member states, and broader comparative research is supported by international datasets such as the Luxembourg Income Study, discussed in Chapter 6. As we shall see in Chapter 4, anti-poverty policy also now is increasingly developed and implemented on an international scale.

In the early 1990s, one hundred years after Seebohm Rowntree's initial research, the Joseph Rowntree Foundation, commissioned a series of major research projects on poverty and inequality in Britain. The findings from this research suggested that despite a century of research the level of poverty remained high and growing (Barclay, 1995; Hills, 1995), a point to which we shall return in Chapter 2. The Rowntree Foundation also supported some research in York in the later 1990s to examine to the extent of poverty there a hundred years after the first research (Huby *et al.*, 1999), although this did not include an empirical survey to compare with that originally carried out under Seebohm Rowntree, as Bradshaw explains in his introduction to the repro-duction of Rowntree's 1901 publication (Rowntree, 2000).

This history of poverty therefore reveals the complex interaction of academic research, political debate and policy development; and this history is discussed in more detail in a fascinating overview of a century of poverty research and policy by Glennerster *et al.* (2004). Research has become more extensive and more sophisticated, as we shall see in Part II, and the evidence reveals that poverty is a complex and extensive problem affecting a wide range of different groups, as we discuss in Part III. The policies that have been developed to combat poverty have also become more varied in both their aims and their practices, and these are explored in more depth in Part IV. Nevertheless the legacies of the past remain as powerful influences on contemporary thinking and future action. The Poor Law may now be consigned to history, but modern policy-makers still wrestle with the concern to balance support for the 'deserving poor' with control and exhortation of the 'undeserving poor'.

Who is Poor?

SUMMARY OF KEY POINTS

- Changing patterns of poverty distribution reveal that there was a significant increase in poverty and inequality in the UK towards the end of the last century.
- At the beginning of the new century there have been some reductions in poverty and inequality and evidence of a shift in the distribution of income growth across society.
- Compared with other similar OECD countries poverty levels in the UK at the beginning of the new century were higher than average.
- Research on the distribution of poverty reveals that different social groups are differentially affected. This is also true for different geographical areas across the country.
- The composition of poverty has changed in recent years with families and children becoming a larger proportion of those in long-term poverty.
- It has been suggested by commentators that some of those in poverty have come to constitute a separate *underclass*; but sociological evidence does not support such a change in social structure in the UK.
- Negative connotations of underclass status are linked to a legacy of pathological approaches to poverty in the UK, and in some other developed nations.

The extent of poverty and inequality

Poverty is a political problem, and therefore the nature of the problem is the result of the particular political context within which it has developed. This inevitably means that discussion of the extent of poverty largely takes place within a particular political context, usually within one country; and that comparison of poverty across national political boundaries cannot easily be undertaken. There are also difficulties of comparison across countries due to the different definitions and measures which may have been adopted, as we discuss in Chapter 4. We cannot just compare the numbers or proportion of people who are poor in Britain today with the numbers in France or the United States, or still less Brazil or Ethiopia.

This is a book about poverty in the UK therefore; and, although it is no longer possible to ignore both international comparison and international policy, most of the discussion in the book concentrates on research evidence and policy practice in the UK. However, in the twenty-first century the UK is no longer a single political or policy entity; the devolution of powers to the separate administrations in Scotland, Wales and Northern Ireland now mean that some significant policy differences have developed where these powers permit. This book concentrates primarily on UK-wide research and policy; but in some cases differences in these separate areas can be found. More detail on such variations can be found from the websites of the three devolved administrations listed at the end of the book.

As well as the problem of geography, there is also the problem of history. Because of the changing political and policy contexts within which the problem of poverty is conceived, as we outlined in Chapter 1, even within the UK measurement of the extent of poverty varies over time. In part this is perhaps a welcome feature – the problem of poverty ought to change as new data and new debates and definitions develop and new policies are introduced. However, these changes make it extremely difficult to compare past data on poverty with present figures in order to make a comparison or judgement about the effects of changes over time.

This was revealed most graphically in Rowntree's three studies of poverty in York in the 1890s, 1930s and 1950s. Although similar methods were used to survey a similar population, on each occasion there were changes in the definition of poverty. As will be discussed in more detail in Chapter 5, these changes were consciously made and readily justifiable, but they did mean that on each occasion different forms of measurement were being taken. Furthermore, when Abel Smith and Townsend (1965) sought to dispute Rowntree's findings on the extent of poverty in the 1950s and 1960s, their argument was based quite explicitly on the use of different criteria to define and measure the same problem. When comparing the extent of poverty over time, therefore, we are not always comparing like with like, as the summary of different measures of poverty employed by researchers over the last hundred years provided by Hills (2004, pp. 44–5) reveals.

Despite these problems some attempts have been made to measure and compare poverty over time, as we discuss below. Fiegehen et al. (1977, ch. 3) used a range of definitions and methods to compare changes in poverty from the end of the Second World War to the mid-1970s, and concluded that the extent and depth of poverty had reduced over this period. In a wide-ranging article in 1988 Piachaud attempted to adapt data from a range of poverty studies to develop a constant relative poverty level that could be used to compare poverty in Britain from 1899 to 1983. Despite the methodological initiatives that Piachaud developed, however, his conclusions about changes in poverty levels over time were fairly tentative. Although there was evidence of a significant decline in poverty following the Second World War, trends since then appeared to have fluctuated and increases were revealed in poverty levels in the early 1980s (Piachaud, 1988). Since then the picture has become more exaggerated as we shall see; and a more recent overview of poverty research by Glennerster *et al.* (2004) has provided further illustration of these long-term trends.

As I mentioned in Chapter 1, in the 1990s the Joseph Rowntree Foundation commissioned a major enquiry into poverty and inequality in Britain one hundred years after Seebohm Rowntree's original poverty research in York. The research therefore provided a symbolic benchmark against which to compare trends in the growth or decline in the extent of poverty. The research projects that comprised the wide-ranging *Inquiry into Income and Wealth* could not extend their period of comparison back to the 1890s, but many of them did compare changes over three decades from the 1960s; and these confirmed the trend of growing poverty in the 1980s identified by Piachaud (see Hills, 1996).

In 1998 Hills updated the evidence on these poverty trends, utilizing data from the government's annual statistical publication *Households Below Average Incomes* (HBAI) and found that these revealed some decline in the numbers of people in poverty in the early 1990s (Hills, 1998). Since then the numbers have stabilised at just below 20 per cent of the population, as can be seen from Figure 2.1, taken from Hills' (2004) most recent review of trends in inequality in the UK. It reveals quite starkly the massive growth in poverty in the UK in the 1980s, during the years of the Thatcher governments. Since the early 1990s the situation has improved and levels for some groups in particular have fallen. Nevertheless there has been no return to the much lower levels of poverty experienced in the 1960s and 1970s.

The data in Figure 2.1 use the measure of 50 per cent of mean average income as a proxy measure for poverty; and, as we shall see in Chapter 4, there are academic and political problems in identifying and agreeing the indirect measures that can be used to define poverty lines in this way.

Moreover, the mean average of income distribution can sometimes be distorted by the existence of relatively small numbers of very rich people – and there are such people in the UK at the beginning of the new century. The government now prefers to use a median average, based on the midpoint in the income distribution, as a measure of poverty therefore, and it is now this which is more widely used in the HBAI and by most commentators on poverty. In fact it is 60 per cent of the median which is usually quoted as a proxy measure of poverty, and this actually gives a proportion of those who

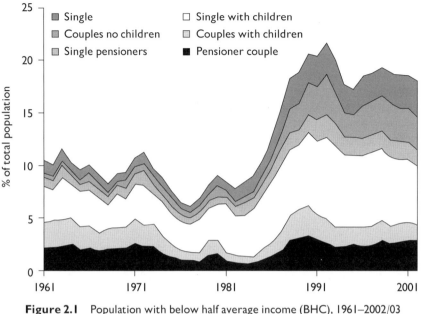

Figure 2.1 Population with below half average income (BHC), 1961–2002/03
Source: Hills (2004), figure 3.1, p. 48.

are poor which compares very closely with the old 50 per cent of mean figure. In 2003/04 the 50 per cent mean figure was 18 per cent and the 60 per cent median 17 per cent (DWP, 2005a, table 3.5). This is the measure also now used by the EU and thus can provide a basis for cross-national comparisons between member nations.

These proportions, and those in Figure 2.1, are based on income before taking into account the housing costs (BHC) which households have to bear. In fact housing costs are a significant element in most weekly household budgets, and yet they vary widely in different parts of the country and are often largely outside the control of households themselves. In recognition of this the government also produces data on the numbers and proportions of people below the above thresholds after their housing costs have been taken into account (AHC). Not surprisingly this reveals a higher proportion in poverty – 22 per cent on the 50 per cent of mean measure and 21 per cent on 60 per cent of median – and, partly for this reason, the government has now moved to using the lower BHC measure in making public comparisons of numbers in poverty. Either way, however, this means a total of 12.3 million, or 12 million, people living in poverty in the UK at the beginning of the twenty-first century (DWP, 2005a, p. 37 and table 3.5); and this situation has been a fairly constant one for most of the last decade.

Of course these numbers based upon proportions of average incomes are relative measures of poverty. This means that as average incomes rise then so will the numbers in poverty, unless inequality more generally is reduced. As suggested in Chapter 1, governments committed to removing or reducing poverty could aim to reduce inequalities to ensure that as few people as

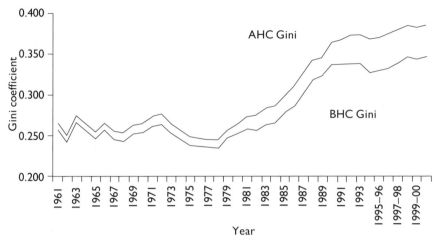

Figure 2.2   Changes in the Gini coefficient measure of inequality in the UK
Source: Goodman and Shephard (2002), figure 5.

possible fall below these thresholds. In fact, however, it seems that in the 1980s, at least, quite the reverse policies were being pursued. Increasing inequalities in incomes were encouraged, or at least tolerated, over this period; and, as Figure 2.2 reveals, the patterns of inequality over the last four decades mirror closely those of poverty, as measured above.

Figure 2.2 uses the Gini coefficient to measure inequality, this is an aggregate measure of the level of inequality within a society based on a scale of 0 to 1, with higher fractions indicating higher levels of inequality, and it is explained more fully in Chapter 6. This figure also directly compares the levels of inequality before taking account of housing costs (BHC) and after (AHC), revealing much higher levels when using the latter measure, with the difference also becoming more accentuated in recent years as housing costs have grown more rapidly than incomes.

One of the arguments advanced by the Conservative governments of the 1980s was that rising inequalities were not necessarily evidence of growth in poverty, because overall living standards were growing. This was the point being made by John Moore in the speech quoted in Chapter 1, when he said that poverty in the 1980s could not be compared to poverty in the 1900s. Of course at times of rises in overall living standards then it is likely that all members of the population will be better off than they were before, and throughout the last hundred years or more this has indeed been the case. This raises the complex issue of *relative* versus *absolute* definitions of poverty, which we will return to examine in more depth in Chapter 4. In terms of the levels, and experience, of poverty in modern society, however, it is pertinent to ask the question whether the continuing increases in living standards in society have in fact been shared equally across all levels of the income distribution; and here the evidence suggests that in reality this has not always been the case.

Between 1979 and 1990 while average incomes grew by about 35 per cent, those at the top of the scale saw their incomes rise by over 60 per cent and

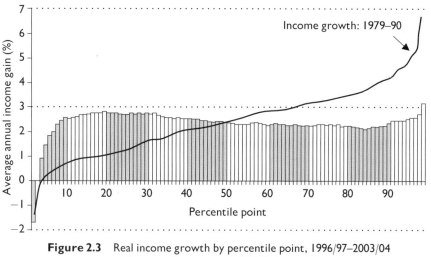

Figure 2.3 Real income growth by percentile point, 1996/97–2003/04
Source: Brewer *et al.* (2005), figure 2.5.

yet those at the bottom experienced a decline in their income of as much as 15 per cent, using the AHC measure (DSS, 1995). This pattern is revealed in a graphical form in Figure 2.3, which shows how incomes changed (BHC) on an annual average basis for each percentile group (that is each 1 per cent) of the population between 1996/97 and 2003/04 and compares this with the earlier period from 1979 to 1990.

The picture is a revealing one. Over the period from 1979 to 1990, we can see that the higher up the income scale the greater the rise in average income. What is more, those at the very bottom of the scale became worse off in these absolute terms compared to their position in 1979. Over this period, therefore, the rich got richer and the poor really did get poorer.

This is in contrast to the period after 1996/97, when the new Labour government came into power. The changes over this period in Figure 2.3 are rather different; the graph slopes the other way revealing that higher levels of income growth were experienced at this time by those lower down the income scale, suggesting a genuine redistribution of wealth towards the less well-off. However, even here the picture at the two extremes is starkly different. The very top 1 per cent again saw a relatively higher rise in their incomes and the bottom few per cent saw much lower increases, with another real decline in standards at the very bottom (the bottom percentile, with −16 per cent growth, has been omitted so as not to skew the graph). Any redistribution of resources at the beginning of the new century has not, therefore, benefited those who are very poor, and has not prevented the ever-increasing wealth of those who are very rich.

It is worth pointing out, of course, that those people at the very top and bottom (and indeed elsewhere) of the income scales in 2004 are not necessarily the same people as those who were there in 1979 or even 1996. Individuals and households do move up, and down, the income distribution over time, and some die or emigrate. These changes in poverty dynamics, as they are now called, are an important element in measuring and understanding poverty, as we will return to discuss in Chapter 7. However, they do not change the point that those at the very bottom of the scale in 2004, whoever they were, were worse off than they hade been over two decades earlier; and this is a depressing statistic for anyone concerned for their plight.

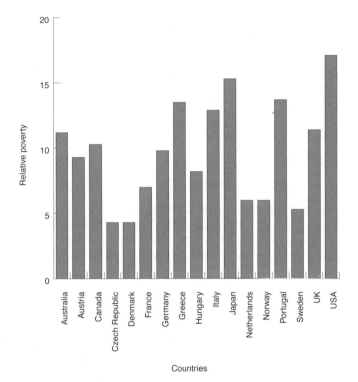

Countries

Figure 2.4   Proportion of the population below the 50 per cent median income poverty threshold in selected OECD countries, 2000
Source: OECD (2005).

The proportions of poverty in the UK also compare interestingly with developments in other advanced industrial countries. International comparisons are fraught with methodological complications, as we shall discuss in more detail in Chapter 4. However, the Organisation for Economic Co-operation and Development (OECD) does now produce data on comparative poverty levels amongst industrial nations which allows national distributions to be contrasted. As Figure 2.4 reveals, at the turn of the century the UK did not compare very favourably with a number of other similar OECD nations using figures based on data from 2000.

The distribution of poverty

Levels of poverty and inequality expanded significantly in the UK towards the end of the last century, therefore, and although they have reduced to some extent since then, they have remained high both by historical standards and when compared geographically to the situation in a number of other OECD nations. Analysis of the statistics on poverty, in particular the HBAI data provided by the government, also reveals that the experience and the risk of poverty are not evenly distributed across all social groups within the country. Some people are more likely to be poor than others.

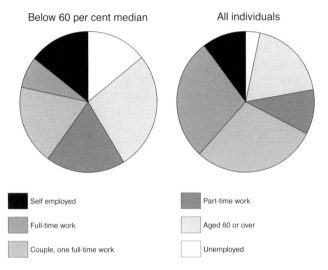

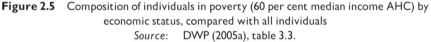

Figure 2.5 Composition of individuals in poverty (60 per cent median income AHC) by economic status, compared with all individuals
Source: DWP (2005a), table 3.3.

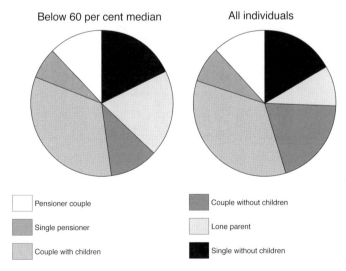

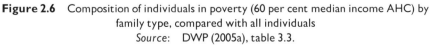

Figure 2.6 Composition of individuals in poverty (60 per cent median income AHC) by family type, compared with all individuals
Source: DWP (2005a), table 3.3.

As we might expect, the risk of poverty is associated with economic status. Using the 60 per cent of median income (AHC) measure discussed above, Figure 2.5 reveals that unemployed or otherwise economically inactive households are much more likely to be in poverty than those in full-time employment.

Poverty is not just unevenly distributed by economic status; it is also linked to family circumstances. Figure 2.6 uses the same database to compare the distribution of poverty across different family types, and reveals that in particular lone parents are at greater risk of poverty. Indeed for lone parents the risk of poverty is 47 per cent, in other words almost half of lone parents are poor by this measure (DWP, 2005a, table, 3.5).

In addition to these issues of economic status and family type, poverty is also unevenly distributed by gender, ethnicity, age and disability; and these are dimensions that we shall return to discuss in more detail in Part III. There is yet another distributional issue which has become a concern of both academics and policy-makers in recent years, however: geographical, or spatial, distribution of poverty across the different localities and regions of the country.

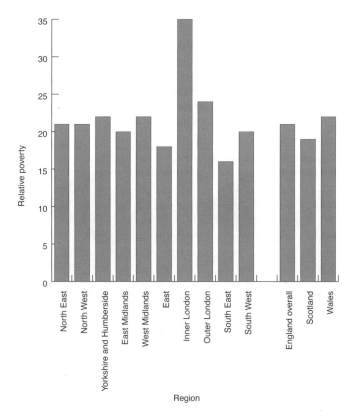

Figure 2.7 Distribution of poverty (60 per cent of median income AHC) by English region and British nation
Source: DWP (2005a), table 3.6.

Discussion of the 'geography of poverty', as this issue is sometimes called, is also a complex and sometimes technical debate about both definition and measurement of poverty across spatial dimensions, as we shall discuss below. Philo's (1995) Child Poverty Action Group (CPAG) book provides a good introduction to some of these debates, and this and more recent evidence suggests that there are significant differences in the extent of poverty within different areas of the country.

These differences can be seen at regional level within Britain. The government's HBAI data now includes information on the distribution of poverty at the regional level and this is revealed in Figure 2.7, which shows higher levels of poverty in London in particular.

However, regions are rather large geographical areas. When smaller local areas are examined the differences in the concentration of poverty become more pronounced. Dorling and Thomas's (2004) major study of the geographical distribution of a wide range of indicators, drawing on the data from the 2001 Census, uses parliamentary constituencies to make comparisons, and here starker differences, for instance in levels of unemployment, are revealed.

The most extensive data on the spatial distribution of poverty is provided by the government's *Indices of Deprivation* (ID2004), produced by the Office of the Deputy Prime Minister. These indices have taken a number of forms over time, but the most recent format dates from a major review which was carried out at the end of the last century by academics at the University of Oxford and led to a new set of indices being produced in 2000 (DETR, 2000a), which were updated and expanded in 2004 (ODPM, 2004). They apply to England only, however, with separate developments taking place in the devolved administrations in Scotland, Wales and Northern Ireland. For instance, Scotland has developed a distinct social inclusion strategy and Wales has appointed a Children's Commissioner.

The English indices used here cover a number of dimensions (or domains) of poverty and deprivation, including employment, health, education, environment and crime, as well as income; and they employ a number of different indicators to measure these, including data on receipt of social security benefits. They also take analysis down to more detailed geographical levels including local authority districts, the electoral wards within these, and in 2004 to Super Output Areas (SOAs) of around 1,500 people. The results are complex and voluminous, and are therefore largely accessible only in CDrom form.

Depending upon which indices are employed, of course, different distributions of poverty and deprivation are revealed. Nevertheless, some clear patterns do emerge, with certain districts usually appearing in the bottom five to ten of all lists. For instance, taking the overall average score across all indicators, the bottom five districts in 2004 were Liverpool (most deprived), Manchester, Knowlsey, Tower Hamlets and Hackney (ODPM, 2004, table 5.4, p. 114).

Much controversy surrounds the construction of spatial measures such as the ID2004, in part because, as with other definitions and measurements of poverty, of the close link that they have in practice to policy action. In the case of the distribution of deprivation revealed in the ID2004 the data are used in part to determine the distribution of certain resources and policy initiatives aimed at combating local poverty and social exclusion, as we will return to discuss in more detail in Chapter 16. Rather like a 'beauty contest in reverse', therefore, being designated as a deprived area can lead to access to additional resources for local policy projects, and these can make a significant difference to local people, and to local politicians.

This raises a more general problem with analysis of the spatial distribution of poverty, sometimes referred to as the 'ecological fallacy'. This is the assumption that the identification of deprived areas will provide us with a spatial distribution of poverty. This is not the case because not all people who are poor do live within the poorest areas, and not all those living in the poor areas are themselves poor. More recently this issue has been taken up as a distinction between 'people poverty' and 'place poverty' (Powell *et al.*, 2001). Spatial distribution of deprivation may tell us about something about place dimensions of poverty, but if our concern is with the people who are poor then we will need to use different measures. And this has particular importance for policies designed to respond to 'place poverty', as we shall see in Chapter 16.

STATISTICS: A NOTE OF WARNING

All of the statistics quoted in this chapter have been taken from recent statistical evidence. Inevitably, however, this evidence is time limited and will be replaced by more up-to-date figures in the future. In the case of much government data, updating is now provided on an annual basis. There are a number of sources of up-to-date information on poverty, and readers should be prepared to make use of these to get the latest figures.

The Child Poverty Action Group produces an extensive review of statistical data on poverty, called *Poverty: The Facts*, which is regularly updated every two to three years. The most recent version is the fifth edition (Flaherty *et al.*, 2004). In addition to this the CPAG publish a quarterly journal, *Poverty*, which often includes summaries of the very latest figures available. Even regular paper publications take relatively long to appear these days, however, and more up-to-date information is generally available on the internet. The best source here is the poverty website maintained by the New Policy Institute and the Joseph Rowntree Foundation; but there are a number of other useful websites which are also regularly updated, including those of the major government departments. These are listed in website references at the end of the book.

Changing patterns of poverty

The extent of poverty in the UK has thus varied over time, and the distribution of poverty reveals that the risk and experience of poverty is different for different social groups. What is more, as we saw in Chapter 1, the history of poverty in Britain is linked to the development of the capitalist economy and the resulting impact of the regime of wage labour. Once removed from the land as a source of support, people were at risk of poverty in a wage-based economy if they did not have capital resources or a wage (and an adequate wage) from employment. Risk of poverty is therefore related to class status. It is those in the working class, and especially those without recognised skills or qualifications on the margins of the labour market, who are most likely to be unemployed and poor. Indeed in a wage economy, for the vast majority of people to be unemployed also means to be poor – although this is not of course an iron law, as unemployed lottery winners and members of the aristocracy reveal.

Unemployment is also disproportionately experienced by particular categories of potential, or hopeful, workers. Those who are sick or suffer from a disability may find it difficult to secure waged labour because it may be assumed that they cannot perform effectively. Members of minority ethnic groups, in particular black people, may also be excluded from the labour market by the prejudice held by employers. Older people are excluded from the labour market by the widely held assumption that after a certain age they will want to, or should be required to, retire from work. All these groups, and others, experience particular problems of poverty, as we shall discuss in more detail in Part III.

However, whilst in a wage labour economy unemployment increases the risk of being poor, at the same time employment provides no guarantee of escaping it. Many workers have found that all needs cannot be met from the low wages which they earn, especially if they have dependants to support. Even those in waged work may therefore be at risk of poverty, and low wages can even fall below the state social security benefit levels. Since 1999 there has been statutory control over low wages through establishment of a national minimum wage (£5.05 an hour for adults in 2005), and this has raised the income of over a million low-paid workers. However, it can still leave those with dependants to support below the poverty line, and, as we shall discuss in Chapter 14, extensive use is now made of tax credits to supplement the wages of low-paid workers to ensure, in principle at least, that none are worse off in work than they would have been if dependant upon social security benefits.

Nevertheless the 'working poor' remain a significant proportion of those living in poverty, as can be seen in Figure 2.5; and this is even more significant when the self-employed are included. A large proportion of self-employed people are in practice living in poverty. These people are not, of course, protected by minimum wage provision and are also less likely to be able to benefit from tax credit support. For them the experience of self-employment is less likely to be the freedom of being one's own boss and more likely to be a constant struggle to pay the bills and keep the business afloat.

The balance between the different groups of people in poverty revealed in Figure 2.5 is one which also changes over time. Research on changing patterns of poverty, for instance that by the Rowntree Inquiry into Income and Wealth (Hills, 1995, p. 34), revealed that the number of employed and self-employed people among those in poverty grew significantly in the 1980s and

1990s. Similarly the number of lone parents, now the group with the highest risk of poverty, was also growing over this time. Also, of course, levels of unemployment grew dramatically over this period. As a result, therefore, the proportion in poverty who were of working age was much higher at the end of the last century than it had been for much of the preceding four or five decades. In the middle of the last century most poor people were older citizens over the retirement age; and, although as we shall discuss in Chapter 11 there are still large numbers of older people in poverty, the balance between these and those of working age has been shifting, with the numbers of families with children living in poverty growing most dramatically.

The changing composition of those in poverty is a reminder that poverty is both created and recreated by the social structures and social policies within which it is situated – it is a product of history. However, the significant growth in the late twentieth century in certain categories of poverty, such as the unemployed and lone parents, has been seen in some quarters as evidence that major social changes in the distribution and causes of poverty have been taking place in recent times in the UK and in other advanced industrial countries, with important implications too for the nature of the policies that should be developed to respond to this.

Temporary and relatively predictable exclusion from the labour market, for example because of sickness and retirement, has been associated with acknowledged risk of poverty linked to life-course events and changes in the life-cycle. These events were identified by Rowntree in his early research on poverty, and we shall discuss them further in Chapter 7. They tend to lead to a form of anti-poverty policy based on the need to protect people against such predictable life-cycle events and resulting in redistribution, through state support, of resources across the life-cycle. Under such redistribution all are expected to make contributions during times of employment and all might expect to benefit at times of labour market exclusion. This is some-times referred to as *horizontal redistribution*, and, as we discuss in Chapter 14, it is linked to a model of social security based on protection through social insurance.

However, many lone parents and the long-term unemployed (the groups growing most rapidly in the 1980s and 1990s) are not temporarily excluded from the labour market in the UK, they are more or less permanently removed from it. For them insurance protection based on benefits in return for contributions is not an effective form of protection as they are unable to make the required contributions whilst in work in the first place. They are thus more likely to depend on means-tested social security benefits, financed out of ordinary taxation and targeted directly at those who are poor, again as we shall see in Chapter 14. Provision of such support is referred to as *vertical redistribution*, a transfer of resources from those in employment (those who have) to those who are outside of the labour market and have no other means of support (those who have not).

The changes in the composition of poverty in the 1980s and 1990s resulted in an increase in the number of people not protected from poverty by social insurance, due to long-term exclusion from the labour market or reliance on inadequate wages within it. And as a result the number of people in poverty having to rely on social assistance benefits grew dramatically towards the end of the last century. The number depending on Income Support, the basic assistance benefit in Britain, increased from four million in the 1970s to ten million in the 1990s, and this phenomenon was repeated in most other European countries (see Room *et al.*, 1989). Some commentators, notably those working within the European Commission, thus began to refer to these growing groups as the 'new poor' (Room *et al.*, 1990) and to suggest that the processes shaping both their risks and their experiences of poverty were different from the life-cycle events affecting previous generations.

The underclass

The changing experiences of new poverty, commentators such as Room argued, moved beyond the narrow confines of material poverty and low income to encompass a broader process of 'social exclusion', which brings disadvantage and discrimination across a wide range of social activities (Room, 1995). We will return to discuss this 'new' phenomenon of social exclusion and its implications for our understanding of poverty and anti-poverty policy in more detail in Chapter 8. However, the supposed identification of a new form of poverty was taken up by some commentators as suggesting that the changes in the distribution of poverty were the product of changes in the activities and attitudes of people who were poor, and that new poverty was not just a product of shifts in types of employment and social security support, but evidence of the development of a new social class of poor or excluded citizens – the *underclass*.

Discussion of an underclass of people who are poor takes on wider and more sinister implications than simply counting and comparing the number of different social groups living in poverty. The growth of new poverty was seen by some as the product of new social forces, which it was argued affected particularly those groups that had come to constitute some of the largest elements among those who were poor – although, as we shall see shortly, these forces are not actually new at all. The identification of such social forces is based to a large extent upon pathological perceptions of the causes and dynamics of poverty within society, as we shall discuss in more detail in Chapter 3. Most importantly, however, they are taken as evidence that the 'new poor' had come to occupy a different place within the class structure of Britain (and over advanced welfare capitalist countries) at the end of the twentieth century. They were no longer the unemployed working class, but a separate underclass.

The idea of an underclass at the bottom of, or even below, the rest of society could be found in the work of a number of key commentators in Britain in the late twentieth century. As early as 1973 Rex had talked of black communities in Britain becoming a segregated underclass, which he later described as being 'cut off from the main class structures of society' (Rex, 1979, p. 86). In his major study of poverty, Townsend (1979, p. 819) suggested that the elderly experienced an 'underclass status', a status that he later (p. 920) extended to include the disabled, the chronically sick, the long-term unemployed and lone-parent families. In a book dealing more generally with the labour market disadvantage of different social groups, Oliver (1991b, p. 133) argued that disabled people constituted an underclass in modern industrial society.

All these writers were using the concept of an underclass to describe the circumstances of particular groups in poverty. Their focus was largely on the exclusion experienced by such groups, their inability to participate in many social activities and their feeling of being trapped in a position of deprivation. Implicit in this, however, was the suggestion that perhaps the circumstances of such groups took them outside traditional class and social stratification approaches, based largely on labour market divisions, and left them as a distinct social class below the working class. This idea of the underclass as a new social class was taken up more directly by Runciman (1990), who linked it to the declining role of employment in manufacturing industry in the late twentieth century and the economic changes that would inevitably flow from this. This was also discussed by some of the contributors to a debate on the concept initiated by the Policy Studies Institute (Smith, 1992).

The concept achieved most prominence in the UK, however, when it was taken up by the Labour MP and former director of the CPAG, Frank Field, in a book published in 1989 entitled *Losing Out? The Emergence of Britain's Underclass*. In this book Field argued that in the 1980s the universal values of citizenship that had underlain the postwar welfare state had been abandoned in favour of policies that had led to social polarisation and the emergence of a new British underclass. He identified the underclass as constituting three groups of people in particular: the long-term unemployed, lone parents and the poorer elderly. Field also identified four causes of the emergence of such an underclass: the rise in unemployment, the widening of class divisions, the exclusion of those in poverty from rising living standards and the change in public attitudes away from altruism and towards self-interest.

Field's account of the emergence of this new British underclass was an outspokenly sympathetic one, and his clear aim in publishing the book was to seek to sway political opinion in favour of shifts in policy that might reverse the trends he had identified. Field was well-known for his views on poverty and social security policy, and later was briefly Minister for Welfare Reform in the 1997 Labour government. He was aware, however, that the notion of an underclass had been taken up and used rather differently by other writers, notably Dahrendorf, who in 1987 had talked of high unemployment as being related to the growth of an underclass in Britain, but who also associated this with undesirable characteristics and fatalistic attitudes amongst those affected.

Field was aware that there was 'a danger of these characteristics being interpreted as the "causes" of the problem itself, and from this it is only a short step to falling into the syndrome of "blaming the victim"' (Field, 1989, p. 6), although he himself later indulged in such causal association and moral judgement in his discussion of the problems of female lone parents who were poor. The 'danger' of associating description of the characteristics of an underclass with explanation of its causes, and moral judgement of the attitudes and behaviour of those within it, is one that is inescapably inter-twined within all attempts to categorise those who experience poverty and deprivation as a separate social category, and popular usage of the term underclass has recently come to encompass particularly perjorative connota-tions. This became clear in the work of some other exponents of the underclass thesis, notably the American writer Charles Murray to whom we return shortly, although in fact the legacy of pathology on which this draws has a much longer history.

The legacy of pathology

The attempt to identify the individual or social characteristics of those who are poor as the source of their poverty implies a pathological model of the causation of poverty, as we shall discuss in Chapter 3; and the association of such pathological approaches with depictions of those in poverty as a separate or isolated group in society has been a recurring feature of debates about the problem of poverty in modern industrial society. Despite the renewed interest, this is not a new phenomenon; and in Britain, as Morris (1994, chs 2 and 3) discussed, the trend can be traced back at least as far as the early studies of poverty of the late nineteenth century.

In his seminal studies of poverty in London, Booth (1889) distinguished a group among the ranks of those in poverty whom he regarded as a 'residuum' of criminal or feckless characters who were a blight on the rest of 'the poor and lower classes'. Stedman Jones (1971), writing about class structure and class struggle in the last two decades of the nineteenth century, described the fears of both middle-class and 'respectable' working-class commentators that the residuum would constitute a threat to social stability by undermining the work ethic and threatening social order. Part of the characterisation of the residuum, and part of the fears they supposedly generated, were the assump-tions that they did not share the values and aspirations of the rest of society and that this cultural alienation, and the poverty that resulted from it, were transmitted within the underclass from generation to generation.

Macnicol (1987) took up the development of this notion of intergenera-tional pathology or inherited deprivation by looking at the investigations by eugenicists during the interwar years into the evidence of genetic transfer of disability or deprivation. In many studies the distinction between physical disability and social deprivation was confused or overlooked, and it was only with the realisation of the horrors that eugenic approaches had led to in Nazi Germany that the prominence of this research began to decline.

In the United States in the 1960s the pathological tradition was taken up once again in response to the rediscovery of poverty within the affluent postwar American society (Morris, 1994, ch. 3). One significant catalyst for this reemphasis on the categorisation of people in poverty was the detailed research carried out by Lewis (1965, 1968) into the lives of Puerto Rican families. Lewis described how such families, and the communities in which they lived, had learned to cope with their high levels of poverty and deprivation in part by suppressing expectations of greater wealth, or even secure employment, and developing a culture that focused on the day-to-day strategies adopted by families and individuals to survive without affluence in an affluent society. Lewis referred to this as a 'culture of poverty' and his main concern was merely to identify and describe it as a social phenomenon.

However, the idea that people who were poor in affluent American society might have a separate culture of poverty, which therefore prevented them from ascribing to or achieving the wealth that was available to others, quickly became adapted as a pathological explanation of the persistence of such poverty. Because poverty in the United States is experienced much more by black people, especially those living in black inner city neighbourhoods, this pathology also acquired a racial, or racist, dimension (Jennings, 1994). For instance Moynihan (1965, p. 5) talked of the 'deterioration of the Negro family' as the cause of poverty among black Americans, and Wilson (1987) identified 'poor blacks' as belonging to an underclass isolated from other sections of the American community.

The reemphasis on pathological explanations of the poverty that was rediscovered in affluent America in the 1960s, in particular the work of Moynihan who was also a leading member of the Federal government at the time, was followed by a significant change in emphasis in the policy responses to the problem, as we shall discuss in Chapter 15. This resulted particularly in a change in policy focus towards the families and communities living in poverty rather than towards the broader social and economic structure of which they were a part.

Such a change was also experienced in Britain in the 1960s and 1970s following the renewal here too of pathological approaches to poverty, based in part on the debates in the United States. Here the reassertion of the pathological approach to poverty was associated in particular with the views of the Conservative minister Keith Joseph and most notably a speech he made to the Pre-School Playgroups Association in 1972 (see Denham and Garnett, 2001). Joseph referred to people in poverty as having 'problems of maladjustment' and suggested that such inadequacies might be transmitted across generations via what he described as a 'cycle of deprivation' (Joseph, 1972). He even initiated a major research programme, funded by the then Social Science Research Council, to explore this cyclical dimension of poverty, although the overall conclusions from the research did not provide any strong evidence of a cycle of deprivation operating across generations (Rutter and Madge, 1976; Brown and Madge, 1982).

Despite these academic misgivings, and the failure of the policy developments in the USA and the UK in the 1970s which we discuss in Chapter 15, this pathological approach to poverty returned in the 1980s, again with direct reference to sections of the population who were poor (and black) as an underclass. This was first seen in the work of Auletta (1982), who talked about nine million people in the USA constituting an underclass with undesirable and socially disruptive values. It was taken up particularly, however, by Murray (1984), a right-wing political scientist, who argued that welfare benefits had helped to create a culture of dependency that attracted some people into underclass status, identifying in particular the supposedly growing number of young female lone parents who had chosen a life of parenthood on welfare benefits rather then accept the responsibilities of marriage. Murray argued that through such – inadequate – single parenting a culture of deprivation and dependency was transmitted to subsequent generations, thus recreating an isolated and hopeless class of welfare recipients.

In 1989 Murray was invited over to the UK by *The Sunday Times* newspaper to investigate the possible development of an underclass in the country similar to that he had identified in the USA. The high level of poverty and welfare dependency had suggested to some that this might be the case. The problem of a potential underclass had been referred to by Dahrendorf in 1987, and a number of incidents of social unrest in inner city areas with high levels of deprivation had resulted in press reports suggesting links between hopelessness and lawlessness among unemployed benefit dependants.

Murray's findings were published by the right-wing policy group, the Institute of Economic Affairs (IEA), together with commentaries by critics (Murray, 1990). His conclusion was that things were not as serious in the UK in the 1980s as they were in the USA, but that a new underclass was emerging as a result of increasing levels of illegitimacy and lone parenthood, high levels of criminality and the dropping-out of the labour force of young unemployed male school-leavers who had never developed the habit of employment. His account was both bleak and forthright, identifying the underclass as a 'type of poverty' and suggesting that the current policy responses were likely to accentuate rather than relieve the problem. It also contained clear moral overtones disapproving of the characteristics he identified as causing under-class status, such as illegitimacy and fecklessness.

These moral issues were taken up by Murray even more directly when he returned to Britain five years later (Murray, 1994; Lister, 1996). This time he singled out lone mothers as the major cause of changing attitudes and values among the new generations of those in poverty, and blamed over-generous social security benefits for encouraging women to become lone parents. As in 1990, Murray's views were challenged by other commentators, who con-demned his pathological approach as an example of blaming the victims of poverty for their plight; but it was Murray's opinions that received the widest coverage in the popular press.

The work of Murray is the clearest and most recent example of a long historical tradition of the pathologisation of poverty in academic research and political debate. It focuses on the culture of poverty as an explanation of the problem of deprivation, and subsequently as a justification for a particular policy response to it, although in reality Murray's most radical ideas have not been translated into concrete policy programmes. As Ryan (1971, p. 8) put it in a book about the policy developments in the USA in the 1960s, entitled *Blaming the Victim*:

> First, identify a social problem. Second, study those affected by the problem and discover in what ways they are different from the rest of us ... Third, define the difference as the cause of the social problem

itself. Finally, of course, assign a government bureaucrat to invent a humanitarian action programme to correct the difference.

In blaming the victim, therefore, poverty becomes the problem of the people who are poor themselves, and identifying them as occupying a distinct status as an underclass as a result of this provides a spurious socio-economic justification for this. Lister expands on this political and ideological (mis)usage of pathology to create a negative image of the problem of poverty and of the people who are poor themselves, referring to it as a process of 'othering' (Lister, 2004, ch. 5).

Of course such a pathological approach is only one way of seeking to explain the causes of poverty in modern society, as we will return to discuss in Chapter 3; and pathological explanations of poverty need not carry with them the strong overtones of moral condemnation found in the work of Murray in particular. For instance, Lewis's (1965, 1968) early research on the 'culture of poverty' was aiming to describe rather than condemn the isolation and separation of those in poverty.

What is more, there is little sociological evidence to support any strong theoretical or empirical argument about the existence of a new underclass in modern British society. Research examining the social circumstances and individual attitudes of people who are poor and on the margins of the labour market has cast doubt on the existence of any separate and isolated social group (Morris, 1995). For instance, there are significant differences within this group between the relatively large number who over time are moving in and out of employment and have close links with the labour market and the smaller number of very-long-term unemployed (Morris and Irwin, 1992). Not all of those outside the labour market are subject to economic exclusion; and therefore, as Gallie (1988) argued, there is no automatic link between economic circumstances and social differentiation.

However, a focus on the potentially cyclical nature of poverty and deprivation, and a concern that the social circumstances of those who are poor may be interacting with the dynamics of their family and community relations to reproduce an acceptance of (or a resignation to) social exclusion within certain communities or neighbourhoods has returned to the policy agenda in the UK, and the USA, in the early twenty-first century. In a special issue of the journal *Benefits*, Deacon (2002b) points out that there are 'Echoes of Sir Keith' [Joseph] in the policy rhetoric of New Labour, and Welshman (2002) explores in more detail the development of the cycle of deprivation and underclass thesis. At the same time, Such and Walker (2002) review more recent empirical research on the cyclical nature of 'transmitted deprivation' and conclude again that the evidence is still partial and inconclusive.

In a more wide-ranging review Deacon (2002a) examines the work of key authors who have addressed the relation between pathology and poverty and its policy implications, including the work of Murray, and develops a typology of these 'perspectives on welfare'. He also goes on to discuss some of the more recent policy initiatives that have flowed from these, such as the welfare reforms of the Clinton administration in the USA and the welfare to work and 'new deal' policies of the Labour governments in the UK. They also underpin the targeted anti-poverty initiatives which we discuss in Chapters 15 and 16, which critics have pointed out continue to involve an implicit pathologisation of the problem of poverty and social exclusion (Hills, 2002; Alcock, 2004a).

Certainly it is the case that the underclass thesis of social exclusion no longer has the prominence in political or academic debate in the new century that it did in the 1980s and 1990s, although it has remained influential especially in UK and US government thinking. And, given the 'long and undistinguished pedigree' (Macnicol, 1987, p. 315) of the concept and its associations with pathological explanations of the problem of poverty, it is no doubt desirable that this 'potent symbol' (Dean, 1991, p. 35) has in practice not led to a complete transformation of poverty analysis or anti-poverty policy. As Deacon (2002a) discusses, however, what the concern with pathology has done is return to the centre of debate about poverty recognition of the balance between structure and agency in understanding social and individual development; and it is to these broader issues that we will return briefly at the beginning of the next chapter.

The Causes of
Poverty

SUMMARY OF KEY POINTS

- All explanations of the causes of poverty involve a balance between the relative roles of *structure* and *agency*.
- Pathological approaches to the causes of poverty stress the role of individuals, families and communities in creating or recreating poverty.
- Structural approaches to the causes of poverty stress the role of public institutions, politicians and broader social and economic forces.
- Ideologies of poverty shape how all of us perceive the problem of poverty.
- Studies of attitudes towards poverty have revealed how popular perceptions are shaped by certain ideologies.
- Only relatively recently have research and debate on poverty sought to include the 'subjective' views and experiences of people who are poor.

Structure and agency

At the heart of all social science is debate, and frequently disagreement, about the relative roles of structure and agency in explaining social order and social change.

- The *structural* approach emphasises the importance of social circumstances and social forces in determining the life-courses and life chances of people. Economic growth, labour market opportunities, educational provision, social security systems and many other structural features of society provide a powerful contextual framework in which our living standards and social relations are created and recreated. And, as many social policy commentators have argued, in order to change these circumstances and relations these structural frameworks must themselves be changed, by policy action.
- The focus on *agency* conversely suggests that we are all ultimately the authors of our own fortunes, or misfortunes. All individuals make choices about the life courses they wish to pursue and the social relations they want to foster, from the clothes that they wear to the subjects they study at university for instance. More importantly in this context, for society to function, individuals must take responsibility for managing their own living standards and social relations, for instance, those who are unemployed should take responsibility for seeking to get a job.

In practice, of course, both of these seemingly opposed approaches have some theoretical truth within them. Social structures do set a social context within which we are placed and from which, by and large, we cannot escape; and even many of the choices that individuals do appear to have often turn out in fact to be largely constrained by structural forces (as attempts to bring choice into the allocation of places in state schools has demonstrated). And yet, at the same time individual agents do make decisions about how to live their lives, and through these decisions can change the circumstances within which they live (as the decision to go to study at university reveals).

The point, as most social scientists recognise, is that life chances and social relations are a product of the interaction of both structure and agency; and the more pertinent question to ask is not, which is the determining factor in any situation, but rather what is the balance of influence of each and how does this change over time and space? To some extent this is an empirical question which can only be answered by carrying out empirical research. However, to some extent the answer will also be determined by the approach that is taken to any research, whatever methodological form that takes. In other words if we look largely for structural explanations and seek largely structural solutions to social problems, then it is structural forces which are likely to emerge as the key factors. Conversely if we focus upon the role of agency then we are more likely to find that individual decisions do matter. It depends on which lens we are looking through, as well as what we are looking at.

This may also be affected by the nature of the activities or the problems under investigation. As Leisering and Leibfried (1999) pointed out in their study of agency and dynamics in poverty in Germany, structural factors are likely to have a greater influence over relations between social groups and social institutions, but individual life-course changes may be more directly affected by the choices that agents make. In general, however, it is the case that research and policy debate on poverty has traditionally been dominated largely by a structural perspective on the problem as found, for instance, in Ferge and Millar's (1987) study of poverty in a range of different European countries entitled the *Dynamics of Deprivation*.

Poverty research has tended to count the numbers of people experiencing poverty and to measure their poverty in terms of economic status, income sources, access to services and such like. Anti-poverty policy has tended to focus upon seeking to change these social circumstances by reforming social relations, for instance by managing or regulating economic forces, redistributing resources to raise incomes, or restructuring social services. There is no doubt that such policies have had significant effects in removing people from poverty or reducing its severity; and they remain central to public commitments to combat poverty today.

However, over the last decade or so the importance of agency in shaping the life-courses and life chances of people in poverty has come into more prominence in academic debate, and expectations about the activities and responsibilities of agents have become a more significant element of policy development. The growing prominence of agency in poverty analysis has accompanied an increase also in concern with the dynamic analysis of the experience of poverty, which we shall return to discuss in Chapter 7. This is linked to theoretical debates about the importance of recognising the need for life-course planning in understanding social relations, and to the greater availability of empirical data on social dynamics provided by panel surveys and other longitudinal datasets (see Dewilde, 2003; Alcock, 2004b). The concern with agency has also been a feature of the perspectives on welfare developed by a number of key commentators on social policy in the broad poverty field, as explored by Deacon (2002a).

The shift in policy emphasis towards agency can be seen most clearly in the welfare reforms introduced in the USA in the 1990s under the Clinton administration. Informed to some extent by the work of Ellwood on the undesirability of long term dependence on cash-based welfare (Bane and Ellwood, 1994; Ellwood, 1998), the aim of these reforms was to challenge welfare dependency by encouraging (and in some cases requiring) claimants to seek self-sufficiency in the labour market, whilst at the same time supplementing low wages with tax credits to make employment a more viable option for those in poverty. Thus people who were poor were to be expected to take responsibility for making life course changes to escape from poverty.

Similar shifts in welfare policy have been introduced by the Labour government in the UK at the beginning of the new century, as we shall discuss in a little more detail in Part IV. These include the welfare-to-work programme to encourage and assist unemployed people to find paid work, and the expansion of tax credits for the low paid. They also include the development of a new balance between public and private provision for pensions under which individuals are expected to take out private pension cover, and a wide range of targeted programmes to provide support and assistance to individuals and communities living in deprived areas, as we discuss in Chapter 16. In all cases, however, these new policy initiatives involve a shift in the balance between structure and agency in combating poverty to place a greater emphasis upon the latter. Although, as some commentators have pointed out (Hills, 2002), the continuing importance of structural forces and structural reforms in anti-poverty policy should not be overlooked.

The relative balance between structure and agency in understanding poverty has taken something of a shift towards agency at the beginning of the twenty-first century therefore. This is reflected not just in policy change. It has also led to an increasing emphasis on the role that agents play in coping with and challenging their poverty, albeit for the most part within structural circumstances which they may be able to do relatively little about. This can be seen in particular in Lister's (2004) analysis of the creation and recreation of poverty in modern society. She discusses in some detail how the 'victims' of poverty are also actors in shaping their experience of it, and how this perspective has often been ignored in research and analysis focusing upon the structural context of poverty. She even produces a useful fourfold classi-fication of the strategies that are adopted by agents to respond to their poverty – referred to as 'getting by', 'getting (back) at', 'getting out' or 'getting organised' (Lister, 2004, ch. 6).

In all cases what this approach underlines is that people in poverty are not passive recipients (or not!) of the outcomes of structural forces or social policies, but rather are active agents in shaping their lives and challenging the constraints within which their poverty is created and recreated. Lister links this to a later discussion of the importance of the experiences and perspectives of people who are poor on our more general (academic) understanding of poverty, a point to which we will return later. What her analysis reveals most clearly, however, is that when we seek to understand and explain poverty we must be aware of both the structural and individual causes of the problem.

Pathological causes

Analysis of the balance between structure and agency in understanding the causes of poverty is not just a twenty-first century phenomenon. In his 1978 study of the explanations of poverty Holman sought to identify and contrast a number of different perspectives, which we can classify as either pathological or structural approaches; and a similar distinction was later made by Spicker (1993, ch. 6). We examine some of these approaches below. The suggestion by Holman and others is that some perspectives may be preferable to others in explaining the causes of poverty. However, in practice any comprehensive explanation of poverty is likely to involve a balance between structure and agency and to include the influence of a number of different, but overlapping, social forces.

The first category of explanation that Holman (1978) refers to in his book is 'individuals and poverty'. This includes the pathological explanations of indolence and fecklessness adopted by some underclass theorists, that we discussed in Chapter 2. It also includes *genetic* explanations, which seek to relate social status with supposedly inherited characteristics such as intelligence, and *psychological* approaches, which explain individuals' (non)achievements by reference to acquired or developed personality traits. These are potential explanations of poverty and they do include a dynamic element, albeit a largely immutable one, deriving from nature (how we are born) rather than nurture (how we develop as people). In many cases such individual explanations imply a rejection of social or structural explanations, and they can be criticised as approaches that seek to blame the victims for their own poverty.

Proponents would argue, however, that genetic or psychological approaches do not imply individual blame, they merely establish causal links. However, there are serious questions as to whether the evidence to support those links has been satisfactorily established, especially since, as Holman (1978) discusses, most of those who might appear to have inherited the characteristics associated with poverty do not themselves become poor.

A second category of explanations, which have also been interpreted by critics as a case of blaming the victims, are those that focus on the family or the community as the cause of poverty. One of the most well-known proponents of such approaches is the former Conservative Social Services Minister Keith Joseph. As we saw in Chapter 2, Joseph (1972) referred to this as a 'cycle of deprivation' in which the inadequate parenting, lowered aspirations and disadvantaged environment of families and communities became internalised as part of the values of their children as they grew up. Thus when these children reached adulthood their expectations and abilities were lowered, and they more readily expected and accepted the poverty and deprivation of their parents and acquaintances.

As discussed earlier, such an approach was very influential in debates on the emergence of an underclass as a product of social isolation and the adoption of a culture of poverty (Welshman, 2002). It is a perspective which has returned to prominence in the policy debates about social exclusion at the beginning of the new century, and it has particular implications for anti-poverty policy, as we shall discuss in Chapter 16. Although this approach avoids ascribing poverty to individuals, it still contains a largely pathological model of the creation and recreation of poverty. It is the people who are poor themselves who, it is implied, are the key agents in producing and reproducing their poverty, albeit at a collective level through family and community cultural relations.

This does not explain the broader circumstances in which families and communities are situated, nor how they came to be poor in the first place. Nor does it explain how some individuals and families manage to escape the culture of poverty. The research commissioned by Joseph in the 1970s to investigate the operation of 'cycles of deprivation' raised just such questions when it concluded that most of the children from poor homes did not repeat the poverty of their families and communities, and that most of those who became poor did not themselves come from such deprived backgrounds (Rutter and Madge, 1976; Brown and Madge, 1982). This suggests that explanation should focus on the creation of such backgrounds, and not just on the behaviour of individuals within them. This takes us beyond the pathological and onto the structural level.

Structural causes

Poverty is a product of dynamic social forces and, as we saw to some extent in Chapter 1, in modern welfare capitalist countries state policies have been developed over time to combat or reduce poverty. If, therefore, despite these policies poverty persists then perhaps explanation should look not to the failings of those in poverty but to the failings of those policies designed to combat it and the structural changes in society that they were supposedly intended to bring about.

In particular, of course, this means the social security system discussed in Chapter 14, and there have been many who have who pointed to the failure of social security to remove poverty (MacGregor, 1981; Donnison, 1982; Spicker, 1993). Despite the improvements in benefit administration in recent years, which we discuss in Chapter 14, many claimants still do not receive the benefits to which they are entitled. Complex rules on entitlement can exclude some in need. What is more, even those who do get their benefits may not in practice receive sufficient to meet their needs as they or others define them.

This should not be taken to suggest, however, that social security policy has had no impact on the level of poverty. Clearly without social security provision the extent and depth of poverty in the UK, and elsewhere, would be much worse. And it should be remembered that social security also has objectives other than the elimination or relief of poverty, as we shall discuss in more detail in Chapter 14. Furthermore social security is not the only area of policy implementation that may be accused of contributing to the reproduction of poverty. Housing policies, in both the public and private sectors, have obviously failed those people who are poor and homeless. Health policies, or the lack of them, may have resulted in sickness and disability, leading to poverty. Social services may have failed to assist with, or may even have added to, the problems that have brought individuals and families into poverty. Indeed all public agencies, be they state, voluntary or those in the private sector, who contribute to the range of social services within the state may be accused of failing in their tasks as long as poverty persists among their clients or potential clients.

To some extent this may be the fault of individual officers within these agencies experiencing low morale or falling down on their jobs – another dimension of the role of agency in determining poverty. Or it may be the fault of the structure and operational practices of agencies, which make them unable to achieve success whatever their workers may wish to do. There may be limitations or failings in the policy guidelines which the agencies have been charged to implement, or shortcomings in the practices developed to carry these out.

More critically perhaps, as some have argued (see Novak, 1984), perhaps our expectations of the achievements of social security are based on a misconception of what such policies are seeking to achieve. Social security systems, for instance, are concerned with controlling and disciplining those in poverty, as well as supporting them. This is not so much a matter of policy practice, however, but rather a focus upon the role and nature of policy itself.

A focus on policy failure, or the failure to develop appropriate policy, is an approach to explaining the dynamics of poverty that moves beyond the level of individuals or community agents, to examine instead the activities of those who, through political action, claim to be prepared and able to change social structures, and the social policies and institutions that they establish to do this. As MacGregor (1981) argued in a book on the *Politics of Poverty*, policies to combat poverty are the product of political decisions; and, as we have discussed, poverty is a political concept. The identification of poverty is linked to political action to eliminate it; thus if poverty remains then perhaps it is because politicians have failed either to identify it accurately or to develop appropriate policies in response to it. In such an approach therefore, poverty is the result of political failure, or the failure of political will.

Of course not all politicians would admit that they had failed to eliminate poverty. Indeed, as we saw in Chapter 1, members of the Conservative governments of the 1980s were outspoken in their claim that poverty, as they defined it, had been eliminated through the policies developed and implemented by themselves and previous governments. Conversely the Labour administrations of the early twenty-first century have expressed their concern about past failures to combat poverty and have committed themselves to removing child poverty in the UK within twenty years (Walker, 1999). What this reveals, as we know, is that political debates on poverty policy cannot be separated from debates on the problem of poverty itself. But this does not negate the value of approaches that seek to explain the causes of poverty within the dynamics of political decision-making. Indeed quite the reverse is true.

The question of who takes political decisions and how their decisions are put into practice is obviously crucial in determining the circumstances of people living within that political system, including those who are poor. There is a powerful logic to the argument that we need look no further than politics and politicians to find the causes of poverty – they run the country, they are responsible for the problems within it. These are the key agents who should be making the right decisions about future action.

For a long time sociologists have pointed out, however, that no matter how powerful politicians may seem, or may even believe themselves to be, they do not control all aspects of the societies they claim to run. Indeed politicians have little or no control over many events, both of a day-to-day nature and of major social and economic importance – and sometimes they are quick to point this out when referring to the actions of other governments or international agencies. Even if politicians may be prepared to accept the blame for the continued existence of poverty, it is far from clear that they are entirely responsible for it.

One of the main reasons why politicians cannot control all aspects of society, or certainly all aspects of welfare capitalist societies such as the UK, is the fact that many of the social events in them are the product of economic forces and economic decision-making that politicians do not control. In practice most politicians would probably admit this and would claim that their aim is merely to *manage* the economy in order to create a context in which social activity can take place. This has certainly been a central feature of the rhetoric of the Labour governments since 1997, and in particular the Chancellor of the Exchequer, Gordon Brown. However, even he would probably have readily admitted that this was an aim which any government could at best only partly achieve; and even that partial achievement may depend to a large extent on what they, or we, mean by 'manage'.

In a largely market-based economy within an international context in which economic planning often takes place at a supranational level, national politicians cannot act freely and cannot change or influence all economic forces. The vagaries of national and international forces thus affect people in ways that politicians cannot control. Such forces can create poverty, which politicians may have intended or hoped to avoid, and conversely they can reduce poverty without direct political action being taken.

This is obviously the case with the poverty associated with the high levels of unemployment resulting from the international economic recessions in the 1930s, 1970s and 1980s. It was also the case for the relatively lower levels of poverty associated with periods of economic boom, such as in the 1950s, when unemployment was low and wages were rising. Poverty is not just the result of unemployment caused by economic recession, however. Economic decline also results in lower wages, leading to poverty for some in employment; earlier retirement and lower pensions, thus increasing poverty among the old; and, perhaps most importantly, pressure to cut public spending on benefits, leading to less state support for the non-employed and employed who are poor.

Changes in national and international economic forces therefore can and do cause poverty. This may suggest a kind of fatalism that assumes because there is nothing even politicians can do about it, and we must simply 'grin and bear it' and hope for better times ahead. Recognition of the importance of economic forces does not necessarily imply fatalism however. Even these economic forces are the products of decisions taken by people, and the consequences of these decisions are to a large extent predictable, as economists argue and seek to demonstrate. Thus they can, or could, be changed. Indeed they can be changed as a result of pressure from politicians. The point to understand is not that politicians cannot control economic forces, but rather that they *must* seek to control economic forces if they wish to influence the events that economic forces largely determine. Policy responses that merely focus on the consequences of economic forces therefore are likely to fail; but policies that seek to prevent these consequences by seeking to influen

economic forces, for instance by reducing inflation and promoting employment, can and indeed do succeed – a goal which, in principle at least, is critical
to the broader government policies in the UK in the early twenty-first century.

As we mentioned in Chapter 1, however, there are those who argue that the
interaction of political will and economic forces cannot solve the problem of
poverty because it is this which is its cause. This is the essence of the argument
developed by Novak in 1988 and to which he has returned since (Novak,
1995; Jones and Novak, 1999). Poverty is produced by the operation of a
capitalist wage labour market because to operate efficiently that wage labour
market needs poverty, or rather people who are poor existing on the fringes of
it. Fear of poverty acts as a disciplinary force on workers and provides
evidence that just as hard work and obedience will bring its rewards, so will
idleness or inactivity lead to punishment. Much the same sort of approach
concludes Holman's (1978) review of explanations of poverty. He refers to it
as a structural explanation in which poverty is merely the converse of wealth
within a stratified society; if we accept the one then we must also be prepared
to accept the other.

There is a danger in adopting wholesale such structural approaches,
however. They can tend to be little more than statements of the obvious.
Poverty is the product of an unequal or capitalist society; therefore only in a
different society will poverty cease to exist. As an explanation of the cause of
poverty this tells us everything and nothing. As a programme for policy action
it is hopelessly unrealistic. Of course it is the socio-economic structure of
society, and the political process that reproduces this, that are critical features
of the causes poverty. But in all societies this structure is complex and ever-
changing, and it is far from immutable, as the evidence of the different
levels of poverty in similar OECD nations in Figure 2.4 reveals. Social
structures can be changed, and particular aspects of these can be reformed
or restructured. Indeed this is what is happening all the time at the micro
level, where individual agents make decisions which alter the course of their
lives, and at the macro level, where politicians introduce new policies or
economic reforms.

Social structures change as a result of the actions of agents, and these
changing structures set a context in which the circumstances, and the
decisions, of future agents are determined. As we said at the beginning of this
chapter it is not a choice between structure and agency; but rather a balance
between the two that we must seek in an attempt to understand, and to
combat, poverty. The search for the causes of poverty cannot therefore be
confined within one or other of the causal frameworks outlined by Holman
(1978) and others; it must encompass the interaction of them all.

Ideologies of poverty

The different frameworks outlined by Holman are not just academic
arguments about social dynamics, they are part of broader ideological
perspectives on poverty which influence how all citizens perceive the problem,

and its solution. Murray's arguments about the existence of an underclass in British society at the end of the last century, discussed in Chapter 2 (see Lister, 1996), are a good example of this broader context. Murray was invited over to the UK by *The Sunday Times* newspaper and some of his work appeared in a popular form in the paper. Newspapers and other news media are critically important in shaping the ideological perspectives within which popular understandings are created and recreated. Whatever our individual views, all of us are influenced by such ideological perspectives, and we contribute to their continued influence through the discussions and articulations of our views in the private and public communications which we all make (including, of course, academic books).

Theoretical arguments are just one particular form of broader ideological frameworks which provide a context, albeit generally a partial one, for our understanding of poverty - although they do not just influence perceptions of poverty. Alcock (2003, ch. 12) discusses their role in shaping understanding of social policy more generally, and George and Wilding (1994) and Mullard and Spicker (1998) provide more detailed guides to the major perspectives which have influenced policy debate.

However, popular public images of poverty are particularly influential in shaping the social context within which poverty is created, as Murray's *Sunday Times* articles were clearly intended to underline. The role of public images in determining private perceptions of poverty was explored in a seminal study of attitudes to social security dependency and abuse in the 1970s by Golding and Middleton (1982). Their study opens with a review of the history of social security and poverty policy in the UK over the previous few centuries, demonstrating, as we saw in Chapter 1, that current perceptions have been shaped by past practices. Not surprisingly perhaps they found that perceived differences between those in work and those not working (the 'deserving and undeserving poor') continued to exercise a powerful influence on public and private ideologies of poverty.

The particular focus of Golding and Middleton's research, however, was on a growing fear of social security abuse in the 1970s, which was being fuelled by stories appearing in the newspapers and popularised by politicians. They explained how media reports of only one or two established incidents of social security abuse were able to carry the implicit, and at times explicit, message that these were only the tip of the iceberg of more widespread abuse. This abuse, the media implied, was the result of idle and feckless claimants seeking to enjoy a comfortable living without working, which they were readily able to do because of the ineffective administration of an over-extensive and over-bureaucratic benefits system. Indeed they suggested that even for those not actually defrauding the system, benefits were so generous that they were encouraging a life of indolent dependency, which could even extend to Spanish holidays on the 'Costa del Dole' (Golding and Middleton, 1982, pp. 106–7).

Two newspaper stories which Golding and Middleton reported provided examples of these ideological images. One, the story of a claimant called Deevy, did involve fraud, reportedly over fifty claims leading to payments of over £36,000 (although in the legal trial no figures anywhere near this were established), which suggested that a naïve and ineffective benefits system was a 'soft touch' for determined fraudsters. The other was the case of a genuine claimant who was supporting both a legal and a common law wife and twenty children in two homes in Devon and living a life of 'gentle glee' (*ibid*., p. 92) at the taxpayer's expense.

The images portrayed by these two stories were those of an overgenerous and easily outwitted social security system providing support, not to alleviate hardship and deprivation, but to maintain a comfortable life of idleness that was far more desirable than that enjoyed by many of those at work who, through the rising taxes on their hard-earned wages, were being expected to finance this. It was a theme that was also taken up by politicians at the time who concluded that something needed to be done to prevent such abuse. In the early 1970s Conservative Secretary of State Keith Joseph had established a committee to investigate the 'abuse of social security benefits' (Fisher Committee, 1973), and later Labour minister Stan Orme established a departmental coordinating committee on abuse (Golding and Middleton, 1982, p. 79). In the 1980s and 1990s these concerns continued and there were a number of attempts to 'crack down' on social security fraud and abuse by deploying additional staff on detection work (see Smith, 1985); and they have been continued by the new Labour governments who have developed targets for the detection of benefit fraud (Sainsbury, 1998).

The media and the political campaigns against social security abuse of the 1970s and 1980s created an ideological climate of hostility to benefit claimants and people in poverty more generally, which even acquired the status of a new moral panic – the problem of scrounging. And from this it is easy to see how the later claims by Murray about the development of an underclass received such popularity.

Golding and Middleton's research explored also the impact of these ideological perspectives on public attitudes, through a survey of attitudes towards welfare conducted in Leicester and Sunderland in 1977. This revealed a high degree of hostility to social security claimants among a large proportion of respondents. In particular, hostility was directed at 'scroungers' and those claimants, in some cases in very large numbers, who were accused of abusing state support. When asked about who deserved to receive social security support most respondents mentioned the old and the sick, only 5.9 per cent quoting the unemployed (Golding and Middleton, 1982, p. 169). Furthermore, the survey revealed that the highest estimates of abuse and the greatest resentment towards claimants came from those in low-paid, low-skilled employment (*ibid*., pp. 169–72).

Not surprisingly, therefore, studies of attitudes towards poverty reveal that the old distinctions between those in and those out of work and the deserving and the undeserving claimants have continued to provide a haunting legacy from past ideologies of poverty and anti-poverty policy in the UK. And this legacy is continually being shaped and reshaped by ideologies of poverty contained in the media and other public forums, as a remark from one of Golding and Middleton's respondents graphically revealed:

There are some genuine ones but the majority just bleed the country dry. The ones who have not worked for a long time should be made to do some kind of work and not claim benefit. 80 per cent are scroungers. It's just what you hear, what's on TV, what's been in the papers over the last few weeks. (Fitter's wife, quoted in *ibid.*, p. 173)

Remarkable, and depressing, though the findings of Golding and Middleton's research into ideologies of poverty were, it remains one of the few attempts to explore the attitudes of ordinary people towards the problem of poverty. As much of the rest of this book reveals, it is academic and political debate which has predominantly shaped our understanding of poverty and the ideological context within which that is generally discussed. This raises another important question about ideologies of poverty, therefore; and that is the extent to which it should be to ordinary people in poverty themselves, rather than academics, politicians or journalists, who we should be looking to provide both a definition and an explanation of what poverty means in modern society.

It might be argued that it ill-becomes academics and politicians to seek to define and explain poverty when few of them are poor or are unlikely ever to have been. This is a point which has been taken up forcefully by Beresford, who has criticised the exclusion of people in poverty from public debate about it (Beresford and Croft, 1995) and has sought to develop research in which the voices of such people are used to provide their own analysis of the 'definition, causes and effects' of poverty (Beresford *et al.*, 1999). This was taken further in the report of the Commission on Poverty, Participation and Power published in 2000, which sought to combine people with 'grassroots' experience of poverty with those more prominent in public life to develop an understanding of how people who were poor might become more involved in policy-making. More recently Bennett and Roberts (2004) have conducted an overview of participatory approaches to involve people with direct experience of poverty in research and give them more influence over how the findings are used.

Bennett and Roberts point out that these approaches can be compared to a range of other more recent initiatives to provide greater 'user involvement' and 'user control' over social policy development and delivery, and they conclude that these processes are inevitably difficult and challenging ones and will take time to feed into mainstream policy practice. We will return to some of the implications of this for the involvement of people who are poor in political activity and campaigning in more detail in Chapter 13. However, there are particular problems involved in attempts to use people's experiences of poverty as a basis for challenging public definitions and explanations of the problem.

These difficulties are explored by Lister (2004) in her book on poverty. As she points out for many people the experience of poverty is a depressing and a disempowering one, which they may be unlikely to see as a basis for engaging positively in public debate. People's experience of poverty is often negative and their reaction to it is likely to be negative too. Indeed, as

Dean and Melrose (1999, p. 29) have also pointed out, this may lead them to shun the 'p' word altogether as 'something blameworthy, threatening and unspeakable'. Or as one of the people involved in Beresford *et al.*'s (1999, p. 152) research put it, 'People don't want to class themselves as poor'.

Lister develops the analysis of this negative experience of poverty, and argues that it is a product of the way in which discourses on poverty have constructed people as poor and shaped their understanding of their plight. The ideologies of poverty that we were discussing above influence people who are poor too. And she goes on to argue that what is needed to challenge this is a change in the politics of poverty to promote instead dignity and respect for the experiences and the views of citizens who are poor, what she calls more generally the 'politics of representation' (Lister, 2004, ch. 5). This is a challenge for academics and policy-makers, however, and one which might involve significant changes in the policies to combat poverty that we discuss in Part IV. What it reminds us is that ideologies of poverty are diverse and contradictory and that the 'objective' analysis of academics and policy-makers discussed in this book must be balanced with the 'subjective' experiences and attitudes of those citizens who are the focus of their concern.

International Dimensions

SUMMARY OF KEY POINTS

- Poverty is a global problem with high levels of deprivation being experienced in many parts of the world.
- The United Nations has committed member states to the goal of eradicating poverty in the world through national and international cooperation.
- Comparisons of poverty levels across nations can be difficult because of the different definitions and measures used in different countries.
- Research on poverty in the European Union is now coordinated by the EU Commission.
- Expansion of the EU has made the achievement of greater harmony in social security and anti-poverty policy more difficult.
- The EU Commission supported a number of anti-poverty programmes in the 1980s and 1990s; but it is now EU policy to require member nations to commit themselves to developing and reviewing National Action Plans to promote social inclusion.

Global poverty and international action

Most discussion of the problem of poverty, and certainly most research into it, takes place within national boundaries. However poverty is an international, or rather a global, problem. There are gross inequalities in the resources available to peoples in different parts of the world and within all countries. These result in widespread deprivation in many relatively affluent countries and in severe deprivation in some less affluent ones with large sections of the population living below the standards which would be accepted in the wider international community. We live in a profoundly unequal world in which the extreme poverty that leads to starvation and early death is unfortunately still quite common in some parts of the world, most notably in sub-Saharan Africa.

Such international inequity and extreme poverty are not new phenomena, but the increasing development of international contact through international agencies and international trade are making it an ever more immediate problem for a wider community of nations. Also the increasing range and accessibility of the communications media are bringing more knowledge of the problem into the homes and consciousness of ever more people across the globe. Poverty is now an international problem, and politicians and academics are increasingly beginning to focus on this broader analysis and the policy implications that flow from it (see George, 1988; Townsend, 1993, 1995; and in particular, Townsend and Gordon, 2002). It has also even begun to attract popular attention amongst ordinary citizens, as revealed in the *Make Poverty History* campaign, which in 2005 sought to promote the cause of global anti-poverty action within the most powerful nations in the developed world, including the UK.

Recognition of the international dimension of the problem of poverty, however, brings with it problems of definition and analysis extending beyond the issues that have dominated national debate and research in countries such as the UK. As discussed in this book, the problem of understanding poverty in a country such as the UK involves appraising a complex range of debates and assessing confusing and sometimes seemingly contradictory evidence. To develop this understanding onto an international scale requires extension and expansion of both theoretical definition and empirical measurement, for which there is insufficient space to do justice here (see Gordon and Townsend, 2000; Townsend and Gordon, 2002).

There is, however, an increasingly vibrant and informed debate about the nature of poverty across the globe, and about the importance of international action to challenge and combat this. Most significant here was the declaration by 117 United Nations states at the World Summit on Social Development in Copenhagen in 1995, quoted at the beginning of this book. The declaration committed the UN to the, 'goal of eradicating poverty in the world through decisive national actions and international co-operation' (Commitment 2, United Nations, 1995). Following this, task forces were set up focusing upon different aspects of global poverty; and in 1997 the United Nations Development Programme (UNDP) reviewed progress and introduced new measures of poverty (Langmore, 2000).

The UNDP has been a key agency in the international response to global poverty. It undertakes a wide range of policy action, supporting all sorts of anti-poverty initiatives in different countries across the world, and since the 1990s has produced an annual report focusing on different aspects of the international dimensions of poverty and development. At the beginning of the twenty-first century, however, there are a number of other international agencies concerned both to define and measure poverty internationally and to support policy action to combat it. These include the major financial institutions of the global economy the International Monetary Fund (IMF) and the World Bank.

The World Bank has often played a high-profile role in developing international understanding of poverty, most notably in their (much criticised) adoption of the below $1 a day (at 1985 prices) definition of inadequate living standards in the world's poorest countries (accompanied by $2 a day in Latin America and $4 a day in transitional economies). They have also been influential in supporting policy responses which rely more heavily upon the promotion of economic development than redistribution; and these have been criticised as inadequate by international poverty campaigners such as Townsend (Townsend and Gordon, 2002).

In addition to the economic focus of the World Bank and the IMF, there are a number of other international agencies actively pursuing international responses to other aspects of global poverty. For instance the International Labour Organisation (ILO) campaigns on issues of employment rights and conditions, and the World Health Organisation (WHO) promotes policy action to combat disease and prevent ill-health. There are also important anti-poverty activities undertaken by major international charities or non-government agencies. These include the longstanding work of organisations such as Oxfam or Christian Aid, who both distribute aid and work to promote economic self-sufficiency, in particular in developing countries in Africa and Asia.

As the work of Oxfam reveals, much of the international action on poverty is not a new phenomenon. However, there is no doubt that the increasing availability of evidence on the plight of people in poverty across the world and the increasing willingness of international agencies and national governments to make global poverty a policy priority has led to a higher level of academic debate about, and policy concern on, the international dimension of poverty at the beginning of the new century. This is revealed most clearly in the recent work of Townsend. As we mentioned in Chapter 1, Townsend's research was influential in developing the definition and measurement of poverty in the UK in the mid-twentieth century. At the beginning of this century he has directed his concern to the problems of defining poverty internationally and, more importantly perhaps, to promoting international action to alleviate it (Townsend, 1993, 1995; Townsend and Gordon, 2002). He has even concluded that what is now needed to combat global poverty is the development of an '*international* welfare state' (Townsend and Gordon, 2002, p. 19, emphasis in original).

International comparisons

In addition to Townsend's work a wider range of research is now being undertaken into the depth and experience of poverty in different countries across the world. For instance, research has recently been published on poverty in Russia (Manning and Tikhonova, 2004) and in China (OECD, 2004). The latter study was carried out under the auspices of the Organisation for Economic Cooperation and Development (OECD). The OECD collects data and undertakes research on economic development and poverty across developed nations and publishes this in paper form and on its website (OECD, 2005). It thus provides a major resource for comparative studies of the international dimensions of poverty. Comparative research is now a significant feature of much academic work on poverty; and a useful guide to some of the key features and concepts of comparative analysis is provided by Gordon and Spicker (1999).

However, as with an understanding of poverty in the UK, international comparisons are inevitably fraught with definitional and methodological difficulties. In a survey of poverty rates in a range of OECD countries, Atkinson (1995a) pointed out that comparisons must take account of the problem of comparability of data across national boundaries, for surveys carried out either independently or by national governments may not necessarily use the same bases for definition or measurement in different countries. This can make comparative analysis more difficult than some of the proponents of international poverty research may realise. Atkinson discussed four of the main problems involved in it in a little more detail. These are:

- The use of different indicators of poverty.
- The application of different poverty lines to income or expenditure distributions.
- The adoption of different units, families or households for measurement.
- The choice of different equivalence scales to compare the resources available within units.

These present problems for the analysis and comparison of data from research studies on a single country, as we shall discuss in Chapter 6; but such problems are magnified several times when analysis or comparison seeks to transcend national boundaries.

Despite these problems, however, significant progress has been made in recent years in the international analysis of data on poverty. Of particular importance in this context is the use of the Luxembourg Income Study (LIS) on income inequality. The LIS was established in 1983, under the sponsorship of the Luxembourg government to develop a database on income distribution from subscribing countries (see Smeeding *et al.*, 1990; de Tombeur and Ladewig, 1994). It contains information on over twenty countries drawing on individual databases going back to 1968. It permits academics or government researchers to access data on these different countries and undertake comparative studies of poverty and income distribution, as Mitchell's (1991) study of ten welfare states demonstrated.

As with many national datasets, the LIS contains mainly 'snapshot' data on income distribution. As we discuss in Chapter 7, such data cannot tell us anything about the dynamic changes in income distribution and poverty experienced over time. Longitudinal datasets can do this, however; and, within Europe at least, such a comparative dataset does exist in the European Community Household Panel Survey (ECHP). This was established by the European Union statistical agency, Eurostat, in 1994 which since then has been collecting data annually from most of the member nations then within the EU. It provides a more detailed source of data for comparative analysis within Western Europe, and one which can be used to track changes over time, so enhancing the basis for comparative studies of poverty. It is also evidence of the importance of the European dimension of research and policy as a result of the policies and institutions of the EU, which also directly affect the UK as a member of the Union.

Poverty in Europe

Despite the existence of wide cultural and political differences, which have often divided Europe over the last hundred years and more, the economic and social development of most Western European countries has followed a pattern that provides for closer comparison and cooperation than exists between many other groups of countries throughout the world. Further, since the collapse of Eastern bloc communism in the late 1980s this pattern has been imported in some form to most of the former communist countries of Eastern Europe, who now look to the West for social, economic and political support and development. Thus the growth of capitalism and industrialisation, the development of political democracy and the establishment of welfare states have produced within European countries patterns of poverty and anti-poverty policy that permit relatively easy comparisons to be made between trends and achievements.

The relative homogeneity of European socio-economic structures has been consolidated considerably since the end of the Second World War by the economic and social unity provided by the creation and development of the EU. Initially covering six countries (France, Italy, West Germany, Belgium, the Netherlands and Luxembourg) the European Economic Community, as it was then called, has since expanded to cover now twenty-five member nations comprising most of Western Europe and extending into Eastern Europe too, with other Eastern European countries aspiring to join in the future. Over this period it has also transformed itself in to a political as well as an economic union – the EU. In the process of this the EU has expanded from being a predominantly economic and trading partnership to become a focus for joint economic and social planning across a wide spectrum of financial and welfare issues at the beginning of the new century (Hantrais, 2000; Geyer, 2000; Kleinman, 2002).

In the EU in particular, therefore, it is possible to identify common problems of poverty and inequality and common strategies for responding to these, which can be compared between different nation states with some degree of accuracy. All countries have experienced the impact of industrialisation and the creation of labour markets, although in some countries the size of the agricultural sector of the economy has remained large compared with others. This has resulted in similar patterns to those in Britain of wage poverty and poverty resulting from unemployment, and also in similar family structures in which the impact of this poverty is experienced differently by men and women at different stages of their life-cycle. As we shall see, therefore, statistical comparisons between countries reveal similar patterns of poverty, even though its extent and depth varies.

Comparative analysis of welfare policies in European countries in particular has been heavily influenced by the seminal work of Esping Andersen (1990) on welfare state regimes as a means of contrasting the similarities and differences in the structure of welfare provision in different countries. Esping Andersen has since developed this work (1996; 1999), and the approach has also been taken up by others (Goodin *et al.*, 1999). There is little direct comparison of poverty and anti-poverty policies in these general accounts, however, although Mitchell (1991) has looked in more depth at income transfer policies across ten advanced welfare states. The regimes which Esping Andersen develops are only 'ideal types', but they do represent approaches to social policy that provide for comparison between similar policy developments in different countries. This is particularly true of the original six EU nations, which all developed versions of corporatist welfare states with very similar social security and other anti-poverty measures based on employment-related insurance benefits, with a range of limited safety-net measures for those not covered by the main scheme. As we shall see below, the development of EU policy and planning has led to increasing pressure for the coordination and harmonisation of social security and anti-poverty policy between member states, even though this is challenged by the increased diversity of an ever-expanding EU.

Despite the similarities in the development of welfare regimes, however, there are rather different traditions of poverty debate and poverty research in different European countries. As George and Lawson (1980) and Walker *et al.* (1984) have pointed out, in the past this has made direct comparisons between countries difficult, even where overall developments reveal similar trends. Obviously the Luxembourg Income Study will help to overcome some of these differences in the future. However, the work of the EU itself, and in particular the central statistical department, Eurostat, has done much to develop a cross-national basis for comparisons of poverty and inequality within EU countries. Eurostat does not itself collect data from respondents but relies on data which is provided to it by the statistical offices of the member nations. It is thus more of a data warehouse than a research agency. However, the data has been widely used to develop comparative studies of poverty, and other social issues, across member nations. In particular researchers have used it to compare poverty levels utilising the measure of different proportions of mean average income (40, 50 and 60 per cent) also used by the UK government discussed in Chapter 2 (Eurostat, 1990; Atkinson, 1998; Atkinson *et al.*, 2002).

Figure 4.1 is taken from such a Eurostat study of comparative poverty rates, although the 1980s data is based on information on expenditure rather than income, a distinction that we shall return to discuss in more detail in Chapter 6. It reveals comparatively high levels of poverty in the UK in the 1990s under this measure, particularly given the overall relative affluence of this country.

The problems of comparisons over time are revealed to some extent in Figure 4.1, with different measures being used across the two decades. It also

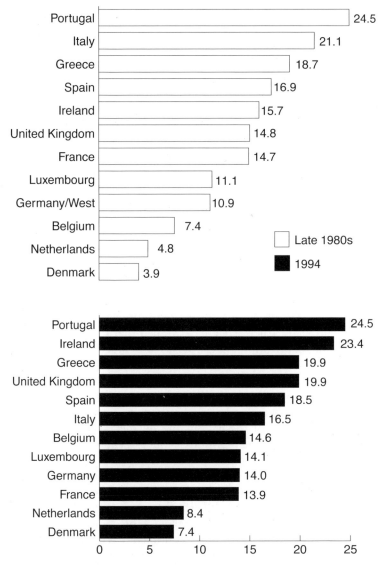

Figure 4.1 Poverty rates (per cent) in the EU in the late 1980s (50 per cent of mean expenditure) and in 1994 (50 per cent of mean income)
Source: Lindqvist (2000), figure 9.1, p. 197.

reveals another of the problems in international comparison: it takes a long time for up-to-date statistics for all countries to be produced and analysed. Eurostat has taken up some of these concerns in the commissioning of a longitudinal dataset for statistical comparisons, the European Community Household Panel (ECHP) mentioned above, and this has been employed by Kuchler and Goebel (2003) to compare trends in poverty incidence and poverty intensity across member states in the 1990s.

Another problem within such cross-national statistical comparisons is the different impact of country-based measures of average income compared to EU wide measures. In relatively affluent nations, such as Germany and the UK, 50 or 60 per cent of the average income is likely to be a much higher absolute figure than in relatively poorer nations such as Portugal or Greece; and yet the adoption of a single central EU average should mean that all citizens are being compared against a common benchmark. Such a common European measure would, of course, be likely to increase the relative levels of poverty in poorer countries and depress the levels in the more affluent ones; and, ironically perhaps, might therefore lessen political concern with the problem of poverty across the Union in affluent countries. In general therefore Eurostat and other comparative researchers tend generally to adopt a country-specific measure when undertaking such comparative analysis, using 50 or 60 per cent of national average income.

These comparisons are made on relative measures, but the EU has also explored the possibility of developing absolute measures of poverty for the purposes of international comparison. The aim was to determine a European baseline level of living (EBL) using a measure of basic needs – European base-line needs (EBN) (see EC, 1989). More recently Gordon and Townsend (2000, ch. 4) have sought to expand on this and develop the concept of 'overall poverty', based on the notion of deprivation or exclusion from those things taken for granted by others in society and drawn from the 1995 UN declaration mentioned earlier. They have argued that this could be measured using research on deprivation indicators as developed in the *Poverty and Social Exclusion* Survey in the UK (Gordon *et al.*, 2000), which we shall discuss in more detail in Chapter 5.

As in the UK, changes in the levels of poverty across Europe have also involved a change in the composition of those in poverty, with a relative decline in the proportion of the elderly and an increase in the unemployed (especially the long-term unemployed), young people, lone parents and migrant labourers. And, as in the UK, this led European commentators to make a distinction between this 'new poverty' and previous life-cycle experience of poverty discussed in Chapter 7 (EC, 1991; Room *et al.*, 1990). This problem is accentuated by the fact that such people are generally excluded from the employment-related benefit protection that is provided by most of the corporatist welfare states of continental Western Europe, leading to a collapse in the comprehensive poverty prevention provided by such schemes and increasing reliance on inadequate and loosely structured assistance measures. This problem has been further exacerbated since a number of the Eastern European former communist countries has joined the

EU, leading to an increasing gap between those covered by comprehensive social security protection and those excluded from it.

These changes are leading to a reassessment of the appropriateness of social security policies within the EU and of the effectiveness of anti-poverty measures, with a growing fear about the potential marginalisation and social exclusion of the expanding group of the 'new poor'. Part of the concern here is with the consequences of the differences between the social security protection offered to poor citizens in different EU countries and with the potential for future harmonisation of these. Differences in protection can lead to the related problems of 'social dumping' and 'social tourism'.

▦ *Social dumping* is the problem of investors and employers moving activities within the EU to seek out locations where social security protection, and other labour market costs and regulations, are least onerous.
▦ *Social tourism* is the converse problem of workers or other citizens moving across countries to seek out those countries where social security protection is greatest.

One obvious consequence of such trends is a mismatch between employment prospects and potential employees. However, they can also have a more general effect on policy development within the EU, creating indirect pressure on all countries to reduce social security and labour market costs in order to attract investment and employment. This is likely to run counter to any commitment to harmonise social security and other protection by building on best practice and seeking to develop comparable levels of protection across all member nations. What is more with the enlargement of the Union to include parts of Eastern Europe these pressures have become potentially more acute.

European anti-poverty policy

In part as a result of these pressures upon any moves towards harmonisation of social security protection within the EU, the Union has for some time been committed to the maintenance of some overview over the development of poverty and social exclusion within member nations and to the implementation of EU-wide measures to combat this – at least to some extent. A general overview of developments in poverty and deprivation throughout the EU was provided in the early 1990s by the EU Observatory on National Policies to Combat Social Exclusion (see Robbins *et al.*, 1994), although this was disbanded in 1994 with the winding-up of the third EU anti-poverty programme, discussed below. Information on poverty in Europe has continued to be provided by the Commission, however, including the Eurostat data discussed above. The EU has also funded an independent agency to coordinate anti-poverty action – the European Anti-Poverty Network (EAPN). The European context of poverty and social exclusion was also discussed in a pamphlet produced by the CPAG in the early 1990s (Simpson and Walker, 1993) and in a collection of papers edited by Room (1995).

The EU started out primarily as an economic union, the European Economic Community, concerned with the development and regulation of trade rather than with the determination of economic or social policies within or across member states. Although this primary economic focus has remained of fundamental importance, by the end of the twentieth century the EU had become more and more concerned with attempts to intervene in national policy planning to develop community-wide initiatives to which all member states must subscribe.

The most well-known of these initiatives were the attempts to harmonise and upgrade employment rights across member nations to combat the effects of social dumping and social tourism. These have been developed over several decades and have included directives from the EU Commission on such issues as health and safety at work and maximum numbers of working hours. They culminated in 1989 in the drafting of the Social Charter (the Community Charter of the Fundamental Social Rights of Workers). The Social Charter was incorporated into the Maastricht Treaty of 1992, although it was then a separate Chapter, from which the UK government was permitted to opt out. After 1997 the Labour government removed the opt-out and adopted in full the commitments in the Charter, which, together with other commitments to EU social and economic policy development, were incorporated into the 1997 Treaty of Amsterdam.

However, EU social and economic policy planning has also included a wide range of policy initiatives that have sought more generally to respond to concerns over the growing levels of poverty and social exclusion within the EU. Set against the massive economic programmes of the EU these social programmes have been relatively small-scale and limited in their scope and effect. Nevertheless they have been important in moving the problem of poverty and anti-poverty policy up the European agenda. Perhaps the most important of these initiatives has been the distribution of EU structural funds. These funds have been used to provide support for particular activities in those member states that come under the broad aegis of the fund. There were initially three separate structural funds (Kleinman, 2002, ch. 5):

- the *European Social Fund* (ESF) for employment and training initiatives;
- the *European Regional Development Fund* (ERDF) to improve infrastructure in depressed regions; and
- the *European Agricultural Guidance and Guarantee Fund* (FEOGA) to assist in rural change and development.

However, these separate funds were extended and integrated in order to maximise their impact within member states, and after Maastricht they were extended further to include a new Cohesion Fund. In effect they now operate as one general programme for employment, infrastructure and agricultural change providing support for projects initiated or supported by national governments in areas of established social need. The targeting of funds is also now determined by the designation of specific regions within countries as priority areas for European support. The effect of this is some element of regional redistribution within the Union, intended to counterbalance some of the effects of the geographical concentration of economic development at the centre of continental Europe, sometimes referred to as the 'golden triangle' of Frankfurt, Paris and Milan. In the last century there were seven such objectives distributing resources across a wide range of areas across the member nations. However, since 2000 these have been reduced to three (Kleinman, 2002, ch. 5):

- *Objective 1* – the most deprived areas.
- *Objective 2* – areas facing industrial decline, rural areas, urban areas and those affecting by fishing industry decline.
- *Objective 3* – assistance to education, training and employment.

Spending on the structural funds grew rapidly in the latter years of the last century to over €32 billion, more than a third of the EU budget (Kleinman, 2002, p. 114). In the 1990s most of this spending also went to the first two objectives, covering around a half of the EU population, although the proportion covered by the first two objectives will decline under the new regime in the new century.

The social programmes will also be affected significantly by the extension of EU membership to the candidate nations in Eastern Europe. These countries already face more serious problems of economic decline and industrial restructuring than most of even the poorer areas of Western Europe. Ironically, therefore, enlargement of the Union may only serve in the short run to accentuate the gap between citizens in the new member nations and those in the prosperous 'golden triangle'; and further pressure will come onto the programmes to promote economic and social development through regional redistribution.

In addition to the more general initiatives arising from the operation of the structural funds there has been a series of specific initiatives designed to tackle directly the problem of poverty within the EU, generally referred to as the three EU poverty programmes. These were a series of very small-scale initiatives, the third programme being the largest with a budget of €55 million (£38 million) over five years from 1989–94, less than the annual budget of a social services department or a university. Nevertheless they were symbolically important in providing an example of community-wide action to combat poverty, and they did lead to the development of some interesting new initiatives in project-based anti-poverty strategy.

The first programme ran from 1975–80 and comprised a small number of pilot schemes and studies in community development (Dennett *et al.*, 1982). After these were completed there were no further projects for a period of four years of 'evaluation and reflection' (EC, 1991, p. 15). Then a second programme was established to run for five years, from 1984–89, with a budget of €29 million. The second programme included 91 local action research projects throughout the then twelve-member states that were designed to build on the actual experience of local anti-poverty work, with the results coordinated in academic institutions in Bath and Louvain (Room *et al.*, 1993).

This work was supplemented by statistical and attitudinal research carried out on a community-wide basis by Eurostat and the EU survey agency Eurobarometer (EC, 1990 and 1994).

The third anti-poverty programme directly followed the second and ran for five years, from 1989–94. The broad aim of the programme was to foster the economic and social integration of the economically and socially least-privileged groups, echoing wider concerns about marginalisation and social exclusion. As in the previous programmes, this was to be achieved primarily by working *with* people in poverty in action research projects based on partnership principles, an approach which has since been taken up more widely in national government policies in the UK as we shall see in Chapter 16. There were 39 projects across the then twelve member-states, those in Britain being based in Belfast, Bristol, Edinburgh and Liverpool, coordinated by a research unit at Warwick University.

Included in 'Poverty 3', as it was called, was the establishment in 1990 of more general research and evaluation work carried out by the EU Observatory on National Policies to Combat Social Exclusion. This included representatives of active poverty researchers from all the participating member states, and produced annual reports detailing both changes in national policies and developments in European poverty trends (for instance, Robbins *et al.*, 1994). In 1994 the Commission proposed replacing 'Poverty 3' with a fourth EU anti-poverty programme, but this was blocked by the representatives of the British and German governments; and since then such high profile cross-national anti-poverty action has not been supported by the EU.

Nevertheless it is worth remembering that the poverty programmes were very small-scale initiatives by European-wide economic standards. By targeting limited resources onto a few local areas little could be done to combat the broader problems of poverty within the member-states – a problem that we will return to discuss in the context of UK policy initiatives in Chapter 16. However, what the action research projects did provide were examples of initiatives to combat poverty and ways of working in partnership with people in poverty that could be utilised to develop more comprehensive strategies in the future, either at the national or the community level. Such targeted activity has continued to be supported by the EU and is specifically mandated in the Amsterdam Treaty of 1997. A range of small scale initiatives has been supported across the Union under the auspices of the Directorate General for Employment and Social Affairs (DGV), and these have become something of a model for targeted anti-poverty action within member-nations too. More generally, formal commitments to combat poverty within the EU have been shifted to national governments, with all the (then) EU members committing themselves at Lisbon in 2000 to draw up National Action Plans on Social Inclusion and to review these on a rolling basis.

Support for anti-poverty action within the EU is now therefore formally a commitment of member-nations. However, coordination and promotion of activity to combat social exclusion is still provided by the EU Commission through a Social Exclusion Action Programme, with a programme committee of representatives of member-nations and commitments to provide analysis, networking and exchange of best practice throughout the EU from 2002 to 2006. Furthermore, the broader social policies such as the structural funds and the development of social security protection and employment rights have remained as significant cross-national activities with support from within the Commission.

It is worth bearing in mind, however, that, although such initiatives may well help to address the problems of poverty and social exclusion within the EU, they are also likely to have the effect of further segregating European countries from the wider international context. High standards of employment and wages in the EU countries are likely to be bought about at the expense of maintaining a high overall balance of trade with other countries throughout the world and of excluding from Europe large numbers of migrant or immigrant workers from low-wage, developing countries. An integrated and protected Europe, therefore, may also become 'Fortress Europe', providing relatively high standards for most of its citizens within an increasingly unequal wider international context of poverty and deprivation. Although, of course, this is part of a much broader debate about the global context of poverty with which we opened this chapter. European protectionism is only one part of a widespread international resistance to major social and economic reform.

Part II

Definition and Measurement

Defining Poverty

SUMMARY OF KEY POINTS

- Definitions of poverty are needed in order to measure its extent within society.
- Distinctions have been made between *absolute* and *relative* definitions of poverty, although in practice most approaches involve a mixture of the two.
- Most research on poverty has aimed to define a 'poverty line' within the income distribution below which people can be said to be poor.
- Budget standards approaches seek to draw a poverty line by defining and measuring the cost of those goods needed to avoid poverty.
- Deprivation indicator approaches seek to draw a poverty line by drawing up a list of those aspects of living standards which respondents identify as necessary.
- Both approaches lead to the identification of a link between low income and lack of necessities, which can be treated as a poverty line.
- Multi-dimensional approaches to the definition and measurement of poverty which do not seek to draw one single poverty line have become more common in recent research and policy debate.

The need for definition

This part of the book deals with the problems of defining and measuring poverty. This chapter concentrates on discussion of attempts to define poverty and the ways in which these definitions have changed and developed over time. Arguably it is the issue of definition that lies at the heart of our task in understanding poverty. We must first know what poverty is before we can identify where and when it is occurring or attempt to measure it, and before we can begin to do anything to alleviate it.

As discussed in Part I, disagreements over the definition of poverty run deep and are closely associated with disagreements over both the causes of poverty and the solutions to it. In practice all these issues of definition, measurement, cause and solution are bound up together, and an understanding of poverty requires an appreciation of the interrelationship between them all. Nevertheless some logical distinctions can be made, and they will have to be if we are to make any progress in analysing the range of theoretical and empirical material these debates have produced.

The need for definition is in fact recognised by most of the major researchers and commentators on poverty issues. In his study of poverty in Britain in the 1960s and 1970s, Townsend opened the report with a definition of poverty that was crucial to his approach to the study and the findings it revealed, and which has been widely used by others since:

> Individuals, families and groups in the population can be said to be in poverty when they lack the resources to obtain the types of diet, participate in the activities and have the living conditions and amenities which are customary . . . in the societies to which they belong. (Townsend, 1979, p. 31)

However, debates in Britain about the appropriate way to define poverty go back at least to the end of the nineteenth century and to the work of the two pioneers of the study of poverty, Booth and Rowntree, discussed in Chapter 1; and throughout much of this time this debate has focused particularly on the fundamental distinction that is alleged to exist between absolute and relative poverty.

Absolute poverty is sometimes claimed to be an objective, even a scientific definition of poverty. It is based on the notion of subsistence. Subsistence is the minimum needed to sustain life, and so being below subsistence level is to be experiencing absolute poverty because one does not have enough to live on. On the face of it this is a contradiction in terms – how do those without enough to live on, live? The answer, according to absolute poverty theorists, is that they do not do so for long; and if they are not provided with enough for subsistence they will starve, or – perhaps more likely in a country such as Britain – in the winter they will freeze. Indeed every winter a significant number of older people in Britain do die of hypothermia because they cannot afford to heat their homes adequately.

The definition of absolute poverty is thus associated with attempts to define subsistence. We need to work out what people need to have in order to survive; then, if we ensure that they are provided with this, we have removed the problem of poverty. This notion of absolute or subsistence poverty has often been associated with the early work of Booth (1889) and Rowntree (1901 and 2000), although Spicker (1990) and Veit-Wilson (1986) have respectively argued that these are mistaken or oversimplified judgements and that in practice both employed more complex, relative definitions in their studies. And this has certainly been the case in the debates and research which have followed them.

Throughout much of the twentieth century, therefore, academic and political debate focused on whether and how poverty could be identified and measured within a relatively affluent welfare society. Towards the end of the century, however, there was something of a return to the absolute or subsistence approach championed by the New Right academics and politicians associated with the Conservative governments led by Margaret Thatcher. An early example of this was the work of Joseph and Sumption, who claimed that 'An absolute standard means one defined by reference to the actual needs of the poor and not by reference to the expenditure of those who are not poor. A family is poor if it cannot afford to eat' (1979, p. 27). This was taken up by the then Secretary of State for Social Services, John Moore, in 1989 in the speech quoted in Chapter 1. He called this speech 'The end of the line for poverty' and in it he castigated relative notions of poverty as 'bizarre', because they seemed to be suggesting that, as poverty was related to average standards of living, it would continue to exist no matter how wealthy a country became, which, he claimed, could surely not be right.

Absolute poverty is thus contrasted with *relative* poverty. This is a more subjective or social standard in that it explicitly recognises that some element of judgement is involved in determining poverty levels, although as we shall see the question of whose judgement this should be is a controversial one. Judgement is required because a relative definition of poverty is based on a comparison between the standard of living of people who are poor and the standard of living of other members of society who are not poor, usually involving some measure of the average standard of the whole of the society in which poverty is being studied.

The relative definition of poverty is associated in particular with the Fabian critics of the postwar achievements of the welfare state in eliminating poverty in Britain, most notably the work of Townsend (1954, 1979) and Abel Smith and Townsend (1965). Their argument was that although state benefits had provided enough to prevent subsistence poverty for most, in terms of their position relative to the average standard of living in society the poorest people were no better off in the 1950s and 1960s than they had been in the 1940s. Thus in a society growing in affluence, as postwar Britain was, remaining as far behind the average as before continued to constitute poverty. As Townsend put it in his 1979 definition, quoted above, relative poverty prevents people from participating in activities that are customary in the society in which they live.

This notion of participation is not only the product of postwar Fabian thinking, however, commentators as long ago and ideologically as far apart as

Adam Smith and Karl Marx appeared to recognise and support it. According to Adam Smith:

> By necessaries, I understand not only the commodities which are indispensibly necessary for the support of life but whatever the custom of the country renders it indecent for creditable people, even of the lowest order, to be without. A linen shirt, for example, is strictly speaking not a necessity of life ... But in the present time ... a creditable day labourer would be ashamed to appear in public without a linen shirt. (Smith, 1776, p. 691)

Similarly in a pamphlet first published in 1891 Marx wrote that 'Our desires and pleasures spring from society; we measure them, therefore, by society ... they are of a relative nature' (Marx, 1952, p. 33).

Of course absolutist critics, such as Moore (1989), argue that these relative differences are merely inequalities which will exist in any society, and that the relativist protagonists are using the notion of poverty illegitimately with the aim of redistributing wealth rather than preventing want. This debate underlies much of the politics and policy of poverty prevention or allevia-tion in modern societies, and we shall discuss it in more detail shortly. Once we do examine what the supporters of both absolute and relative defini-tions of poverty mean, however, we will begin to realise that the distinction is in fact largely a false one. As mentioned, Veit Wilson (1986) has demon-strated how Rowntree, often thought of as the architect of the absolute definition of poverty, in reality utilised relative measures. This is because the bald distinction between absolute and relative poverty is in practice an over-simplification of much more complex definitional problems; which are discussed at more length in Lister's (2004, ch. 1) book on poverty.

Absolute and relative poverty

Absolute definitions do appear to have some sort of objective logic to them based around the notion of subsistence – having enough to sustain life. But this begs the question, what is life? What we require for life will in practice differ depending on place and time. For instance what is adequate shelter depends on the ambient climate and the availability of materials for con-struction – even the homeless people living in what has sometimes been called London's 'Cardboard City' arguably are only able to survive because of the availability of cardboard. Adequate fuel for warmth also depends on the climate, the time of year, the condition of someone's dwelling and their state of health. Adequate diet depends on the availability of types of food, the ability to cook food, the nature of the work for which sustenance is required and (at least according to Rowntree, who allowed more in his basic diet for men than for women) on gender. Diet might also depend on taste – Rowntree included tea in his basic British diet, although it is of negligible nutritional value.

Thus different people need different things in different places according to differing circumstances. Differing individual needs will also be affected by the living or sharing arrangements people have with other individuals in families or households, an issue to which we will return in Chapter 6. What is more people's circumstances will in practice be determined by their ability to utilise the resources they do have in order to provide adequately for themselves. Although Rowntree attempted to use the independent judgement of nutritionists in order to determine a basic diet to act as a subsistence definition of poverty, he still distinguished between primary and secondary poverty. *Primary* poverty referred to those who did not have access to the resources to meet their subsistence needs, *secondary* poverty to those who seemingly did have the resources but were still unable to utilise these to raise themselves above the subsistence level. Although Rowntree distinguished between these, he referred to both as poverty.

As mentioned, Rowntree included 'non-necessities' such as tea in his subsistence measure. In his second study in 1936 he also included the cost of a radio, a newspaper, presents for children and holidays (Rowntree, 1941). This was not only a recognition that absolute standards may not be the same thing as avoidance of starvation, but also that these standards changed over time. In their review of definitions and measurements of poverty, Fiegehen *et al.* (1977) noted that for all apparently absolute definitions there is a tendency to raise minimum levels as living standards improve. This was revealed starkly in an attempt by Stitt and Grant (1993) to use Rowntree's subsistence methodology to produce an absolute measure of poverty for the 1990s, which included significant weekly sums for swimming, trips to the cinema and other leisure activities – important needs perhaps, but certainly debatable as necessary for subsistence.

Of course Stitt and Grant were using their knowledge of cultural needs in the 1990s to determine the weekly budget upon which their research was based. As Veit-Wilson (1986) argued, Rowntree's studies of poverty also relied primarily on a similarly arbitrary assessment of lifestyle in York at the time of the surveys, drawn from the judgement of Rowntree and his interviewers. This is an inherent problem in the setting of budgets based on needs, to which we shall return shortly. However, we cannot simply conclude from it that absolute definitions of poverty are wrong and relative ones right. There are problems with the relativist case too, and many of these were exposed by Sen (1983) in a persuasive attack on the orthodoxy of relativism.

If poverty levels change as society becomes more affluent, then it is not clear how the position of those who are poor can be distinguished from others who are merely less well-off in an unequal social order. This raises the question of where, and how, to draw a line between those in poverty and the rest. This was taken up in Piachaud's (1981a) critique of Townsend's 1979 study of relative poverty, which we discuss below. In essence the argument is that any cut-off line is arbitrary and merely involves the imposition of a subjective judgement of what is an acceptable minimum standard at any particular time.

Sen takes this further with the suggestion that if the relative position of the line remained the same, then during a period of recession in which overall standards drop there may be no increase in poverty; or conversely in a very wealthy society people would still be poor if, say, they could not afford a new motor car every year. This, he suggests, is clearly absurd: there must be some absolute measure against which relativities can be assessed. In searching for this Sen returns to Adam Smith's reference to the 'need' for a linen shirt. He argues that this provides a basis for an absolute, rather than a relative, definition of poverty, because Smith refers to the lack of the shirt as destroying a person's dignity – it is shameful.

It is this experience of shame or, as Sen later argued, the lack of capability that it exemplifies, that makes a person poor. By capability he meant the extent to which people could function as individual members of a social order. Such capability is essential in any social order, but the commodities needed to exercise it vary from society to society and within one society depending on the circumstances of individuals. But *lack* of capability is absolute and it is this, Sen argues, that constitutes poverty. Thus poverty is a separate status that is different from simply being less well-off. Lister (2004, ch. 1) explores this argument in more detail in her book on poverty, linking it also to debates about the concept of 'need' and the extent to which, as Doyal and Gough (1991) have argued, we might be able to arrive at absolute definitions of human needs.

However, in practice Sen had trouble defining lack of capability. He attempted to base this on a Rawlsian notion of social justice. This is the idea that what we are prepared to argue is 'just' is the minimum state that we ourselves would accept as tolerable within the existing social order. So that those incapable of achieving such a standard experience social injustice and are therefore poor. But this is a rather abstract and philosophical approach to social values, and it has never been successfully applied to social policy debate or planning. Indeed such a notion of justice is essentially a matter of judgement or debate or political preference – and not an objective or scientific fact. For instance Sen implies that starvation is objectively recognisable as poverty, yet as discussed above attempts to arrive at a definition of an adequate diet to avoid starvation have been fraught with disagreements.

Thus absolute definitions of poverty necessarily involve relative judgements to apply them to any particular society; and relative definitions require some absolute core in order to distinguish them from broader inequalities. Both it seems have major disadvantages, and in pure terms neither is acceptable or workable as a definition of poverty. If we wish to retain poverty as a basis for analysis, measurement and ultimately political action, therefore, we need to avoid the disadvantages of both, or rather to capitalise on their advantages.

In practice most attempts to define poverty do combine both, as Fiegehen *et al.* (1977) noted, usually by selecting a poverty standard, expressing it in income terms and then applying it to the income distribution of a particular society in order to reveal the proportion in poverty. Strictly speaking, of course, this is a measure of poverty rather than a definition, but to some extent the issues overlap. Once we accept an element of relativity in the definition of poverty, then we need to develop a means of deciding where within the distribution of resources across society the line which separates off those in poverty can be drawn. What we need to do therefore is define a 'poverty line'.

The most frequently used approach to this in the UK has often been to use the level of basic assistance benefits (currently Income Support), as this is clearly an example of what the government regards as necessary to combat poverty at any particular time. It is a readily available definition, it is related to household size with equivalent amounts specified for different household members (see Chapter 6), and, as we shall see, fractions or multiples of it can be used to measure those below the level or just above it. Atkinson (1990) discussed the history of the minimum level implied by benefit scales in Britain, pointing out that they include a mixture of absolute and relative features, and Bradshaw and Lynes (1995) took this up in more detail in a study of the links between benefit ratings and living standards.

However, as Veit-Wilson (1987) has pointed out, the use of benefit rates to define poverty lines is in a sense tautological. In political terms it cannot provide a basis upon which to act as it is already the product of political action. If there are those below it, and most studies of poverty find that there are, then they could be classed as poor; but this does not give a meaningful picture – either absolutely or relatively – of their poverty. Furthermore, as John Moore (1989) argued in his speech attacking relative definitions of poverty, it means that if the government were to raise the level of benefit in response to political pressure to alleviate poverty, then the extent of poverty might appear to increase; and if it were to lower the level as a result of a decision to reduce state support, then the number in poverty might be reduced. A logical approach ought to operate in exactly the reverse direction to this.

More recently Veit-Wilson (1998) undertook research to compare the ways in which ten different countries across the developed world sought to establish minimum income standards. As he pointed out, the way in which these were developed depended upon the political and policy context in which they were constructed, or the 'discourses of poverty' as he referred to these. As with UK benefit levels, they were intended to embody the notion of a standard of adequacy rather than a definition of poverty. They included minimum wage and minimum benefit levels, calculations of consumption levels or average budgets, and statistical constructs based on levels of average income or expenditure. In some cases, therefore, these minimum income standards were clearly relative measures based on the outcomes of policy processes in determining wage or benefit levels. In others, however, they did aim to develop a 'scientific approach' (*ibid.*, p. 16) towards the definition of poverty based on the notion of an observable threshold below which adequate standards of living could not be maintained.

These approaches to the definition of poverty lines have also been developed by academic researchers within the UK. They include in particular the 'budget standard' method, drawing on the Rowntree absolutist tradition of a list of necessities, and 'deprivation indicator' method, drawing on the Townsend relativist tradition of deprived lifestyle. In practice, both combine both absolutist and relativist dimensions, and end up producing rather similar results utilising similar methods of measuring living standards and drawing poverty lines; and more recently researchers have begun to look to combine these different approaches to create multi-dimensional or 'overall' definitions of poverty (Finch and Bradshaw, 2003). As we shall see in Chapter 8 this has been taken further in debate about the broader concept of social exclusion, where a range of multiple indicators are generally used to replace a single poverty line or point of measurement.

Budget standards

Budget standards approaches are based on attempts to determine a list of necessities, the absence of which can then be used as a poverty line below which, presumably, people should not be permitted to fall. They are thus absolutist in structure; but, as many including Bradshaw (Bradshaw *et al.*, 1987) have argued, budgets can also represent socially determined needs. Budget standards definitions are usually based on the notion of a (weekly) basket of goods. The idea was pioneered by Rowntree in his studies of poverty in York (1901, 1941; Rowntree and Lavers, 1951), where a weekly diet was constructed based on the advice of nutritionists.

Rowntree's was a long and detailed list of goods including, in the 1950 version, 10 ounces of rice at 5*d*, 6 pounds of swedes at 1*s* 3*d*, 1 egg at 3*d* and, of course, half a pound of tea at 1*s* 8*d*. Nevertheless it provided only for an extremely frugal standard of living, as he admitted in 1901:

> A family living on the scale allowed for must never spend a penny on railway fare or omnibus. They must never go into the country unless they walk. They must never purchase a halfpenny newspaper or spend a penny to buy a ticket for a popular concert ... and what is bought must be of the plainest and most economical description. (Rowntree, 1901, p. 167)

The narrow-minded meanness of this basket-of-goods approach was expertly exposed in 1922 by Ernest Bevin, then the leader of the dockworkers' trade union, in an incident described by Atkinson (1989, p. 27). During an enquiry into dockworkers' pay, evidence as to need had been presented by a researcher in a description of a minimum basket of goods. Bevin had gone out and bought the recommended diet of scraps of bacon, fish and bread and then presented them to the researcher, asking whether he thought it sufficient for a man who had to carry heavy bags of grain all day.

Of course baskets of goods need not be so frugal, especially if they are explicitly based on an attempt to define a socially determined standard. There is a long tradition in the USA of attempts to define and cost the required living standard for a worker's family, going back to the Bureau of Labour Statistics' (BLS) work of the early twentieth century. The approach has been adapted and developed by other researchers utilising different standards, for instance by the New York Community Council, which maintained a variant of the BLS budget. However, there are inevitable problems associated with the use of baskets of goods determined by experts because this involves the imposition of arbitrary and, as Bevin demonstrated, often hopelessly unrealistic judgements by those who probably have no experience of living on them. They are thus unworkable in practice when compared with the expenditure patterns of real people, as Rowntree's researchers found out (Veit-Wilson, 1986).

Since budget standards are supposed to represent required expenditure patterns, surely it would be preferable to base them on actual patterns of expenditure rather than on hypothetical expert judgement? This is what the Watts Committee in the United States tried to do. Statistical evidence on expenditure patterns was used to draw up different levels of expenditure. There was a 'prevailing family standard', fixed at a median level, but also a 'social minimum standard' at 50 per cent below this and a 'social abundance standard' at 50 per cent above it. Bradshaw *et al.* (1987) compared these to British standards, using purchasing power parities to avoid exchange rate variations, and found similarities between the social minimum standard and assistance benefit levels in Britain.

A similar approach was pioneered in the UK by Piachaud (1979) in the latter part of the last century to seek to arrive at the budget that would be needed to provide adequate support for children – provocatively entitled by the CPAG, who published it, *The Cost of a Child*. Piachaud used a budget standard approach to establish expenditure-based budgets for children, which were above the levels of benefit then provided for children in the basic Supplementary Benefit scheme. He then used this to measure the number of children in poverty (Piachaud, 1981b). These were politically important findings, especially of course for the CPAG; and they have been repeated since, albeit in a somewhat different forms (Oldfield and Yu, 1993; Ridge, 2002).

Piachaud's work had a clear political message about the unacceptable levels of child poverty that he claimed to find in late twentieth-century Britain, and, as we shall see, this is a message which has now led to significant policy commitments to reduce child poverty in the early decades of the new century. The approach which he developed, however, was also taken up more widely in attempts to use expenditure patterns to determine acceptable standards of living for adults too. And these too have begun to have a more and more significant impact upon policy debates.

The leading figure in this research has been Jonathan Bradshaw from the University of York. In the 1980s he began work in Britain using the expenditure patterns and weekly budgets of people living on assistance benefit (Bradshaw and Morgan, 1987) and those of benefit claimants in the north-east of England (Bradshaw and Holmes, 1989). His work demonstrated that the weekly budgets derived from these expenditure patterns provided inadequate resources for those living on these incomes – for example leaving just 94p a week for a woman to spend on clothing, a diet deficient by 6,500 calories and only enough money for one haircut a year (Bradshaw *et al.*, 1987, pp. 180–1).

Since then Bradshaw has continued and much extended this budget standards research. In the early 1990s he established the Family Budget Unit (FBU), which used expert judgements and expenditure patterns to determine a range of different budgets for certain different family types, as in the BLS work in the United States (Bradshaw, 1993a, 1993b). Detailed calculations were made of consumption needs and expenditure patterns to draw up weekly budgets for a range of different family and household types. These were also based on different relative standards of living to provide a guide to the incomes that would be needed to support such standards. These included a 'modest but adequate' budget, based on average 'normal' living costs, and a scaled down 'low-cost but acceptable' budget, which could be taken as a relative measure of a subsistence or poverty standard based on budget calculations and expenditure patterns within affluent society. The different budget calculations for different family types utilising these different standards of living can now be viewed on the FBU website at York University, listed at the end of the book.

The assumption underlying both Piachaud's and Bradshaw's work of course is that anyone seeing the evidence of the inadequacy of the weekly budget constructed from their research will recognise the existence of poverty – as in Bevin's 'docker's breakfast'. But this is still a matter of judgement about the acceptability of different relative standards of living, which in practice comes either from the views of experts (Bradshaw and Piachaud), or non-experts (their readers). Such budget standards also do not overcome the problem of Rowntree's distinction between primary and secondary poverty. In practice many households do spend some money on 'non-necessities' such as alcohol and tobacco (see Bradshaw and Morgan, 1987, p. 14), so that they may be living below the budget standard level even though in theory they have sufficient weekly income to stay above it.

One way to avoid this dilemma may be to adopt what Veit-Wilson (1987, p. 201) once called a 'sociological' approach to budget setting and accept that ordinary people's living patterns include non-necessary expenditure. Hence the poverty level should be the income at which people, following their ordinary expenditure patterns, would have sufficient for necessities. This is effectively what Rowntree means by his notion of secondary poverty. It does not get round the problem of defining necessities, nor the relativities issue of how much non-necessary expenditure is acceptable as ordinary (keeping pets, running a car, pursuing a hobby?); but it does suggest that some broader averaging out of expenditure patterns and weekly budgets may permit researchers to take account of the expenditure patterns of real households in setting the acceptable level of weekly budgets.

This has sometimes been called the *income proxy* approach to budget setting. It can be traced back to the attempts by the Watts Committee in the United States to base definitions of standards on the income levels necessary to maintain various weekly living norms. But it was the work of Orshanksy in 1965 for the American Social Security Administration which really established income proxies as a new method of determining threshold standards for various family sizes, which could be used as the basis for future poverty research and policy development. Following the nineteenth-century German researcher Ernst Engel, she compared the expenditure patterns of families at different income levels, and found that lower-income families spent a greater proportion of their income on necessities. The proportion of income spent on necessities thus declined as income rose and more non-necessities were purchased. This is referred to as the 'Engel curve' (Figure 5.1).

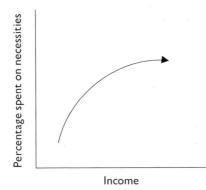

Figure 5.1   The Engel curve

Orshansky argued that average expenditure devoted to necessities could thus be used to determine the poverty level, suggesting that people were in poverty if more than 30 per cent of the household budget was spent on food (Orshansky, 1969; see Bradshaw *et al.*, 1987, p. 173). This provides an income proxy for poverty, based on the purchase of necessities. And of course the cut-off point need not necessarily be 30 per cent, and the measure need not only be expenditure on food; for instance in Canada a level of 62 per cent of spending on food, clothing and shelter has been used. However, instead of fixing the point arbitrarily it could be discerned from the Engel curve itself. Engel curves are not usually a simple curve, but are more of an 'S' shape, representing more complex changes in patterns of expenditure (Figure 5.2).

The inflection points, marked by the arrows in Figure 5.2, are where the marginal propensity to consume more of a particular type of good accelerates or slows down – the 'turnover point'. Above the first point, higher income makes a wider range of expenditures possible; later points are likely to represent stages where the variety of new expenditure is exhausted and the quality of goods bought becomes an issue in determining patterns. The turnover point therefore gives the level at which choice replaces need when determining expenditure – the poverty level. And Bradshaw *et al.* (1987) have argued that

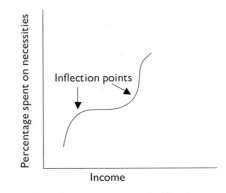

Figure 5.2   Inflection points on the Engel curve

it is possible to derive such a point for all household types based on recorded expenditure on items such as food, clothing and fuel.

In practice, as we shall see, this is similar in conception and operation to the poverty threshold derived by Townsend and others from the deprivation indicator approach discussed below. Like Townsend's method it is a *behaviourist* approach, constructed from evidence of behaviour patterns revealed in surveys of household or family expenditure. However, it is still dependent to some extent on a judgement by experts as to what constitute the necessities against which expenditure is measured. Other income proxy researchers have sought to overcome this by developing a *consensual* definition of needs and the incomes required to meet them and thus avoid poverty, by asking survey respondents about their views on necessities as well as their expenditure practices.

Early development of this can be found in the work of Van Praag and his colleagues at the University of Leyden in the Netherlands (Van Praag *et al.*, 1982). In a series of major social surveys conducted in a number of European countries, they asked the respondents what level of income they would need in order to make ends meet and avoid poverty. They also asked what cash income the respondents would attribute to various standards of living, described on a scale from very bad to very good. Fairly complex statistical analysis was then employed to derive poverty lines from the two sets of responses, based on what the respondents had said was necessary for an adequate standard – referred to as the 'Leyden poverty line' (see Veit-Wilson, 1987, pp. 190–1).

Thus an income proxy approach was utilised to define a consensual poverty line, based on the notion of an adequate budget. This was a significant move beyond the arbitrary weekly minimum levels fixed by experts and nutritionists found in some in earlier studies. It was also clearly adopting a relative perspective on the notion of necessities and living standards, based on the attitudes of respondents in surveys of living standards. In practice this is very similar to the deprivation indicator approach to poverty, which draws more directly on the relativist tradition of poverty research; and more recently Bradshaw has also collaborated in research within this tradition (see Gordon *et al.*, 2000).

Deprivation indicators

Townsend, in his work on poverty in Britain in the 1960s, was the pioneer of the deprivation indicator method of poverty definition. As with his overall approach to poverty, it was drawn from the relativist critiques of the postwar complacency about the supposed removal of absolute poverty in Britain. In particular this complacency was based on Rowntree's third and final study of poverty in York (Rowntree and Lavers, 1951), which had revealed a much lower level of poverty than the previous studies and appeared to confirm the view that welfare state reforms, based on the recommendations of Beveridge, together with growing affluence, meant that no one in Britain was any longer in need.

Townsend championed the idea that need, or rather deprivation, was relative, as is revealed in the quotation at the start of this chapter from the beginning of his 1979 report on poverty. However he believed that relative need, expressed as exclusion from everyday living patterns, was not a matter of mere arbitrary judgement but could be objectively determined and measured. This was to be done by drawing up a list of key indicators of standard of living, the lack of which would be evidence of deprivation.

In the survey upon which the 1979 study was based, sixty such indicators expressed as yes/no questions were presented to over two thousand households. Around forty of these elicited yes/no answer patterns highly correlated with income. From these Townsend constructed a 'deprivation index' based on twelve indicators, such as the lack of a refrigerator, no holiday away from home in the last twelve months and the lack of a cooked breakfast most days of week, all of which correlated highly with low income (see Townsend, 1979, table 6.3, p. 250). From this index deprivation scores were then calculated for different households and these were compared with the incomes of households. These incomes were expressed as a proportion of the benefit entitlement for those households, because Townsend wanted to compare deprivation with benefit levels. These were then plotted onto a graph, where here they fell into two clear lines (Figure 5.3); one line represented the changing position on the deprivation index of the bottom five income groups as income rose, while

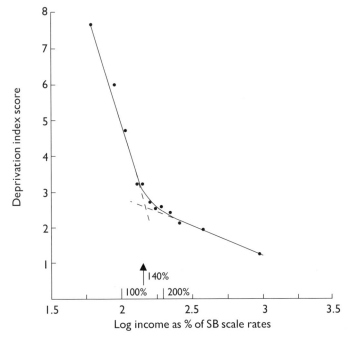

Figure 5.3 Deprivation by logarithm of income as a percentage of Supplementary Benefit rates

Source: Townsend (1979), figure 6.4, p. 261.

the other represented the changing position of the top seven. The bottom five income groups were those with a household income below 140 per cent of the then Supplementary Benefit level.

From this Townsend claimed that the point where the lines met, or to put it another way where the curve 'turned over', constituted a 'threshold of deprivation ... that is, a point in descending the income scale below which deprivation increased disproportionately to the fall in income' (*ibid.*, p. 271). More generally, Townsend claimed, here was an objective means of defining a relative poverty line; and the fact that the threshold, or poverty line, was at about 140 per cent of benefit entitlement confirmed previous claims by Townsend and others that those immediately above the benefit levels would still be in poverty in an affluent country such as Britain. What is more, of course, it also provided a powerful case for the introduction of an easy solution to the problem, at least in theory – by raising the benefit levels by 40 per cent.

This was a ground-breaking step in the pursuit of a relative definition of poverty, but it was not without its problems, or its critics. The most famous critique was that published by Piachaud in the journal *New Society* (Piachaud, 1981a; see also Desai, 1986). Piachaud criticised Townsend's list of deprivation indicators, which made it appear as though Townsend was setting himself up as an expert of what was an acceptable standard of life (for instance a cooked breakfast every day) and was taking no account of taste as an explanation for the lack of particular indicators (for instance vegetarians will not want a joint of meat on Sunday, the lack of which Townsend saw as an indicator of deprivation). Piachaud also made a more technical criticism of the statistical technique, which had produced the threshold by the use of modal values, as this did not take account of variations around average points, which would have left the lines on the graph much less clear-cut.

Desai discusses these criticisms in some depth, but he also demonstrates that a reanalysis of Townsend's data that takes them into account still produces the same threshold, thus apparently confirming the validity of Townsend's overall approach. However the approach and the threshold are at best a behavioural and not a consensual definition of the poverty line – as with the income proxy measures drawn from spending patterns. They also centrally involve the judgement of experts, in this case Townsend himself, in the determination of acceptable indicators of deprivation from which to derive the line.

These deficiencies, however, have been taken into account in later studies that have adapted and developed Townsend's deprivation indicator method. The most significant of these was the research sponsored by the London Weekend Television (LWT) company for a television series called *Breadline Britain*. The programmes were based on a major survey of a representative sample of people which was carried out in 1983 and was subsequently published as a book (Mack and Lansley, 1985). The survey was then repeated in 1990, using the same methodology, and screened as a second series of programmes (Frayman, 1992). The data from the second survey was not initially used for extensive academic analysis, but this was eventually taken up in a collection of papers edited by Gordon and Pantazis (1997).

The Breadline Britain surveys, like Townsend, used a list of indicators expressed as survey questions, but the development and the use of the list was much more sophisticated. In each case the researchers asked their respondents whether or not they thought each potential indicator was necessary to avoid hardship, eliciting their views on these in much the same way that Van Praag et al. (1982) had done for the necessities in their research on budgets. They then asked not only whether the respondents lacked those indicators, but also whether this lack was due to the lack of resources to purchase them (as opposed to a choice not to expend resources on these items).

From this a list of consensually agreed indicators, similar to but rather longer than Townsend's (Mack and Lansley, 1985, table 4.1, p. 89), was drawn up to act as an index which could then be applied to the population in the survey. However, this index avoided the problems both of expert determination of acceptable indicators and of variations in the taste of respondents in choosing to go without particular things. Just as in Townsend's study, however, the Breadline Britain data revealed a threshold between the bottom (four) and the top (eight) groups, although in their case the break occurred at around 135 per cent of the benefit entitlement level. Thus, even using this more sophisticated approach based on consensual definitions of need and lack, the existence of a poverty line separating those unable to sustain an acceptable standard of living from the rest of society appeared to be confirmed.

Interestingly, too, in the second survey the views of respondents as to the unacceptable lack of necessary items had slightly, but perceptibly, changed to include such things as a decent state of decoration at home, an insurance policy and fresh fruit. This confirmed what Townsend had earlier argued, and what Rowntree had in effect conceded, that customary standards change as society develops. Rather depressingly the 1990 survey also revealed that a higher proportion of respondents were suffering from deprivation than in 1983 – an increase from 14 per cent to 21 per cent of households who were lacking three or more of the consensually defined necessities.

Media sponsorship for such detailed research on poverty was an exceptional case of journalistic interest in academic debate. Perhaps not surprisingly, it has not been repeated since; and LWT has since been taken over and merged into much larger conglomerate television companies. However, the deprivation indicator approach has remained a central feature of research on poverty, and in particular has been further developed by the Townsend Centre for International Poverty Research at the University of Bristol, established and led by Townsend himself. In 1999 they carried out a third major survey utilising the Breadline Britain methodology and used the findings, inter alia, to compare the situation at the end of the decade with the results from the earlier surveys (Gordon et al., 2000).

In fact the 1999 Poverty and Social Exclusion (PSE) Survey, as it was called, was not quite the same as the earlier LWT research. The General Household Survey (GHS) for 1998/99 was used to provide data on economic circumstances and incomes, and then the Office of National Statistics (ONS) Omnibus Survey was used to collect data on what were viewed as necessities, with a follow-up survey of a smaller sub-sample of lower-income households used to establish lack of items identified as necessities and other information on poverty and social exclusion. 'Piggy-backing' on other surveys in this way reduced the potential costs of the PSE survey, because academic funders were not able to support initial research in the way the LWT had in the 1980s.

The PSE survey produced a similar list of items, regarded by respondents as necessities, to the earlier surveys, with 35 items considered by 50 per cent or more to be necessary for an acceptable standard of living in Britain at the end of the twentieth century. More detailed analysis of those who lacked some of these items because they could not afford them was then carried out and statistical tests done to determine whether a separate group of poor people could be identified in this way, as they had been in the earlier surveys. From this the researchers concluded that people could be classified as poor if there were two or more socially defined necessities that they were unable to afford, although they also identified other groups above this level who were 'vulnerable to poverty' or had recently 'risen out of poverty' (*ibid.*, p. 18).

On this measure 25.6 per cent of the population were poor. Using the three or more measure employed by the earlier surveys the proportion was 24 per cent, a further increase on the 21 per cent identified by this measure in 1990. Although, as in the earlier surveys too, the list of items considered necessities had also altered to some extent, with carpets, telephones and new clothes now being seen as necessitous (*ibid.*, p. 44). The conclusion of the researchers was that this major survey had once again vindicated the value of the deprivation indicator approach to the defining of poverty, and provided telling evidence of the continuing and growing levels of poverty and deprivation in the country at the turn of the century.

Nevertheless critics of the deprivation indicator approach do remain. Taking up some of the early criticisms made by Piachaud (1981a) of Townsend's initial work, McKay (2004) has used further statistical analysis of the PSE survey to argue that the consensus on necessities is not as clear cut as the original authors have made out, and that the designation of those lacking two or more such necessities as poor is problematic, as in most cases these households could also afford an average of eight non-necessities. This raises again the question of choice versus need in expenditure patterns, and hence Rowntree's initial distinction between primary and secondary poverty. It also suggests that there are inevitably likely to be both theoretical and methodological difficulties in arriving at one single mechanism for defining poverty scientifically.

Multi-dimensional approaches

It is revealing that both the budget standard and deprivation indicator approaches to the definition of poverty have led to the use of similar survey-based attempts to develop consensual indicators of poverty and deprivation. The ability of households to afford these items is then compared with income distributions to reveal the extent to which low incomes can be associated with deprivation or reduced living standards, sometimes employing the plotting of this relationship on a graph. In effect, therefore, these approaches are adopting a multi-dimensional approach, utilising both lack of socially perceived necessities and low income. The PSE survey also in fact employed a third measure in its follow-up survey, asking people about their experiences of social exclusion and the extent to which they felt that they were (or had been) poor.

It has not been common in poverty research, however, for these different measures to be used in combination. This issue was taken up by Finch and Bradshaw (2003) in an article which explored the potential for examining overlapping dimensions of poverty. They concluded that there was actually relatively little overlap between the people defined as poor by the three different measures of deprivation from perceived necessities, subjective poverty and low-income poverty in the PSE survey. This suggests that there may in fact be different problems of poverty here rather then one single definition or line. However, they also employed the three measures cumulatively to look at the overlapping impact of these dimensions. Here they found that there were differences between those who were poor on multiple dimensions and those who were poor on only one.

Finch and Bradshaw therefore argued that it may not be safe, in scientific terms, to rely upon only one measure of poverty, but rather that different measures should be employed in combination. This multi-dimensional approach is increasingly recognised by both policy-makers and academic researchers at the beginning of the new century. The Copenhagen Declaration of 1995 (United Nations, 1995) talked about the importance of developing a conception of 'overall poverty' to capture the different dimensions of poverty in different international settings. This overall poverty approach has been taken up by Gordon and Townsend (2000) who have argued that the PSE research could be used to develop such a multi-dimensional approach to the definition and measurement of poverty in Europe.

The importance of multiple measures of poverty has also been recognised by the UK government in the early twenty-first century. In 2003 they engaged in consultation over how to measure child poverty in the country, following their commitment to reduce levels of child poverty and remove it by 2020, as we discuss in Chapter 11. Following this they announced that in future a combination of three measures would be adopted, although their use of the term absolute is different from that discussed earlier (DWP, 2003):

- Absolute low income – 60 per cent of median average income in 1998/99 in real terms, to compare whether there were improvements against a fixed benchmark.
- Relative low income – 60 per cent of contemporary median income, to compare poor families against general rises in incomes.
- Material deprivation and low income combined – including a measure of lack of material necessities, to compare living standards more broadly.

The government also now publish an annual review of poverty and social exclusion, entitled *Opportunity for All* (DWP, 2004a), which we discuss in

Chapter 8. This includes a long list of over fifty indicators of poverty and exclusion against which trends are measured on an annual basis. These indicators vary from low income levels, to educational achievement and fear of crime.

This use of multiple indicators was endorsed by Spicker (2004) in a article in which he argued that attempts to combine different indicators in summary indices or definitions inevitably involved combining different, and potentially incompatible, measures of poverty and deprivation; and that multiple indicators should in practice be used as just that. In other words multiple indicators capture the different dimensions of different aspects of poverty, and are likely to have different implications for the focus and direction of anti-poverty policy. We should accept that poverty, and anti-poverty policy, are therefore multi-faceted phenomena and recognise that no single definition or poverty line can ever capture all these dimensions. This has important consequences for anti-poverty policy, as we shall see in Part IV. It has important implications for attempts to measure poverty too.

Measuring Poverty

SUMMARY OF KEY POINTS

- Measurement of poverty needs to distinguish between a focus on either expenditure or income, although in practice it is usually the latter which is employed in most research.
- There is an important difference between *head count* and *poverty gap* measures of poverty.
- Measurement can be based on income or expenditure of individuals, families or households, although each will reveal different patterns.
- Equivalence scales can be used to compare households of different sizes and composition.
- Studies of intra-household income transfers reveal that resources are often not equally shared within families or households.
- Quantitative measurement of poverty can be based on either existing data sources or new survey research; but comparison across different datasets is always potentially problematic.
- Measurement of inequality can employ simple graphical devices such as *Lorenz curves* and *Gini coefficients*.
- Qualitative research provides description and detail which cannot be found in statistical analysis.
- Qualitative analysis can provide a basis for people in poverty to articulate their own experiences and gain some control over the presentation of research on poverty.

The problem of measurement

For most academics and researchers, as well as most politicians, the purpose of attempting to define poverty is to be able to measure its extent within or across societies, the implication being that where poverty is extensive, it should then be the focus of concern and policies should be developed to remove or ameliorate it. It is primarily because of this policy context that the task of defining poverty and drawing poverty lines is, of course, so problematic. For the same reason the question of measuring poverty is fraught with difficulties and disagreements. Fundamental to the debate on measurement, as with the debate on definitions, is the question of whether what is being measured is a separate category of poverty or merely a predetermined aspect of the broader measurement of levels of inequality, such as a line or threshold drawn towards the bottom of the income or wealth scale. However, the issue is further complicated, as Ringen (1988) pointed out, by confusion over the use of both direct and indirect measures to draw the lines.

The emphasis on relative deprivation and standard of living when determining poverty levels, developed by Townsend (1979), Mack and Lansley (1985) and Gordon *et al.* (2000), focuses attention on expenditure, or more accurately consumption, as a measure of poverty. However, most studies of poverty, particularly those seeking to establish the number living below a given poverty line use income as a measure, as indeed do Gordon *et al.* and the others when seeking to identify groups who may be defined as poor. Ringen's argument is that, given that it is consumption that determines the standard living, the measurement of poverty should be based on direct measures of this. Any measurement of poverty based on income is employing an indirect measure, since income cannot be used as a proxy for consumption as many aspects of consumption are not determined solely by income.

This is true for the consumption of non-commodified services, those that cannot be purchased in a market such as health care and education, as well as other public services which influence standards of living such as crime prevention, environment and access to transport. However, it is also true for the consumption of many material goods which also influence our daily lives, from housing (locations, size and standard) and private transport (ownership of a motor car) to consumer goods, such as washing machines and telephones. Access to or possession of such services and goods is not just determined by income, and therefore an income-based measure of poverty is likely to overlook or understate the importance of such consumption factors in determining the extent and depth of poverty. This was explored in more depth in research by Saunders *et al.* who concluded that income and expenditure measures were tapping into 'quite different dimensions of economic well-being' (2002, p. 230).

This has been recognised in public discourse about poverty in particular. For instance, as we shall return to discuss, it can be seen in the more recent concerns with the broader issues of social exclusion. It is also taken up in attempts through research to measure standards of living. For instance, the government sponsored Family Expenditure Survey (FES), now the Expenditure and

Food Survey (EFS), which is the major source of statistical information about living standards in the UK, collects data on expenditure as well as income because this is seen as a more direct measure of poverty and deprivation. However, measurement of expenditure is much more difficult, and therefore more expensive, than measurement of income, as the later discussion of the impact of savings and debt reveals. It is partly for this practical reason therefore that much quantitative research on poverty continues to rely upon income measures, despite the inherent limitations of them.

However, the use of income measures is not without its problems. For a start it is necessary to distinguish between *gross* income (usually wages paid before income tax, National Insurance and other unavoidable deductions are made) and *net* income (the amount of money actually available for people to spend each week). The amount of resources available for daily household living is also critically affected by the cost of housing. Rents or mortgage payments are by far the largest items in most household budgets, and to a large extent they are out of the control of households on a weekly basis. Statistics on incomes and expenditure frequently make a distinction therefore between income *before* housing costs have been deducted (BHC) and *after* these have been accounted for (AHC). This is true of the main HBAI figures, as we saw in Chapter 2, where the distinction creates a significant difference to the levels of poverty revealed, with many more households found to be poor (when compared to average incomes) on the AHC measure, because of the relatively high impact of housing costs on low-income households.

Then there is the question of what period to measure income over. Most people probably plan much of their expenditure on a weekly basis, and the research on budget standards discussed in Chapter 5 has largely operated with weekly household budgets. It also used to be quite common for workers to be paid on a weekly basis, and social security benefit levels are set weekly. However, a large number of workers are now paid monthly and even social security benefits are sometimes paid on a fortnightly or monthly basis. Yet many people in practice think about their incomes in annual terms, and this is certainly the way these are often presented and expressed in wage and salary negotiations. And, as we shall see, the period over which income is received and spent can make a difference to regular living standards, although research by Boheim and Jenkins (2000) found that both current income (that received at the time of the survey) and annual income (the average over the last year) measures provided broadly similar pictures of income distribution.

Certainly it is the case that income is not all consumed on a weekly basis. Purchase of consumer goods such as washing machines and telephones is done far less frequently, and when incurred may well take expenditure over weekly income limits. Past purchase of such goods, and other assets, will also conversely mean that these will reduce pressures on expenditure, and hence income, on a weekly basis (ownership of a washing machine means no weekly trips to the launderette). This is linked to saving, and even investment. Obviously those who are able to save money from their weekly or monthly income to provide for irregular purchases or commitments will have a lower weekly expenditure but a higher overall standard of living. Taking a longer term, life-course, perspective on this, investment of current income for future needs, for instance through a private or occupational pension scheme, can be critical in determining the lifetime risk of poverty – and, indeed, current social security policy in the UK and elsewhere assumes that this is just what most future pensioners will be doing, as we shall see in Chapter 14. Savings, and other forms of accumulated wealth, can mean that many people with little or no regular incomes are not in practice threatened by poverty, and may even live lavish lifestyles. Conversely, lack of access to such assets will increase the risk of poverty, even where regular income is received. These issues are now central to analysis of poverty dynamics to which we shall return in Chapter 7.

The opposite of savings is debt. The use of credit to finance all manner of consumption goods is now widespread in modern society, most obviously in the case of owner-occupied housing subject to a mortgage. Levels of credit and debt are higher in the early twenty-first century than they have ever been before in Britain. For many people this is not a problem; but for some, levels of personal debt may become unsustainable. And when debts cannot be repaid this undermines the ability of people to get by on their regular income and can accelerate or accentuate the experience of poverty. There are other dimensions of problematic credit and debt which can also contribute to poverty, not least the emotional pressures of indebtedness. Some of these were explored in a major review of credit and debt in the 1990s (Berthoud and Kempson, 1992), and more recently have been taken up in research on financial exclusion (Collard et al., 2001; Collard et al., 2003) which we shall return to discuss in Chapter 8.

In short, therefore, adopting income, even as a proxy measure, for standard of living does not resolve the problem of how to measure poverty, for there needs to be some agreement over the period for which income is assumed to be available to households; and the benefit of income has to be balanced against access to wealth or pressure of debt. However, this does not mean that we cannot, or should not, seek to measure poverty in this way. As Atkinson in particular has consistently argued and demonstrated (for instance Atkinson, 1983, 1989), if care is taken to recognise the problems involved there is quite a lot we can say from data on income and expenditure about the extent of poverty and inequality in the UK, and in other advanced industrial countries too.

Indeed the major definition of poverty in the UK, and now across the European Union, is based on a measure of the proportion of people with incomes below a fixed proportion of average incomes, usually now 60 per cent of median income, as we saw in Chapter 2. For all its limitations this is a clear and easily accessible poverty line, which does involve a relative definition which can be compared over time and across different populations. It also has clear policy implications, suggesting that if large numbers of people are living below this line, then income distribution should be changed to alter this. And, to some extent, this is just what the UK government have committed themselves to do with their policies on ending child poverty, which we discuss in Chapter 11.

There are complications even with this measure, however. In particular there is the difference which such a poverty line can disguise between the 'head count' and the 'poverty gap'.

- The *head count* refers to the numbers of people below the poverty line, for example 60 per cent of median income. This is the measure commonly used and it also sets a clear target for combating poverty. By raising the incomes of those below the line to above it the numbers of people in poverty can be reduced.
- The *poverty gap* refers to the distance below the line of the incomes of those who are poor. There is a rather significant difference between an income of 58 per cent of the average and one of 30 per cent, and yet on a head-count measure both would be treated as poverty in the same way. This, too, has policy implications. It is easier and probably less costly to move those just below the line to just above it, than it is to move those who are some way below it (see Bradshaw, 2001). Arguably it is these poorer people who ought to be a more pressing policy priority, and yet in practice large-scale reductions in poverty are more likely to be achieved by concentrating policy action onto those who are not-so-poor.

In Chapter 4 we discussed the recent trends towards multi-dimensional approaches to defining poverty, recognising that poverty can mean different things in different circumstances and have different dimensions for different people. This applies to how we measure poverty too. Both head count and poverty gap measures are important, and will tell us something about different dimensions of the problem of poverty. Both income and expenditure measures can also reveal the different dimensions of spending power and spending patterns, and this is recognised in the PSE survey research (Gordon *et al.*, 2000) and the new measures of child poverty (DWP, 2003). Even here, however, there are further considerations to be borne in mind when measuring poverty, in particular the extent to which income or expenditure should be counted at individual or household levels.

Individuals and households

It is individual people who experience poverty. However, by and large individual people do not always live as individuals, and in particular they do not do so throughout all of their lives. In fact most individuals live with other individuals in families or households, where they pool their resources to some extent and share their wealth, or their poverty, with other family or household members. Thus if we want to measure poverty then we need to take account of the household or family structure in which people live and in which resources are distributed and consumed. A weekly income of £100 means something rather different if it is received by a single person than if it is received by a couple with two young children; and measures of income that do not take account of this will not tell us much about the real experience of poverty or deprivation.

In a collection of studies comparing the differing needs and resources of different household and family structures, Walker and Parker (1988) pointed out the importance of both differing household structure and life-cycle changes in this; and the various contributors to the book took up differing aspects of these issues. The question was also discussed by Townsend in his major poverty survey (Townsend, 1979, ch. 7). The most important initial issue raised by both is the need to distinguish between households and families, although on many occasions of course the two may overlap and the boundaries between them may not always be clear.

The logical (or sociological) distinction between the two is that unlike households, families consist of people with a more or less explicit commitment to joint living and sharing based on emotional, as well as empirical, interdependency. Marriage is the most obvious symbolic representation of this, but the concept of family is not restricted to married couples – it includes the dependent children of such couples and non-married partners (not necessarily heterosexual) who have made, or appear to have made, quasi-marital commitments. This narrow form of family is sometimes referred to as the 'nuclear family' to distinguish it from broader family and kinship ties between adult parents and children, or adult siblings.

The expectation is that members of families will pool and share resources and will expect, and welcome, interdependency; although, as will be discussed below, this is not always the case. This expectation is also enforced through the law, in particular in the rules covering entitlement to means-tested benefits in the UK, where those 'living together as husband and wife', together with their dependent children, are treated as an income unit and are paid at a lower (couple) rate than two separate individuals would be. The assumption is that two or more people together can live more cheaply than one alone, and there is obviously some sense in this. For instance heating and cleaning costs will probably be commensurably reduced, although how these savings should be measured is a controversial issue to which we shall return shortly in a discussion of equivalence scales.

Reduced living costs such as these, however, will also be experienced by those sharing residential accommodation even if they share no family ties or commitments – hence the argument that households, too, constitute a basis for a presumed pooling of resources. Since households are not based on any explicit emotional commitment, then the equivalent of marriage or civil partnership cannot serve as a definitional guide, and what constitutes a household can vary enormously. For instance a household may consist of a family with adult children still living at home, or aged parents living with their adult sons or daughters – in effect forms of extended family. Alternatively a household could be made up of non-relatives living within one house and sharing some living accommodation for convenience, or more usually because of financial necessity, for example young single adults sharing a rented house.

Obviously there is a distinction to be drawn between family-based or household groupings. Arguably the former have made some interpersonal commitment to sharing resources, whereas the latter probably have not. Although of course the distinction between the extended-family household and the single-adult household confuses the difference considerably. The distinction is also important when attempting to compare the resources of different groups since households are generally a broader and larger category than families. This difference in size is likely to be significant. Having stated a preference for households as a basis for measurement, Beckerman and Clark (1982, p. 17) went on to show that, using the family unit, in 1975 3.2 per cent of the population were living below the basic assistance benefit level, compared with 2.3 per cent when the household unit was used. As Piachaud (1982a, p. 342) argued, 'It is well known that the extent of poverty based on larger units is less than that based on smaller units since, for example, many poor individuals share households with better-off relatives'.

The distinction took on an important formal dimension in 1988 when the government introduced a change in the collection and presentation of official statistics covering low incomes. The change involved a switch from the previous basis of publishing the figures relating to low-income families (LIF) to publishing the figures relating to households with below average incomes (HBAI), which has since become the basis for all the annual statistical measures of income and expenditure. The reasons behind the change were complex and at the time controversial. They stemmed in part from the claim by government that sharing within households was commonplace (DSS, 1988). However, this was not supported by any direct evidence of such sharing, and yet, as critics pointed out, it led to an apparent reduction in overall levels of poverty. The Institute for Fiscal Studies (IFS) compared the figures under the new HBAI measure in 1988 with what these would have been under the old LIF (Johnson and Webb, 1990). Their analysis showed that the switch of basis from family to household reduced the percentage of people with low incomes and thus produced a measure that appeared to demonstrate reduced inequality, resulting from the assumption of greater levels of income-sharing.

Thus the difference between household and family measures is important, not just in the assumptions different measures make about how we organise our domestic lives (which of course can only be assumptions) but also in the consequences these have for the extent of poverty or inequality revealed by the different measures. For some time, therefore, researchers have tried to develop ways of including within statistical measures some mechanism for taking account of the reduced cost of pooled resources in families or households, so that comparisons can be made between the circumstances of those living in differing domestic arrangements. This has been done through the development of equivalence scales.

Equivalence scales

Equivalence scales are an attempt to express in proportional terms the presumed costs-of-living reductions experienced by members of households sharing resources, and they have been widely used in studies of poverty. Rowntree's first 1899 survey (Rowntree, 1901) was based on an equivalence scale drawn from presumed dietary needs, under which the amount allowed for children in a household was estimated at between a third and a quarter of that for an adult. Thus a household containing one adult and one child would require an income that was between 1.25 and 1.33 times the income of a single adult household to achieve the same standard of living.

The most well-known and widely used equivalence scales today are the Income Support (IS) scale rates, where the lower rate for a couple compared with two single persons and the reduced rate for children produce an equivalence scale, using a base of 1.0 for a couple, of roughly 0.65 the second adult in a household, and 0.45 for a child. There used to be a finer grading of the rates for children (and hence the equivalence scales for them) with lower fractions for younger children; but these have now been replaced with a single, higher, child rate. These are of course arbitrary fractions based on the (changing) judgement of government; and in practice they change slightly as the scales are uprated every year. However, they are widely understood, if perhaps implicitly by many; and, of course, they have clear policy implications for family support – with the move to a single rate for children leading to a significant increase in the benefits levels for families with young children (see Piachaud and Sutherland, 2002).

How to determine what fractions to use in equivalence scales is, not surprisingly, a controversial issue. Fiegehen *et al.* (1977, ch. 7) discussed different models and the consequences of these. They used data from the Family Expenditure Survey to determine the costs of different household members such as children, and compared the scales based on these expenditure patterns to those then assumed in benefit rates, finding that in practice there was little difference between the two. Other scales do treat the notional costs of additional adults and children differently, however; and such differences can make comparison between data on different distributions of income and different measures of poverty rather complex. Atkinson discussed this in the context of international comparisons of poverty rates, pointing out that the scale for a child adopted in different countries varied from 0.15 to 0.75 (Atkinson, 1995a, p. 89).

Coordination of scales across countries can help here, and this is done to some extent by the Luxembourg Income Study (LIS) and the OECD. However, even here inconsistencies may arise, with the OECD recently modifying its equivalence scales to reduce the scale for additional adults from 0.7 to 0.5 and for children from 0.5 to 0.3. Changes such as this can have a significant effect upon the scale of poverty – lower proportions for additional adults and children give the impression that a lower overall income can support the same household adequately. They can also influence the apparent distribution of poverty, with the recent OECD change reducing the numbers of children measured as poor compared to the numbers of adults (since all single person households would be likely to be adult only).

Nevertheless, equivalence scales do permit us to compare households or families of different structures or sizes more accurately, in particular in terms of changes in expenditure patterns at different levels of income. Thus analysis utilising Engel curves (the points in income scales at which expenditure on necessary items changes, discussed in Chapter 5) can be constructed and comparisons made between families of different types. Fiegehen *et al.* (1977, ch. 7) used this to show how Engel curves vary for households with and without dependent children, confirming our common-sense expectation that for households with children expenditure on necessities claims a higher proportion of income, especially at low income levels.

Intra-household transfers

Different household and family formations therefore result in different needs and expenditure patterns; and, as we shall see, these needs and patterns vary over time. Equivalence scales are a means of comparing different households or families by formalising assumptions about the reduced needs and expenditure that result from the sharing of resources within the household. However, the comparisons based on reduced costs due to sharing in households are founded on two important assumptions, both of which can be subjected to critical debate. The first assumption is that sharing or the aggregation of resources does take place within households, and that this interdependency is non-problematic. The second is that two or more people can live less expensively than one and maintain the same standard.

The assumption of aggregation is a long-standing feature of both academic analysis and policy development; and it is obviously not without foundation. For instance, although most children have no income of their own we know that most parents expect to use a part of their income to provide for their children. Nevertheless it is far from clear whether all parents share all their resources with their children on an equal basis – and indeed common sense suggests that it is most unlikely that they do. When it comes to sharing between adults the assumption of equal sharing is even more questionable.

Obviously obtaining reliable information on the distribution of incomes within households is problematic, a point to which we shall return shortly; but studies that have attempted to do this suggest that unequal sharing is likely to be the norm. In 1982 Piachaud (1982b, p. 481) concluded that 'the distribution of incomes within families is highly unequal'. Later in the 1980s Pahl (1989) carried out research based on interviews with both husbands and wives to investigate in detail the different patterns of income distribution within families and found that patterns varied significantly, and frequently exhibited inequalities both in share of income and control over expenditure. More recently she has conducted further research looking at the impact of new forms of electronic banking and credit on this (Pahl, 1999). Similar variations were also revealed in further qualitative research with families living on benefits carried out in the 1990s by Goode *et al.* (1998).

One of the reasons why the women in these families felt poor was because they did not control the resources – it was not their income that provided for the family and by and large they could not determine expenditure (*ibid.*). This feeling of dependency is a central feature of inequality within households, and it is compounded by the assumptions about aggregation and sharing of living costs incorporated into benefit policy (see Esam and

Berthoud, 1991). It is a social and an emotional as well as a material inequality, and it is a significant yet widely overlooked feature of poverty amid affluence to which we shall return in Chapter 9. Even when married women are in paid employment, family inequalities are not necessarily removed, for as Morris (1989) has shown, their income is generally lower and more likely to be spent on supplementing an inadequate housekeeping budget.

Of course poverty and inequality within households is not exclusively a female problem. The enforced dependency contained in policies that aggregate family and household incomes has consequences for sick and disabled adults forced to rely on others at home, as we shall discuss in Chapter 12. It is also extended to young adults, now sometimes up to the age of 25. The minimum wage level for young adults is below that for older people and, under benefit regulations, they receive lower levels of benefit and are assumed to be able to share their households with others.

The second assumption underlying the household basis for poverty measurement is that of the reduction in living costs that is associated with sharing. Again there is obviously some basis for this – heating can be shared, as can furniture and many other household items. However, many of the reductions supposedly associated with shared living are indirect savings based on unpaid work performed within the household, usually by women. Piachaud (1987) famously contrasted the cost of oven-ready chips with home-prepared chips – the end result is more or less the same but one costs more to the household in terms of money and the other more in terms of time. For the high-flying executive we know that 'time is money', but this equation is equally valid for the housewife at home.

The standard of living of many households is maintained by, usually women's, unpaid labour at home cooking and cleaning. This can act as a substitute for a reduced family income, but at a cost to the family member performing the work. As Lister (1990 and 2004, ch. 3) has argued, this loss of time, 'time poverty', is a significant deprivation in the lives of many women and one that is disguised within the household measure of income and expenditure.

When unpaid work at home extends to caring for other dependants, such as children, the cost in time rises astronomically. In a well-publicised pamphlet Piachaud (1984) estimated that this averaged out at around fifty hours a week for the ordinary young child. This is more than the average working week in paid employment and a significant feature of a broader conceptualisation of the intra-household distribution of resources.

Both the direct cost (cash) and indirect costs (emotional dependency, loss of control and time poverty) of intrahousehold distribution have often been ignored in studies of poverty. Indeed it is only fairly recently that research has attempted to obtain information about such distributions, and work in the area is still developing. Although it hardly provides a justification, this may in part be due to recognition of the difficulties inherent in securing reliable data on such a potentially sensitive issue (respondents may wish to hide, even from themselves, the real costs of their family lives). Pahl's work was based on qualitative interviews with very small samples of households. The results were revealing, but they were not necessarily representative. Conducting large-scale quantitative research within households can be difficult to organise, although quantitative research by Vogler (1994) found that only a fifth of households conformed to an 'orthodox model' of egalitarian decision-making units. In fact, of course, both quantitative and qualitative approaches have their advantages and limitations, as we shall discuss in a little more detail below.

Quantitative measures

Much of the work on measuring poverty has been quantitative in nature, using statistical techniques to count the number of people in poverty or to measure the extent of inequality. Indeed in the UK in particular this arithmetic tradition has a long and well-established history in academic circles and political debate, stemming from the seminal studies of Booth (1889) and Rowntree (1901) at the end of the nineteenth century.

The great advantage of quantitative measures is their scale and their anonymity. A statistical survey, if it is large enough and if the sample of respondents providing the data is carefully chosen, can provide an objective, and arguably scientific, picture of the broader group or society from which it has been selected, particularly if standard measures of the statistical significance of the data have been reached. Quantitative measures have always been at the centre of poverty research and measurement therefore. These can be based on existing statistical information collected by government or other agencies for different purposes, or they can be based on original data collected directly by researchers using survey methods to question a sample of the population. Both approaches have been widely used in poverty and inequality research in Britain.

Using existing data sets

The main sources of existing data are government statistics, collected by government Departments or the Office of National Statistics (ONS), formerly the Central Statistical Office. In the past these used to include the *Blue Books* – national income and expenditure blue books produced from Inland Revenue data and other official sources, which provided a more or less consistent source of data on these from 1952 until the mid-1970s and were widely relied on by researchers and politicians. Since 1957 the government has conducted a regular Family Expenditure Survey (FES) based on detailed information on the expenditure patterns of a relatively large sample of the population, now called the Expenditure and Food Survey (EFS). The DWP also conducts a Family Resources Survey covering such things as receipt of benefits, asset holdings and pension protection.

Early versions of these government surveys were used by Abel Smith and Townsend (1965) in their famous study, *The Poor and the Poorest*, which demonstrated that high levels of poverty persisted in the UK despite the introduction of the welfare reforms of the postwar period. And since the

1970s, the DHSS, now the Department for Work and Pensions (DWP), has been using this data to publish the details of families and households with low incomes, now available annually in the report on Households Below Average Incomes (HBAI) (DWP, 2005a). These statistics are all now widely available on government department websites, in particular the statistics website maintained by the Office of National Statistics (ONS), listed at the end of the book.

The most comprehensive official statistics dealing with incomes, including low incomes, however, were those produced by the Royal Commission on the Distribution of Income and Wealth, the Diamond Commission, which produced regular reports culminating in 1980 when they were discontinued by the Conservative government (Royal Commission, 1980); and it was partly to replace the income distribution data once provided by the Diamond Commission that the Rowntree Foundation established its Inquiry into Income and Wealth in the early 1990s (Barclay, 1995; Hills, 1995). This was an extensive and expensive research project, however (see Hills, 1996), and has not been continued into the new century, although Hills himself still monitors statistical data on inequality. He has produced another book analysing the latest trends on inequality (Hills, 2004) and has worked with colleagues at the LSE to review the achievements of the Labour governments in tackling inequalities (Hills and Stewart, 2005).

The great advantages of government statistics, of course, are that access to them is free and they carry the authority of their official status. They are thus the most widely used source of quantitative data. Despite their apparent authority, however, there are limitations in the official statistics that need to be borne in mind in any attempt to utilise them as a poverty measure. For instance the FES/EFS sample is only about one in 2,500, it covers only those in households (thus excluding the homeless or those in institutions), it has a roughly 30 per cent non-response rate, and, given the way the data is gathered, it is very likely to understate income. Thus not everyone or everything is covered, and poverty and low income in particular may be under-represented in the figures.

Conducting survey research

It is partly because of limitations such as these, therefore, that some researchers have sought to collect their own quantitative data on poverty and deprivation. Such original data has the advantage of being able to cover a breadth and depth of detail not included in government and other official statistics. Some of the most significant studies of poverty have thus been based on surveys conducted by, or on behalf of, the investigators themselves. Rowntree (1901, 1941) and Townsend (1979) employed research workers to interview respondents and collect data. Mack and Lansley (1985), through London Weekend Television (LWT), used a contract research agency (MORI) to conduct a survey for them.

In a later study of poverty in London, Townsend (Townsend et al., 1987) combined a survey of a sample of the population with cooperation and consultation with representative bodies in the local borough councils and the now abolished Greater London Council (GLC). Such locally based surveys of poverty grew dramatically in number in the 1990s as local authorities used them to supplement existing data sources to develop a profile of the extent and distribution of poverty in their local area (Alcock and Craig, 2000).

Of course all the problems of sample size, non-response, and so on apply to the collection and use of original data too. Nevertheless the control over the construction of questionnaires and the samples of respondents that original research provides permit a much greater range of data to be collected and analysed, as was demonstrated in Townsend's major 1960s and 1970s survey (Townsend, 1979). But collecting original data is costly. Townsend's study in particular struggled with a budget that, though large by some research standards, was barely adequate for the task to which it was addressed; and the more recent Poverty and Social Exclusion (PSE) survey had to rely largely on data already collected in the national General Household Survey (GHS) (Gordon *et al.*, 2000).

Despite these problems some very useful and significant studies have managed to collect original data with relatively small budgets by using various opportunities arising from other activities. In the 1960s Coates and Silburn's (1970) classic study of poverty in an inner city area of Nottingham (St Ann's) was based on data collected by Workers Educational Association students and undergraduates at Nottingham University as part of their social studies curriculum.

Comparing data

One of the broader limitations of original data, however, is its potential incompatibility with data from other studies, either of different populations or at different times. One of reasons why Abel Smith and Townsend (1965) were able to discover higher levels of poverty in Britain in the 1950s than those revealed in Rowntree's final 1950 survey in York (Rowntree and Lavers, 1951) was because their work was based on a different and more extensive data source. Thus the difference was arguably as much to do with how the data relied on was collected as it was to do with different levels of poverty and inequality in British society. When making comparisons over time this problem of comparability of data can become a significant one, as Piachaud (1988) has argued; although, as he also showed, adjustments can usually be made to the data to reveal some comparability if this is approached carefully.

If we want to make comparisons between levels of poverty and inequality in different countries, then the problem of comparability of data is also a potential problem, as mentioned in Chapter 4. Even in official statistics there are differences in policy over what information is collected, and differences in culture and convention over how this is done, and how it is analysed and presented. However, as we discussed in Chapter 4, the increasing activity of international agencies in collecting and storing data within conventional and comparable frameworks has made this much easier, with international data being held by the EU (through Eurostat), the LIS and the OECD.

Information and communication technology has also now made access to and use of such data much easier, and has much expanded the scope for analysis, and reanalysis, of it. As Atkinson (1989, p. 38), the leading British expert on quantitative measurement of poverty and inequality, argued some time ago, if such data can be made accessible then it can expand the opportunities for such research. What is more researchers can then, if they wish, reanalyse such data using their own poverty lines or poverty measures, thus avoiding some of the problems and disagreements over this discussed in Chapter 5.

In order to do this, however, definitions of poverty must be expressed in a form that can be applied as an indicator of poverty to a statistical database of income or expenditure. In most cases this takes the form of algebraic formulae, which can then be applied to the data to reveal the numbers and proportions in poverty. This use of indicators is a complex science, generally referred to as 'econometrics', and it requires an understanding of algebra that is likely to be beyond many social scientists. Atkinson discusses some of the conceptual and practical issues involved in this in two famous papers reproduced in 1989 (Atkinson, 1989, chs 1 and 2). The use of algebraic formulae permits us to make measurements of poverty, according to different definitions, from data on income or expenditure inequality and to compare these across countries or over time. Thus they can help to turn definitions into measures – although they cannot overcome the problem of disagreement over the definitions themselves.

Measuring inequality

It is measures of inequality, therefore, that are at the heart of quantitative studies of poverty. Measuring inequality, and changing patterns of income or expenditure distribution, provides us with the broad picture of relativities of wealth and deprivation into which discussion about where to draw the poverty line can be introduced (see Hills, 2004, ch. 3). Thus in order better to understand debates about poverty we need to spend a little time examining how measures of inequality operate and what kind of information they provide.

The most graphic demonstration of the power of inequality measures is Pen's famous *Parade of Dwarfs* (Pen, 1971). In a fascinating popularisation of the distribution of income in British society, Pen characterised the spread of incomes as an hour-long parade of people whose height was symbolic of their relative place in the distribution of resources in society, with average income being represented by persons of average height. As the title of the paper suggests, under this representation the vast majority of people were very short – only twelve minutes before the end of the hour did persons of average height appear. However after that, in the last ten minutes, heights grew dramatically, with doctors and accountants seven to eight yards high, and finally at the end a few people who were a mile high or more. Seen in this way the measurement of inequality is indeed staggering. Pen also presented it as a graph, which revealed in visual form the fact that so many are below the

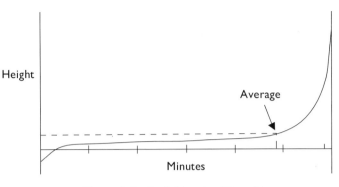

Figure 6.1   Pen's 'Parade of Dwarfs'
Source: Pen (1971).

average, and that a few are far above it (Figure 6.1). The political importance of the relationship between inequality and poverty measures becomes much clearer when we recognise that the large majority of people receive below average resources.

The idea behind Pen's parade was taken up again in the 1990s in the presentation of the findings from the Rowntree Foundation's research on income and wealth. Hills (1995) produced an 'Income Parade' for the UK for 1990/91, which compared the incomes of various different ideal family types throughout the population, and revealed that average income was only exceeded by the top 30 per cent of households.

A more conventional, and adaptable, way of expressing the distribution described in Pen's parade is through the construction of what are called *Lorenz curves*. These are used to represent, in simple graphical form, the distribution of incomes in a particular country against what would be a hypothetical distribution of completely identical incomes. They are discussed by Atkinson (1983, pp. 15–17), who provided the following example based on the distribution of income in the UK in 1978–79 (Figure 6.2).

The curve representing distribution in Britain lay below the straight line representing hypothetical identical income levels. Thus if all incomes had been equal, 40 per cent of income units would have received 40 per cent of total income – line ACD. In fact, however, distribution was not equal, it followed the curve below the line, and thus 40 per cent of people received below 20 per cent of income – line ABE. The trajectory of the curve below the line thus expresses the extent of inequality in society. The further away from the diagonal line the curve is, the greater the extent of inequality; thus a curve below that in Figure 6.2 would show 40 per cent of the population getting much less then 20 per cent of total income.

Lorenz curves not only have the advantage of expressing measures of inequality in a simple, visual form, they also allow comparisons to be made easily between different distributions (and thus inequalities) in different societies (see Atkinson, 1983, pp. 54–5). Thus if the United States has a Lorenz curve below that of the UK, then we can say that in general it is a more

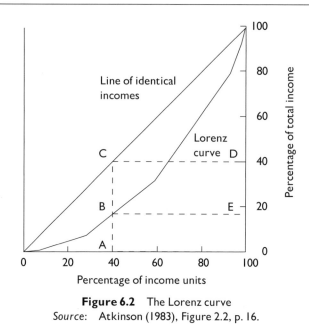

Figure 6.2 The Lorenz curve
Source: Atkinson (1983), Figure 2.2, p. 16.

unequal society. This relationship can also be expressed in numerical form by calculating from a Lorenz curve a figure known as the *Gini coefficient*. This is the fraction that represents the relationship found in the graph between the area between the curve and the diagonal and the total area under the diagonal. Thus:

$$\text{Gini coefficient} = \frac{\text{area between Lorenz curve and diagonal}}{\text{total area under diagonal}}$$

This will always be a decimal fraction, for instance 0.4, because in all societies the curve will lie somewhere below the diagonal. But the closer to the diagonal the curve is, and thus the less the overall inequality, the smaller the fraction will be. Thus a society with a Gini coefficient of 0.4 has less inequality than one with a Gini coefficient of 0.6.

The Gini coefficient is a very simple comparative measure of inequality, but it is also a very crude one. In particular it cannot represent one potentially important feature of different distributions that can be represented by Lorenz curves, that is the spread of inequality. Atkinson (1983, p. 55) demonstrated this by comparing the Lorenz curves for the UK and West Germany (Figure 6.3).

As can be seen, here the curves were both below the line, but they intersected. The Gini coefficients for both countries in fact were more or less the same, but the distribution of income in each was significantly different. Thus, according to Atkinson, at that time there were more people in West Germany with low incomes than there were in the UK, but conversely those in the middle in West Germany enjoyed a comparatively higher relative position to those in the middle in the UK.

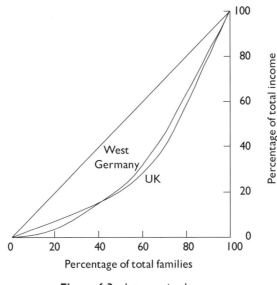

Figure 6.3 Intersecting Lorenz curves
Source: Atkinson (1983), figure 3.2, p. 55.

Measures of inequality therefore concern not just the relationship between those at the top and those at the bottom, they also tell us about the relationships between all those in between, and here patterns may and do vary significantly between different countries as expressed by the intersection of comparative Lorenz curves. This is a similar distinction to that between the head-count and poverty-gap measures of poverty referred to earlier – both are important and may lead to important differences in policy to respond to the patterns they reveal. Of course distributions will also vary within one country over time, particularly if policy measures are introduced that aim to reduce, or increase, the extent of inequality. Measures of inequality compared over time can thus tell us something about the success or failure of such policies. And the increases in the level of poverty and inequality in the UK towards then end of the last century, discussed in Chapter 2, provide a clear picture of policy outcomes here (see Hills, 2004).

However, as suggested earlier, measuring poverty involves more than just the collection of statistics and the application of algebraic formulae; it must also encompass examination of what these dry figures mean for the real lives of real people. These limitations were graphically illustrated as early as 1920 in the interchange between Bowley, one of the British pioneers of poverty measurement, and Bevin, the trade union leader and later Foreign Secretary, over the 'docker's breakfast', discussed in Chapter 5. As Bevin's biographer pointed out, the trade union leader's (qualitative) measure of the meagre diet of bread, bacon and fish was worth 'volumes of statistics' in its effect on public opinion (Atkinson, 1989, p. 38). Therefore to gain a fuller understanding of poverty and inequality in the UK, or indeed anywhere else, we need to employ qualitative measures in addition to statistical surveys.

Qualitative analysis

It is probably true to say that quantitative measures of poverty and the collection and analysis of statistics dominated research and debate on poverty in Britain throughout much of the twentieth century. However, the use of statistics has not prevented the development of a strong tradition of qualitative description and analysis of the experience of poverty that has sought to give life and meaning to the sometimes complex tables and graphs of the arithmetic tradition.

Both Rowntree and Booth included descriptive material on the standard of living of the local people covered by their surveys, further underlining the inaccuracy of claims that they were operating only with crude notions of absolute poverty. Townsend, in his major 1960s and 1970s survey of poverty in Britain, specifically focused part of his research, and a chapter of the book based on the study (Townsend, 1979, ch. 8), on what he called the impact of poverty. For instance here is an extract from a description of the impact of poverty on a young family suffering disability and with a handicapped child:

> Mr and Mrs Nelson, 35 and 32, live with their three sons of 13, 9 and 6 in a four-roomed council flat in a poor district of Oldham, overlooked by a rubber factory belching smoke all day long and near a canal. They believe the flat is a danger to their health. 'One bedroom is so damp that it stripped itself'. The living room has a fire but they can only afford a one-bar electric fire to heat the bedrooms because they are terribly damp. The fire is taken from one room to the next. At Christmas the bedroom window was smashed by a brick. Because the family cannot afford new glass, the room gets too cold and the boys sleep in one bedroom. (Townsend, 1979, p. 305)

More recently a review of the experience of poverty in the 1990s published by the CPAG, called *Hardship Britain*, used interviews with people living in poverty to provide a depressing picture of the struggles in their lives. For instance,

> The family have no telephone, vacuum cleaner, electric kettle, or freezer and their fridge is in poor condition, as are all their other household goods. Although they try to give the children two hot meals a day, and often feel obliged to give them fruit and sweets (even though this stretches their budget), their lifestyle is in all other respects spartan. For example, the Chaudrys do not have a set of warm winter clothes or two pairs of all-weather shoes for everyone; the children get no treats and the family cannot afford to go and visit friends and relatives in other towns. (Cohen *et al.*, 1992, p. 19)

As with this CPAG review of poverty in Britain, some of the most interesting and most significant qualitative analyses of poverty have been based largely or entirely on descriptive material. These include early more journalistic works such as Mayhew's *London's Poor* and Orwell's *Road to Wigan Pier*, and more recent works such as Harrison's (1983) *Inside the Inner City* and Seabrook's (1984) *Landscapes of Poverty*. They also include a range of smaller but more detailed research studies published by organisations such as the CPAG and focusing on particular aspects of poverty, such as McClelland's (1982) *A Little Pride and Dignity* looking at child-care costs, or on poverty in particular localities, such as Evason's (1980) *Ends That Won't Meet* examining poverty in Belfast. In the 1990s Kempson *et al.* (1994) produced a compelling analysis of the lives of families struggling to survive on state benefits, called *Hard Times*; and Kempson (1996) also published a review of qualitative research supported by the Rowntree Foundation, called *Life on a Low Income*. In the new century qualitative studies have focussed on the experiences of those living in areas of high deprivation, such as Lupton's (2003) *Poverty Street*, Mumford and Power's (2003) *East Enders* and Smith's (2005) *On the Margins*. Qualitative studies generally seem to have more evocative titles than do statistical analyses too.

Of course qualitative studies are generally not large-scale, and the descriptions they offer cannot claim to be representative of poverty in any scientific sense. Despite their popular persuasive power they can therefore be more readily dismissed by critical academics or unsympathetic politicians, although in practice, of course, politicians may be influenced more by popular opinion, or by attempts to manipulate it, than they are by statistical rigour. However, qualitative data can be linked directly to quantitative measures to harness the complementary strengths of measurement and description, as Rowntree's (1901) and Townsend's (1979) seminal studies revealed so graphically. Deprivation can be measured quantitatively, but an important part of what is being measured is lost in the process.

Like statistical analysis, qualitative description is also continually developing. The development of new information technologies has transformed qualitative representation of poverty as well as quantitative measurement of it. Here it is the development and growth of television, video and DVD that have been powerful influences. Television and video or DVD descriptions of poverty, either real or fictional, can be seen and heard in the homes of a huge audience.

There have been a number of influential televised studies of poverty. Perhaps the most famous was the fictional 1960s drama on the homelessness and poverty of a young family, entitled *Cathy Come Home*. However, probably the most important example of this new genre of qualitative research presentation was the television series for which Mack and Lansley's important studies of relative poverty were undertaken in 1983 and 1990 (Mack and Lansley, 1985; Frayman, 1992). The studies were originally commissioned by London Weekend Television and were screened as a series of television programmes called *Breadline Britain*. Like the survey itself, the programmes were largely based on interviews with respondents in their own homes. These were screened as a series of vignettes in which the people described their struggle to manage on the breadline. This made for harrowing viewing and presented to a wide audience the human costs of the statistical measures of poverty detailed in the survey, although, given the late-night screening time the audience was probably not as large as it might have been earlier in the evening.

The use of television to enable people in poverty to describe their deprivation raises the broader issue of the role of their determination of and control over the qualitative measurement of their poverty, and the presentation of this to the wider world. There is a strong element of paternalism in all academic studies of poverty and deprivation, which is most clearly revealed in qualitative descriptions or depictions of the lives of those who are poor. It has been argued by some, in particular by the one-time academic and later community worker in Glasgow's Easterhouse estate, Bob Holman, that people living in poverty should be permitted, or encouraged, to speak for themselves about their experiences. Autobiography should replace biography, he has consistently argued, not necessarily because it is a more accurate or convincing message, but because it places the power and control over the message in the hands of those experiencing the problem.

The desirability of involving people who are poor in qualitative research on poverty has been taken up more proactively by Beresford (see Beresford and Croft, 1995). Like Holman he argues that involvement of people directly in the development and the presentation of poverty research not only provides insights that academic researchers would never have been able to make, but also establishes some control over the conduct and use of research on poverty by those who are so often the victims of it, and more generally helps to empower people through participation. In an innovative research project, published by the CPAG (Beresford *et al.*, 1999), Beresford sought to do this by encouraging people in poverty to 'speak for themselves'. However, this revealed in particular one of the difficulties with self-perceptions of poverty – many of those conventionally regarded as poor may not themselves welcome being identified and labelled in this way. One participant commented that poverty was, 'a horrid word because I think straight away you conjure up this person sitting huddled in the cold'; and another agreed that, 'it does label you, there's no question about it' (*ibid.*, p. 64).

These concerns were taken up in the work of the Commission on Poverty, Participation and Power at the end of the last century, whose report, entitled *Listen Hear: The Right to be Heard* (Commission on Poverty, Participation and Power, 2000), commented on the active role that people living in poverty had been encouraged to play in a series of fora and events organised by the Commission and listed a number of recommendations to ensure that people experiencing poverty would be able to participate in the decision-making processes affecting their lives. The issue is also discussed by Lister (2004) in her book on poverty; and Bennett and Roberts (2004) have conducted an overview of participatory approaches to research on poverty in the UK. But in this they concluded that, although such approaches were being developed more widely, they had not yet become mainstream elements of policy and practice.

In part this is because of the time taken to develop such participation and the financial costs of conducting such activity. Participatory research cannot escape the practical problems which face all attempts to measure poverty either quantitatively or qualitatively – all such research requires time and commitment of resources. Whatever the academic, or political, desirability of new forms of definition or measurement of poverty, therefore, financial support will be needed to make these operational. This is an issue that applies in particular if such financial commitments are required to support research over a long period of time too; and yet recent debate on the measurement of poverty has begun to suggest that this is exactly what is required to improve our understanding of the problem.

The Dynamics
of Poverty

SUMMARY OF KEY POINTS

- Research on poverty now recognises that risk of poverty changes over time and across the course of people's lives.
- It is important to distinguish the *life-cycle* changes which can affect all from the *life-course* analysis of how the circumstances of individuals actually change.
- Longitudinal analysis, utilising research data on dynamic changes in the lives of respondents is needed to understand this.
- Longitudinal analysis reveals that many people experience only relatively short spells of poverty, although some may return to further spells in the future.
- For the smaller numbers who experience poverty over a longer period of time the cumulative effects of such deprivation may be particularly debilitating.
- Dynamic analysis emphasises the importance of constructing 'routes out of poverty', although these will involve both agency-based and structural responses.

Poverty over time

People's lives change over time. This is perhaps a self-evident statement; but it is one which until relatively recently has not been fully recognised and understood in academic research and political debate on poverty – and indeed society more generally. Much sociological and social policy research has tended to collect information about social structures and the impact of social policies at particular points in time. This is of course understandable. We tend to see the world as it is today; and respondents to surveys, whether quantitative or qualitative, will tell us about their current circumstances.

What this means, however, is that such research can only provide us with a 'snapshot' of social life and the extent of poverty; and yet our lives change over time. If we want to understand how these changes affect our social circumstances, including our risk of and experience of poverty, then we need not snapshots but 'moving pictures'. More recently social scientists in general, and poverty researchers in particular, have begun to recognise the need for such moving pictures in order to understand what is generally now referred to as the 'dynamics of poverty'. Dynamic analysis has begun to influence both theoretical debate about poverty and empirical research on it; and it has also begun to have a significant influence on anti-poverty policies too.

The theoretical context of the importance of dynamism for understanding social relations flows from the work of leading sociologists who have been exploring the changing nature of social lives in modern society. Most notable here is the work of the German sociologist Beck (1992) and the British sociologist Giddens (1991). Both have argued that modern (post-industrial) society is characterised by much greater levels of social mobility and fluidity than was the case in earlier periods of industrialisation, and in particular that the impact of welfare policies and global economic forces mean that class and occupational positions are not fixed so that individuals can expect to move up or down the social hierarchy to a much greater extent than might have been the case in the early part of the last century. People's lives are changing ever more rapidly.

These commentators also suggest that such mobility is more clearly linked to individual aspirations, abilities and achievements. Individuals can now more readily expect to move from their class of origin and to alter their place in the social structure. In part this is because they are likely to be subject to such changes throughout their life-cycle as economic, family or other circumstances change around them. In other words structures are more fluid. However, it is also in part because they can negotiate their movement through these changes through their own efforts and achievements – for instance, through the acquisition of knowledge and skills. In other words there is an enhanced role for individuals as agents in shaping their life chances.

Beck (1992) conceptualised these changing modern social relations as constituting a 'risk society' in which individuals would have to negotiate their routes through changing social circumstances by the taking of risks. Beck thus envisaged a dynamic, 'individualised' approach to social research and social analysis emphasising the role of agency. This has had particular implications for poverty research and for anti-poverty policy, as we discussed in Chapter 3. It suggests that poverty should not be seen as a more or less permanent product of structural social relations and location within these, but rather is likely to be a temporary phenomenon (short term, long term or recurrent) encountered by different individuals in different circumstances or at different times in their life course. Leisering and Leibfried (1999, ch. 10) have argued that this leads us to develop a life-course approach to poverty dynamics in which they identify three key principles: temporalisation, democratisation and biographisation.

▨ *Temporalisation* refers to the experience of poverty in different temporal forms (short, medium and long) and in single or repeated spells. Poverty can no longer therefore be equated with pre-ordained economic categories.
▨ *Democratisation* is linked to Beck's (1992) notion of a risk society, within which a wider cross-section of the population must expect to undertake risk and experience spells of relative deprivation.
▨ *Biographisation* refers to the subjective dimension of temporalised poverty in individual biographies, in other words the different ways in which poverty and deprivation are experienced and evaluated in relation to the specific life courses of different individuals.

In short, more people are experiencing poverty, they are experiencing it in more different ways, and their perceptions of that experience vary from individual to individual.

The extent to which modern social relations do constitute more of a 'risk society' for individuals is, of course, debatable. Certainly social mobility and social uncertainty are not entirely new or recent phenomena. What is more, as we discussed in Chapter 3, there has always been a role for agency in determining the risk and the experience of poverty. At most therefore what Beck and Giddens are drawing our attention to is a relative shift in the stability of social structures. Nevertheless any such shift is likely to throw into clearer relief the need to understand the changes that are affecting people's lives over time, and in particular the extent to which we should be focusing upon not current circumstances but life-cycle changes.

Life-cycle changes

The notion that the risk of poverty varies across individuals and across the life-cycle has in fact been a feature of poverty research for over a century. Rowntree's initial study of poverty at the end of the nineteenth century identified the life-cycle characteristics of poverty linked to 'five alternating periods of want and comparative plenty' in the life of 'the labourer', which would mean that there was a greater risk of individual poverty in childhood and the early years of parenthood, when wages from work might not support the needs of a family, and in old age, when the productivity of workers declined or they were required to leave the labour market (Rowntree, 1901, pp. 136–7). Rowntree saw these changes as critically determined by people's participation in labour markets, and he realised that this had significant implications for anti-poverty policy – the need to ensure that those outside the labour market were protected by other means such as social security, as we shall return to discuss in Chapter 14.

More recently this link between life-cycle events and risk of poverty has been taken up by Dewilde (2003) in a review of the role of life-course analysis in developing an understanding of social exclusion and poverty. She sets her discussion in the context of the changes to social structures (labour markets, family relations and so on) associated with post-industrial society, as argued by Beck and Giddens, and refers to the historical legacy of dynamic analysis flowing from Rowntree's conclusions over a century ago. She also points out the important impact of new empirical datasets on the current development of dynamic analysis, a point to which we shall return shortly.

However, Dewilde makes a distinction between the life-cycle changes initially identified by Rowntree and the life-course perspective which has become important in more recent debate. The *life-cycle*, or family cycle, approach assumes that all are affected in similar ways by similar life-cycle events, such as parenthood or employment. These can then be recognised and responded to in policy development, as anticipated by Rowntree, for instance through child support and pensions.

The importance of such demographic changes has been discussed and analysed by a number of authors, most notably Falkingham and Hills (1995). Changes such as marriage or divorce and age at childbirth, will affect individuals' earning capacity and income, and thus spending needs and spending and saving patterns. What is more, as other commentators have pointed out, modern life-cycle changes are likely to be more complex than the five phases outlined by Rowntree. O'Higgins *et al.* (1988) identified ten life-cycle groups linked to changing experience of labour markets and family structures, and, in recognition of changes in marriage and divorce, they added an eleventh risk group, lone parents.

The *life-course* perspective, however, focuses more closely on the individualised experiences of different individuals, as outlined by Leisering and Leibfried (1999) above. As Dewilde (2003) points out, life-course experiences will be affected by a wider range of structural contexts, in particular, for instance there will be cohort effects, with those born in more recent times finding their lives constrained within very different social and economic circumstances to those of their predecessors.

Variations in demographic trends, such as shifts in the overall number of births and deaths, can significantly alter the lifetime experiences of different cohorts of the population. For instance a downturn in the birth rate will be represented fifteen or twenty years later by a reduced number of school-leavers entering the employment market. This may well mean enhanced employment prospects, and hence reduced poverty prospects, for these young adults, irrespective of any individual effort or talent on their part or any policy changes introduced by the government. Conversely those born during the periods of so-called 'baby booms' may face greater difficulties in providing for themselves as they grow older as they will be part of a larger number of people reaching retirement age at more or less the same time. Such contextual influence must be balanced against the ways in which individual life courses are constructed within these.

Dewilde outlines three different approaches to such a life-course analysis: the traditional, institutional and political economy approaches:

- The *traditional* approach focuses upon the impact of age, career and family and household structures on construction of the life course.
- The *institutional* approach examines the impact of social institutions, in particular state welfare services such as education and pensions, in regulating and structuring our lives.
- The *political economy* approach seeks to coordinate both of these individual and institutional levels, together with cohort and social group effects, to explore the issue of stratification *over* the life course (*ibid.*, p. 122).

The latter, in particular, she argues underlines the need for longitudinal analysis on an individualised basis of the risks and experiences of poverty and social exclusion. This has been made more feasible by the growing availability of longitudinal research on life course changes using new forms of data gathering and analysis.

Longitudinal analysis

To observe dynamic change we need access to longitudinal data on social relations. This is now widely recognised by social scientists studying social relations; and empirical research has in recent years begun to turn its attention to the need to develop longitudinal data-sets. However, this in itself is far from a simple exercise and the scale and scope of available longitudinal data varies significantly. The Office for National Statistics (ONS, 1999) has provided a useful guide to such sources, available on their website. This makes a distinction in particular between prospective and retrospective collection of data.

Prospective surveys collect data about a sample (or cohort) of respondents as their life unfolds after a start point date when the survey was set up. Depending on the size and representativeness of the cohort and the range of information collected, they can provide a picture of the changing life courses of individuals over the period covered, although not, of course, the experiences which people had before that date. These are sometime referred to as 'panel surveys', although that can be a little misleading as they take a number of different forms. For instance, there are the Census cohorts, which use the decennial Census to follow a 1 per cent sample of the national population from the 1971 Census onwards. There are also age specific (or birth cohort) panels collecting data on a cohort of people all born at the same time. These include the National Child Development Study following a cohort of people all born in March 1958 and gathering information about their development at (so far) five points in their life course, and more recently the Millennium Cohort Study following a sample of 15,000 babies born in the UK in 2000 (for a brief guide to these and other UK datasets, see Wasoff, 2003).

However, the more significant new prospective data-sets now being used for the dynamic analysis of poverty in particular are the full household panels, which collect information about a representative cohort of the population at regular intervals, usually on an annual basis. As Walker and Leisering (1998) explain in their review of data sources for dynamic analysis, such surveys can provide us with some guide to the changing circumstances and experiences of those within the panel – and, if it is a representative survey, then hence of society more generally. The first major such panel survey was pioneered in the USA in the Panel Study of Income Dynamics (PSID), which was initiated in 1968 and is now able to provide evidence of social mobility over a period of around thirty years.

Panel surveys in Europe are less common, and more recent. In the UK there is the British Household Panel Survey (BHPS), which has collected data annually from 1991. Much analysis has been carried out on this data including a wide-ranging analysis of the first seven years of the survey (Berthoud and Gershuny, 2000). There is also the European Community Household Panel (ECHP) which provides a base for longitudinal analysis across the European Union. There are also national household panels in many EU member-countries.

Inevitably, however, there are limitations to the information which panel surveys can provide. For a start their recent development means that they mainly have a limited time span and can thus provide a moving picture over only a short time scale, and of course one focusing only on recent years and hence recent social dynamics. In part this is because of the relative expense of carrying out such research. Unlike a snapshot survey which, however large, can be subject to a fixed and time-limited budget, a panel survey requires the commitment of significant resources (and research infrastructure) over a long (and in principle indefinite) period of time. It is really only governments or major public agencies which can command such resources and commit them over time. Hence panel surveys really require explicit political support, and this partly explains their relatively slow and recent development.

However, there are other problems with panel surveys, as Walker and Leisering (1998) discuss in their review of longitudinal data. The difficulties of securing and retaining a representative cohort may limit the viability and validity of analysis. This is particularly the case because of the attrition rates experienced by panel surveys (the loss of respondents over time) and the likelihood that lost respondents may constitute a significant subgroup with important (but unobservable) characteristics, especially for the analysis of poverty dynamics. More generally the broad sweep of panel surveys may mean that they cannot contain sufficient information about small subgroups of the population, such as those who are poor or socially marginalised (see also Dewilde, 2003, pp. 114–15). Here specific or dedicated panel surveys may be needed. An example of this is the Bremen Longitudinal Study on Social Assistance discussed by Leisering and Leibfried (1999); but there are few other comparable databases.

Some of these problems can be overcome by use of *administrative* data to track changes in circumstances. Administrative data is the term employed to refer to the use of information routinely collected by government or other public agencies in their work with citizens, which can then be accessed and analysed by social researchers. Of most relevance to poverty dynamics here is the analysis of the records of social security claimants receiving social assistance and other social security benefits. These are now available on both a national and a local basis, and have been used to explore the impact of benefit dependency upon patterns of poverty, in particular by researchers at the University of Oxford working with Noble (see Noble *et al.*, 1998; and Evans *et al.*, 2002).

The limited time frame of panel surveys and administrative data is one of the reasons why *retrospective* collection of longitudinal data can also be useful, however. This generally involves collecting data, usually at one point in time, from respondents about their past experiences and life changes. This can be done through surveys, such as the Family and Working Lives Survey, a representative sample of almost 10,000 conducted in the 1990s. It avoids the problems of short time frames and attrition rates associated with prospective data collection; and data from such surveys has been used by authors like Rowlingson and McKay (2002) to track the life courses of groups, such as lone parents, experiencing high levels of poverty and deprivation.

The use of retrospective, autobiographical accounts can provide considerable detail about life-course circumstances and experiences, and they are generally cheaper to conduct than prospective surveys, as only one round of interviews is required. Although both can, of course be combined. The BHPS used some element of retrospective data collection from its initial sample, including information about employment and family history up to the start of the panel survey questionnaire. However, retrospective datasets do have limitations flowing in particular from their reliance upon the memory recall and honesty of respondents, and the scale and scope of interview questions.

In all cases, however, there are problems in drawing out causal explanations of social change from *quantitative* data about the events experienced by people across a period of their life-cycle. Correlations can be identified between particular events; but no firm explanatory pattern can be established. This is in part a product of the immense complexity of social life – all events are the product of a range of factors, some underlying and some precipitate, and even relatively detailed (and expensive) longitudinal datasets cannot address all aspects of our many-sided social milieu. And, in particular, although such data can tell us some things about the balance between structure and agency in driving social change, it cannot provide a definitive answer to the question of where that balance lies.

In part, however, these limitations are also a product of the more general limitations within quantitative analysis of social relations. Quantitative data inevitably focuses upon discrete and measurable social events and is collected through simple questions that can be computer-coded for statistical analysis. Social life, and the life courses of social agents, cannot be reduced to such a few pieces of data. What is more, if our concern is to explore social dynamics, and in particular the decisions and actions which have shaped peoples' lives, we need to address questions of experience, attitude and motivation which cannot be captured in quantitative surveys.

As a result of this, researchers have sought to employ *qualitative* research methods, generally focusing upon biographical accounts of individual life courses. However, there are limitations to the viability and validity of qualitative data too. Biographical data, whether quantitative or qualitative, relies upon the memory and honesty of respondents, which inevitably can be partial and flawed. This can be overcome, of course, through the employment of longitudinal qualitative data collection, although such research is thus far not well-developed in the UK. Qualitative data gathering also relies upon the skills and sensitivity of the researcher, and their interpretation of the data they have secured.

More generally, however, qualitative studies are even more expensive than quantitative studies to carry out, and qualitative longitudinal research doubly so. For this reason, and because of the nature of the data they generate, qualitative studies are therefore necessarily small scale. This means that only limited, and generally selected, groups of respondents can be approached and only certain events or issues explored with them. Qualitative studies are therefore almost always focused upon particular social issues and their impact upon selected subgroups of individuals. These can provide significant and important insights into the dynamics of these issues and the experiences of these subgroups; but inevitably they will not cover broader social structural factors or the interrelation between different aspects of respondents' complex lives.

Periods of poverty

Dynamic analysis of longitudinal data can provide us with a much fuller picture of the problem and the experience of poverty than the static surveys which have dominated much of past research. Snapshots of poverty only tell us who is poor now. If there is social mobility within society then different people are likely to be poor at different points of their life course. People will move in and out of poverty, they will remain poor for different periods of time, and they may return to further periods of poverty with greater or lesser frequency. To use the jargon of economics there is a difference between the *stocks* of those in poverty at any one time and the *flows* into and out of poverty over time.

Research on the dynamics of poverty in recent years has revealed that static pictures of poverty do provide only a partial understanding (see Leisering and Leibfried, 1999; and Leisering and Walker, 1998). People do move into and out of poverty and therefore the numbers affected by poverty over time are much greater than the numbers revealed in any particular static overview (Muffels *et al.*, 1999). This means that a much greater proportion of the population is likely to experience a period of poverty at some point in their lives. Poverty is therefore a larger, and more widely shared, problem than we might otherwise have thought.

What is more, because people can move into and out of poverty, we know that it should not necessarily be conceived as a permanent problem. This is encouraging for society more generally and for those individuals currently poor in particular. It also suggests that the claims of some anti-welfare critics such as Murray (1984; Lister, 1996), that welfare support creates an under-class of people who have drifted down the social hierarchy and opted for a life of welfare dependency, are not supported by any empirical evidence. In fact dynamic analysis reveals that movement into and out of poverty is a very complex affair and that the life-course experience of poverty is different for different groups within society, with some at greater risk than others and some experiencing longer periods of poverty (Leisering and Leibfried, 1999; Muffels *et al.*, 1999).

Dynamic analysis of poverty and social exclusion has also been undertaken at the Centre for Analysis of Social Exclusion (CASE) at the London School of Economics (LSE) in the UK (Hills *et al.*, 2002). Here Burgess and Propper (2002) employed BHPS data to examine movements between income groups within the population over time and identified a number of different types of income trajectory, including those rising out of poverty, those falling into it and those experiencing 'blips' into and out of poverty. They concluded that there was considerable movement into and out of poverty, and that this could have a negative as well as a positive dimension. Some people do not escape poverty for very long – what has been referred to as the problem of the 'revolving door'. At the same time they found that for a significant group poverty could be a persisting problem, and that most of those poor at any one time were likely to experience a lot of poverty.

This was confirmed by comparative research across Europe using the ECHP by Whelan *et al.* (2003). They found that such longitudinal analysis did reveal the existence of a 'sub-set' of individuals who were poor experiencing higher levels of deprivation and relatively longer periods of poverty, which they referred to as 'persistent poverty'. They concluded that this measure of persistence was a significant advance on static cross-sectional income measures.

Both of these studies reveal that dynamic analysis can shed significant new light on our understanding of poverty, in particular by demonstrating that the extent and experience of poverty varies over time. There are, however, some other important messages about the experience of periods of poverty revealed by such analysis. Most people may experience only short periods of poverty, but some do experience relatively long periods. For those who do experience poverty for longer periods of time the consequences may be much more debilitating and desperate. In longer periods of poverty past savings are depleted, household goods deteriorate and cannot be replaced, and debts accrue and become unsustainable.

Current longitudinal data still does not tell us much about the experiences of those who do experience longer periods of poverty; but qualitative data on the experience of poverty over time may help here, by exploring in more depth some of these debilitating consequences of long periods of poverty and low income. As we mentioned in Chapter 6, some of this research was summarised by Kempson (1996, p. 47) who concluded that:

People's experiences change the longer they live on a low income from acute worry initially, through a period when they feel they are coping with the situation, and finally to chronic despair when they can see no light at the end of the tunnel.

She also identified different types of experience of the dynamics of poverty and, employing an analogy with swimmers, distinguishing those that were 'keeping their heads above water' or 'struggling to the surface' from those that were 'sinking' or 'drowning' (*ibid.*, p. 28). And in an earlier study she developed a hierarchy of approaches to managing in poverty that would be likely to be resorted to over time as periods of poverty became more extended:

Hierarchy of approaches

Find (better paid) full-time work
Spend 'savings'
Claim benefit
Sell non-essential possessions
Find part-time work within earnings disregard
Use consumer credit for regular expenditure
Delay paying bills
Take casual work (often above earnings disregard)
Cash insurance policies
Pawn valuables
Sell essential possessions
Charity
Petty crime
Begging (*not considered acceptable*)

Source: Kempson *et al.* (1994), p. 275 (italics added).

The message from dynamic analysis of poverty is not therefore a universally positive one. The knowledge that some can, and do, escape poverty must be balanced with the realisation that for some this may only be a temporary respite and that for others the experience of long periods of deprivation can be especially debilitating. Nevertheless the increasing focus on the dynamic understanding of poverty and social exclusion has important some implications for policy development, and these too have become more widely recognised in the UK, and beyond, in recent years.

Routes out of poverty

Dynamic analysis of poverty emphasises in particular the balance between agency and structure in determining the risk and the experience of poverty, as we discussed in Chapter 3. Individual agents can, and do, make choices which affect their life courses, from deciding to get married or have children to deciding to go to university or apply for a particular job. These choices also affect people's risk of poverty. Dynamic analysis of poverty and social exclusion therefore leads to a greater recognition of the importance of life-course planning in determining the risks and the experience of poverty.

This can be seen in policy development within the UK, and other advanced industrial economies, at the beginning of the new century, most notably in a range of policies which the government broadly refers to as 'welfare to work'. These include support and encouragement for unemployed people to enter paid employment, most significantly through the 'New Deal' initiatives providing training and job placement for certain unemployed claimants, together with contact with a personal adviser in the local Jobcentre Plus (see Millar, 2000). They also include measures to raise the incomes of low-paid workers in order to make employment an attractive and effective route out of poverty, such as the statutory minimum wage and the use of tax credits to subsidise low wages, which I discuss in Chapter 14.

Measures such as these are increasingly conceived as aiming to provide 'pathways' or 'ladders' out of poverty, emphasising the element of individual movement involved, and the upward trajectory that people are being encouraged to take. Research has examined the impact of these measures in providing routes out of poverty for people in twenty-first century Britain, and concluded that there is considerable movement out of poverty from one year to the next, although the people involved do not generally move far up the income scale (Kemp *et al.*, 2004). There are also of course people moving down as well as up the income scale, and there are a small, though significant, number who remain persistently poor (Burgess and Propper, 2002; Whelan *et al.*, 2003), and, as we shall discuss in Part IV, different policies may be required for these.

The implications of dynamic analysis extend beyond the encouragement of and support for employment. Life-course planning within a 'risk society' encompasses changing family relations and preparation for old age, and requires us to investigate the effect of incentives and opportunities across people's lifetimes (Evans and Eyre, 2004). The UK government both encourages agents to take their own steps to limit the risk of poverty here, for instance through investment in private pensions, and provides support for certain life-cycle events, such as child benefit and child tax credits for families, as we shall discuss in Chapter 11.

However, there is a danger in shifting the emphasis within the anti-poverty debate entirely onto individual agents and the decisions and plans that they can make to avoid or escape poverty. Dynamic analysis also reveals the continuing relevance of structural factors in shaping or constraining the life-course choices open to individuals; and, as Hills (2002) points out in the final chapter of the CASE book on social exclusion, structural factors remain important in determining risk of poverty. The patterns of distribution of poverty cannot be accounted for as the random effects of a series of individual life-course decisions. Structural factors also remain important, therefore, in any policy responses to poverty dynamics.

Hills explores the implications of a dynamic understanding of poverty and social exclusion in a little more detail. He suggests that these lead us to classify policy responses to this into four broad categories (Hills, 2002, p. 232):

- *Prevention* or reduction of the risks of entering poverty, for instance through education or training to make employment more secure.
- *Promotion* of escape from poverty, for instance through 'welfare to work' policies to equip unemployed people for jobs.
- *Protection* from the experience of poverty, for instance through paying benefits to the unemployed.
- *Propulsion* into better-supported circumstances, for instance through the use of in-work benefits to subsidise low wages.

The first two clearly involve policies to support and promote agents in avoiding or escaping poverty, what Hills refers to as *active* measures. The second two, however, are responses to the consequences of events and involve structural provision of resources to support those who are, or may become, poor. Hills refers to these as *passive* or redistributive measures. It is important to avoid pejorative judgements of the relative value of such active and passive measures based on the connotations of the words themselves. Both are equally significant and important. All four, Hills argues, can be found within the policy framework of the UK government in the twenty-first century, and all four are needed to provide a comprehensive response to the risks of poverty. Dynamic understanding of poverty does not therefore lead to an abandonment of more traditional concerns with structural measures to combat poverty. The activation of individual agents can be supported by the redistribution and reshaping of structural support.

Social Exclusion

SUMMARY OF KEY POINTS

■ Relative deprivation focuses our attention upon a wider range of non-monetary dimensions of poverty including lifestyle matters such as access to leisure, financial services, information technology and democratic participation.

■ These broader social problems are generally referred to as social exclusion, a concept that has its roots outside the UK, in particular in European policy debate.

■ Social exclusion is, like poverty, a multidimensional phenomenon and there is much debate about its conceptual basis and practical application.

■ Research and policy debate on social exclusion generally seeks to measure this across a range of social indicators.

■ Social exclusion is also identified as a spatial phenomenon, although there is much confusion over the different implications of 'people poverty' and 'place poverty'.

■ Social exclusion policy has often focused upon the 'victims' of exclusion rather than the agencies and processes leading to their exclusion.

■ Social exclusion is also a product of broader social and economic forces which have national and international dimensions and lead to more general problems of social differentiation and social polarisation within modern society.

Relative deprivation

One of the main problems underlying the attempts to define and measure poverty discussed the previous few chapters is the impossibility of establishing one poverty line on which all can agree. This has led to an increasing tendency to seek multi-dimensional approaches in particular to the measurement of poverty, as exemplified in the three-dimensional measure of child poverty adopted by the government following consultation on the problem, as we discussed in Chapter 5 (DWP, 2003). Multi-dimensional approaches involve a focus upon issues beyond simply income and expenditure levels, or what we might call monetary poverty – a focus on what we *have or do not have*. They include also attempts to examine the social and economic situations of individuals and families, and the extent to which these situations circumscribe the activities and life chances that people experience. This broader focus on social circumstances has in the past been referred to as a concern with deprivation – an appreciation of what we *do or do not do*.

The most important early proponent of the notion of deprivation in the UK and beyond was Townsend, who linked it to his attempts to define and measure relative poverty. He argued that understanding relative poverty involved understanding the related phenomenon of deprivation, and the recognition that this too was a relative concept, determined (and experienced) by the social context in which it was located. In an article published in 1987 he distinguished three different forms of relative deprivation (Townsend, 1987):

- Lacking the diet, clothing and other facilities that are customary and approved in society.
- Falling below the majority or socially accepted standard of living.
- Falling below what could be the majority standard given a better redistribution or restructuring of society.

The first two directed attention towards access to social services (both public and private) which can affect our standard of living irrespective of our level of cash income, and also towards the use that is made of such services and the extent to which this means that people are able to do what is socially expected of them. The latter, he argued, is largely utilised in studies of developing countries, and suggests an attempt to impose relative standards that are not part of current custom and experience.

This raises the issue of the relationship between subjective and objective approaches to deprivation, which has also been the source of some debate. If relative deprivation is about perceptions of needs and lacks, then one implication might be that it only exists to the extent to which people perceive themselves to have needs that are not met, or are unable to do things they think they ought to be able to do. If you do not need or want such things, then in what sense can you be deprived of them?

This *subjective* dimension was explored in a seminal study by Runciman (1966), who examined different perceptions of deprivation. He found that many people did not perceive themselves as relatively deprived, over a quarter of his sample saying that there were no others who were better-off than themselves (*ibid.*, p. 227). Even those who did experience relative deprivation often compared themselves to those not necessarily much better-off than themselves, for instance people with no children, people on shift work, university researchers or people able to let out a part of their home (*ibid.*, p. 229). In an unequal society such as 1960s Britain, therefore, people's sense of social justice was a rather limited one.

Of course this was hardly a surprising discovery. People's knowledge of the standards of others, especially of the luxuries of the rich, are fairly limited – not the least because the better-off do not always flaunt their wealth and may even, for a variety of obvious reasons, seek to disguise it. Furthermore we all have to live, and mainly do live, within our current circumstances – we learn to get by. Thus for many people, to maintain alongside such an accommodation a deep and burning grievance about what they are deprived of is neither comfortable nor healthy.

Townsend also explored subjective perceptions in his major study of poverty in the 1960s and found that although a large number (over a half) of those 'living in poverty' did not feel poor, 'most of them none the less recognised in other ways that they were worse off than people with high or middle incomes, or than they had been themselves in previous life' (Townsend, 1979, p. 431). He concluded that there was a strong correlation between such subjective perceptions and his measures of objective poverty. More recent attempts to include people's subjective experiences of poverty within research, such as the work of Beresford *et al.* (1999, ch. 3) which we discussed in Chapter 6, reveal that although people do sometimes reject the negative labels associated with poverty, they are often very much aware of the social deprivation and disadvantage that they suffer and indeed may be more willing to embrace these as descriptions of the problems they face.

Townsend has consistently maintained that, in its focus on the conditions of life rather than on the distribution of resources, deprivation should be distinguished from the narrower concept of poverty. However, he argues, this does not mean that it cannot be objectively defined and measured. He discussed criteria for the measurement of deprivation in his 1987 article on the subject. Here, as in his earlier survey research (Townsend, 1979), he distinguished between material and social deprivation – perhaps in implicit recognition of the absolute and relative dimensions of the phenomenon. He then went on to outline a list of indicators that could be used to determine and measure levels of deprivation, covering such things as diet, home circumstances, working conditions, family activity, community integration and social participation, deprivation of which could be used to derive scores for different individuals or groups. Of course the list of indicators is open to the same challenge of expert judgement as the list of indicators used to determine the poverty threshold discussed in Chapter 5. It is an objective measure, but not necessarily a consensual or even a behavioural one.

However, the list demonstrates the potentially broader remit of the notion of relative deprivation. In complex and affluent societies necessities are not just food, clothing and shelter; and incomes or expenditure are not the only measures of standard of living. Where we live, where we work, how we work, how we spend our leisure time (if we have any), what services we have access to or receive – all these, and not merely our personal or household weekly budgets, affect our lives; and deprivation can extend into any or all of these broader aspects of lifestyle. Indeed it is this broader and richer (or poorer, for some) notion of 'lifestyle', rather than simply 'standard of living', with which discussion of deprivation has become associated. It is debatable whether lifestyle can be objectively defined and measured, but an understanding of how our lifestyles can alternatively be enriched or deprived is central to an understanding of poverty in affluent societies.

Most obvious here is the impact of housing on living standards and lifestyle. A secure, comfortable and appropriately sized home is likely to be high on the list of anyone's lifestyle preferences. Conversely the lack of these – an inadequate or unfit home, or no home at all – is likely to lead to significant deprivation. Money can buy a good home, of course, but for many people, particularly in the rented sector, housing conditions are not only a product of income status. What is more the cost of housing varies considerably with location and type of housing, and this too is often out of the control of households, hence the difference between the levels of poverty revealed by before and after housing cost income measures discussed in Chapter 2.

Health, and ill-health, are also key dimensions of deprivation. Poor health, in particular chronic sickness or disability, can considerably undermine quality of life, no matter how high or low ones weekly income. Combating, or preventing, ill-health is of course a complex problem, which there is not the space to explore here. However, there has for some time been compelling evidence that poor health is not evenly distributed across the social spectrum. Government research on the 'Health Divide' in the 1980s, published privately by Penguin Books (Townsend et al., 1988) revealed that poor health was closely linked to other aspects of poverty and inequality. These findings were repeated in a later official inquiry in the 1990s (Acheson Report, 1998), and have been explored and developed in other academic research, which revealed a widening of the health gap between rich and poor towards the end of the last century (Shaw et al., 1999).

Relative deprivation also extends to what we know or have learnt. There are significant differences in the opportunities and experiences of education which we receive as children or adults (Smith and Noble, 1995). These differences have been recognised as key policy priorities for government – most famously in Tony Blair's address to the Labour Party conference in 1996 when he listed as the three priorities for the future Labour government, 'education, education and education'. Of course deprivation in education can later result in deprivation in opportunities and experiences at work (at least for those who have paid employment); and in work too deprivation may be experienced beyond the level of monetary income.

Some people work in conditions that are considerably more deprived than others, even though the pay differentials may not be that great. The working environments of builders and office clerks provide an obvious contrast here, even though the former may earn more than the latter. Townsend (1979) identified four aspects of deprivation at work: the severity of the job itself (outdoors or indoors, standing or seated), the security of the job, the conditions and amenities of work, and the provision of welfare or fringe benefits.

Most of the problems of deprivation here are pretty obvious, although the issue of fringe benefits has assumed much greater importance in recent years. Many jobs – often the more secure, pleasant and better paid ones – now include significant benefits, such as a long holiday entitlement, generous sick pay and maternity leave, occupational pensions, private health insurance, subsidised travel or even free accommodation (for instance No. 10 Downing Street, although here security may be a less significant feature!). Occupational welfare provisions such as pension schemes are particularly important for they continue the advantages – and the disadvantages – of differential employment situations beyond the period of the employment contract itself. As Mann and Anstee (1989) discussed, they became of increasing importance towards the end of the last century and now contribute to the broader social divisions and deprivations that result from privileged or non-privileged access to the labour market.

Those in secure positions in the *core* of the labour market are thus increasingly experiencing different standards from those on irregular and part-time contracts on the *periphery* (Toynbee, 2003). This raises more general questions about the extent to which deprivation is linked to social circumstances and one's place in society – or exclusion from it.

Poverty and social exclusion

In the mid-1980s the contributors to a CPAG publication drew attention to a range of new and broader aspects of deprivation that they argued were growing in importance in modern society (Golding, 1986). These included activities that had not traditionally been associated with either the experience or the definition of poverty, but in modern (or post-modern) society would be likely to be increasingly associated with deprived lifestyles.

One of these new issues was leisure. With reduced working time now a reality for all, albeit differentially distributed, what we do or do not do with our leisure time may be an important source of inequality and deprivation. The leisure industry, especially sport and culture or entertainment, is now a major feature of modern society – indeed it has been a major growth industry in Britain over the last two decades. Yet access to, and enjoyment of, leisure facilities are subject to wide differences and deprivations. Tomlinson (1986) quoted squash, a rapidly growing and yet expensive and inflexible sport, and Alton Towers, a vast but expensive and inaccessible leisure park now copied in many other places, as examples of restricted access to leisure.

Lack of access to our increasingly complex information and communications networks can also be a significant source of deprivation in modern Britain. Television, telephones, fax machines and now electronic mail have come more and more to dominate our lives – or rather the lives of some. Our cultural and leisure lives are dominated by television, and for those without access to television, and increasingly these days multi-channel digital tele-vision, cultural exclusion (for instance in the school playground) can be sharp. Telephones, and now in particular mobile phones, have become essential forms of communication for many, and here too exclusion can be a source of deprivation. And in the twenty-first century the use of the internet, or World Wide Web, has come to dominate both cultural and commercial relations, with dating and shopping taking place on the web – but not for those with no access to it.

Along with leisure and communications the other growth industry of the recent years has been financial services – banking, investment, credit, insurance and so on. In particular the development of cheques, credit cards and direct debit cards has transformed the process of buying and selling. For those without access to these facilities therefore, such financial exclusion can be significant. Toporowski (1986) found that only 69 per cent of adults had current bank accounts in 1985, and for those in social class E (the bottom) the proportion was 41 per cent. More recent research by Kempson and Whyley (1999) discovered that around one and a half million households in the UK were lacking basic financial products, such as a current account and home contents insurance, and that a further 4.4 million were on the margins of financial services provision.

However, the disadvantages of credit can also lead to, or compound, deprivation. When credit can no longer be repaid it becomes debt, and the problems associated with debt have become more serious and widespread in twenty-first century Britain. Research by Parker (1988), Ford (1991) and Berthoud and Kempson (1992) has explored the problems associated with high levels of multiple debt among the less well-off. Such forms of debt are often combined with high rates of interest, thus they cost more; and when they are not repaid they can lead to pressure and threats from creditors and can cause insecurity and anxiety among debtors. Debt can therefore be a source of physical and emotional, and well as financial, insecurity.

Another form of hardship disproportionately experienced by those in poverty is the threat – or even the fear – of being a victim of crime. Having property stolen or damaged, or worse still being a victim of assault or attack, is a severe depletion of quality of life; and the threat of this happening again provides a nagging sense of insecurity that can only fully be appreciated by those who have suffered from it. Crime statistics, and more especially surveys asking victims about crime, such as the National Crime Survey, have revealed that the highest levels of criminal activity and criminal threats are experienced amongst generally deprived groups living in deprived areas. Furthermore this can have particular consequences for the most vulnerable groups in society, with older people, women, young children and members of some ethnic minorities perhaps feeling unable to venture outside their homes in certain neighbourhoods at certain times of the day (or night) for fear of being victims of crime. Such fears are often exaggerated in practice; but their consequence is still to exclude people from the forms of social exchange that others might take for granted, and so to some extent from society itself.

Ward's (1986) contribution to the CPAG book mentioned above discussed the political dimensions of deprivation in a democratic society. Taking an active part in political organisations may not be widely regarded as an essential part of lifestyle in modern Britain; but it is an essential element of any effective democracy. Those who are excluded from it by lack of money, time, knowledge or experience are deprived of the opportunity to participate in the democratic process. That such non-participation is significantly associated with those groups also disproportionately experiencing other aspects of deprivation – the unemployed, the low paid, women at home, the elderly and ethnic minority communities – suggests that the impact of this is a significant feature of deprivation, and one with a disturbing self-perpetuating potential.

The democratic and social deficit associated with exclusion from political processes and practices has become a major focus of academic research and political concern in recent years – captured in the concept of *social capital.* Research by the American political scientist, Robert Putnam, in Italy suggested that reduced involvement of people in voluntary organisations and social activities in the south of the country was associated with reduced political participation in regional government there (Putnam, 1993). And in later research in the USA he argued that a declining participation in clubs and associations was linked to a declining engagement with democratic government across that country too (Putnam, 2000). What is going on here he argued is a declining investment by individuals in social capital – the stock of relations between people within society (see Field, 2003).

Declining levels of social capital can be closely linked to increasing levels of social exclusion, of which political participation is but one, albeit significant, part. Following on from his research, Putnam has been invited to advise governments, including the UK government, about the consequences of such a decline, and the political and policy initiatives which might be taken to overcome or reverse it. Such broader concern with social exclusion has become a much more significant feature of political and policy debate about the dimensions of poverty and deprivation in modern society, and the measures that should be adopted to respond to this.

The CPAG book, mentioned earlier, which introduced some of these dimensions to UK debate, was called *Excluding the Poor*; and in his contribution Williams (1986) focused on this wider aspect of deprivation as exclusion. He pointed out that the notion of deprivation as a form of social exclusion in fact drew upon ideas and concepts that had some of their roots in continental, and specifically French, research on poverty and deprivation. It had also been taken up and developed by EU researchers and policy-makers before it came to prominence in the UK. This is explored by the contributors to a book on social exclusion edited by Room (1995), which includes a contribution from the French social scientist Paugam, often associated with the development of the idea of social exclusion as a broadening out of the problem of poverty in modern society (Paugam, 1991).

Social exclusion became a dimension of the EU anti-poverty programmes of the 1980s and 1990s, discussed in Chapter 4. The problem was addressed as an issue in the second EU anti-poverty programme in 1988 and was mentioned in the preamble to European Social Charter a year later (see Berghman, 1995, p. 11). The observatory established by the EU Commission as part of the third programme was explicitly directed at the monitoring of national policies to combat social exclusion (Room *et al.*, 1991; Robbins *et al.*, 1994); and since 2000 all member states have committed themselves to drawing up and regularly reviewing National Action Plans to combat social exclusion.

What the EU policy-makers were seeking to do in their embracement of the problem of social exclusion was to broaden debate about, and research on, poverty and deprivation beyond the confines of the circumstances and experiences of those who were poor to encompass the reaction to poverty by other social agencies and individuals throughout society. Rather than being a *state of affairs*, they were suggesting, social exclusion is really a *process* involving us all. Unlike poverty and deprivation, therefore, exclusion focuses our attention on what others *do to us*.

In the mid-1990s J.-P. Tricart, a senior officer in the DGV, the section of the Commission responsible for social affairs, argued that:

> Today, the concept of social exclusion is taking over from poverty, which is more static than dynamic and seen far more often as exclusively monetary poverty ... Social exclusion does not only mean insufficient income, and it even goes beyond participation in working life ... More generally, in stressing the rupture of the social link, it suggests something more than social inequality and therefore carries with it the risk of a two tier society, or the relegation to the status of a welfare dependent. (Robbins *et al.*, 1994, p. 12)

Lister (2004, ch. 4) discusses the conceptual basis of social exclusion and its relation to poverty in her book on poverty. She explores the historical and international roots of the term and points out that, like poverty, it is also very much a contested concept with different dimensions and competing political implications. This was discussed in more detail by Levitas (1998) in an earlier book on the subject, in which she outlined the contrasting political implications of different discourses on inclusion and exclusion, which we return to examine in more detail in Chapter 17. Like poverty, therefore, social exclusion is a multi-dimensional social phenomenon.

Dimensions of social exclusion

The growing academic interest in social exclusion in the UK was exemplified by the establishment in 1997 of a publicly funded research centre on the topic (the Centre for Analysis of Social Exclusion, CASE) at the London School of Economics. In an early pamphlet from CASE, Atkinson and Hills (1998), sought to define what the researchers there understood by the notion of social exclusion, by emphasising three features which characterised the broader social context within which it was constructed and maintained:

- *Relativity* – social exclusion is manifest in social relations not individual circumstances;
- *Agency* – social exclusion is the result of actions taken by those who exclude others; and
- *Dynamics* – social exclusion is the result of experience over time and can be transmitted across generations.

More recently the LSE researchers have extended and developed their discussion of the concept, within the context of a range of empirical research on the dimensions and experiences of social exclusion carried out within the centre (Hills *et al.*, 2002). In here Burchardt *et al.* (2002) develop this earlier definition arguing that individuals are socially excluded if they do not participate in key activities in society. They identify four such areas of activity:

- *Consumption* – purchasing of goods and services;
- *Production* – participating in economically or socially valuable activity;
- *Political engagement* – involvement in local or national decision-making;
- *Social interaction* – with family, friends and communities.

The researchers then used data from the BHPS to measure the proportions of the working-age population excluded across a number of these dimensions. This revealed large numbers of people experiencing some level of exclusion over the period examined, but very few experiencing high levels of exclusion over a number of years. Whelan *et al.* (2002) have conducted similar analysis across a number of European countries using the ECHP. They too concluded that multiple deprivation and persistent poverty did not interact in a significant fashion to create a cleavage between a minority of excluded people and a comfortable majority of society.

These findings have broader analytical and political implications because they challenge any notion that social exclusion can be linked to a more general breakdown in social structures and in particular to the construction of the kind of *underclass* discussed in Chapter 2. Social exclusion is not associated with a permanent separation from society affecting a particular group of individuals, therefore, as we shall return to explore in a little more detail shortly. Rather, as we said above, it has a range of dimensions, affecting different people at different times and in different ways.

The poverty and social exclusion (PSE) survey, developing the early Breadline Britain research on indicators of deprivation, provides an example of this. The researchers here identified four broad aspects of social exclusion: inadequate income, labour market exclusion, service exclusion, and exclusion from social relations. They identified a range of socially perceived necessities, which included activities such as visits for family or friends and having a hobby or leisure activity (Gordon *et al.*, 2000, p. 14); and they argued that these could be combined to give multi-dimensional measure of such exclusion. They also contrasted this measure with income, and with subjective perceptions of poverty and discovered, as Whelan *et al.* (2002) had, that these different dimensions impacted differently on different sections of the community, with very few experiencing deprivation on all three measures simultaneously.

A somewhat similar approach has been undertaken by another group of independent researchers at the New Policy Institute (NPI). They too developed a range of indicators of poverty and social exclusion covering a range of different dimensions. They came to a total of fifty, with different dimensions for children, young adults and older people, including such things as: infant mortality, problems with drug use and overcrowded housing (Palmer *et al.*, 2003). One of the ideas behind this NPI initiative was to assess progress on the combating or reducing of these indicators on an annual basis; and this they have been doing with the support of the Joseph Rowntree Foundation since 1998. Each year a summary is provided of overall progress against each indicator, recorded as 'improved, steady or worsened' (with the 2004 report available online only on the NPI website). Although this reveals many areas of improvement, it also shows some areas of exclusion worsening (for instance, problems with drug use). Since 2002 the NPI have also provided a separate report on poverty and social exclusion in Scotland, utilising a similar list of forty indicators (Palmer *et al.*, 2004).

Since 1997, alongside their commitment to end child poverty, the government in the UK have also taken up a commitment to combat social exclusion and to measure progress in addressing this. This has led to a wide range of new policy initiatives and organisations and to new commitments to monitor and evaluate the activities of these.

Most significant here was the establishment of the *Social Exclusion Unit* (SEU) at the beginning of 1998 within months of the government taking office. The SEU was the result of a direct initiative by the Prime Minister himself and was originally located in the Cabinet Office, reporting straight to No. 10. It comprised civil servants from different government departments, together with representatives of relevant external agencies. It did not have a large budget and was intended primarily to coordinate and develop the work of government and other public agencies rather than to establish new service areas – described by the Prime Minister as the need for 'joined-up solutions to joined-up problems'.

The work of combating social exclusion and coordinating policy action could potentially range very widely of course; and in practice the work of the SEU has been focused upon a series of key priorities for social action, determined by government, such as rough sleeping, school exclusions and teenage pregnancies. The SEU was also later transferred to the Office of the Deputy Prime Minister (ODPM), where many of the other area-based social exclusion initiatives, which we discuss in Chapter 16, were also largely located. Nevertheless the 'flagship' role of the SEU in the political and policy commitment to combating poverty and social exclusion has been a significant feature of the new policy landscape at the beginning of the new century, including a clear statement by government of how the problem is now conceived:

Social exclusion is about more than income poverty.

Social exclusion happens when people or places suffer from a series of problems such as unemployment, discrimination, poor skills, low incomes, poor housing, high crime, ill health and family breakdown. When such problems combine they can create a vicious circle.

Social exclusion can happen as a result of problems that face one person in their life. But it can also start from birth. Being born into poverty or to parents with low skills has a major influence on future life chances. (*What is Social Exclusion?*, SEU website)

This suggests that the UK government is operating with the multi-dimensional approach to social exclusion developed by researchers and with some aspects of the relativity, agency and dynamics identified by the academics in CASE. And with this recognition goes a commitment to combat social exclusion and to monitor progress on this on a formal basis within government. The most important element in this monitoring is the annual report on activities and achievements published by the Department for Work and Pensions under the title *Opportunity for All* (DWP, 2004a).

This reporting process was established in 1999 and included a list of then 32 indicators of social exclusion, which have since been expanded to over 50. Like the NPI list they include different dimensions for different social groups and include a range of different aspects of exclusion such as, educational attainment, smoking rates and fear of crime (some of the broader dimensions of deprivation discussed above). Also, as with the NPI list, performance in combating exclusion over the year is summarised as positive, negative or neutral. In the *Opportunity for All* indicators therefore, there is official recognition by government of the need for a multi-dimensional approach to the measurement and monitoring of social exclusion in modern UK society, extending across monetary resources, access to services and participation in social relations. The focus of policy concern is no longer just on income poverty in households. It is also no longer just on individuals or households.

Spatial dimensions of exclusion

In the mid-1990s the CPAG published another significant collection of writings on poverty, this time focusing upon what they called 'the social geography of poverty' (Philo 1995). The theme of this book was the spatial distribution of poverty, and the conclusion of the contributors was that poverty was not evenly distributed on a geographical basis across the UK. In other words, some places were poorer than others. Recognition of this spatial dimension to poverty and social exclusion has come to occupy a more and more prominent place in academic work and policy planning in the UK at the beginning of the new century, supported in part by the development and use of new computer software, geographical information systems (GIS), which can more easily map poverty geographically using statistical data. .

In fact, however, although the CPAG book and the growth in use of GIS has prompted an enhanced interest in the geography of poverty in the last decade, this was not the first time that the uneven spatial distribution of poverty and deprivation had been identified or measured. Similar points were made by the contributors to another collection of writing by geographers in the 1970s (Herbert and Smith, 1979). The geographical concentration of poverty had also been a focus of policy development and implementation in the USA and the UK in the 1960s, as we shall discuss in Chapter 15, one of the consequences of which were a range of policy initiatives aimed at targeting resources onto areas identified as having concentrations of poverty, sometimes referred to in the 1960s as 'pockets of poverty'.

This raises a series of practical and methodological questions, of course, about how to define geographical areas and how to determine the distribution of poverty across them. There is much disagreement about this amongst both academics and policy-makers. In the UK the easiest local areas to focus on are local authority districts, for here there are political and administrative bodies responsible for a discrete area and able to gather knowledge about the extent of poverty and social exclusion within it. It is also local authority districts which have generally been the main areas used in government responses to the spatial distribution of poverty, for instance, in the Urban Programme and other twentieth century anti-poverty initiatives discussed in Chapter 15.

In order to determine the distribution of such targeted resources to local authority areas, therefore, the government needed to develop a measure of the distribution of poverty across districts. This was done by establishing an Index of Deprivation, which was a composite measure incorporating together a number of different indicators of local deprivation. Different indicators were selected at different times to comprise this, and different statistical methods were used to arrive at a single composite index. What is more these changed over time from the DoE81 in the 1980s to the DoE91 or 'Index of Local Conditions' in the 1990s (DOE, 1994). A useful summary of these and other official measures of local deprivation was provided by Lee *et al.* (1995); and this confirmed that in practice (as with many other national measures of poverty) it is multi-dimensional indicators which must form the basis of any overall measure.

In addition to the measures employed by national government, many local authorities themselves began to develop local profiles of poverty in their areas in the 1980s and 1990s. Often these were linked to local policies from combat poverty undertaken independently of central government, and frequently therefore they employed different indicators and different measures from central government. This provided some excellent examples of local data collection and analysis (see Alcock and Craig, 2000); but it made any comparison across local areas on the basis these local profiles rather difficult.

In 2000 the government commissioned a major review and revision of the national basis for measuring local deprivation. This led to a new series of indices, including a wider range of indicators across a number of different domains (such as income, employment, health and education), which, in addition to providing an overall geographical measure (the Index of Multiple Deprivation, IMD), could also be combined in different ways to provide different indices of different aspects of local deprivation (DETR, 2000a). In 2004 these indices were revised and developed further to include additional domains such as crime and environment (ODPM, 2004).

Another innovation of the new indices after 2000 was that they could also provide information on the distribution of poverty at a smaller area level than local authority districts. The ID2004 provided data on 'Super Output Areas' (SOAs), drawn from the decennial Census, which are based on populations as small as 1,500 people (ODPM, 2004, p. 16). This is important because both academics and policy-makers have been critical of the use of larger areas such as local authority districts to map poverty and social exclusion. For example, the largest local authority in England, Birmingham City Council, has around one million inhabitants. It is generally revealed as a relatively deprived area on most geographical measures; but, although it contains some very poor neighbourhoods, it also contains some very wealthy ones.

Spatial measures which concentrate on smaller local areas are therefore likely to be of more use in helping us to understand the geographical distribution of poverty and exclusion. However, even here there are some fundamental conceptual and methodological issues at the heart of any spatial analysis of poverty and social exclusion. In particular there is the problem of what has sometimes been referred to as the 'ecological fallacy' (see Hamnett, 1979), or the conflation of the issue of poverty with the issue of place mentioned in Chapter 2. Many 'poor people' do live in 'poor areas', but so too do many people who are not poor, and (perhaps more importantly) many people who are poor live outside such areas. Any attempt to measure poverty spatially therefore will be ignoring many people who are poor.

This was taken up in a more sophisticated form more recently by Powell et al. (2001) in a discussion of the difference between 'people poverty' and 'place poverty'. They argued that the two were often confused, with measures of concentrations of people poverty (for instance, income and employment levels) being used as a proxy for place poverty, as was the case in many of the contributions to Philo's (1995) collection. Here the ecological fallacy is a real problem. For the concentrations of individual or household poverty do not necessarily make a place poor, and in particular do not justify the targeting of anti-poverty measures onto an area just because some poor people live within it – an issue to which we shall return in Chapter 16. Conversely, if we do seek to develop a measure of place poverty, which Powell et al. (2001, pp. 249–52) do by using a measure of social expenditure in the area, then we find that very different areas emerge as poor from those on the people measure. People poverty and place poverty are not the same things therefore, either conceptually or empirically, and spatial analysis of poverty needs to be capable of taking account of both.

Related to the ecological fallacy is the problem of differences within the measurement, and the experience, of poverty across different types of geographical areas. Most spatial analysis of poverty has revealed that concentrations of people living in poverty are generally found in urban areas, and in particular inner city housing estates. From this it has sometimes been concluded that poverty is largely an urban phenomenon (Herbert and Smith, 1979), and as a consequence much targeted anti-poverty activity has been focused on urban areas, as we shall see in Chapter 15.

This ignores poverty in rural areas, however; and, more importantly, it ignores the different dimensions which poverty and social exclusion might take in these areas. Access to services, both public services such as schools or health centres and private services such as shops, is generally much easier in urban areas; and public transport is also relatively frequent and reliable. In rural areas this is often not the case; and this may contribute to a peculiarly rural form of exclusion, which will be compounded for those without access to private transport here. Shucksmith (2000) reviewed a range of research projects on rural living in the UK and concluded that there were a number of particular dimensions to rural social exclusion, such as transport and afford-able housing, which were very different from those experienced in urban areas. There are clear policy implications in these differences too, although in practice little has been done in the UK to respond to many of the specifically rural dimensions of social exclusion.

More generally, however, the recent accentuation of concern with the spatial distribution of poverty and social exclusion has had a significant impact upon the development of policy in the UK, and elsewhere. One of the early reports from the SEU, provocatively entitled *Bringing Britain Together* (SEU, 1998), argued strongly that the problem of social exclusion was linked to the concentration of deprivation in poor areas. This was followed by proposals for a National Strategy for Neighbourhood Renewal to coordinate measures to combat poverty and exclusion through local policy action in such deprived areas (SEU, 2000). These ideas have been taken up and developed by the Labour government through the introduction of a range of new policy programmes to target additional resources onto poor areas in order to combat social exclusion. These are now generally referred to as area-based initiatives (ABIs), and we shall return to discuss them in more detail in Chapter 16.

Exclusion or polarisation?

The concern with people living in deprived neighbourhoods has become a widely shared conception of the problems of poverty and social exclusion in modern society; and academic research has recently begun to explore in more depth this local dimension of exclusion. The CASE researchers at the LSE initiated a detailed qualitative analysis of the experiences of social exclusion in deprived areas in Leeds, Sheffield and East London (Mumford and Power, 2003), although this is a longitudinal study and will only produce detailed results after a number of years. Lupton (2003), also based in CASE, has examined the dynamics of neighbourhood decline and renewal in twelve different disadvantaged areas in England and Wales and provided a fascinat-ing review of the experiences of exclusion within those areas and the impact of policies aimed at combating them. The local experience of poverty and social exclusion has also become a major focus of policy action, as we shall see in Part IV.

However, such an approach directs both academic analysis and policy action onto the 'victims' of social exclusion rather than the wider social circumstances and processes which lead to their exclusion; and this has particularly been the case with much of the recent UK government policy action discussed in Chapter 16. If social exclusion is a multi-dimensional product of a range of different dynamic social processes, then our understanding of this should focus upon these processes rather than the people who are excluded by them. The danger with policy action in poor neighbourhoods is that it does not address the roles that agencies based outside of those neighbourhoods may be playing in creating and recreating such exclusion. This applies to private sector agencies who may withdraw investment (and in effect therefore employment opportunities) or outlets (such as local branches of retail chains) from areas of deprivation, and to public sector agencies such as health and social services or education who may fail to support adequate local access to services in such areas. However, it is not just public and private agencies that can be the drivers of social exclusion, broader social and economic forces may also be in play here.

This broader context has been taken up by some academic commentators on social exclusion, who have pointed out that it has become an integral feature of the social structure in most advanced industrial societies at the turn of the century and should really be seen as a product of the broader trends in social and economic development within these societies, and indeed beyond them. Jordan (1996) took both a historical and a comparative approach to an analysis of poverty and social exclusion to argue that current problems are the product of historical changes in social structure and social solidarity, and of international political and economic forces. In particular he argued that the impact of global markets of capitalist investment and consumption had undermined past mass solidarities and institutional systems, and had replaced them with a more competitive and individualised culture in which the risk of social exclusion for some was more accentuated.

Byrne's (1999) analysis focused more on theoretical exploration of the meaning of social exclusion; but he too linked this to the changing nature of economic development in modern industrial societies such as the UK towards the end of the twentieth century. In particular he argued that a new 'post-industrial' order was emerging based on the exploitation of low-paid workers and the fragmentation of previous class solidarities. Both Jordan and Byrne are clear that the causes of social exclusion lay in national, or rather international, economic forces, rather than with the activities (or non-activities) of people living in inner-city estates. Therefore policy responses which focused only on the victims of social exclusion would be unlikely to provide much hope for significant change.

The limitations of a focus only on the victims of social exclusion was also taken up by Barry (2002) in his contribution to the CASE collection on *Understanding Social Exclusion* (Hills *et al.*, 2002). He pointed out that exclusion from participation in social relations and social institutions is not something reserved for those in poverty. Wealthy people too exclude themselves from many aspects of society, for instance, from public education and health services through use of exclusive private provision, and even from regular social interaction through locating their homes in gated communities or exclusive rural retreats. Such exclusion is optional rather than enforced, and therefore may not be of concern to many analysts and politicians. However, as Barry pointed out, it can have broader consequences for social relations, and in particular for social solidarity.

He argued that social exclusion should be seen alongside the related issues of social differentiation and social polarisation. *Social differentiation* (the very different experiences and circumstances of different groups within society) can be found in all societies, but when it takes on particular forms it can threaten social inclusion – most notably perhaps in the former apartheid regime in South Africa. *Social polarisation* (the existence of wide and growing gaps between these different social groups) can challenge social justice and social solidarity. Therefore the isolation of rich citizens in private schools and hospitals means that they are able to purchase social advantages denied to others, and that their support (both financial and political) for broader public services is likely to be reduced or removed. This is linked to inequality, Barry argued, for a more polarised social order is likely to be a more unequal one. This is similar to the trends identified by Jordan and Byrne, and seems to be supported by the evidence on the growing levels of inequality experienced in the UK towards the end of the last century discussed in Chapter 2 (and see Hills, 2004).

What this makes clear is that social exclusion is not just a problem for those who are excluded, it is a problem for social structure and social solidarity more generally. If significant numbers of people are excluded from enjoyment of the fruits of economic and social development, from use of social services, or from participation in social relations, then social order will be likely to become more polarised and more unequal – and ultimately perhaps more unstable for all.

Part III

Social Divisions
and Poverty

Gender and Poverty

SUMMARY OF KEY POINTS

- Research on poverty has revealed that women are generally at greater risk of poverty than men, and that when poor their experience of poverty can be different to that of men.
- Women's greater risk of poverty is partly a product of their unequal status within the labour market and their generally lower pay and career prospects.
- Social security protection used to discriminate against women by excluding them from entitlement to benefits in their own right. Such discrimination has now been removed; but women remain more likely to be reliant upon less generous, means-tested benefits.
- Women's weaker labour market position has also meant that they are less likely to benefit from private and occupational protection, notably pensions. Yet the majority of pensioners (around two-thirds) are women.
- Women's greater responsibility for caring for children and dependent adults also exposes them to greater risk of poverty.
- Overall, women's 'dependency' on men produces an ideological framework which can reinforce their experience of poverty.

The feminisation of poverty

Most attempts to measure poverty use household or family income or expenditure as the basis for counting or calculating the extent of poverty, as discussed in Chapter 6. Even when individual income is used, measurement tends to treat all individuals similarly as recipients of income without comparing their different circumstances or obligations. Insofar as this is explained or justified, and generally it is not, the assumption is that whilst income and expenditure are matters of public knowledge and concern and thus amenable to public scrutiny and measurement, household and family circumstances and obligations are private matters that cannot and should not be the focus of public research. We will return later to the significance of this alleged public/private divide in structuring our knowledge and perceptions of individual and family poverty. It is increasingly widely recognised, however, that differences in individual and family circumstances are crucial to determining the impact and extent of poverty, and that rather than being excluded or ignored they should be a central feature of any understanding of poverty. This is particularly true of the differences associated with gender.

The predominant focus on household and family income has obscured, or in Millar and Glendinning's (1989) words rendered 'invisible', the differences between men's and women's experiences of poverty, and differences in the extent and depth of poverty between men and women. The effect of this has most frequently been seen in the tendency to assume that women who are poor are the wives or partners of (low-paid or unemployed) men who are poor rather than the poor (low-paid or unemployed) wives or partners of men who may themselves be in well-paid employment. Even when women, as heads of households or breadwinners, are included, the particular problems that may be associated with their gender, for instance problems of discrimination or disadvantage within the labour market, are often ignored.

More recently feminist critiques have begun to question and challenge this 'gender blindness' and to argue that focusing on the differences between men and women in research and policy analysis would reveal that women suffer poverty on a more widespread basis than men, and that their experience of poverty is quite different as a result of expectations about gender roles. Of particular importance here was the collection of papers edited by Glendinning and Millar for their reader, *Women and Poverty in Britain*, first published in 1987 and updated in 1992.

This new (or renewed) concern with women's experience of poverty has sometimes been referred to as the 'feminisation of poverty' (see Lister, 2004, ch. 3). As Millar (1989) pointed out, the phrase came from the USA, and it is a particularly ambiguous one. It could be taken to refer simply to the fact that as poverty levels increase more women are likely to experience poverty, or it could refer to a greater risk of poverty for women and thus a change in the balance between the genders, or indeed it could refer merely to an increased emphasis in research and policy on the poverty experienced by women. These were alternatively analysed as the 'invisibility', 'gender balance' and 'reconceptualisation' theses in a critique of feminist approaches by Dey

(1996). The phrase is probably used in practice to mean all three of these, and the predominant evidence is that in societies such as the USA and the UK all three are to some extent true. Indeed, according to a United Nations report quoted by Lister (2004, ch. 3) this is a worldwide phenomenon with 70 per cent of the people in poverty in the world estimated to be female.

Certainly if poverty levels generally are increasing which, as we saw in Chapter 2, they were in the UK in the 1980s and 1990s, then this will have affected women as well as men. There is also evidence that some of the changes associated with such recent increases may have resulted in a greater proportion of this new poverty being experienced by women. For instance, demographic changes resulting in greater numbers of single elderly women, and marital breakdown resulting in lone-parent households, have increased the number of households comprising predominantly women and these are heavily represented among those who are poor, with 21 per cent of single female pensioners (compared to 14 per cent of male) and 47 per cent of lone parents poor by the 60 per cent of median income measure (AHC) in 2003/04 (DWP, 2005a, table 3.5). More generally 20 per cent of women are poor by this measure compared to 18 per cent of men (*ibid.*); and in an analysis of the PSE survey, discussed in Chapter 5 (Gordon *et al.*, 2000), women were found to have a 5 per cent higher chance of experiencing poverty than men (Bradshaw *et al.*, 2003).

Furthermore although, as we shall see, there has been a general increase in women's participation in the labour market, this has not led to equal status with male employees, and the growing impact of labour market changes has affected female workers disproportionately (Pillinger, 1992; Lewis, 1993). At a more general level still, the restrictions that have been introduced into public welfare services since the 1970s have had a disproportionate effect on women who, as Edgell and Duke (1983) pointed out, are the major beneficiaries of such services. The increase in private, voluntary and informal welfare has both excluded women from preferential treatment through the market, because of their position of economic disadvantage within it, and increased the burden on women at home to compensate for the growing gaps and inadequacies in public services. Changes in the welfare mix have thus contributed to a position of potentially deepening deprivation for women.

The increased focus on the gender dimension of poverty in recent years has directed greater public attention towards the poverty experienced by women. However, it should not be concluded from this that women's poverty is a recent phenomenon, or that the disproportionate distribution of the experience of poverty between the genders is a result only of changes introduced in the late twentieth century. As Lewis and Piachaud (1992) pointed out, this maldistribution of poverty was a feature of British society throughout the twentieth century. It was partly a product of the fact that households headed by women are more likely to be poor because of lower wages or a disproportionate reliance on benefits. However, it was also due to the fact that, even in households comprising men and women with apparently adequate overall incomes, the distribution of resources within the household may be uneven, as we saw in Chapter 6, and may leave some, usually women, experiencing poverty.

A study by Graham (1986) of women in families revealed that many experienced poverty, and over a half of those who then separated from their partners felt they were financially better-off on their own. Even when their only income was state benefit, their perception of their position changed. One lone mother interviewed by Graham said:

> I'm much better off. Definitely. I know where I am now, because I get our money each week and I can control what I spend. Oh, he was earning more than I get but I was worse off than I am now. I am not so poor on £43 Supplementary Benefit a week for everything for me and the two children as I was then. At least I know where the money's being spent and where it's not being spent. It might not last as long but at least it's being put into provisions for the home.

Pahl's (1989) research on the distribution of household income also revealed that inequitable family budgeting could leave women proportionately disadvantaged; and this was confirmed in later research of Goode *et al.* (1998) mentioned in Chapter 6.

However, it is not just the inequitable distribution of resources within households and families that contributes to women's experience of poverty. There is also the issue of who controls the resources and directs or determines expenditure, as revealed in the above extract. When the primary household income is acquired by men they can exercise control over how it is spent, and this may enhance the power they already hold within the household. Men's incomes are more likely than women's incomes to lift families out of poverty (Millar, 2003); and, when women in paid employment do bring their own resources into the household, the value of these is often not recognised and they are used to subsidise shortfalls in the housekeeping budget (Morris, 1989) or are targeted on particular additional goods or services (Piachaud, 1982b).

What is more, although it may frequently be the case that men control the resources, it is generally women who have to *manage* them, and who have to face the stark choice of determining priorities when living on a low income. This was revealed graphically in research by Kempson *et al.* (1994, p. 116) on families living on low incomes, which listed numerous examples of women having to make hard decisions on budgeting – and generally having to go without as a result. For instance one mother said:

> To be honest with you, the last time I bought for myself was for my husband's funeral. I don't buy anything at all for myself. My sister-in-law passes clothes on to me or they buy new things for my birthday ... I've got nothing, but I don't go nowhere.

This is one example of a number of instances of research evidence revealing the extent to which women will deny themselves even basic needs in order to cope with inadequate or reduced household budgets. Kempson *et al.* (1994)

also found that women would eat smaller portions of food and go without meals, or hot meals, whilst at home alone during the day. In an earlier study Graham (1986) discovered that women may even go without heating, as the following quote from a mother in a low-income household reveals: 'I turn it off when I'm on my own and put a blanket on myself. Sometimes we both do in the evening but my husband doesn't like being cold and puts the heating back on' (Graham, 1992, p. 220). As Land and Rose (1985, p. 86) once put it, 'self denial is still seen as women's special share of poverty', and referred to this as self-sacrifice or 'compulsory altruism'.

This self-denial includes the time women spend on unpaid work at home to supplement inadequate household budgets, for instance Piachaud's (1987) example of the differing costs of home-made as opposed to oven-ready chips, discussed in Chapter 6. Much of the 'time poverty' (Lister, 1990 and 2004, ch. 3) associated with such domestic work is disproportionately experienced by women. It is also linked to longer-term consequences for women's economic and social position that result in particular from the absence from the labour market associated with domestic work, for instance in the loss of career advancement and the accumulation of occupational benefits or protection, which we discuss below.

In general terms, therefore, women's poverty is not only greater and disproportionately more widespread than men's, it is in many ways a quite different experience – and thus in a sense it is a different problem. Poverty, as we have seen, is a political concept, and this political context extends to the politics of gender too. The feminist criticism of the gender blindness of much poverty research and analysis is not just that it has failed to measure or has underplayed the poverty experienced by women, but that it has ignored, and in practice concealed, the gendered experience of poverty and the different circumstances in which women are poor and deprived. This point was emphasised by Millar and Glendinning in 1989, and is exemplified too in more recent research on women's poverty (Bradshaw et al., 2003; Millar, 2003).

Employment and low pay

Paid employment is the main source of income for the majority of people in modern British society. Thus access to the labour market and the wages received from it are crucial in determining resources for individuals and households, and for providing security and control over those resources. Women's position in the labour market is thus a central determinant of their wealth, or poverty; and research has consistently demonstrated that the position of women here is significantly different from that of men (see Dex, 1985; Beechey, 1987; Pillinger, 1992).

Although during the early period of industrialisation women were employed alongside men in the rapidly growing number of factories and workshops, there was a trend away from equal employment during the nineteenth century that involved the direct exclusion, via 'protective' legislation, of women from some forms of employment, such as coalmining. Women were also excluded more generally by discriminatory employment practices, which were supported by male employees, who in return demanded a 'family wage' sufficient to support a dependent wife and children.

The effect of these pressures was to exclude large numbers of, especially married, women from paid employment and to force them into dependency on men. They did not result, however, in the complete removal of women from paid employment. Many women continued to work, and for many families the male 'family wage' was never sufficient to provide for the household without the addition of women's supplementary earnings.

Nevertheless large numbers of women did leave the labour market in the nineteenth and early twentieth centuries. By 1891 women's participation rate in paid employment was only 35 per cent compared with men's at 84 per cent (Lewis and Piachaud, 1992, p. 37). Furthermore, women's employment came to be seen by employers, male employees, and even women themselves, as secondary employment operating to supplement male wages or provide minor household luxuries – 'pin money'. Thus women's wages were much lower than men's. For all industries they were 51.5 per cent of the average wage for a male manual worker in 1886 (*ibid.*, p. 39). This created a vicious circle of secondary wage status that indirectly forced women into dependence, at least partially, on men, especially when they had children to support.

By the beginning of the twentieth century, therefore, women's separate and secondary position in the labour market was entrenched, reinforced and recreated by powerful ideological expectations about women's different responsibilities within the presumed family structure (see Gittins, 1993). During the twentieth century, however, and particularly after the Second World War, women's participation in the labour market began to grow again (Wilson, 1994). By 1971 women comprised 38 per cent of the labour force, and by 2003 this had risen to 45 per cent (Flaherty *et al.*, 2004, p. 174); and these changes have been accompanied by some moves towards more equal pay and equal treatment at work, although this has been a long, slow and far from complete process.

Since the 1970s legislation in the form of the Equal Pay and the Sex Discrimination Acts have required equal pay and treatment for women at work. Despite this, however, women's average hourly earnings have only risen to 81 per cent of that of their male counterparts (*ibid.*, p. 175). The reasons for the failure of the law requiring equal treatment are complex and multifaceted. In part they are a product of the nature of the legislation itself and the mechanisms for enforcing it (see Morris and Nott, 1991). However, more generally the failure reflects the fact that the broader structure of women's participation in the labour market, whilst it has grown overall, has remained quite different from that of men – and these differences remain a major cause of women's greater risk and different experience of poverty.

Therefore even though more women do now work, they tend to work in different jobs and under different conditions from men (Lonsdale, 1992; Wilson, 1994). Thus women are much more likely than men to be working part-time, 42 per cent of women are part-timers compared with 9 per cent of men (Flaherty *et al.*, 2004, p. 177); and much of the growth in women's labour market participation can be accounted for by increased part-time working. Yet part-time work generally attracts lower rates of pay and gives rise to fewer contractual and statutory rights and protections. Women's part-time work also includes some of the worst-rewarded and yet most labour-intensive paid work in the form of 'home working', for example assembling clothing at home, processing mail orders or undertaking paid child care on a formal or informal basis.

Even when women are in full-time work, however, they are frequently engaged in different work and under different conditions from men. For instance female employees predominate in secretarial and clerical work, in nursing, in residential care and in primary school teaching. The Labour Force Survey for 2002/03 revealed that around 40 per cent of women were working in public administration, education and health, about 25 per cent were working in administrative and secretarial posts (compared to 5 per cent of men), and 14 per cent were working in personal social services (compared to 2 per cent of men) (*ibid.*, p. 174). These are generally low-status and lower-paid employment sectors; and yet, in the higher-status jobs in the same areas, men tend to predominate, for instance as accountants, doctors, managers and head teachers. Furthermore, within factory production in the private sector women tend to work in different sectors from men, for example in clothing and hosiery production or food and drink preparation. Even within the same factory they are likely to be placed in different sections of the production process, for instance in the packing department; and again the jobs occupied by women are frequently those with lower status and lower pay.

Within a segmented labour market, therefore, women are generally employed in different and less desirable sectors than men (see Flaherty *et al.*, 2004, p. 175). And following this their less-secure and less-consistent connection with the labour market is also likely to exclude them from many of the increasingly important occupational protections and benefits provided to secure male workers, such as sickness pay, pensions schemes or share-ownership schemes. All of these can provide a cushion against poverty and deprivation beyond the period of employment; and this is particularly the case with occupational pensions, as we shall see in Chapter 11. Research on women and occupational pensions has revealed the need to reconsider the consequences of the relative exclusion of women from this major source of income and security in later life (Evason and Spence, 2003).

However, the main point about women's secondary status in the labour market is that it is also related to more general ideological expectations about their responsibilities for domestic work, which remain strongly rooted in British society (Kiernan, 1991). As Morris (1991) pointed out, women's disadvantaged position in the labour market is reinforced by the dual roles that many women occupy as both paid worker and unpaid housewife. It is because women have to undertake this 'double shift' that they more frequently work part-time and thus experience worse pay and conditions. Yet at the same time it is because women who work experience worse pay and conditions that there is potentially so much pressure on married women to see their paid work as secondary to that of their husbands. This can force married women indirectly into dependence on their husbands. It can also be a source of single women's greater risk of poverty, whether as single young women at work, as divorced or separated lone parents, or as single or widowed elderly pensioners with no occupational or earnings-related pension support. For some women, therefore, the experience may be one of being trapped in marriage or trapped in poverty – or both.

Social security

Social security protection has always been based on support for the wage labour market and the use of benefits as a wage substitute, or a wage subsidy – an issue to which we shall return in Chapter 14. As a result of this the treatment of women within social security provision has in practice largely been determined by their treatment within, or outside, the labour market, and their presumed dependency on men. This could be seen in the nineteenth-century Poor Law, where entry into the workhouse for unemployed women was reserved for those whose husbands would not provide for them, and better treatment was reserved for widows for whom the alternative of family support did not exist.

When insurance-based benefits were developed in the early part of the twentieth century, the fact that they depended on contributions made whilst in paid employment effectively excluded most married women from protection. However even those women who were in paid work were treated differently from men, paying lower contributions and receiving lower benefits – generally around 80 per cent of the full rate. Even this reduced protection was challenged during the recession of the 1930s through the introduction of an Anomalies Act to prevent married women who were 'not really unemployed' from claiming unemployment benefit merely to enhance their married lives. The assumption of course, as in the case of the workhouse, was that married women did not need social security support because they could depend on their husbands. This assumption was reinforced in the means-tested Unemployment Assistance schemes that replaced the Poor Law in the 1930s, and it was extended to include dependence on other close family members, such as parents or children, with the result that single women, too, were effectively denied support in most circumstances.

The separate treatment and secondary status for women within benefit provision became entrenched in social security after the reform of the system following the Second World War. The Beveridge Report, which underlay the reforms, made specific reference to the need for separate treatment for married women under the proposed insurance scheme on account of their responsibility for 'other duties' (Beveridge, 1942, p. 51). Beveridge's assumption was that married women would be engaged in unpaid work at home and thus would not need protection under the scheme other than through a dependant's benefit paid to their husbands. Only when a husband could no longer act as provider for his wife, in widowhood, would a payment (Widow's Benefit) be made directly to her. Beveridge had originally also suggested a payment to women after divorce, but this was not taken up by the postwar government for fear of encouraging marital breakdown. Thus although single women at work did pay contributions and could receive benefits in the same way as men, married women in employment could only make a reduced contribution in return for which no benefits were paid.

The means-tested assistance scheme that accompanied the introduction of insurance protection also continued the assumption of women's dependence on their husbands through the aggregation of family incomes as the basis for determining entitlement. If men had an income their wives could not independently claim benefit. This presumed dependency was extended to single women living with men, to avoid a situation in which they might be treated more favourably than their married sisters, giving rise to the need for questioning and investigation to determine whether single women claimants were in practice cohabitating with a man. Aggregation and dependence were restricted after the war to spouses or cohabitees, however, and did not extend, as the prewar scheme had, to other close family members.

What this implied was that for the purposes of safety-net support women were presumed to be dependent on male partners. Beveridge's intention had been that the assistance scheme would be of marginal and declining importance compared with the provision of benefit support through insurance. As we shall see in Chapter 14, however, this has not proved to be the case. Reliance on the means-tested assistance scheme has grown inexorably since the 1960s; and its reinforcement of family dependency has had particular consequences for women who, although they have always constituted the majority of benefit dependants, were until the 1980s excluded from claiming in their own right unless they were single.

In the 1970s and 1980s changes were introduced into social security legislation to remove, at least formally, some of the discriminatory treatment experienced by women. In the 1970s insurance protection was reformed to permit married women to contribute and receive benefits on the same basis as men, although because of their past exclusion many women could still never establish full contribution records for long-term benefits such as pensions. In the 1980s means-tested benefits were reformed to permit either men or women to act as the claimant and receive the family benefit. However, aggregation and family dependency remained within means-testing and the other disadvantages of such support continue to impact most heavily upon women. What is more the gradual decline in the scope of the support provided by NI benefits has potentially increased women's reliance upon aggregated means-tested support, at a time when their independent entitlement to NI support was growing following the reforms to this (see Bennett, 2005)

Since the turn of the century there has been further expansion of means-testing and its extension into the taxation system through the use of tax credits, as we shall see in Chapter 14. There was much debate in political circles about whether such support should be paid directly to (male) employees or (female) carers – into 'the wallet' rather than 'the purse'. In the event, couples were given the choice, and since 2003 tax credits for child-care costs have been paid direct to the main carer. The result has been in practice a transfer of resources from men (as employees) to women (as carers), although the disincentives inherent in the scheme mean that Working Tax Credit may discourage some women from entering the labour market as the second earners in couples (see Chapter 14, and Bennett, 2005).

The other recent extension of means-testing which has also had a particular impact on women has been the introduction of the minimum income guarantee for pensioners. As we shall see in Chapter 11, many pensioners still experience poverty, and this is generally the case where they do not have access to the additional support provided by private or occupational pension schemes. It is women who disproportionately experience such exclusion because of the disadvantaged labour market position that many have experienced, as we discussed above. As commentators have pointed out this gives rise to more general gender discrimination within private pension provision (Evason and Spence, 2003), and means that it is female pensioners who are more likely to be entirely dependent the basic state pension. Because of the recognised inadequacy of this basic pension the government have introduced a means-tested supplement, the minimum income guarantee. This does raise the incomes of those receiving it significantly, and this is of particular benefit to the women pensioners who are the majority of claimants. However, as we shall return to discuss in Chapter 14, the problems with the take-up of means-tested benefits, which result in many of those potentially entitled not receiving the benefits which they need, apply in particular to the income guarantee; and so there are many pensioners still dependent only upon the lower basic state pension – and that the majority of these are women (see Bennett, 2005).

Social security has been the main anti-poverty policy measure in the UK throughout the last century or longer. However the benefits it provides, whether through insurance or means-testing within state provision or various forms of private protection, have largely been predicated on and structured to support family units in which men and women occupy specific and distinct gender roles. One of the major effects of this has been the exclusion, either directly or indirectly, of many women from receipt of social security benefits, and thus an increase in their risk of poverty. This exclusion has often been associated with assumptions about women's caring responsibilities and their status as dependants.

The costs of caring

Women's secondary status in the labour market and the social security scheme is closely related to assumptions about gender roles within families, and in particular women's responsibility for caring work. Young children and adults with illnesses or disabilities need close and regular personal attention; and, although there is some limited public and private collective provision for such care, the majority of it is carried out in the home – and by and large it is carried out by women.

It has even been suggested that women are somehow uniquely equipped to undertake caring roles (see Henwood *et al.*, 1987), and such an assumption has been influential in the development of public support for such work. The papers in Finch and Groves' (1983) book on caring for adults, *A Labour of Love*, discussed this gender stereotyping and pointed out that the expectation that women will provide care at home is inextricably linked to their emotional ties to their children or other family members. For women, therefore, caring *about* someone also means being willing to care *for* them, and this is an expectation that many women in practice share, even though they are aware of the heavy costs it involves.

These costs extend beyond the provision of support itself, however, for they also give rise to a greater risk of poverty for women. Those needing care themselves are obviously at risk of poverty, primarily because they are unable to secure support through paid employment or employment-related benefits. This is most clearly the case for children, who in most cases must be supported by their parents, hence the greater risk of poverty for families with children discussed in Chapter 11. However, the women who are engaged in such caring work, especially when caring for young children or those with severe disabilities, are similarly excluded from the labour market and hence they too are at risk of poverty. As Graham (1987, p. 223) remarked, 'Poverty and caring are for many women two sides of the same coin'.

For women as parents this risk of poverty is especially acute where they are acting as lone parents. Around 47 per cent of lone parents in the UK are poor, on the 60 per cent of median income measure (AHC), compared to 20 per cent of couples with children (DWP, 2005a, table 3.5). The vast majority, around 90 per cent, of lone parents are women, and here women's secondary labour market status compounds the more general problems of trying to balance caring responsibilities against paid employment to support a family. Millar has argued that gender is the crucial factor in lone parent poverty – 'it is precisely because lone mothers are women that they have a very high risk of poverty', she claimed (1992, p. 149), and she pointed out that the relatively small number of lone fathers were less likely to be poor.

The wider availability of collective child care and the availability of tax credits to contribute to the costs for paying for this now aim to make it easier for lone parents to enter paid employment; and targeted support and advice for them to do so are provided under the New Deal. What is more the Child Support Agency now exists to facilitate, or enforce, the payment of maintenance for child-care costs from absent parents (usually in practice fathers). However, lone parents with children under school age are not required to seek employment as a condition of receiving social security support, and many remain reliant upon social security as a major source of income. Furthermore the Child Support Agency has failed in practice to secure regular and reliable maintenance from most fathers. So around a half of lone parents, mostly women, remain poor.

It is not only child care that may trap women in poverty; adults with serious illnesses or disabilities also require care. With growing longevity and improved medical standards the demand for this care has been growing significantly – in particular since the move in the 1990s to replace institutional care for dependent adults with 'community care', which in practice has nearly always meant care at home in the family. Providing such care is again likely to remove carers from the labour market and thus increase their risk of poverty and dependency, as we discuss in more detail in Chapter 12. Indeed it is somewhat ironic that, as earlier childbearing and smaller families have reduced the scale of the burden of child care for women, the growing demand for adult care has to some extent taken its place, resulting in what Roll (1989, p. 25) once called the development of a 'cycle of caring' for many women.

It is not just low income that contributes to the poverty experienced by carers, however. As we have seen, the experience of deprivation and social exclusion covers a range of social and individual needs that people in certain circumstances may lack; and those involved in caring work frequently experience significant deprivation beyond the loss of adequate cash income. In particular they are likely to be trapped within the home for long periods of time and be engaged in monotonous, tiring and potentially emotionally draining work. This is especially the case for those caring for dependent adults – for whilst children will grow up and leave home, dependent adults are more likely to be in a deteriorating condition that will only be ended by their death. The loss of control over their time on a day-to-day basis is thus a significant feature of deprivation for carers. For them the notion of 'time poverty' may be particularly pertinent.

What is more, as Joshi (1992) has argued, the cost of caring does not just include those deprivations experienced at the time. Absence from the labour market, for mothers perhaps at a crucial point in their lives, is likely to lead to longer-term deprivation resulting from lost occupational benefits, lost training and career opportunities, and perhaps lost opportunities for saving and investment too. These are sometimes described as the 'opportunity costs' of caring work (Joshi, 1988) and they can add up to significant losses, which women in general are likely to experience at some point in their lives. The assumption of course is that such costs can be borne because at such points women will be supported by their husbands. However this assumption of dependency in reality may be more of a cause of women's poverty than a solution to it.

Dependency

At the heart of women's social and economic situation, and thus their greater risk of poverty, is their assumed position of dependency on men within the family. It is because it is assumed that women can depend on their husbands for material support that they have traditionally been excluded from full participation in the labour market and social security provision. As we saw in Chapter 6, however, the allocation of resources within households and families is not always equitable and may leave many women living below the standard enjoyed by their partners. Furthermore, the incomes received by men may often not be sufficient to provide adequately for a dependent wife (and children), and so women have had to engage in paid work to supplement the family income and avoid poverty, although they may also work to secure an independent income (Machin and Waldfogel, 1994; Millar, 2003). Yet this secondary income status for women has the effect of reproducing and reinforcing their lower wages, and their secondary employment situation in the labour market.

The problem of dependency can thus operate as a vicious circle for women who, when young and single, may feel themselves pressured into marriage, in part at least because of the poor prospects for employment and pay, and once married (and especially after child bearing) are trapped into dependency on their husbands. However, women's dependence on their husbands is an ideological as well as an economic feature of gender stereotyping. It is closely tied to broader ideologies of family structure and family roles, which, as feminists have argued, sometimes involve clear differentiation and discrimination between men and women (see Gittins, 1993; Barrett and Macintosh, 1982).

This differentiation, and the inequality and poverty that flow from it, are largely disguised from public view. As Lister (2004, ch. 3) argues, women's dependency is frequently linked to a 'hidden poverty', with the implication that what goes on inside the private world of the family should not be of concern to researchers or policy-makers. Research such as Pahl's (1989) on household income distribution has now begun to penetrate this private world of the family; and feminist scholarship has begun to challenge the false nature of the public/private divide, in particular from the position of women at home for whom the private world of the home is also their public world. Lister (2004) has argued that any attempts to challenge or combat women's poverty must take up this ideological dimension as well as the economic needs of women who are poor. The inequality and exclusion associated with dependency need to be counterposed with a demand for *autonomy*, which in turn his is linked to a more general concern with the position of women as 'citizens' within society (Lister, 2003). A claim for equal citizenship for women in UK society, she has argued, could be a vehicle for challenging both ideological and economic aspects of women's greater risk of poverty.

Racism and Poverty

SUMMARY OF KEY POINTS

- Black and minority ethnic people living in the UK experience 'racist' discrimination and disadvantage which increase their risk of poverty.
- Some of this disadvantage is the product of the history of immigration of black people into the country, which has left high concentrations of black and minority ethnic groups living in some of the poorest geographical areas.
- There are demographic differences between different ethnic groups in the UK, with some ethnic minorities having higher proportions of larger families with greater risk of poverty.
- Black and minority ethnic people experience disadvantage in the labour market with higher levels of low pay or unemployment within some groups.
- There is some evidence that ethnic minorities are also disadvantaged within social security provision because they may be excluded from receipt of some benefits and are also likely to experience lower rates of take-up of others.
- Social exclusion in housing, health and education is also structured by race and ethnicity; and the experience of racism itself compounds other aspects of social exclusion for many black and minority ethnic people.

Racism and ethnic minority inequality

The UK in the twenty-first century remains to a significant extent a racist society in that there is continuing evidence that black and other minority ethnic communities experience discrimination and disadvantage on a dispropor-tionate basis, and this cannot be explained merely as result of chance or misfortune (see Solomos, 2003). This does not make British society unique, nor in a sense is it all that surprising. Discrimination and disadvantage for ethnic minority groups is common in many, if not most, social structures, and certainly there is overt evidence of racism similar to, and in some cases more exaggerated than, that found in the UK in most other European and Western capitalist countries.

However, widespread evidence of racism elsewhere should not lead us to overlook the particular features and particular causes of racism in British society, which have produced a unique pattern of discrimination and dis-advantage resulting in significant inequality and higher levels of poverty for certain groups within society. Nor of course should the widespread experi-ence of racism be interpreted as suggesting its consequences are not a problem, or not a problem amenable to analysis and policy response. Indeed it is because 'race' is such an important feature of the structure of poverty and inequality that its impact must be included in understanding, and tackled by policy development.

What is meant by race in this context, however, has been the subject of some debate, both on terminology and on the use of terms adopted. It is probably not a debate that can be entirely satisfactorily resolved either because, as to some extent with the debates on the definition of poverty, meaning is inextricably linked to broader theoretical and political questions about the nature of the problem and the appropriate response to it. In the case of modern Britain this debate is founded in the country's imperial past, its subjuga-tion of colonial populations and the assumption of 'white supremacy' that arose from this.

Thus in Britain 'race' is often taken to mean skin colour, and in particular the difference between white and black skin. This has been accentuated by the entry into the country of a significant number of black ex-colonial residents, in particular after the Second World War. These immigrants and their offspring often vary in cultural backgrounds and skin colour. However they are all potential victims of discrimination or disadvantage based on skin colour. They are therefore often generically referred to as 'black' when compared with the indigenous 'white' population, and discussion of the disadvantages associated with race often distinguishes between the circumstances and experiences of blacks and whites.

Within Britain's black population, however, there is a range of different communities with different ethnic, cultural and religious traditions. These are sometimes referred to as 'ethnic minority communities'; and they also include non-black communities such as Jews, Arabs, Eastern Europeans and others, all of whom may experience discrimination or disadvantage because of their culture, language or religion. Analysis of the experiences of racism and in particular its links to poverty and social exclusion needs to take account of the different experiences and circumstances of these different ethnic minority groups. However, in order to do this we need data about them which distinguishes citizens according to such criteria. Not all research, either official government information or independent academic investigation, does this, and so there are practical limits to what we can say about the experiences of different ethnic groups.

Nevertheless, growing concern with racism and with the importance of ethnic diversity within the country has led to greater availability of data on the experience of different ethnic groups in recent years. The Censuses in 1991 and 2001 included questions about the ethnicity of respondents. Information about ethnicity has also been included in the Labour Force Survey (on employment patterns) and the Family Resources Survey (on living standards) since the 1980s and 1990s respectively; and in 1993 the fourth in a series of National Surveys of Ethnic Minorities was carried out by the Policy Studies Institute and provided a range of statistical information about the shape and distribution of the ethnic minority population in the UK (Modood *et al.*, 1997).

This data generally provides information about the circumstances of different ethnic groups and, as we shall see, there are some important variations and contrasts here, with some groups faring much worse than others (Berthoud, 1998a). In some cases, however, distinctions are only made between the generic white and black populations; and to some extent this broader distinction does reflect the racism experienced by Britain's the black population, which overlays their situation as minority ethnic communities. It is this racism, and not skin colour or cultural difference, that is a major part of the problems experienced by black people and contributes to their poverty and exclusion.

History

The racism faced by Britain's black population has a history as long as that of the population itself, certainly extending back to the early days of overseas trade and Britain's involvement in the slave trade during the growth of colonisation. Early black immigrants to the country were generally associated with trading and seafaring activities, and tended to be concentrated in ports such as Cardiff, Liverpool and London. This geographical concentration was a trend that was followed by later groups of black immigrants to Britain, primarily as a result of discrimination in housing and employment markets, which forced the new residents into poor inner city areas that were less popular among the indigenous population. However, such concentration may have compounded the problem of racism by appearing to minimise the wider integration of black people into other parts of British society, and as we shall see it has certainly contributed to the problems of poverty that have flowed from this.

In the early part of the twentieth century immigration by Jews and Eastern Europeans introduced new ethnic minority communities into Britain, and many of these faced discrimination and hostility from sections of the indigenous population. After the Second World War, however, and following the conversion of the British Empire into a commonwealth of independent countries with close links with Britain, larger numbers of black immigrants from the former colonies were encouraged to come to Britain, mainly in order to fill menial and poorly paid jobs that an indigenous population enjoying 'full employment' did not find attractive.

It was these immigrants in particular who experienced the discrimination and hostility that forced them into the poorer areas of London and the large cities of the Midlands, Lancashire and Yorkshire. It was also they who, because of their black skins and former colonial status, became the focus of a new racism among the white community, which began to surface in the form of hostility, abuse, harassment and even violence in the late 1950s. By the 1960s this racism, allied to the weaker economic and geographical situation of the new black populations, was beginning to coalesce into a broader structure of discrimination and disadvantage based on race.

The major period of black immigration into the UK was relatively short, and by the 1960s fears about unemployment and reduced economic growth had resulted in the imposition of immigration controls aimed at reducing the numbers of new migrants to the UK, in particular from the commonwealth countries which had until then had had free access to residence in the UK. In fact overall levels of immigration were not great either before or after the imposition of these controls because immigration was balanced up by emigration to other countries from the UK. Indeed before the 1980s emigration flows exceeded immigration, and, though there was a rise in net immigration after 1990, this flattened out to around 150,000 a year after 2000 (ONS, 2005a). Set in the context of growing migration around the world towards the latter part of the last century, migration patterns within the UK were not significantly high and indeed were below those in many other advanced industrial countries.

The immigration controls which were introduced in the UK in the 1960s and 1970s applied to all potential immigrants into Britain, of course, and not only black commonwealth citizens. Although, after 1973 when Britain joined the (then) European Economic Community, controls no longer applied to the citizens of EU countries, who had freedom of movement across member states. However, there is no doubt that the controls did impact most directly on commonwealth citizens who previously had free access to the UK; and what is more there is evidence that these controls were enforced with particular severity against black migrants (see Moore and Wallace, 1975). One effect of this was to compound the hostility and suspicion experienced by the resident black population, all of whom could thus be labelled as potential unwanted or illegal immigrants.

More recently this hostility has been directed towards asylum-seekers, who are seeking entry to the UK in order to avoid violence and oppression in their home countries. Where such fears are genuine, applicants will be granted permission to stay; but there is suspicion that some applicants are simply seeking to gain entry for economic reasons. This suspicion can be tested by immigration officials and challenged through the legal process; but it is shared, and promulgated, by the popular press who are often hostile to asylum-seekers and seek to brand them as unwanted or illegal immigrants. Not all asylum-seekers are black, indeed many now come from Eastern Europe and former Soviet states; but the negative reaction to them has to some degree extended racist anti-immigration sentiments to such a wider group, blurring the boundaries of this dimension of racism to include all non-Anglo-Saxon 'foreigners'.

At the same time the size of black population has been growing in number both in absolute terms and as a proportion of the overall UK population. This is a product of the birth in the UK of 'second-generation' black children, who now outnumber those who arrived in the country through immigration, and of the continuing numbers of immigrants who are still able to enter to join their families here. Between the 1991 and 2001 Censuses the number of all minority ethnic groups rose from 3 million to 4.6 million, although even then they only constituted 8 per cent of the overall population (see Table 10.1).

The history of immigration, ethnic diversity and a growing black population in the UK is thus a complex one, and, as we shall see, the demographic implications of this have particular consequences for the risk and experience of poverty amongst ethnic minority citizens. However, it has contributed to the more general problem of racism within the country, which extends to some extent to all black people in the country, even those born here as

Table 10.1   Size of ethnic groups in Britain 2001 (with 1991 for comparison)

	1991 population (000s)	2001 population (000s)	% of total population 2001	% of minority ethnic population 2001
White	51,873	52,481	92	
All minority ethnic groups	**3,014**	**4,623**	**8**	**100**
Black Caribbean	500	566	1	12
Black African	212	485	1	10
Black other	178	97	0	2
Indian	840	1,052	2	23
Pakistani	477	747	1	16
Bangladeshi	163	283	0	6
Other Asian	197	247	0	5
Chinese	157	243	0	5
Other	290	229	0	5
Mixed race	0	674	1	15

Note: Columns do not sum to 100% due to rounding.
Source: 2001 Census: Key Statistics Table 6.

British citizens, and to all potential immigrants, or at least those coming from different ethnic or cultural backgrounds and seeking asylum or residence in this country. And this racism can further compound the problems of poverty and social exclusion experienced by those who are its victims.

Demography and geography

Ethnic minorities make up about 8 per cent of the UK population according to the 2001 Census. Table 10.1 shows the distribution of these across the major ethnic groups, and reveals that Indians and Pakistanis make up the largest groups followed by black Caribbeans and black Africans.

As Table 10.1 also reveals, the numbers of the ethnic minority population are growing in most ethnic groups. This is a product of immigration but also of the larger size of families in some ethnic groups. Average family size within the Pakistani (4.2) and Bangladeshi (4.7) population is much greater than amongst black Caribbeans and whites. By contrast, lone-parent households are more common amongst black Caribbeans at 54 per cent of all families, compared to 23 per cent of white families and 9 per cent of Asian families (Flaherty *et al.*, 2004, p.189). Given the relatively high levels of child poverty in the UK, which we discuss in Chapter 11, this means that all these families are particularly at risk. The highest levels of poverty are associated with larger families and lone-parent households, and therefore these ethnic groups are more likely to experience poverty because of this.

Higher risk of poverty is also linked to old age. Here demographic trends may favour ethnic minorities for there are smaller numbers of elderly people here compared to the white population (Platt, 2002, p. 84). This is largely a reflection of patterns of immigration: the relatively young people who came to the UK in the 1950s and 1960s have not yet reached the average ages of the indigenous population. However, it can disguise the relatively high levels of poverty which do exist amongst the, smaller, ethnic minority elderly population. These people are less likely to have generous occupational pensions, because of the labour market disadvantages which we discuss below. They are also less likely to have full NI pension records if they came to the country during their working lives and have perhaps since then again spent time abroad (Platt, 2002, p. 85). Thus ethnic minority pensioners are more likely to be dependent upon means-tested social security support, and more likely to be poor than their white counterparts.

The demographic profile of Britain's ethnic minority population therefore contributes to their greater risk of experiencing poverty. This is also true of their geographical distribution. As we mentioned above early immigrants to the UK tended to concentrate in the dockland areas in which they arrived, most notably in London. The relatively large numbers of new immigrants in the postwar era, however, came to the country in search of employment in the burgeoning UK economy. Much of this employment was found in low-paid manufacturing employment and, to a lesser extent, in new public services such as transport and the NHS. The effect of this was to concentrate these new immigrants in the urban industrial areas of the Midlands, the North-West and Yorkshire, and again in London.

Since that time these patterns of geographical dispersal have to some extent had a reinforcing effect on the later distribution of the ethnic minority population. Later immigrants have often come to join or live close to relatives or colleagues here. Second-generation ethnic minority citizens have been born in these areas and often remained in them. More generally racism and discrimination in public and private housing markets and in employment opportunities have restricted the ability of many black people to move outside of these areas of relatively high concentration.

The result is that the geographical distribution of Britain's ethnic minority communities is highly skewed towards a relatively small number of urban areas. This is clearly revealed in a briefing paper from researchers at the LSE (Lupton and Power, 2004), which shows continuing concentrations in London (especially), the Midlands, the North-West and Yorkshire, with smaller pockets in other urban centres such as Bristol, Newcastle, Edinburgh and Glasgow. Lupton and Power explore the geographical distribution of different ethnic groups and find that concentration is also influenced by ethnic and cultural background; for instance, within the West Midlands, Pakistanis are the predominant minority ethnic group in Birmingham and Indians in Wolverhampton. What is more, within these areas the concentration of ethnic minority populations is frequently even more acute, with some London boroughs such as Newham and Brent having a majority of the population from ethnic minorities (Lupton and Power, 2004, table 3).

Such geographical concentration is a significant feature of the life experiences and social circumstances of different ethnic groups; however, it is also closely linked to the greater risk of poverty and social exclusion that is associated with race and ethnicity in the UK. The areas where most ethnic minority communities are located are also those with the highest levels of poverty and deprivation – 70 per cent of ethnic minority citizens live in the 88 most deprived local authority districts in England (Flaherty *et al.*, 2004, p. 196), with similar patterns within the other devolved administrations. These 88 districts are the focus of neighbourhood renewal support in recognition of the higher levels of deprivation found within them, as measured in the *Indices of Deprivation* using data on benefit dependency, employment levels, educational achievement and health inequalities (ODPM, 2004). The higher levels of deprivation in these areas are naturally going to accentuate the risk of poverty for the higher levels of ethnic minority people living within them (see Pilkington, 2003, ch. 4).

As we discussed in Chapter 8, there is a difference between the people and the place dimensions of the geographical distribution of poverty. Inequalities in employment, education and health are linked to a more general greater risk of poverty for all black *people*, as we discuss below. The *place* dimension remains important, however. For instance, social renting and poor quality housing is disproportionately concentrated in these areas and is also disproportionately occupied by ethnic minority groups. Thus, 57 per cent of Bangladeshis and 50 per cent of black Africans live in social rented housing;

three times more Bangladeshis and Pakistanis live in unfit housing than whites; and 15 per cent of ethnic minority households live in overcrowded accommodation compared to 2 per cent of whites (Flaherty *et al.*, 2004, p. 197).

More generally, high concentrations of ethnic minority groups in particular areas, though these can provide some cultural sharing and support, can also add to the risks of harassment and intimidation that all black people face in the UK (Platt, 2002, p. 69). In the early years of the new century this took an extreme form with the development of riots in towns such as Bradford and Oldham where high concentrations of ethnic minority people could be found, and with a rise in support in some of these areas for far right, racist, political parties such as the National Front. There is even the danger of the links between racial inequality and geographical location becoming a self-fulfilling prophesy of deprivation, as can be found in the so-called *ghettos* in many urban centres in the USA. This creates a challenge for social inclusion policies which, to succeed, must promote simultaneously both racial equality and area regeneration.

Employment and unemployment

Many of the ethnic minority immigrants to Britain in the 1950s and 1960s came to pursue employment in a buoyant labour market, but one in which they were largely placed in the least attractive and least well-paid jobs. The black people who came to Britain were initially concentrated in low-paid, low-status, public-service manual work and in low-paid shift work in labour-intensive manufacturing processes such as textiles and hosiery. Despite the significant changes in the labour market since these times, more recent evidence from the Labour Force Survey and other government data on labour market distribution suggests that these concentrations have continued since (Pilkington, 2003, ch. 3). Around 50 per cent of Bangladeshi and Chinese men work in the catering industry (Platt, 2002, p. 102); Pakistani men are twice as likely as white men to be in semi-skilled or unskilled work; and black Africans and Caribbeans are over-represented in manual work in transport and communications (Falherty *et al.*, 2004, p. 192). Family patterns and cultural traditions also mean that ethnic minority women have not benefited from the growth in female employment, with around a half of Bangladeshi and Pakistani women not in employment or seeking work, compared to under 10 per cent of whites (Platt, 2002, p. 90).

The result of this relative labour market segregation is that average earnings are lower for black people than for white people. For instance the average hourly pay for Pakistani and Bangladeshi men and women in 1998 was £6.87 and £6.33, compared to around £9.00 an hour for white men (Platt, 2002, p. 102), and by 2002 the same groups had pay levels 52 per cent and 45 per cent below those of their white counterparts (Flaherty *et al.*, 2004, p. 193). With lower proportions of women in these groups in employment, this suggests that for these groups in particular poverty linked to low pay is quite widespread. What is more this can be compounded by the larger average family size for some, especially Asian, workers to support, and the possibility that wages will also be used to support family members outside the household. An earlier PSI survey found that 40 per cent of West Indian households and 30 per cent of Asian households had sent money to dependants outside the household (Brown, 1984, p. 302). Of course low wages for families may be supplemented by means-tested benefits, but, as we will discuss below, there is evidence that black people are less likely than white people to be claiming these.

Black people's disadvantaged position in the labour market is also mirrored by their position outside it. Many of the low-status, labour-intensive jobs in manufacturing and public services into which black immigrant workers were recruited were those that were disproportionately affected by the impact of recession on manufacturing industry and the public expenditure cuts of the 1970s and 1980s. This has led to higher levels of unemployment among black people throughout the country, and this has been accentuated by the discrimination in recruitment experienced by black people seeking jobs, especially young British-born blacks leaving education and unable to find any employment.

Thus unemployment rates are higher for black people in Britain than for whites. In 2001/02 the overall unemployment rate for most minority ethnic groups was two to three times higher than that for whites. But for some ethnic groups the situation was much worse, with Bangladeshi men experiencing 21 per cent unemployment and Pakistani and black African men 16 per cent, compared to 5 per cent for white British men (ONS, 2005b). Unemployment is particularly high for many young ethnic minority school leavers, with young Bangladeshi men under 25 experiencing over 40 per cent unemployment and Pakistani and black African men and women over 20 per cent (*ibid.*), although there are significant differences in the experience of some minority ethnic groups here, with Chinese and Indian young people doing better (Flaherty *et al.*, 2004, pp. 194–5). Black and minority ethnic young people also seem to benefit less from employment policy initiatives with only 31 per cent of ethnic minority young people leaving the New Deal for sustained employment compared to over 40 per cent of whites (*ibid.*, p. 191).

The disadvantaged position of black people within the UK labour market is the product of a range of factors, including the labour market segregation and the weak employment security that accompanied patterns of immigration and settlement in the last century. It is also to some extent, though, a product of discrimination by employers within the labour market. Direct discrimination on the basis of race has been outlawed by legislation since the 1970s in Britain; but there is some evidence that indirect and 'institutional' discrimination continues to exist. For instance, the recent Macpherson Report (1999) into the police investigation of the Stephen Lawrence murder concluded that institutional racism characterised most major organisations in British society (see Pilkington, 2003, p. 85 *et seq*). Whatever the causes, however, such disadvantage has exposed black people to a greater risk of poverty. It has also resulted in higher levels of benefit dependency among black people.

Benefits

Direct evidence of the number of black people dependent on benefits has been difficult to obtain because social security statistics do not record the ethnic origin of claimants, although the Family Resources Survey, which the DWP commissions, does now provide information on benefit receipt and ethnic origin. This confirms previous evidence that within the state benefit system black claimants are likely to be disproportionately dependent on less-generous and lower-status means-tested benefits. Black claimants of income-related benefits made up 34 per cent of families in 2000/01, compared to 20 per cent for white claimants (Platt, 2002, p. 70).

The reason for this segregation within benefits is because, as with much of postwar welfare provision in Britain, the Beveridge social security system failed to recognise the ways in which its structures could operate to exclude certain groups of people. This is particularly true of insurance benefits, which are paid in return for contributions made during employment. Black people's relative exclusion from secure and well-paid employment is also likely to exclude them from insurance benefits, especially pensions which are based on contributions made throughout a working life that could be broken by periods of absence abroad as well as unemployment. Other apparently neutral qualifications for benefit entitlement may also operate against black people because of their immigrant status. This applies in particular to the residence tests that are applied to some of the non-contributory disability benefits, discussed in Chapter 12. These have now all been reduced to a period of six months residence in Britain prior to claiming, although in the past periods of up to ten years were required for some.

This all means that black households on benefits are much more likely than white households to be in receipt of means-tested benefits such as Income Support and Housing Benefit. The extension of means-tested support into the labour market through tax credits for low pay has further expanded the numbers and proportion of black and ethnic minority people dependent on these benefits for, as we have seen, low pay is more widely experienced by black employees. Most means-tested benefits are lower than those within the insurance scheme, and they are also subject to other restrictions that have a disproportionately disadvantageous impact on black claimants.

Means-tested benefits are only available to those ordinarily resident in Britain, and claimants are thus technically required to establish this when they make a claim. Normally speaking this is a formality, but as some recent immigrants are excluded from such entitlement evidence of resident status may be required. This has resulted on some occasions in the practice of checking the passports of all 'suspicious' black claimants in social security offices. Passport checking can operate as an invidious disincentive to any black claimants to seek benefit support, whatever their residence status, and can lead to problems if passports are not readily obtainable. Benefits officers are now instructed not to request passports routinely as proof of entitlement, but as Gordon and Newnham (1985, p. 24–5) found, the practice had become so widespread in the past that 'many black claimants volunteer their passports believing it is only a matter of time before they are asked to produce them'.

The requirement to produce passports as evidence of entitlement can act as a particular disincentive for many black claimants because of its link with immigration control. Most important here is the 'habitual residence test' used to determine entitlement to means-tested benefits for immigrants. There is evidence that inappropriate administration of this rule has disproportionately affected black and Asian claimants (Falherty *et al.*, 2004, p. 199). However, the more disconcerting wider impact of the rule is its role as an indirect disincentive (based on a mistaken belief about exclusion from entitlement) for any black claimants, especially family dependants, to claim benefits, even insurance benefits to which they do have independent rights. And this disincentive can be compounded by direct or indirect discrimination against black claimants in the more general administration of benefits. A survey of black clients using Citizens' Advice Bureaux in 1990 revealed a number of such practices, including delays in processing benefit claims while (unnecessary) checks were carried out to determine entitlement, and intrusive questioning to establish certain personal details such as marital status when marriages had been contracted abroad. They were described by the NACAB (1991) in their report as 'barriers to benefit'. More recently the House of Commons Work and Pensions Committee inquiry into the delivery of benefit to black and minority ethnic groups and refugees concluded that there was no doubt that ethnic minority claimants did experience different treatment (DWP, 2005c, para. 211).

Such barriers can contribute to reduced levels of take-up of benefits amongst ethnic minority citizens; and there is some evidence that this also is a significant problem. A survey of claimants by National Opinion Polls for the National Audit Office in the 1990s revealed lower levels of take-up of means-tested education and health benefits among non-British/Irish respondents (see Amin and Oppenheim, 1992, pp. 54–5). Research in Leeds in 1993 revealed problems of take-up among Chinese and Bangladeshi communities (Law *et al.*, 1994); and the House of Commons Work and Pensions Committee argued in 2005 that, although more data was needed on take-up by different ethnic groups, there was evidence of continuing problems, in particular because of the limited availability of information and support on benefits in minority languages.

Language can also be a significant barrier; social security benefits are administered in English; English is spoken in all offices; forms are printed in English and must be completed in English. Leaflets and publicity material on benefit entitlement are also printed in English, although some are available in minority languages. For those who do not speak or write English fluently, which is still quite common in some Asian communities, this can be a major barrier to receipt of support, This was revealed in the NACAB (1991) survey, and it is still relatively rare for benefits offices to be able to provide interpreter services for non-English speakers to pursue their entitlement adequately (DWP, 2005c, para. 174). However, it is equally likely that the absence of publicity and other literature in ethnic minority languages means that for many potential claimants even this point of contact is never reached. Cultural differences stemming from socialisation in different social structures may also lead people to fail to identify a right to state benefits as a potential source of support at times of deprivation (Cohen and Tarpey, 1986; Law *et al.*, 1994).

More recent concern over the unequal treatment of ethnic minority claimants within the benefits system has focused in particular on the problems experienced by asylum-seekers. Because of their precarious economic and social situation asylum-seekers are at particular risk of poverty, with survey evidence suggesting that as many as 85 per cent experienced hunger and 95 per cent could not afford to buy clothes (Flaherty *et al.*, 2004, p. 200). And this is likely to lead in particular to high levels of poverty for children in asylum-seeker families (Fitzpatrick, 2005) and for the children of gypsies and travellers (Cemlyn and Clark, 2005). However, asylum-seekers are prohibited from working until a decision has been made about their case and they do not have full access to social security support. The requirement that asylum-seekers should use vouchers rather than cash to buy food and clothing was withdrawn following a Home Office review in 2002; but asylum-seekers are not entitled to 'universal' child benefit and receive around 25 per cent less in means-tested benefits than equivalent resident families (Flaherty *et al.*, 2004, p. 200; Fitzpatrick, 2005).

Disadvantage and social exclusion

The problem of poverty is not just a problem of insecure or inadequate cash incomes due to labour-market exclusion or benefit discrimination. As we saw in Chapter 8, deprivation and social exclusion include a broader range of disadvantage, denial and exclusion that can result in a reduced quality of life for some. For black people in Britain the existence of racism at all levels of the social structure means that many of these broader features of deprivation are also likely to affect them disproportionately. This broader range of problems is discussed in more depth by specialist authors such as Law (1996), Platt (2002) and Pilkington (2003). It includes disadvantage in education, health and personal social services – all of which are overlaid with the problem of racism itself.

Participation and achievement in education is now recognized by government as a critical factor in contributing to social exclusion and to the means of combating it. As well as being a form of deprivation in itself, failure or underachievement in education can lead to poverty and inequality later in life. Educational disadvantage is also closely linked to the generally poorer services to be found in the inner city areas where large numbers of black people live. It is compounded both by direct discrimination within the education system, such as stereotyping black pupils as troublemakers or low achievers, and by the indirect exclusion that results from the ethnocentrism of the school curriculum. The Swann Report (1985) on the education of children from ethnic-minority groups laid much of the blame for inequalities within education on racism within the wider community, but there is continuing evidence that black children are up to three times more likely to be excluded from school than white children (Flaherty *et al.*, 2004, p. 194) and that some ethnic-minority people (notably Bangladeshis and Pakistanis) have lower levels of qualifications than the population at large (Platt, 2002, p. 111).

Inequalities in health are also frequently associated with severe deprivation. Skellington and Morris (1992, ch. 5) reported evidence of higher rates of mortality, including perinatal and infant mortality, among sections of the black community. This is generally associated with poorer health, although black people also suffer specifically from some debilitating diseases that do not affect the indigenous population, such as sickle-cell anaemia among people of black African descent. Caribbean women also have 80 per cent higher rates for high blood pressure that whites (Flaherty *et al.*, 2004, p. 198). Inequalities in health can be further compounded by unequal use of health care and social services by black people; and there is evidence that major services including community care do in practice operate disadvantageously for many ethnic-minority communities (see Ahmad and Atkin, 1996) – for instance, Bangladeshi women are half as likely as average to attend cervical cancer screenings (Flaherty *et al.*, 2004, p. 198).

In personal social services there have been concerns about both the 'over-representation' of ethnic minorities as 'problem' families, with black children disproportionately being taken into care, and their 'under-representation' in the take-up of services including support for child and adult community care (Law, 1996, ch. 4). There have also been debates about the best forms of support for ethnic minority and black clients, both in terms of the ethnic sensitivity of services for community care support and the placing of black children for fostering and adoption. In all of these areas, however, the difficulties experienced by vulnerable individuals and families in accessing appropriate services at times of critical need can contribute to the more general problems of poverty and exclusion which they may face.

Deprivation in housing, health and education add significantly to the financial inequality of black and ethnic minority people in Britain, and they have remained important despite the introduction since the 1960s of race relations legislation designed to prevent direct and indirect discrimination and promote equality of opportunity. However, these indirect consequences may be compounded by some of the more direct scars of racism in ways that may severely deplete the quality of life enjoyed, or endured, by those who suffer under them. Racial harassment is part of a daily burden borne by most, it not all, black people in Britain. It is a burden that white people can never fully understand and many do not even recognise – although they may be contributing to it. Harassment ranges from being made to feel different and excluded, to being a victim of violence and disturbance in public or at home. This can discourage black people and other ethnic minorities from sharing public spaces and can bring enduring fear and insecurity to the heart of their daily lives, combining experiences of both exclusion and entrapment.

Age and Poverty

SUMMARY OF KEY POINTS

- Risk of poverty varies at different points in the life-cycle and in particular is associated with childhood and old age.
- Child poverty is not a new phenomenon; but rates of child poverty were increasing in the UK towards the end of the last century.
- In 1999 the government pledged to end child poverty by 2020 and to reduce it by a quarter by 2005.
- Risk of poverty has also generally been higher for older people, although at the beginning of the new century the risk of poverty in old age had declined in comparison with other social groups.
- Retirement from the labour force may push people into poverty, especially where pension protection is limited.
- Pension protection is now intended to be a partnership between limited state support and private and occupational provision; but significant numbers of pensioners do not benefit from private protection and thus are likely to rely on means-tested support and be at risk of poverty.
- The growing proportion of the population who will be over pension age has led to fears that these will post a 'burden' on future generations; but in practice the balance of economic contributions across the generations has always been a changing one.

Poverty and the life-cycle

The risk and experience of poverty not only varies with gender and race, it also varies with age. At different stages in our life courses we experience greater or lesser risk of poverty; and the effect of this is that the distribution of poverty within society is disproportionately concentrated on those within particular age groups. This disproportionate risk of poverty is a longstanding phenomenon, and it was identified by Rowntree in his first study of poverty in York at the end of the nineteenth century. Rowntree argued that there was a structural link between the life-cycle and the risk of poverty, which he captured in a famous diagram (see Figure 11.1). This demonstrated, he suggested, that poverty was in particular associated with childhood, early middle life (when the presence of children in the household put pressure on the family budget), and old age.

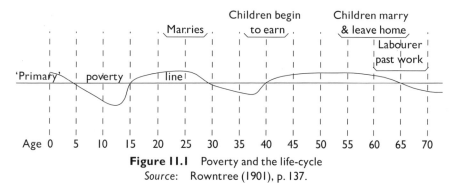

Figure 11.1   Poverty and the life-cycle
Source: Rowntree (1901), p. 137.

As we discussed in Chapter 7, changes in the economy and in family life have made this simple life-cycle model less appropriate as an accurate depiction of the life-cycle experiences of individuals in the twenty-first century. A similar diagram today would probably incorporate a more fluctuating and fractured line through the life-cycle. Nevertheless, the links between poverty and childhood (and therefore families with young children) and poverty and old age are still major features of the distribution of poverty in the UK today – and indeed in most other advanced industrial countries.

What is more, as we shall return to discuss in Chapter 14, central elements of anti-poverty policy, and in particular social security policy, have recognised this pattern of risk and sought to address it through the redistribution of resources within the tax and benefit systems. Child Benefit, and more recently Child Tax Credits, direct resources to families; and pensions provide income support for the elderly. These two areas remain the largest aspects of social security expenditure, although as we shall see shortly they have not prevented poverty continuing to be concentrated on children and those over pension age.

Child poverty

The link between childhood and poverty established by Rowntree was confirmed in many later studies of poverty in the UK; and a comprehensive overview of the historical development of research and policy debate on child poverty going back to 1800 has been produced by Platt (2005). In the early twentieth century, research on the period from 1912 to 1937 consistently showed higher rates of poverty for a family with three children than for a single man (Glennerster *et al.*, 2004, figure 4, p. 44). The social security reforms of the 1940s, based on the recommendations of the Beveridge Report (1942), were intended to combat poverty through the provision of benefit support; and they included the payment of Family Allowances to provide additional support for children, which had been strongly supported by Beveridge. In fact Family Allowances were initially paid only to families with more than one child; but they were later converted into Child Benefit and paid for all children (and after 1998 at a higher rate for the first child).

However, as the 'rediscovery of poverty' in the 1960s revealed, the Beveridge reforms had not removed the experience of poverty from later twentieth-century Britain. What is more, Abel Smith and Townsend's (1965) famous study of poverty in affluent Britain revealed that it was poverty amongst families with young children that remained a continuing feature of the poverty landscape. It was in part as a result of the evidence from this research that concern about the plight of children and families in poverty became a focus for political campaigning in the 1960s. Together with a number of other leading social policy academics and practitioners, Townsend worked to establish an independent pressure group to campaign for policy reforms to combat child poverty – the Child Poverty Action Group (CPAG), which soon became one of the most respected voices arguing for policy reform on poverty in the UK, as we discuss in Chapter 13 (see McCarthy, 1986).

Whatever the efforts and achievements of the CPAG in the latter part of the last century, however, they were not able to secure any significant improvement in the levels of child poverty in the country. Indeed, as Figure 11.2 reveals, after a period of fluctuation in the 1960s and 1970s, levels of child poverty began to rise dramatically in the 1980s and 1990s, and even to rise more rapidly than the average increase across the overall population.

Figure 11.2 uses the 50 per cent of mean income point as a measure of poverty. As I explained in Chapter 2, it is more common now to use 60 per cent of median income as a measure, although the difference between the two in practice is not great. The most recent HBAI figures show that on this measure, 21 per cent (BHC) and 28 per cent (AHC) of children are poor. These are higher proportions than the population in general, where the levels are 17 and 21 per cent respectively (DWP, 2005a, table 3.5).

At the beginning of the twenty-first century, therefore, child poverty is a greater problem than it was over two decades ago, and it is a more acute problem than that of poverty more generally. This is not just a UK phenomenon. A major study of child poverty in rich countries, carried out by UNICEF using OECD data, concluded that the proportion of children living in poverty had risen in a majority of the world's developed economies (UNICEF, 2005). Given the continuing economic growth in most OECD countries this report makes grim reading. The international comparison which it provides also reveals that the UK record is a relatively poor one, with 15.4

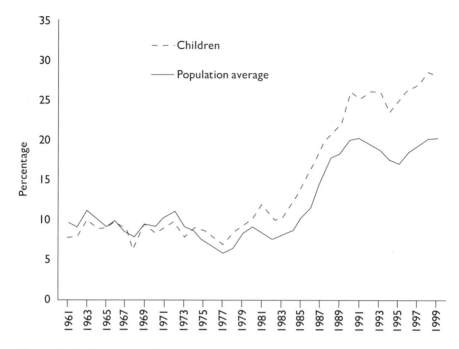

Figure 11.2   Proportion of children living in households with incomes below 50 per cent of mean income, before housing costs, 1961–99
Sources: Webb (2002), chart 8.19; and Piachaud and Webb (2004), figure 6.

per cent of children poor on the 50 per cent of median income measure that UNICEF use. This compares with 14.7 per cent in Australia, 10.2 per cent in Germany, 7.5 per cent in France and 2.4 per cent in Denmark. In a league table of the 26 richest countries the UK is 7th from the bottom, although some way above the USA on 21.9 per cent (UNICEF, 2005, p. 4).

When changes in the levels of child poverty over the last decade of the last century are compared, however, the UK does much better. Here the data show a 3.1 per cent reduction in child poverty in this country in the 1990s, the highest for any of the countries listed, with the majority actually showing an increase in levels of child poverty. The UK may have one of the poorest records of OECD countries in recent years, but it is also now showing the highest level of improvement, which the UNICEF report attributes to the recent developments in policies on child poverty discussed below (UNICEF, 2005, p. 15).

The median and mean figures are, of course, only one way of measuring poverty, as we discussed in Chapters 2 and 6. Other research using other measures has also sought to discover the levels of poverty amongst children. Research examining the experience of poverty over time, using BHPS data, found that 29 per cent of children were persistently poor and 13 per cent were severely poor for at least one year (Adelman *et al.*, 2003). The PSE survey researchers defined children as poor if they were lacking one or more necessities because their parents could not afford them. On this measure they found 34 per cent lacking one or more items and 18 per cent lacking two or more (Gordon *et al.*, 2000, p. 35); and Adelman *et al.* (2003) found that parents in families who were poor often 'protected' their children by going without necessities themselves in order to provide the best they could for the children.

There has also been research exploring the more general problems of social exclusion faced by children and the families in which they live. Smith and Noble (1995) looked at disadvantage in education in the 1990s; and Dennehy *et al.* (1997) and Dowler *et al.* (2001) looked at poverty and health. The contributors to Preston's (2005) collection on child poverty explored the differential risks of poverty experienced by various social groups and revealed significant differences here. Even where there are policy benefits aimed directly at some aspects of poverty and deprivation amongst children, however, they are not always effective in combating problems. For instance, evidence shows that 20 per cent of the children entitled to free school meals do not take these up (Flaherty *et al.*, 2004, p. 150).

In a more wide-ranging study of poverty and social exclusion amongst children, Ridge (2002) focused not only upon material deprivation and access to resources, but also upon more intangible problems of 'fitting in' and 'joining in' (including the problems of acceptable clothing and leisure pursuits) and upon the experience of children in school and in other public settings. This book aimed in particular to provide a child's perspective on poverty and exclusion, to complement the growing availability of qualitative work centred on the experiences and views of those who are themselves experiencing poverty – arguing that children's views had been missing from poverty discourse throughout the research carried out in the last century.

Eradicating child poverty

The establishment of the CPAG in 1966 was intended to provide a campaigning profile for the particular problems of child poverty and to persuade the government in the UK to act directly to remove child poverty. Central to the case which the CPAG have consistently argued since is that child poverty is particularly problematic because the experience of poverty in childhood can significantly reduce the life chances and the life expectations of future generations. This is a view that was endorsed by UNICEF in their international study of child poverty:

> Children living in poverty experience deprivation of the material, spiritual and emotional resources needed to survive, develop and thrive, leaving them unable to enjoy their rights, to achieve their full potential or participate as full and equal members of society. (UNICEF, 2005, p. 10)

Child poverty is a problem for the future as well as the present; and there is a growing body of evidence that deprivation experienced in childhood does indeed affect future life chances (see Gregg *et al.*, 1999; Sigle-Rushton, 2004). What is more, as we saw above, child poverty has become a more significant problem than poverty more generally in the UK, and in other developed countries, at the beginning of the new century.

This problem was recognised by the Labour government in the UK in 1999. In a lecture recalling the legacy of Beveridge, delivered at Toynbee Hall in London, the Prime Minister, Tony Blair, made the pledge to eradicate child poverty quoted in Chapter 1, though he added that, 'it will take a generation. It is a 20-year mission but I believe it can be done' (Blair, 1999, p. 7). This was a significant political commitment, quite unlike any previous policy statements on poverty. Never before has a government made such a clear and direct statement of their goal – although, as a twenty-year mission, it is a goal on which not only the current Labour government will be judged; Blair has challenged future governments to take on the commitment too.

The pledge to eradicate child poverty has developed beyond these general words, however. In order to achieve the aim of eradicating child poverty, policies had to be put in place straight away which would begin to reduce child poverty and move towards the 2020 target. In practice a range of policy initiatives have been developed aimed directly or indirectly at reducing child poverty.

These include increases in state support for families with children through rises in Child Benefit and in the Income Support rates for children in families dependent upon social security benefits. Additional support also now goes to working families through Child Tax Credits for those on lower earnings. This started out as the Working Families Tax Credit (WFTC), a replacement and expansion of the previous Family Credit scheme; but the tax support for children was later separated from the support for adults on low wages and became a separately identified credit for all families falling below a relatively generous earnings threshold.

More generally, however, the measures to combat poverty through welfare to work discussed in Chapter 14 have also had the aim, and the effect, of reducing the numbers of children in poverty by providing employment opportunities for parents. These include the New Deal provisions, which contain specific measures for advice and guidance on employment for lone parents; as well as the provisions for guaranteed minimum wages and tax credits for low-wage workers, which make employment more attractive for some parents and carers.

Taken together with the broader benefits of economic growth in the early years of the new century, these measures did begin to reduce the numbers of children in poverty, as the UNICEF report records. This meant that the government could set more specific targets for the reductions in child poverty to be achieved; and explicit subsidiary targets of reducing poverty levels by 25 per cent by 2005 and a half by 2010 were set (see Walker, 1999; Dornan, 2004).

Given the complexity of both definitions and measures of poverty, as we discussed in Chapters 5 and 6, however, there has been much debate since 1999 about exactly what is meant by the pledge to reduce and then remove child poverty; and how the moves towards achieving it can be measured. As we have seen there are many ways of measuring poverty, including child poverty, and different measures are likely to yield different results. The government themselves have relied largely on HBAI data on the numbers below 60 per cent of median income; and now generally the before-housing-costs (BHC) figures which give a lower overall number of children in poverty.

As the UNICEF (2005) report commented there have been significant achievements in the UK here. A number of researchers therefore concluded that the government should be able to meet its 2005 target of a 25 per cent reduction (for instance, Brewer, 2004). Sutherland *et al.* (2003) used micro-simulation techniques to predict the numbers of children in poverty and also concluded that the government was on-track to meet its target; but in fact they have not and will have to extend policies significantly to move on to the 50 per cent target by 2010. Not surprisingly it is those just below the poverty line whom it is easiest to move above it.

There has also been much debate about whether the measure of success should be based on the proportion of children poor by current measures or by the standards applying in the baseline year 1998/9. With the rising living standards experienced in the new century these will change, and therefore the numbers of children poor by 1999 standards would be likely to decline whatever specific policy measures were undertaken. Conversely, on a relative measure more general rises in incomes will not help to reduce child poverty. Rising living standards thus mean that anti-poverty policy is chasing a moving target. It can be important to know how things have improved since a fixed benchmark point (see Sutherland *et al.*, 2003), but relative measures of poverty are now widely accepted and used, and so it is against a current income figure that achievements are likely to be judged in practice.

These debates about the appropriate measures of reductions in child poverty furthermore prompted the government to initiate a formal review of the official measures to be used in the future. This involved consultation with academics and researchers, with the results being published by the Department for Work and Pensions (DWP, 2003). The conclusion they reached was that in future a multi-dimensional approach should be adopted based on the three measures of absolute and relative income and material deprivation listed in Chapter 5.

Under these measures poverty will only be deemed to be falling if all three indicators are moving in the right direction. The government has planned to introduce them from 2004/05, following changes to the Family Resources Survey, and after the assessment of the first five years of the child poverty pledge. The new measures were not applied to the first five years, therefore, but are to be applied to the next five, and beyond.

Alongside the review of the measure of child poverty has been the broader recognition by government of the importance of the different dimensions of poverty and social exclusion, which we discussed in Chapter 8. These apply to child poverty too, and this is recognised explicitly in the indicators used to measure reductions in poverty and social exclusion reported on each year in *Opportunity for All* (DWP, 2004a). Here there are separate indicators relating to children and young people including such measures as infant mortality, school achievement levels, truancy and school exclusions. And this means that policies to address these broader aspects of social exclusion will need to extend beyond the employment and income support measures discussed above in the context of the pledge to eradicate child poverty. Removing the poverty and exclusion associated with childhood is thus a complex and a wide-ranging challenge.

Poverty and social exclusion in old age

Rowntree's discussion of the life-cycle risks of poverty identified old age as the second age-related dimension of poverty in late nineteenth century York. Booth's (1892, 1894) famous work on poverty in London at the end of the nineteenth century had also revealed a much higher level of poverty among the elderly than in the rest of the population; and the evidence is that this link continued into the last century. Similar conclusions about the extent of poverty in old age were reached by Townsend (1979) in his major 1960s study of poverty in Britain; and later Alan Walker (1980, 1993; Walker and Phillipson, 1986) wrote widely on the link between old age and poverty and the reasons for this.

Townsend's research (1979, p. 787) found that a much higher proportion of elderly people (64 per cent) than non-elderly people (26 per cent) had an income that was less than 140 per cent of benefit entitlement, which was roughly equivalent to his definition of poverty. In the 1960s and 1970s poverty was associated closely with old age, in particular because of the limited support provided by the basic state pension scheme on which most relied. Since then, however, there has been growing poverty among younger un-employed and low-paid families, and the relative position of older people has improved somewhat.

In 1979, 31 per cent of the poorest decile of the income distribution were pensioners. By 2001/02 this had fallen to 11 per cent (Flaherty *et al.*, 2004, p. 45). In 2003/04, 22 per cent of single pensioners and 20 per cent of pensioner couples were below the 60 per cent of median income threshold (BHC), and 20 per cent of couples and 19 per cent of single pensioners were below this threshold (AHC) (DWP, 2005a, table 3.5). This compares with 17 per cent (BHC) and 21 per cent (AHC) for the population more generally. The position of older people has improved in recent years, therefore, and indeed the lower average housing costs of most pensioners (linked in some cases to mortgages which have been paid off) means that after taking account of these they are now slightly below the average poverty levels. They remain above average on the BHC measure, however, so to some extent old age remains associated with a greater risk of poverty.

Elderly people's lower incomes and greater risk of poverty are obviously closely linked to their sources of income. In general elderly people derive a much higher proportion of their income from benefits than from earnings compared with the rest of the population, because for the most part they have left employment in the labour market and are reliant upon pensions, and, as we shall see, despite the growth in private pension protection many older people are still relying upon inadequate state pension support.

Furthermore, as we have discussed before, inadequate income is only one dimension of poverty and social exclusion. Many of the other broader aspects of deprivation and exclusion can disproportionately affect older people. For instance, research by Scharf *et al.* (2002) revealed that older people living in more deprived urban areas experienced problems relating to crime, environment and isolation. The indicators of social exclusion incorporated in the government's annual *Opportunity for All* reports also now have a separate list for older people (DWP, 2004a). These include low income and contribution to non-state pensions (really an indicator for future older people), and also the need for home-based or community care, housing falling below decency standards, and fear of crime.

Retirement

Much of the poverty and social exclusion associated with old age is linked to retirement from the labour market. The notion that people should retire from work at a certain age is a relatively recent one, and it only developed in advanced industrial countries over the last century alongside the development of pension payments for the retired. Although retirement is a life-course event that many, especially younger, people take for granted, it is in fact an extremely complex issue and one that only began to grow significantly in importance in the latter half of the twentieth century because of increased longevity following medical and health advances, and because of the availability of support from pensions to provide an income after work.

Earlier in the century it was not common for older workers to retire automatically from employment. Indeed during the immediate postwar period, at a time of 'full employment', much store was placed on the value of older experienced workers, and in 1951 around a third of men aged over 65 were still economically active (Phillipson, 1993). However, since that time the number of older people in full-time employment has declined significantly, in particular because of the imposition of what is in effect a compulsory retirement age for most workers at the age at which state pension entitlement commences (currently 60 for women, 65 for men) – after this age workers are not protected by law from dismissal. By the mid-1980s only one in fifteen men over the age of 65 was still in employment.

In practice, when older people do work they are not, unlike other marginalised groups such as women, black people or those with disabilities, concentrated in particular segments of the labour market, primarily of course because older people in employment did not enter it as older people, but have simply carried on with previous patterns of employment. The marginalisation of women, black people and others in employment is, however, carried over into old age; and these labour market inequalities also structure inequality and poverty in old age.

However, there is some evidence that when older workers, even those below the pension age, are seeking employment they experience discrimination and marginalisation (Harris, 1991) – a phenomenon that is part of the increasingly recognised problem of 'ageism' (see Bytheway and Johnson, 1990). Discrimination on the basis of age can apply at any stage in the life-cycle, but particular problems are faced by older people seeking access to the labour market who, it may be assumed because of their entitlement to pension support, are less in need of employment than younger people. There is no New Deal support for pensioners to move from welfare to work, for instance. This can be compounded where employers think that older people may also be less efficient or less flexible workers, and so may discriminate against them for these reasons.

Ageism has also been experienced in the increased pressure that was first brought to bear on older workers during the economic recessions of the 1980s and 1990s to leave employment early to protect the jobs of younger people. Although many older workers, in particular those with significant personal pension entitlements, may have welcomed the opportunity to end their working life early, there were many others for whom such retirement was in effect a form of redundancy – and one with little prospect of further work (Harris, 1991). What is more this type of redundancy has begun to affect workers earlier and earlier in their working lives, and it has now become quite common for 'early-retirement' schemes to be offered to workers in their 50s and early 60s. And once outside the labour market many may find it difficult to return because of ageist discrimination against taking on older employees.

For those who have accrued significant savings over their lives and are entitled to a relatively substantial retirement pension, leaving work can be an opportunity to enjoy a relaxed and leisurely lifestyle. For those in unrewarding jobs that require strength and stamina rather than experience the opportunity to replace dependency on wages with dependency on pensions may also be attractive, and when illness, frailty or disability compound the problem of earning from work this may be particularly important.

However, exclusion from the labour market can also have serious deleterious consequences that significantly reduce the quality of life of older people. For instance experience and knowledge are no longer valued – indeed they are usually ignored; contact with colleagues and friends at work is arbitrarily severed; and the status and respect that go with employment and productivity are taken away. As we have seen before, social exclusion is a significant feature of deprivation in modern societies. This is a problem that disproportionately affects older people through the experience of retirement; and for the still significant number of older people who do not have an adequate pension entitlement, absence from the labour market also means loss of an adequate income and thus a greatly increased risk of poverty and dependency.

The concept of retirement, of course, only applies to paid employment. Unpaid work, especially that done in the home, continues after retirement or job release. In this context retirement is therefore something of a male notion, or perhaps more accurately a male problem. For older women, who are less likely than their younger sisters to be in full-time employment and more likely to be responsible for the bulk of home work, retirement is something that happens to their husbands. Indeed for some, unpaid work at home may frequently increase in old age because of the demands created by increased frailty and disability. Most of the elderly people needing care in their home receive it from family members, and in practice in many cases this work is done by other elderly persons in the family, usually a spouse (McGlone, 1992). Exclusion from the labour market may therefore not mean increased access to leisure, and it may not mean cessation of work. Rather it may mean a transfer of work and leisure into the home – together with a reduction of income.

Pensions

In the nineteenth century, at a time when life expectancy was much shorter than today, no specific provision was made for income support in old age. Thus although some trade unions and friendly societies, and even some employers, provided limited pension protection for older members, the majority who reached old age had no right to financial support. If these people were unable to support themselves through employment, then the only alternative open to them was dependency on the Poor Law, and thus the workhouse. It was the poverty among older people that resulted from this that was highlighted by Booth (1892, 1894) in his surveys at the end of the century, and it led to some pressure on the government to provide directly for the elderly poor.

Following the example of Germany, therefore, pensions were introduced for certain older people in 1908. The original pension of 5 shillings a week, paid only to those over 70, was not based on contributions made during employment, and was subject to an income test – '5 shillings a week for cheating death', as one popular song put it. In 1911 a contributory social security scheme was introduced, and in 1925 pensions based on contributions were paid to those over 65.

Following the Beveridge Report (1942) on social security reform the postwar government introduced a supposedly comprehensive insurance-based pension scheme whereby all men over 65 and women over 60 were paid flat-rate pensions, with additions for dependants, based on their contribution records during their working lives. However, because all current pensioners would have been automatically excluded from such a scheme as a result of their incomplete contribution record, the contribution conditions were effectively waived for them and full pensions were paid immediately, which, as we shall see in Chapter 14, prevented the scheme from ever operating from a funded insurance base.

In order to ensure that pensions were adequate to support the older people depending on them, Beveridge based his recommended rates on Rowntree's (1901 and 1941) nutritional guidelines for minimum subsistence. However, to avoid a situation in which pensions and other benefits might exceed earnings and thus discourage employment, and to encourage the development of additional private protection, which Beveridge saw as desirable, they were fixed at *only* this subsistence level. They were thus barely adequate and provided little protection against poverty. When Abel Smith and Townsend (1965) discovered large numbers of people living below the means-tested benefit poverty line in the 1950s and 1960s, the majority of these were pensioners living on state pensions that were not adequate to provide them even with the equivalent of this safety net income – although many of the pensioner claimants were also not in receipt of the means-tested supplements to which they might have been entitled at the time.

In absolute terms, however, the value of pensions increased in the 1950s and 1960s; and in the 1970s in particular pensions increased in relative terms when compared with benefits for the younger unemployed. In the late 1970s this gap began to widen because the basic insurance pension was increased in line with rises in prices or earnings, whichever was the higher, whilst other benefits were increased in line with prices only. After 1980, however, even this relative position of advantage against other claimants was removed when basic pension increases were restricted, like other benefits, to price inflation only. Since 1997 state pensions have again been increased more than other benefits and above price inflation; but this has not restored entirely the relativities with average incomes found in the 1970s.

Throughout its history the basic pension has thus been kept at a relatively low level. This is in part because, like the benefits for those not in employment, it acts as a wage substitute and is kept below wage levels in order to deter voluntary departure from the labour market. However, the link between pension entitlement and retirement, especially after the spread of early and compulsory retirement in the latter part of the twentieth century, has significantly undermined the logic of this unequal treatment. Pensioners who have been required to leave the labour market hardly require financial incentives to seek support through wages, and this may partly explain the relatively advantaged status that pensioners have enjoyed compared with other benefit claimants over this later period.

The low level of pension payments was also, however, a product of the basis on which the postwar social security scheme was established. By admitting all elderly claimants directly into the insurance scheme the financing was effectively based on a 'pay-as-you-go' basis, with current contributions being used to pay for current benefits, as opposed to being saved or invested as a deferred payment to existing contributors. Payment of current pensions out of current contributions thus created an inevitable pressure to keep pension levels down in order to keep the contribution levels for current contributors as low as possible. As the number of pensioners has grown throughout the postwar period this pressure has become stronger, a point to which we shall return below.

A low basic pension also acts as an important incentive for employed people to seek additional private financial protection for their old age. Beveridge (1942) had always hoped that state pensions would be supplemented by voluntary private insurance, and thus argued that, provided the basic pension levels were 'adequate', there need be no concern that they were below wage levels since those in work could use their higher wages to purchase additional pension protection. Taken together with the pay-as-you-go basis of state insurance pensions, this meant that the notion of pensions as deferred earnings, rather than as a wage substitute for those no longer able to provide for themselves, was restricted to private-sector pension protection.

In practice, occupational pensions – additional private protection provided by employers through contributions paid by employees into a separate pension scheme – grew rapidly in the 1950s and 1960s as employers sought to attract workers by offering the advantages of pension protection through work. Sometimes referred to as 'superannuation', these early occupational pension schemes flourished mainly in private-sector employment and the number of workers covered grew from 4.3 million in 1956 to 12.2 million in 1967 (Walker, 1986, p. 202). After that point the number of people covered by these private schemes began to decline, down to 5.5 million by 1983 (Walker, 1986, p. 203). By this time, however, occupational pension cover was widespread in the growing public sector, so the numbers covered by such provision continued to rise overall.

Many of the occupational pension schemes, especially those in the private sector, did not provide very generous protection after retirement, however; and most could not readily be transferred from one job to another – thus the rights accrued could be lost if employment changed. Also, most pensions were not 'index linked' – that is, they did not rise with subsequent inflation, rendering payment levels increasingly inadequate during the high inflation climate of the late twentieth century. Furthermore, occupational pension protection frequently assumed male career patterns of continuous contribution over a working life, with the final pension level being based on earnings at the end of the working life. This could seriously disadvantage women workers who had taken career breaks and any employees for whom final earnings were not the highest they had received.

The limitations on occupational pensions have thus meant that many of those contributing did not receive significant financial returns from them. In some cases entitlement amounted to little more than a couple of pounds a week. This limited protection, together with the continued exclusion of many from even limited occupational provision, was one of the main reasons for the introduction of the State Earnings Related Pensions Scheme (SERPS) in 1978. SERPS was a complex extension of NI pensions to provide a measure of additional pension income on top of the basic pension based on contributions made during the working life. This additional protection applied provisionally to all contributors, but in order not to undermine the protection provided by some occupational schemes, contributors to approved occupational schemes could 'opt out' of SERPS, paying reduced contributions and receiving only the basic state pension on retirement (see Atkinson, 1991).

SERPS was introduced by the Labour government in the 1970s, but it had a measure of cross-party support because of its coalition with occupational protection. The additional protection it provided was not due to reach maturity until 1998 because only contributions paid after the starting date of 1978 were eligible for inclusion in the calculation of the earnings-related additional payment. This meant that the scheme was of little or no benefit to existing pensioners, and in the short to medium term it was able to do little to alleviate the risk of poverty in old age.

SERPS also began to contribute significantly to fears about the potentially high cost of future state pension payments, because like the original pension scheme, payments were made on a pay-as-you-go basis. Partly because of such fears, but also linked to their more general support for private protection through the market, the Conservative governments of the 1980s began to encourage more widespread investment in occupational and private pensions. Private, as opposed to occupational, pension schemes developed little during the early postwar period, although they could have had the potential benefit of avoiding the limitations of occupational and employment-related schemes. In the 1980s, therefore, the government began to provide significant incentives for those investing in private pensions in the form of tax relief and investment bonuses, and after this private pension protection grew rapidly in scope and coverage.

At the beginning of the twenty-first century private and occupational pension provision provided a significant potential supplementary income for large numbers of future pensioners. Although the potential value of some private protection was highly dependent upon the investment of contributions within the stockmarket, and as the overall value of these markets began to decline so did the value of some pensions. Together with the highly publicised collapse of some prominent private schemes (for instance, the finance company Equitable Life), this prompted the Labour government to introduce some regulatory controls over private pension providers to ensure that certain minimum standards of investment practice were pursued; but, despite this regulation, private investments cannot provide a guarantee of future income in all circumstances

In contrast, for those outside private and occupational protection, SERPS was by the turn of the century providing additional earnings-related pension protection for significant numbers of new pensioners. However, the additional costs of providing this on a widespread basis to growing numbers of pensioners on a pay-as-you-go basis was putting pressure on public expenditure on pensions. This was compounded by the growing numbers of older people within the population both absolutely (as longevity increased) and relatively (as the numbers of the working age population was declining). This prompted the Labour government to initiate a formal review of pension provision shortly after they came to power in 1997, published as a Green Paper (DSS, 1998).

The Green Paper was subtitled *Partnership in Pensions*, and the conclusion that it reached was that future pension protection would need to be built upon a clearer, and perhaps rebalanced, partnership between public and private pension protection. The outcome of this was the replacement of SERPS with a smaller Second State Pension (SSP) aimed at providing additional protection above the basic state pension only for low-paid workers who could not be expected to take out private or occupational protection. This would reduce the cost of public pensions over time; and it would permit the basic state pension for all to be raised at a more rapid rate than price inflation, although not significantly so. For the majority of people of working age, however, the expectation is that they will invest in occupational or private pension protection to provide a supplement to their basic state pension on retirement.

Such private pension provision remained optional, although some commentators (most significantly former Minister for Welfare Reform, Frank Field) had suggested that it should be made compulsory in order to ensure that all those eligible did take out protection. A review of private protection in 2004 suggested that many people were still not taking out adequate private protection and that more should be done to advise and encourage them to do so (DWP, 2004b), and in 2005 an independent Pensions Commission was established to investigate the future needs for pension protection. This led to a debate about the need to raise the basic state pension and to delay the retirement age for future pensioners.

Thus there are improved prospects for some current and future pensioners, but this has not removed the risk or the fear of poverty in old age for the many current pensioners who do not benefit significantly from such additional protection on retirement. For these pensioners, dependent only upon the basic state pension, their income is likely to be low enough to entitle them to means-tested income support. Such means-tested support has now been incorporated into a formal Minimum Income Guarantee for pensioners falling below the means-test threshold, although evidence suggests that large numbers still do not claim this additional means-tested element. For those just above the threshold, for instance, as a result of small additional private pension payments, there is also a Pension Credit which provides a means-tested top-up to such income, up to a ceiling beyond which it tapers away.

Despite this additional protection now available for those dependent on state pensions, however, what the existence of private and occupational pensions does in practice is to reproduce in old age many of the inequalities and deprivations associated with the inequities of the labour market earlier in life. As early as 1955 Titmuss had referred to the fear that occupational protection could lead to the development of 'two nations' in retirement – one relatively affluent group enjoying the benefits of deferred earnings in the form of insurance payments and private pensions, and one generally poor group dependent on the inadequate basic state pension (Titmuss, 1958).

Inequality also results from the continuation into old age of other deprivations and exclusions experienced earlier in life. This means that class differences in income, housing, health and so on continue to divide people after retirement, as do gender differences and the dependence that family relationships frequently produce. As Britain's black population grows older differences arising from race and racism are also reproduced among the elderly. Thus poverty in old age, like poverty earlier in the life-cycle, reflects broader social divisions.

Inequalities during working life, and particularly those that affect pension entitlement, are also influenced by the overall life-cycle experiences of different cohorts of elderly people. As Atkinson and Sutherland (1991) have discussed, this means for instance that the generation of elderly people whose working lives were affected by the depression of the 1930s and the Second World War had very different pre-retirement opportunities from subsequent generations, who have experienced relatively high levels of unbroken employment. The former group thus experienced lower incomes and a greater risk of poverty in old age.

As such groups grow older still their circumstances may worsen further, as any savings become depleted and possessions grow older and cannot be replaced. This problem is more generally reflected in differences and divisions between the 'young old' and the 'old old', where the risk of poverty and the experience of deprivation are more acute among the latter at a time when their need for support and care may be at its greatest. Thus class, gender, race and age structure the risk and the experience of poverty in old age, and these divisions have been heightened rather than reduced by developments in pension provision.

The social construction of dependency

The link between old age and risk of poverty is long-established in the UK, and this pattern is reproduced in most other advanced industrial countries (Walker, 1993). But this link is not a consequence of old age itself (not all older people are poor), rather it is a consequences of social structures and social policies which increase the risk of poverty, in particular after retirement age. This led commentators such as Walker (1980) to argue that the risk of poverty in old age was 'socially constructed', by the assumptions (frequently unjustified and inaccurate) that were made about the circumstances or the needs of elderly people, and by policies that have been developed to respond to these assumptions, which may compound the problems faced by many older people.

Perhaps the most pervasive and most long-standing assumption about elderly people is that, because of their age, they are no longer able to contribute to society and may even be unable to care for themselves. This may be presented sympathetically as a justification for support from the rest of society as a 'reward' for their previous contribution. However it is a contradictory notion that may also be interpreted as implying that elderly people are a burden on society, which willingly or unwillingly the rest of us have to bear.

In practice only a small proportion of elderly people do need care and support in order to remain independent, and many if not most are quite able to contribute to society if they are provided with the opportunity to do so. However, some of the policies designed to provide care for elderly people operate to accentuate their dependent status rather than reduce it, in particular the denial of autonomy and control in many residential establishments and the inadequate provision of genuine support services to assist people to survive in the community. Minor disability can thus result in dependency and poverty in old age, which alternative policy initiatives could have prevented (McGlone, 1992).

Nevertheless, concerns about the 'burden' of costs for elderly people are growing as the numbers of those over pension age grow both absolutely and relatively. The demographic basis for this changing pattern of the age profile of the population is sometimes referred to as the *gerontic ratio*; and a broader examination of this ratio reveals that in fact it has been changing over a long period of time. The proportion of elderly persons in the population was increasing throughout the last century, rising from 12 per 100 people of working age in 1901 to 34 per 100 in 1981; and it is projected to reach 38 per 100 by 2021 (Falkingham, 1989, p. 218). The future changes will therefore not be so significant compared with the past, and in practice they are likely to be less than those anticipated in many other welfare capitalist countries with much higher levels of state pension protection (see Walker, 1993).

Furthermore, the simplistic link between demography and dependency ignores a wide range of other factors that may or may not result in a need to redistribute resources towards elderly people. These include overall levels of productivity and the ability of older people to provide for themselves, both of which factors changed significantly in the early part of the twentieth century, when the gerontic ratio changed more dramatically than it will over the first few decades of the new one. And this has led to debate in the new century about the desirability of deferring the state pension age in the light of increasing longevity. However, there is also the question of the ability and willingness of younger generations to continue to contribute to the state pension scheme in the anticipation that they too will benefit from this in the future.

Current debates about the balance between private pension protection and state support can sometimes confuse the issue of who will pay for future pensions, however, and can contribute to a continuation of the problem of 'two nations' in retirement. In practice all people will continue to benefit from state pensions, and even at current basic levels these will continue to provide a significant income on which all can rely. However, these future pensions will be paid for by future workers. We are all engaged in an implicit contract across the generations to redistribute resources across the life-cycle here, and it is one from which we will all potentially benefit.

Private and occupational pensions can supplement this basic income for many, but many of these depend upon elements of state subsidy, for instance tax relief on the contributions made to many occupational schemes. More generally, however, both the value and the use of private pensions will ultimately depend upon the value of investments when these are drawn on and the ability of the broader economy to provide the goods and services that people need at prices which they can afford to pay. There is a generational contract underlying these expectations, too, albeit one that for most people remains even more implicit than that underpinning state pensions.

Future pension provision and the future risk of poverty for older people thus depends upon the way in which financial investments and economic trends develop, and the way in which policies are adapted and implemented to respond to these. Neither wealth nor poverty in old age is guaranteed.

As Walker put it in 1980 (p. 73), 'So it is not *chronological age* that is significant in causing poverty and dependency ... but the relationship between the *social construction* of age and the social division of labour' (emphasis in original). That relationship changed dramatically over the last century; it can change again in the new one.

Disability and Poverty

SUMMARY OF KEY POINTS

■ Disability covers a wide range of individual circumstances; but significant disability is associated with greater risk of poverty.

■ The risk of poverty for disabled people is increased by the additional costs associated with different levels of disability.

■ Like poverty, disability is not necessarily a permanent state; and the relationship between poverty and disability is complex.

■ Disabled people suffer disadvantage and discrimination in the labour market and are more likely to be reliant upon social security benefits.

■ There are benefits targeted at the particular needs of some disabled people, but take-up of these benefits is low.

■ Those caring for disabled people are also at greater risk of poverty and social exclusion.

■ Much of the deprivation associated with disability could be reduced by the provision of more direct public support to meet the particular needs of disabled people.

The costs of disability

Disability is an umbrella term used to cover a wide range of physical conditions and social circumstances in which people may experience difficulties or problems in providing for themselves or participating in social activity. Loss or impairment of physical functions can be problematic: people who cannot see, hear, walk or clothe themselves obviously have to learn to adapt to their limited capabilities. However physical conditions such as these need not necessarily lead to social problems or social exclusion, and indeed they do not always do so. When assistance or support can be purchased or provided disabled people can and do participate fully in modern society. If they do not participate, and if they experience poverty and exclusion, it is because of their need to survive within structures that assume people are 'able-bodied' and that provide inadequate support for those who are not – or may even directly exclude them.

It is thus discrimination, rather than disability itself, which as the heart of the exclusion experienced by disabled people; and linked to this is a greater risk of poverty and exclusion for disabled people. On average the incomes of disabled people are 20 per cent lower then those of non-disabled people of working age (Burchardt, 2000a). The result of this is that it is often the case that, as Groves once (1988, p. 171) put it, 'Poverty is disability's close companion'.

The problems arising from disability, both directly and indirectly, vary widely however, because so too does the nature of disability itself. Disabilities can include the loss or impairment of physical functions such as mobility, sensory deprivation such as blindness or deafness, or mental disabilities such as learning difficulties. These different disabilities lead to very different social needs and social problems. They have also resulted in much academic and political debate about how to define disability – and this debate remains largely unresolved and controversial.

In the 1960s a government-sponsored survey of disability carried out by the OPCS sought to distinguish three different conditions (see Oliver, 1991a):

- *Impairment* – meaning loss of function.
- *Disability* – meaning restriction of activity.
- *Handicap* – meaning a physical disadvantage that limits individual fulfilment.

In his major study of poverty in the 1960s, Townsend (1979, ch. 20) went further than this and included chronic sickness in his discussion of the poverty and deprivation associated with disability. In the mid-1980s the OPCS (Martin *et al.*, 1988; Martin and White, 1988) carried out another survey of disability in which they developed a scale of severity of disability ranging from one (the lowest level of impairment) to ten (the highest level). This was a more sophisticated approach, although it included in the lower categories people who might not be regarded by some as having a disability.

Different studies of the links between poverty and disability may therefore be using different definitions of disability – and perhaps different definitions of poverty too – making comparisons between findings problematic. The OPCS ten-point scale provides both the broadest and the most sophisticated approach, however, and it has been largely taken up in most of the recent discussions on the issue. Using the scale, the OPCS found that there were over 6.5 million people with disabilities in Britain in 1985, ranging from 1.2 million in category one to 240,000 in category ten (see Dalley, 1991, pp. 7–8). In 2002, Department of Health figures estimated that there were 6.8 million people with disabilities, with over 3 million reporting three or more impairments (Flaherty *et al.*, 2004, p. 89).

The link between poverty and disability is not new, of course, indeed it goes back to the nineteenth century and in particular to the growth of urbanisation (see Topliss, 1979). It was recognised by Townsend in his survey of poverty in the 1960s (Townsend, 1979, ch. 20); and in the 1990s the OPCS research estimated that 47 per cent of disabled adults were living in poverty (Berthoud *et al.*, 1993). More recently the government's HBAI statistics reveal that households containing one or more disabled people are at a greater risk of poverty than those without a disabled person – 22 per cent compared to 15 per cent (BHC), and 26 per cent compared to 19 per cent (AHC), using the 60 per cent of median income measure (DWP, 2005a, table 3.6).

These figures may actually understate the extent of poverty and deprivation experienced by people with disabilities, however, because for many low income can be compounded by the extra costs associated with living with a disability. These include the purchase of physical aids or adaptations to the home, the cost of medicines or ointments, the need to consume more fuel in order to heat the home full-time, and perhaps the need to pay for care or support within the home. Without additional income to cover such extra costs the standard of living of people with disabilities surviving on low incomes is likely to be further reduced, although calculating the extent to which such costs do influence poverty and living standards can be a complex and controversial affair.

Research carried out with disabled people to determine their real living costs, provocatively subtitled *More than you would think* (Smith *et al.*, 2004), estimated weekly budget standards for disabled people ranging from £1,513 for those with high mobility and support needs to £389 for those with low to medium needs. In another research project Zaidi and Burchardt (2003) attempted to estimate these additional costs as a proportion of income for different groups of disabled people with different levels of severity of disability. In all cases they found that there was a significant difference in costs and that these operated to raise the income needed to maintain an equivalent standard of living by between about 16 and 50 per cent. As a result they argued that the numbers of disabled people in poverty were likely to be much greater than those revealed in the HBAI figures which relied on average incomes only, leading to somewhere between 35 to 60 per cent of households with disabled people likely to be poor.

Extra expenditure on certain goods, particularly capital expenditure, is also likely to produce a greater risk of debt for disabled people (Grant, 1995). However, as discussed earlier, poverty is not just a function of low cash income and financial restrictions; there are also broader features of deprivation and exclusion that disproportionately affect people with disabilities. Townsend's (1979, ch. 20) study revealed that people with disabilities experienced poorer housing conditions and were less likely to have regular holidays. Disability is also frequently associated with ill-health, both as a cause and a consequence. Furthermore, participation in social activities and leisure pursuits may be restricted by reduced mobility or sensory deprivation, leading to an overall reduction in the quality of life of people with disabilities compared with most non-disabled people.

The poverty and social exclusion associated with disability, like poverty more generally, also have a dynamic dimension. Longitudinal analysis of the onset and duration of disability is now possible employing datasets such as the BHPS, and researchers such as Burchardt (2000a and 2000b) and Jenkins and Rigg (2003) have used these to explore the experience of disability over time and its link with poverty.

Perhaps the most significant finding here is that, despite popular misconceptions, for most people disability is not a permanent or long-term phenomenon. Burchardt found that over a half of adults experiencing life-limiting disability effects endured these for spells of less than two years. Like poverty disability is for most a time-limited experience. However, again like poverty, there is a minority who do experience longer periods. Burchardt found that few who were disabled for over four years ever recovered and that at any one time these long-term disabled made up a high proportion of all disabled people (2000b, p. 645).

Research also shows that there is a dynamic link between the experiences of disability and poverty. For many the onset of disability was associated with a decline in income and employment and hence an increased risk of poverty. However, those who were disadvantaged when disabled were also more likely to have come from that section of the population already experiencing higher levels of deprivation. Burchardt (2003) found that those in the poorest fifth of the income distribution were two and a half times more likely to become disabled than those in the top fifth. Deprivation may also precede disability therefore; and the relationship between cause and effect in disability and poverty is thus complex and frequently two-way – as captured in the words of Groves (1988, p. 171) quoted above about poverty being disability's 'companion'.

Employment

Exclusion from the labour market means exclusion from receipt of wages, which are the main source of income in modern industrial societies and thus the main means of avoiding poverty. For the nearly 50 per cent of people with disabilities who have passed the retirement age, exclusion from work may be as much a function of age as it is of disability, as we discussed in Chapter 11. However, for younger people of working age there is evidence that those with disabilities are at greater risk of unemployment and inactivity than the rest of the population, and hence at greater risk of poverty.

The OPCS survey in the 1980s found that only 31 per cent of people with disabilities were in work then, as opposed to 69 per cent of the general population (Martin and White, 1988). More recent figures on those in work put the employment rate for disabled women at 46 per cent and disabled men at 51 per cent, compared to 75 per cent and 85 per cent for the non-disabled, with the unemployment rate for the disabled twice that for the non-disabled (Flaherty *et al.*, 2004, p. 92). And even when disabled people are working they are more likely to be in manual employment and lower paid (*ibid.*, p. 93).

Exclusion from the labour market is in part the result of direct discrimination by employers against people with disabilities, who they believe to be unsuitable for many kinds of work and possibly unreliable on health grounds. However, this is compounded by other, potentially more important structural barriers to employment, in particular the failure of employers to adapt workplaces or work practices to permit the participation of people with disabilities. People with physical or sensory disabilities are perfectly capable of working within the limitations of their condition (as high-profile figures such as the Labour politician, David Blunkett, demonstrate), and yet, because of the structure of many working environments, many are excluded from realising their potential to do so.

The direct and indirect discrimination that disabled people face in the workplace has been addressed through policy measures of various kinds for a number of years. These date back to the Disabled Persons Act of 1944, which introduced a statutory requirement that a set quota, at least 3 per cent, of the workforce of organisations with more than twenty employees should be people registered as disabled. This was an impractical and ineffective measure, however. Many disabled people were not registered under the Act, the quota system was inadequately enforced, and the average proportion of disabled employees in organisations within the scheme was found to be nearer to 1 per cent (Floyd, 1991, p. 216).

Until the end of the last century there was no legislation to prevent discrimination against disabled people, unlike the areas of gender and race; but this was altered by the introduction of the Disability Discrimination Act (1995). The Act made direct discrimination unlawful and also promoted more general indirect action against unfair disadvantage through the establishment of a Disability Rights Commission (2000). In the early years of the new century these provisions were extended further to include a widening of the definition of disability and to place a duty on public sector organizations to promote equal treatment of disabled people. In principle at least, therefore, many of the dis-advantages that disabled people face in entering and remaining in the labour market should now be being addressed

The 1990s also saw the introduction of a social security benefit aimed directly at improving the labour-market participation of disabled people – the Disability Working Allowance (DWA). The DWA was closely modelled on Family Credit and it provided a supplement to the low wages of those who were defined as disabled according to certain criteria. It was not entirely successful in terms of take-up and impact, though was much valued by those who did receive it (see Cockett, 2003); and in 1999 it was replaced by the Disabled Person's Tax Credit (DPTC), at the same time as other in-work benefits were converted to tax credits. In 2003 this support was replaced by the addition of extra disability payments to the Child and Working Tax Credits (see Chapter 14). Disabled people were also included as one of the target groups in the New Deal provisions for advice and support to assist people into the labour market, where the role of personal advisers for claimants was first piloted, and later spread to all New Deal clients.

These new measures have done much to improve the policy framework underpinning moves to encourage better labour market participation by disabled people, and hence to reduce the risk of poverty. Nevertheless, people with disabilities still remain relatively speaking in low-status and low-paid employment, or are excluded from the labour market altogether. This exclusion not only prevents them from receiving the financial benefits of employment, it also excludes them from the indirect advantages of employment in the form of fringe benefits, occupational pensions and sick pay, and so on. Security for those disabled people who can work, therefore, to use the terms now adopted by government, is still far from being achieved for all. Security for those who cannot work depends upon those forms of support that are available outside the labour market.

Benefits and dependency

Security for those who cannot work is provided by social security benefits, and in practice larger numbers of disabled people are wholly or partly dependent upon benefits for their income than is the case with the population generally. In practice, what is more, benefit provision for disabled people is complex, with different benefits providing different forms of support for people in different circumstances. Benefit provision for people with disabilities has had a fairly chequered history in Britain, and its history has been one of piecemeal reform and *ad hoc* adaptation rather than consistent development. This has resulted in the growth of significant anomalies between the way people with disabilities and others are treated, and even between the different treatments accorded to different groups among the disabled themselves (see Barnes and Baldwin, 1999).

People with disabilities who meet the criteria for ordinary benefits can of course claim these in the same way as other people. Indeed benefits such as Retirement Pension or Income Support are the main source of income for a large number of people with disabilities who are not entitled to separate or additional provision as a result of their disability. However, ever since the Workmen's Compensation Act in the early part of the twentieth century, separate and additional benefits have been provided for some people, depending on the cause of their disability.

Because of the link with employment and the perceived need to ensure adequate compensation for those disabled by accidents or illness at work, throughout much of the last century benefit provision for those who were disabled through employment was more generous than that for those whose disability arose in other circumstances, for instance through birth or in childhood. However, during the 1990s many of the more generous aspects of employment-based provision were removed or reduced, and provision for disabled people made more equitable – albeit largely as a result of a levelling down to the protection enjoyed by the least well-off.

The postwar Beveridge insurance scheme made no specific provision for people with disabilities; but in the latter part of the last century alterations and additions to aspects of benefit provision were made to provide some support for some recognised extra needs resulting from disability. These included a higher National Insurance benefit (Invalidity Benefit) for those unable to work due to illness or disability for over six months. At the end of the century the numbers dependent upon Invalidity Benefit began to grow and in 1995 it was replaced with a less generous National Insurance-based provision (Incapacity Benefit), which was also subject to more stringent tests of ability, or inability, to work.

The expectation was that this would lead to reductions in reliance upon this benefit, with those able to work either gaining employment or moving onto the Jobseekers' Allowance as unemployed. However, this did not happen, and indeed the numbers of Incapacity Benefit claimants continued to grow, from just over 800,000 in 1981/2 to over 1.7 million in 2001/02 (*Social Trends*, 31, 2005, table 8.18). There has been considerable debate about the extent to which this growth is the result of a growth in disability itself or is a reflection of more general trends in the labour market, where higher levels of unemployment have led to more people suffering long-term illness or disability being excluded from work. Some researchers have referred to this growth in dependency on Incapacity Benefit as 'hidden unemployment', and have suggested that many of those claiming the benefit would in fact be willing and able to work if jobs were available for them but, because of their health or disability problems, had abandoned the search for work (Alcock *et al.*, 2003).

This problem became a concern of the Labour government, which has introduced a number of changes to Incapacity Benefit in order to discourage long-term reliance upon it. These have included tightening the conditions for entitlement to the benefit through payment of National Insurance contributions and reducing entitlement for those with other income above £85 a week. Positive interventions through the New Deal provisions for disabled people have also sought to help Incapacity Benefit claimants to find work. Despite these measures the number of dependents has remained high, and in particular is higher in areas where levels of unemployment more generally are higher, suggesting that benefit dependency is linked to labour market conditions as well as physical disability. Further measures to encourage employment and restrict dependency are therefore planned, including the introduction of a new lower rate of Incapacity Benefit for new claimants with lower levels of incapacity (estimated at around 80 per cent of potential claimants under current rules) who would then be required to attend interviews to assist them to seek work – whilst in effect recognising that many older, long-term claimants may be unlikely ever to be able to return to work.

Entitlement to Invalidity and Incapacity Benefit was initially determined in part by National Insurance contributions. Disabled people out of work without NI contribution records were thus excluded from this benefit, but were able to claim an alternative, Severe Disablement Allowance (SDA), paid at a lower rate (around 60 per cent) than the NI benefits. In 1999, however, SDA was abolished and replaced with a new entitlement to Incapacity Benefit for those disabled during childhood and access to Income Support for those disabled as adults with no other means of support. These changes, too, have contributed to the swelling numbers dependent on long-term Incapacity Benefit, therefore, and mean that however effective support for work search may be, it needs to be recognised that there are likely to be a large number of disabled people relying long-term upon social security support.

As mentioned above, for many disabled people even the more generous levels of NI benefits may not be sufficient to meet their needs because of the additional costs that they experience as a result of their disability. Since the 1970s, however, benefits have been available to meet some of these extra costs of disability. Initially these took the form of two separate benefits:

- Attendance Allowance (AA) for the additional costs incurred by those who needed someone to care for them during the day or the night, or both.
- Mobility Allowance (MA) for the costs of basic mobility for those unable or virtually unable to walk.

In the 1990s they were merged to form one new benefit, Disability Living Allowance (DLA). This included separate components for care and mobility needs, in effect replacing AA and MA; but it also introduced a lower rate payment for less severely disabled people (see Hadjipateras, 1992). Those over pension age, however, are excluded from DLA and remain entitled only to AA, where they have significant care needs. Initially DLA was also not available to children with disabilities, but it has now been extended to children over the age of three.

Both DLA and AA are flat rate and, because they are linked to additional needs, are paid in addition to any other income; but they are not very generous and in practice are most unlikely to meet the full costs of those with severe disabilities. They are also subject to stringent medical tests, which mean that many people with minor disabilities are excluded from receiving them. Despite this there was a concern that the growing numbers of claimants for DLA was evidence of over-generous award of these benefits, and a review of the procedures for determining entitlement was carried out by government in the late 1990s.

In practice, however, research evidence suggests that the small numbers of these who may be receiving DLA when they are not entitled to it is overshadowed by the larger number of disabled people who may be entitled to such extra costs benefits but are not receiving them (Berthoud, 1998b).

Non-take-up of DLA and AA is a significant problem, and this is probably contributing to high levels of poverty amongst people with disabilities. It has been estimated that only between 30 and 50 per cent of people who are eligible take up DLA, and between 40 and 60 per cent take up AA (Craig and Greenslade, 1998).

Social security benefits targeted at people with disabilities and their particular needs do go some way to providing security for those who cannot work. However, because of the low levels of benefit payment and the high costs of disability, and the high levels of non-take-up, they may not go very far in alleviating or preventing poverty. What is more there is a potentially dangerous tension here for extending benefit provision rather than providing real opportunities for employment and services at work and at home to permit people to provide for themselves may operate in practice to trap people through their disability – and therefore perhaps in poverty – rather than free them to participate fully in society. And this problem does not just affect people with disabilities, it is also visited on those who remain at home to care for them and may find that they, too, are trapped in their role.

Poverty for carers

Disability, as we have seen, is a wide-ranging concept covering a number of serious and not so serious physical or mental debilities. Taking the wider definition employed by the OPCS in the 1980s, many of those who may be classed as having a disability are quite able to look after themselves, to get about unaided and to work productively. Nevertheless there is a significant number of people whose disability means they need help in performing sometimes quite basic bodily tasks. In order to survive therefore they need, at least for some of the time, the care provided by another person. The dependency that frequently accompanies this can severely reduce the quality of life of disabled people – however, it can also have deleterious consequences for those providing the care.

Public care for people with disabilities is provided in residential institutions designed specifically for the purpose, and in severe cases this will mean a hospital bed. However, very few people require such intensive care, and very few get it. The OPCS survey found that only 7 per cent of all adults with disabilities lived in residential institutions in the 1980s (Martin et al., 1988). This was accentuated by the policy shift to encourage community, rather than residential, care in the 1990s. Thus for the vast majority of people care is provided in the community, with eight out of ten elderly people who need significant domestic help relying on care from relatives and neighbours at home (Howard, 2001, p. 2). Carers in the home are normally family members – spouses, daughters or sons – and the majority, 58 per cent, are women (ibid., p. 6).

According to the 2001 Census there are over 5.3 million such carers in England and Wales, of which over a million are providing over 50 hours of support a week and a further half a million are providing between 20 and 49 hours (Census, 2001). For these carers, at least, their responsibilities are likely to mean that they have to withdraw from the labour market. Caring thus becomes full-time work. Even those who are able to remain in employment, however, may find that their work is limited in terms of time, place and career opportunities. The effect of this is that carers are less likely to be active in the labour market and more likely to have a lower income than the population at large. Thus caring for disability, as well as disability itself, is associated with a higher risk of poverty, as Howard (2001) in her examination of poverty and social exclusion amongst carers reveals.

The risk of poverty for carers is obviously closely linked to the poverty associated with disability itself. In practice both are likely to live in the same household and experience the harsh consequences of reduced household income. In such situations the dependency of one party on the other is likely to accentuate the problems arising from reduced income. When the carer is working the person with the disability is likely to be the dependent party; but when the carer is not in paid employment it is often they who are dependent on the person for whom they are caring because the household income, probably social security benefits, is likely to be determined primarily by the extent and cause of the disability (*ibid.*, p. 93).

Exclusion from the labour market and dependence upon benefits means that carers' incomes, along with the incomes of those they care for, are likely to be low, resulting in a greater risk of poverty and deprivation. It is not only this type of financial deprivation that is associated with caring responsibilities, however; caring can lead to social exclusion as well as poverty. Leaving paid employment in order to care not only results in an immediate drop in income, it also results in the broader 'opportunity costs' of lost promotion prospects and occupational benefits (Joshi, 1992). In addition to this are the less quantifiable costs of the anxiety of care, worries over the provision of the correct medicines and ointments for instance, and the self-sacrifice that home-based caring work inevitably involves.

In general terms the quality of life enjoyed by someone engaged in significant caring responsibilities within the home is likely to be almost as constrained, and constraining, as that of the disabled person – as one carer quoted in Howard (2001, p. 29) put it, 'Your social life finishes completely ... We're very lonely'. Caring work can be hard, monotonous and demanding. It can also lead to anxiety, distress and perhaps even conflict; and yet it is also frequently bound up with dependency, both financial and emotional. Caring for adults with disabilities can also have a longer term negative dimension – unlike children they will not grow up and become independent, indeed their condition is more likely to deteriorate than to improve.

Disability and deprivation

As we have seen, both persons with disabilities and those who provide care and support for them are at greater risk of poverty and are more likely to experience the deprivation and exclusion associated with a reduced standard of living in our modern society than other people. For persons with disabilities and their carers this may be experienced as a 'dependency trap' – reinforced by exclusion from the labour market, reliance on inadequate benefits and the problem of struggling to cope with the additional costs of being disabled in an 'able-bodied' world.

The problem of disability can thus become a problem of deprivation too. As with age-related poverty, however, there is danger of perceiving a false causal link here. Disabilities may restrict the capabilities of those who suffer from them and may even reduce their quality of life because of this; but they are not the cause of poverty. Deprivation and exclusion are socially created problems, and if they are disproportionately associated with the experience of disability, it is because the social reaction, or non-reaction, to disability has created this link.

In the case of disability it is very much a case of non-reaction leading to problems for persons with disabilities. Modern industrial societies, and even modern welfare states, have largely been constructed on the basis that the people who inhabit them, who produce and reproduce them and benefit from them, are non-disabled. This is true of workplaces, public and private buildings, transport systems, information and communication networks, retail outlets – indeed almost all venues for social interaction. Increasingly attempts are now being made to adapt buildings and organisations to accommodate persons with some disabilities, and such positive measures may now be legal requirements under the disability discrimination legislation; but it will be some time indeed before they are able to transform the physical and social world in which disability is generally experienced.

Radical disability campaigners have sometimes pointed out that most of the problems associated with disability are created, and recreated, not by disability itself but by the failure of social and physical policy planning to recognise or take account of the practical needs experienced by people with disabilities (see Oliver, 1990). As they have argued, the poverty, and the dependency, associated with disability is the consequence, both directly and indirectly, of the failure to respond to these basic needs; and the effect of this has been to prevent many disabled people from providing for themselves in the same ways that other people are expected to do.

Part IV

The Policy Framework

The Politics of Poverty

SUMMARY OF KEY POINTS

- The Fabian tradition of using academic research to influence political debate has brought poverty onto the policy agenda in the UK for over a hundred years.
- In the 1980s the UK government was less inclined to respond to such research evidence; but since 1997 poverty and social exclusion have again become major concerns of public policy.
- The 'poverty lobby' is composed of campaigning groups such as the CPAG.
- Campaigning activity also involves the use of communications media, such as television, to popularise the problem of poverty.
- Some critics have argued that many anti-poverty campaigns do not in practice involve people who are themselves experiencing poverty.
- Some attempts have been made more recently to involve people who are poor in campaigning; but there may be a danger in assuming that only people in poverty have an interest in campaigning against it.

The arithmetic tradition

Poverty, as we discussed in Chapter 1, is a political concept. Thus academic interest in defining and measuring poverty, and academic research into the extent of poverty, have always been closely related to attempts to utilise such academic work to influence policy development or reform. Moreover, political debate on poverty and anti-poverty policy has always been a contested and even a conflictual arena. Thus the problem of poverty has produced political activity, and this has been true for at least the last 150–200 years of industrial society in the UK and elsewhere. Indeed the political activity generated by the problem of poverty has been growing gradually, although with increasing rapidity, over the last century or so. It has also become more organised and more varied, and increasingly the debate has focused not just on whether to politicise poverty, or what poverty to politicise, but also on how to organise political activity and who should be involved in this. We shall return to look at these issues in a little more detail shortly.

The pioneers of modern poverty research at the end of the nineteenth century, Booth and Rowntree, engaged in quite detailed calculations of the extent and distribution of poverty in the expectation that their evidence of the existence of the problem would create pressure on the government to develop policies to remove it. In the early twentieth century this strategy of using empirical evidence to influence political opinion was developed into a more organised form of political pressure through the work of reformers such as Sidney and Beatrice Webb, who consciously set out to combine academic work with political activity. The Webbs were instrumental in the establishment of the Fabian Society, a political group committed to working for welfare reform through political influence, in particular on the emerging Labour Party. They were also involved in the founding of the London School of Economics (LSE), an academic institution with a focus on research and education in social and economic planning (Alcock, 2003, ch. 1).

Through the work of the Webbs and the Fabian Society, therefore, the link between academic debate and political activity became established within the British institutional and political context. Their aim was to use evidence of poverty and social deprivation to expose the failure of the capitalist economic system and to challenge the political domination of the classical liberal tradition of political thought and its emphasis on the non-involvement and non-responsibility of government in economic and social reform. The growth in power of the labour movement and the Labour Party, where Fabian influence was primarily directed, and the gradual expansion of research on the definition and measurement of poverty carried out by growing numbers of researchers extended this challenge both quantitatively, in terms of the empirical evidence produced, and qualitatively, in terms of its impact on political and especially government thinking. This has sometimes been referred as the 'arithmetic tradition', capturing the concern with measurement as a basis for influence.

With the introduction of the welfare state reforms of the postwar period by the Labour government of the late 1940s, it appeared that this tradition had finally become the decisive influence on economic and social planning.

Beveridge's proposals for insurance benefits to prevent 'want' drew heavily on Rowntree's research into the nature and extent of poverty. It even seemed that these reforms had been successful in removing poverty, as the Fabians had argued they would be. Further research by Rowntree (Rowntree and Lavers, 1951), carried out after the introduction of the welfare changes, suggested that the number of people in poverty were very small compared with the those cited in earlier studies.

However, this belief in the achievements of the postwar welfare reforms was challenged in the 1960s by 'rediscovery' of poverty in affluent Britain through the new research carried out by Abel Smith and Townsend (1965) and others which we mentioned in Chapter 1. This research was based on a reassessment of the definition of poverty and a revitalisation of the tradition of empirical research to measure its extent and provide pressure on government to respond to it. It was thus a continuation of the arithmetic tradition of the Fabian Society, albeit with a more sophisticated approach that was directed not so much at the politics of classical liberalism, but rather at the complacent assumption of much postwar politics that welfare reforms could be, and indeed had been, successful in removing poverty (Alcock, 1999).

The rediscovery of poverty led to a growth in the scale and sophistication of academic research on poverty, which has continued into the new century. However, it continued with the arithmetic tradition of Fabian political influence and the belief that the governments of welfare states should utilise the machinery of the state to resolve, or at least relieve, social problems such as poverty – in other words that there was a political consensus on the role of the state in the prevention of poverty. This was linked to a constitutionalist assumption about the desirability and viability of a strategy based on exerting pressure on Parliament and government departments to persuade them of the need for reform. In the latter decades of the last century these assumptions began to come into question.

The Thatcher governments of the 1980s were openly critical of the assumption that an expansion of state welfare was the only way to bring about social and economic change. They challenged the idea that such welfare reform would necessarily benefit poorer people, and argued that seeking support for extensions of state expenditure might even threaten the support for private investment in economic markets upon which future economic growth rested. It was economic growth they argued that would create benefits for all, including those at the bottom to whom growth at the top would eventually 'trickle down'.

Support for such a free-market notion of benefits for all through economic growth and trickle-down also began to be voiced by a new range of organisations outside government in the 1980s, openly challenging the dominance that the Fabians has previously enjoyed in political debate about poverty. These organisations were sometimes referred to as the 'new right' (see Levitas, 1986), and they included the Institute of Economic Affairs (IEA), founded in 1957 but revitalised in the 1980s, the Centre for Policy Studies, established by Keith Joseph and Margaret Thatcher, and the Adam Smith Institute (ASI), which produced a range of proposals for the radical reform of social security provision in the 1980s (ASI, 1984 and 1989).

Faced with such a challenge from the right, and with a largely un-sympathetic and unyielding government, adherents to the Fabian arithmetic tradition experienced a significant setback in the 1980s in their strategy to prevent poverty. Their arguments were challenged and their influence severely reduced. As a result of this the politics of poverty in Britain underwent a major transformation during this period. No longer was it possible to assume that poverty and deprivation were problems recognisable by all in British society, and that the government was under an obligation to respond to evidence that such problems continued to exist in the midst of growing affluence. The focus of debate thus shifted from what *could* be done to what *should* be done, and in this climate detailed empirical research was not such an important factor in the argument.

Nevertheless this shift in the terms of debate did not lead to the abandonment of the Fabian strategy or the research on which it had been based. Academic research into the definition and extent of poverty continued, and in the 1990s was given new impetus by the work of the researchers on the Rowntree Inquiry into Income and Wealth (Barclay 1995; Hills, 1995). The work of EU researchers and commentators also began to have an increasing influence on political debate in Britain, in particular debate on the new problems of social exclusion and social polarisation (Room, 1995). And with the election of the Labour government under Tony Blair in 1997 political debate and academic research on poverty began to move into a new and different phase.

Labour openly challenged the Conservative assertion that poverty was no longer a problem in modern Britain and resurrected the use of the 'p' word (as some pundits put it) in political debate and policy planning. What is more Labour made clear commitments to combat poverty, most notably their pledge to end child poverty by 2020, discussed in Chapter 11. They also promoted new debate and research about definition and measurement of poverty, for instance, through the consultation on the measures of child poverty (DWP, 2003); and initiated an annual review of anti-poverty policies and their impact on various indicators of poverty and exclusion (DWP, 2004a).

Since 1997 the terms of political debate on poverty have also been developed and adapted. In particular the Labour government extended the focus of research and policy onto the broader concept of social exclusion. As we discussed in Chapter 8, research and policy on social exclusion extends beyond the measurement of cash poverty to include a wide range of other social dimensions of deprivation. In such a context the tradition of arithmetic research has in practice been supplemented by other methods and measures. In this new context the language of politics and policy has also changed to focus on concerns with security and opportunity, and this has led to a range of new policy initiatives, which we will return to discuss in Chapters 14 and 16.

The poverty lobby

Central to the Fabian strategy of utilising academic argument and academic research to secure change and development in government policy was an attempt to foster close and influential relationships with government ministers and departments; and particularly during the periods of Labour government in the 1960s and 1970s this was a relatively successful strategy. In the 1960s and 1970s Abel Smith was an adviser to the Secretary of State for Social Services and Piachaud was a member of the Prime Minister's political unit. During this time Donnison was also appointed as chair of the Supplementary Benefits Commission. Prominent Fabians also entered Parliament directly as elected members, most notably in 1979 Frank Field, who had been the Director of the CPAG and later became Minister for Welfare Reform in the early days of the 1997 Labour government.

However, gaining direct political influence by entering the corridors and committee rooms of power has been supplemented in the politics of poverty by the indirect pressure exerted by campaigning activity outside the exclusive worlds of Westminster and Whitehall. In addition to the research and formal political influence of the arithmetic tradition, academics have combined with political activists and members of various organisations representing different special interests and demands to establish independent groups to campaign for a range of policy changes. These have sometimes been referred to by political scientists as 'pressure groups'.

An early example of such pressure group activity was the 1917 Committee, later renamed the Family Endowment Committee, which was established by Eleanor Rathbone and others to campaign for the introduction of Family Allowances to reduce poverty among families and children (Macnicol, 1980). The committee was wound up in the 1940s after its eventual success in persuading the government to institute a Family Allowance scheme, although the scheme was not quite in the form the campaigners had wanted, nor was it entirely the product of their campaigning efforts.

After the rediscovery of poverty in the 1960s, however, and the revitalisation of the arithmetic tradition, Fabian academics began to look again at the possibility of establishing independent campaigning organisations to carry the message of reform outside the narrow confines of academic debate and political influence. Their aim was to establish vehicles outside government and the civil service, and outside academic institutions, to voice opinions on the need for reform and policy development that were informed by academic argument and research, but not limited by the need to appease narrow political interests. This, it was hoped, would get poverty, and the need for anti-poverty policy, onto the political agenda and provide a voice for proposing policy reforms that were not necessarily currently accepted within government or opposition political circles.

Abel Smith and Townsend, the authors of the influential book on the persistence of poverty in affluent Britain (1965), were involved in the establishment of a group to campaign for improved support for poor families and children. The group was initially called the Family Poverty Group, but was shortly renamed the Child Poverty Action Group (CPAG) in 1966 (McCarthy, 1986). From these modest but influential roots the CPAG grew fairly rapidly into a well-informed, well-respected campaigning organisation. It had active and effective leaders in Tony Lynes and his successors, such as Frank Field and Ruth Lister, and was successful both in attracting the recognition of politicians and civil servants and in helping to put the problem of poverty onto the political agenda (see Whiteley and Winyard, 1983). By 1981 MacGregor (pp. 141–2) was writing that the CPAG had become 'part of the fabric of British politics'.

Getting poverty onto the political agenda was just one of the aims of the CPAG, however, and arguably not the most important one. They were also concerned to bring about genuine policy change to reduce or remove poverty, especially among children and families. This of course was a more difficult task, especially after the mid-1960s when the increasing pressure of economic recession gave governments little room, they claimed, to increase welfare provision. Nevertheless some important policy changes were introduced for which the CPAG could claim a fair measure of indirect responsibility. In particular this included the introduction of Child Benefit in the 1970s, which turned out to be a hard-fought battle indeed. Cabinet leaks and trade union influence were orchestrated by the CPAG to maintain the pressure for reform on a government that was seriously considering abandoning its promises to implement the scheme (see Field, 1982).

The CPAG is perhaps the most important and most widely respected group campaigning for reform in the poverty field (Whiteley and Winyard, 1983, p. 18). But it is not the only group – there are many others representing different special interests or promoting various policy reforms. These include Age Concern, the Disability Alliance, the National Council for One-Parent Families, and Shelter, which campaigns against homelessness. In their discussion of these campaign groups Whiteley and Winyard distinguished between *promotional* groups, comprising professionals or volunteers campaigning for reform on behalf of others, and *representational* groups, representatives of those experiencing poverty or deprivation who are campaigning to improve provision for all those like them. They pointed out that both forms of organisation can be found campaigning in the poverty field, and that both have their advantages and their disadvantages in the political arena. As a whole, however, by the 1970s these groups had begun to develop a collective identity forged out of their shared concern for policy reform and had come to be called the 'poverty lobby'.

The poverty lobby did not just share a common concern for certain policy reforms however. When their concerns were sufficiently close, various organisations combined to form joint campaigning organisations to publicise particular shared interests or press for particular policy reforms. There have been a range of such 'umbrella' organisations operating at different times within the UK, for instance, the *End Child Poverty* consortium aimed at putting pressure on the government over its child poverty pledge in the early 2000s. There are also umbrella groups operating on an international basis to lobby both governments and international agencies on poverty issues, such as the *Make Poverty History* campaign which attracted widespread support in the UK and across the developed world at the beginning of the new century.

The campaigning work of the poverty lobby groups includes a wide range of activities aimed at securing maximum publicity and maximum influence for the ideas they wish to promote. The CPAG, for instance, conducts its own research and publishes this together with other research findings in a series of high-profile policy texts (for instance, Dornan, 2004; Preston, 2005). The group also regularly submits evidence and memoranda directly to government departments and ministers, organises meetings and conferences to discuss and publicise proposals at both national and local level, and attempts to utilise the established media – the press, radio and television – to present ideas to a wider audience.

The power of public expression through the media has become of increasing importance to all political campaigners. The media operate both to publicise ideas and to shape them, and their influence in defining the problem and the politics of poverty cannot be ignored. Poverty lobby organisations therefore regularly provide press releases to publicise their work and respond to requests for interviews on radio or television. However journalists and broadcasters can themselves initiate influential political debate by reporting evidence of deprivation or even using the problem of poverty as a theme in fictional dramas. In the 1960s and 1970s there were a few highly influential television dramas focusing on the problems of poverty in Britain, notably *Cathy Come Home* and *The Spongers*; and in the 1980s and 1990s the televised presentation of important new research on poverty by London Weekend Television in the *Breadline Britain* programmes took sophisticated arguments on the definition and measurement of poverty to a potentially mass audience.

In their assessment of the influence and achievements of the poverty lobby, Whiteley and Winyard (1983) pointed out that the success of campaigning work depended on a number of factors, not all of which are within the control of campaigning groups. They highlighted in particular the political environment within which groups are operating, the strategies they choose to promote their ideas and the resources they have to support their work. These influences vary from group to group and over time. The resources supporting the CPAG have enabled it to survive as an influential campaign group for forty years, and its broadly based strategies have permitted it to maintain pressure for reform across a range of fronts, whilst it has adapted to the changing complexion of political power and policy debate.

Despite a sometimes hostile climate, therefore, the poverty lobby has continued to grow and develop, incorporating an increasingly wide range of specialist groups and umbrella organisations. Most, however, are mainly composed of professional campaigners employed to carry out the campaigning aims of the various groups. They are campaigners '*for* the poor' rather than campaigners '*from* the poor'. The politics of poverty also includes the political activities of those who are poor themselves.

Campaigning by those who are poor

Having identified a distinction between promotional and representational groups, Whiteley and Winyard (1983) concluded that most organisations within the poverty lobby in fact were promotional. That is they were neither composed of nor representative of people who were poor or benefit claimants. The major poverty campaign group, the CPAG, is a promotional organisation: its National Executive Committee is primarily composed of professionals elected at the open Annual General Meeting, and the daily work of the organisation is carried out by full-time salaried workers.

However, the CPAG also has a structure of local branches based in cities and towns up and down the country, which can annually elect representatives to the organisation's national executive. These local branches may include claimants and people in poverty, as well as other local campaigners. The involvement of people who are poor in the activities of organisations such as the CPAG raises the question of whether the poverty lobby should not be more actively representative of people who are themselves poor. This issue of campaigning *by* those in poverty, as opposed to *for* those in poverty, is an important one in any discussion of the politics of poverty, and it has been a controversial one in some debates among concerned parties – both those who are poor and those who are not.

One influential protagonist of the case for prioritising campaigning by those who are poor in the promotion of anti-poverty policies has been Holman, one-time Professor of Social Policy, author of an earlier textbook on poverty (Holman, 1978) and later community worker on a large housing estate in Easterhouse Glasgow. In numerous articles in publications such as the *Guardian* newspaper Holman has argued that poverty campaigning should concentrate on 'letting people in poverty speak'. His argument is that only those who experience poverty can know what it is like, and tell it like it is; and therefore that their testimony is both the most authentic and the most effective evidence of the problems that need to be addressed. What is more, if poverty campaigning is seeking to promote the cause of policy reform to address such problems, then the nature of the reforms promoted should be determined not by academics and politicians, even though they may be sympathetic to those in poverty, but by those who know through experience what they need. There-fore Holman also argues that the resources dedicated to combating poverty should be placed under the control of people who are poor themselves, and their community representatives, rather than professionals and policy-makers employed by the state.

In fact the issue of campaigns by rather than for people in poverty is not a new one. In the nineteenth century the government and reformers alike feared the collective action of the disaffected 'residuum' (see Stedman Jones, 1971). In the twentieth century, between the wars, unemployed claimants organised themselves into the National Unemployed Workers' Movement and sought to join or to cooperate with the trade unions representing employed workers in the TUC. There was much tension and distrust in this liaison, although it produced some important and influential campaigning activity, most notably the 'hunger marches' and the Jarrow crusade (see Vincent, 1991, pp. 56 *et seq*).

In the 1970s and 1980s unemployed claimants again established member-ship organisations, now called 'Claimants' Unions', which attempted to develop political links with other labour organisations and poverty lobby groups and were coordinated for a time by an umbrella organisation called the National Federation of Claimants' Unions. The great strengths of the Claimants' Unions – their basis in the spontaneous collective spirit of the unemployed and a membership made up exclusively of benefit claimants – were also their major weaknesses however, at least in organisational terms. Active membership was difficult to sustain over long periods of time and in the face of little prospect of significant improvement in the circumstances of most unemployed people – unless they became employed, at which point they would become ineligible for membership. Individual claimants' unions were usually temporary phenomena therefore, and the national umbrella organisation was unable to maintain a permanent profile in the political arena.

What the organisational difficulties experienced by the claimants' unions revealed were the genuine problems involved in sustained and coordinated campaigning by people in poverty. For a variety of reasons related both to the financial deprivation with which they must constantly struggle and to the social isolation that frequently results from this, people who are poor do not find it easy to engage in organised political activity, and organised political groups have not found it easy to involve them. Lister (2004, p. 153) discusses some of these problems of the 'institutional, political and cultural barriers' faced by people who are poor, within the context of her more general analysis of the role of agency in the experience of poverty, discussed in Chapter 3, where she refers to such collective action as 'getting organised'.

Lister was also involved, with Beresford, in an earlier attempt to bring together academics and professional poverty campaigners and representatives of people in poverty at a forum on *Working Together Against Poverty* in York in 1990 (Lister and Beresford, 1991). Financial hardship, limited knowledge, the experience of stigma and lack of energy and confidence were all identified at the forum as factors inhibiting people who were poor from involvement in campaigning activity. As one participant at the forum put it, 'We may not feel we've got much energy left for anything else. We don't want to speak out when we are unsure of a good response' (*ibid.*, p. 7).

More recently Lister and Beresford have developed this further in their work for the CPAG book, *Poverty First Hand*, which was an attempt to provide a platform for 'poor people to speak for themselves' (Beresford *et al.*, 1999). This included a two-year project to bring together anti-poverty professionals and people with experience of poverty to explore the causes and effects of poverty, the experiences of poverty and the policy recommendations that should flow from these. Similar issues were also explored by the Commission on Poverty, Participation and Power (2000), set up by the UK Coalition Against Poverty in 1999, which concluded that true participation and equal process for people in poverty could be stressful and time-consuming and required high levels of commitment from all concerned.

Involvement of ordinary people, and in particular the 'users' of public services, in political and policy debate about the development and delivery of these services is now much more widely recognised as a valuable and important dimension of the policy process (see Miller, 2004, ch. 8). Within this context Bennett and Roberts (2004) undertook a review of participatory approaches to poverty and anti-poverty policy. They concluded that such approaches were now gaining ground, but that more change would be needed to strengthen the voice of people living in poverty and mainstream this into policy practice. In part, of course, this is because of the difficulties that poverty itself creates. In a study of the consequences of poverty for participation in political activity, Ward (1986) pointed out the *direct* costs of such participation, including membership fees, transport, socialising and keeping up to date, and the *indirect* consequences of poor health, poor environment and lack of time, which inhibit involvement in any organised and active pursuits. The experience of poverty is itself part of the problem.

Perhaps most important of all, however, there are some political contradictions at the heart of poverty campaigning by people in poverty. As we discussed in Chapter 1, poverty is a political concept. As such it is a problem, an undesirable state of affairs about which something should be, but is not being, done. To identify oneself as poor, therefore, is to identify oneself as having a problem and being in need of help. This is a negative categorisation, which people desperately trying to survive, perhaps with dignity, in a hostile world may not willingly and openly wish to adopt – or may indeed believe does not apply to them. One participant at the York forum expressed this clearly, 'Nobody wants to be poor. It's not something we want everyone to know. Some people don't want to tell others they are poor or even admit it to themselves' (Lister and Beresford, 1991, p. 10). And another participant in the later study commented, 'I don't like complaining a great deal because I know full well that I've got food to eat and that I can get by' (Beresford *et al.*, 1999, p. 63).

What is more, important though the issue of the involvement of people experiencing poverty in political campaigning is, there is a problem with the implicit assumption perhaps made by some critics of professional domination of poverty debate, such as Holman, that only such people can act as advocates of the cause of anti-poverty. Clearly poverty and the experience of deprivation is an issue for people who are poor, but it is not *only* an issue for them; and there are political and policy problems which flow from identifying poverty only with the experiences and perceptions of those who are poor.

Poverty campaigning that is limited to the experiences and initiatives of people in poverty runs the risk of being self-defeating, because many people who are themselves poor may not identify with or participate in it. They may not, in Lister's (2004) terms, be 'getting organised'. Identifying the politics of poverty only with the politics of 'the poor' also ignores the fact that poverty is a problem for others in society too – both *in particular*, in terms of self-interest because those not poor now may become poor in the future, and *in general* because the existence of poverty in society may be unacceptable to those who wish to be part of a social order in which others do not suffer deprivation and exclusion. This issue has become much clearer and starker with the increasing availability of evidence of the social polarisation of British society in the twenty-first century.

Indeed it is to a shared belief in greater social justice that the politics of poverty needs to appeal if it is to secure support for policy changes to remove poverty; and this is unlikely to be achieved if poverty is perceived and presented as a problem only for those who are poor. The participation of people experiencing poverty in campaigning against poverty has now become an important challenge to the more general activities of academics, politicians and professionals. It may fatally limit anti-poverty campaigning, however, if it were to become a substitute for them.

Social Security Policy

SUMMARY OF KEY POINTS

- Social security has been the major form of anti-poverty policy in the UK, and in other welfare capitalist countries, for over a century; but social security does not only aim to combat poverty.
- Redistribution though social security can be either *horizontal* of *vertical*, although both may operate to prevent or relieve poverty.
- The development of social security in the UK has seen the gradual replacement of the Poor Law with more comprehensive provision through social insurance and social assistance.
- At the beginning of the new century social security remains a complex mix of different forms and structures of benefit support.
- Social insurance pays benefits in return for contributions made by employees and employers.
- Social assistance pays benefits to those who are poor and involves the application of means-tests to determine entitlement.
- Tax credits provide means-tested support to those in work on low pay.
- Universal benefits are paid to all citizens; the only significant universal benefit in the UK is Child Benefit.
- Problems of error and non-take-up can lead to many claimants not receiving the benefits to which they may be entitled.
- The unemployment and poverty traps are examples of the potential disincentives which flow from targeting social security support on those who are poor.

The principles of social security

Defining and identifying poverty in advanced industrial societies involves an implicit argument that state policy should be developed to remove poverty or prevent it from occurring, as we discussed in Chapter 1. The politics of poverty, therefore, is effectively the politics of anti-poverty policy; and, just as the politics of poverty can be traced back to the development of industrial society, so too can anti-poverty policy. What such a historical review reveals is that throughout this period the major focus of anti-poverty policy in the UK, and indeed in all other industrial societies, has been social security policy.

The idea behind social security policy is the use of support, collected in the form of contributions or taxes from those in employment, to provide an income for those who cannot secure adequate resources for themselves and thus are at risk of poverty. Social security is therefore a form of redistribution of resources from those who have more than sufficient to provide for themselves to those who do not have enough. The resources redistributed in this way are generally cash, in the form of taxes and benefits, but they can and sometimes do include support in kind, for instance the provision of free school meals to the children of poor parents.

Redistribution can take two forms, as we mentioned in Chapter 2:

- *Horizontal* redistribution is primarily concerned to tackle the life-cycle poverty identified by Rowntree (1901, p. 137) through the provision of benefits to people during periods of need, financed by contributions collected from them at times of relative sufficiency (mainly during employment). In such a model all are potential contributors and potential beneficiaries, and resources are redistributed within society across people at different stages of their life-cycle.
- *Vertical* redistribution operates to redirect resources from those with sufficient to those in need without any expectation of a link between payment and receipt. In this model those in need may never even be in a position to contribute and may require support at any time, and for long periods of time. What is more, those who pay may not expect to benefit from their contributions.

These different forms of redistribution lead to different aims for social security policy and different forms of provision. Horizontal redistribution is by and large the aim underlying social insurance approaches to social security, and vertical redistribution is the aim underlying social assistance; and we shall return to examine these in more depth shortly.

By and large this redistribution has been organised by the state; but redistribution not only takes place through public tax and benefit transfers. Private provision for pensions has been a significant element of redistribution across the life course for some, with private and occupational pensions becoming much more extensive and significant over the last two decades. Private insurance provision can also provide for other forms of redistribution at times of need; for instance, many people now have private insurance cover for their mortgage payments in case they lose their jobs – and public support for this has been reduced as a result of the availability of such private provision. Private protection is also provided by employers for their workers, for instance through sick pay or maternity pay. Indeed employers are required by law to provide such support, at least up to a fixed minimum level.

Redistribution of resources to combat poverty also takes place through charitable giving within the voluntary sector. Such transfers, generally referred to as *philanthropy*, were a major source of anti-poverty policy and practice in the nineteenth century, prior to the development of much state social security protection, as we shall discuss below (see Fraser, 2003, ch. 6). However, voluntary support for redistribution remains significant in the twenty-first century. The major international charity Oxfam has a programme of support for those experiencing problems of poverty in the UK, and high-profile public campaigns, such as Children in Need, continue to promote charitable giving to alleviate poverty.

Redistribution and poverty prevention also takes place informally through transfers of resources within families and across generations. Most children escape poverty because their parents can provide for them, and parental support for children often continues when those children grow up and become young adults. Inheritance of resources from parents when they die is also a major form of informal redistribution of resources within families – at least for some.

Nevertheless it is public provision which is by far the most significant in terms of redistribution of income, with the annual budget for social security expenditure exceeding £100 billion in the early years of the twenty-first century. It is also, therefore, social security which is most effective in preventing or combating poverty. However, it is important to note that combating poverty is not the only aim of social security expenditure in the UK, or in other welfare capitalist countries. There are a range of aims and objectives which have underpinned the development and implementation of social security provision including insuring against risk, supporting family relations and promoting social cohesion (see McKay and Rowlingson, 1999, ch. 1; Walker, 2005, ch. 2). And discussion of the role of social security in combating poverty needs to bear this broader policy context in mind. Nevertheless, combating poverty is a key aim of social security provision, although there is some confusion, and some debate, about what social security should be aiming to do here, and how it should go about doing it.

For a start there is the question of whether social security should be aiming to prevent or to relieve poverty:

- *Prevention* of poverty implies the attempt to ensure that no-one gets into circumstances in which they experience poverty. This means identifying those circumstances where there is a risk of poverty (unemployment or retirement, for instance) and providing social security support to all in those circumstances at levels adequate enough to ensure that they are not poor. This requires a *proactive* role for social security policy.
- *Relief* of poverty means restricting the provision of social security protection to those who are poor, in order to lift them out of, or relieve,

their experience of poverty. This is potentially a more restrictive aim, as only those who actually are poor receive benefits. It also implies a *reactive* role for benefits, paying these only when people have become poor and can prove that they are in need.

Another area of debate over the role of social security policy in combating poverty is the extent to which the goal of benefit provision should be to support or to control those who are poor:

- *Support* for people who are poor, in particular where this is seeking to prevent poverty, implies a positive policy intervention designed to combat deprivation and exclusion and to promote social cohesion.
- *Control* of those who are poor is an altogether more negative goal. It is based on the assumption that the problem of poverty is in part a problem of the people who are poor and that they should be encouraged, or coerced, into self-improvement through the provision of minimal social security support. This is the principle of *less-eligibility*, which under-pinned the nineteenth century Poor Law (see Chapter 1), and it means in particular that social security benefits should not compete with wages in the labour market and that receipt of social security support should be conditional upon a demonstrable willingness to seek security through employment on whatever terms are available.

Some critics of social security have gone even further than this and have argued that the controlling aim of social security is really its overriding function within capitalist societies (Novak, 1984 and 1988; Jones and Novak, 1999; Squires, 1990). Social security provision is minimal, conditional and punitive, they argue, because its purpose is to control 'the poor' and to dis-cipline them into seeking employment. What is more, its indirect aim is to use the example of control in order to impose more general discipline within society, or at least certain sections of it, by ensuring that the experiences of those in poverty are a (less eligible) example of what happens to those who fall outside of the preferred social order.

This is perhaps a rather conspiratorial model of social policy-making and implementation, and it seems to ignore the very real benefits that many recipi-ents of social security provision may experience. For many recipients social security does relieve, or even prevent, poverty. However, control is an element of social security policy operating alongside support, as the administration of the requirement for unemployment benefit claimants (now called jobseekers) to seek employment demonstrates (Deacon, 1976). The aim of social security is not support or control, but *both*.

As an anti-poverty policy, therefore, the aims which underlie social security in Britain are more complex and contradictory than one might expect. They are the product of potentially conflicting goals and they have resulted in different principles and structures for provision; and within these, policies and priorities have shifted over time. Of course this is because social security policy itself has been created through political process, not scientific analysis.

Changes in political power have resulted in changes in the aims behind social security policy and these have fed through into policy development and policy practice. Such changes have ebbed and flowed over time, and generally without the results of previous policies being abandoned or overhauled. Like all social phenomena social security policy is a product of history, not logic; and its aims and achievements in combating poverty must be assessed within that historical context.

The development of state support

Social security policy in modern British society can be traced back to the early seventeenth century and the introduction of the Poor Law in 1601, as we saw in Chapter 1. The Poor Law was a form of locally administered poverty relief providing support, plus discipline, to vagrants and beggars. It was initially a loosely structured system operating within a rural agrarian economy. With the growth of industrialisation it came under increasing pressure, and the 1834 reforms resulted in tighter national control over Poor Law provision and the introduction of clearer elements of labour market discipline.

The most significant element of this discipline was the principle of 'less eligibility' – the requirement that any support provided by the state must be set below the circumstances of the lowest wage labourer in order to ensure that dependence on state support remained undesirable. Linked to this was the assumption of family support – husbands, wives, parents and children were expected to provide mutual support during times of need to obviate the need to turn to the state. These restrictions on entitlement to state support were reinforced by the 'workhouse test', the grim and rigorous residential regime to which only those with no other potential source of support would subject themselves. Life in the workhouse was unpleasant – and it was intended to be. It also attracted fear and stigma. These elements of control were a central feature of early social security provision and, albeit in a less stringent form, they have remained at the centre of social security policy ever since.

Not surprisingly, therefore, the Poor Law was not a popular form of state support among the rapidly growing nineteenth-century working class. In practice it was also unable to provide support for all those who were unable to provide adequately for themselves; and in many areas workhouse provision was supplemented by direct provision of outdoor relief, despite the fact that this was intended to end after 1834. For more established workers, how-ever, even this form of relief was undesirable, or largely unnecessary; and the latter half of the century saw the development of a range of private and voluntary schemes to provide income protection for such workers in times of labour market failure.

Most of these schemes were run by friendly societies or trade unions established within the working class. In return for contributions made during periods of employment they provided income support in times of sickness or in old age (see Thane, 1996, ch. 2). They often based the payment level on past contribution records, thus establishing the broader aim of income protection through benefit protection. Schemes such as these were limited in scope, however, and they were generally confined to particular industries or sections of workers. For the majority of workers, especially low-paid ones, there was no such protection.

By the end of the century additional support was also being provided for some of the increasing number of workers and their families who were poor by a range of charitable ventures organised and controlled on a voluntary basis by concerned members of the middle class. This voluntary provision had a strong philanthropic dimension (Fraser, 2003, ch. 6). Although partly motivated by concern for the deprivation experienced by the new urban working class in Britain's industrial cities, charitable support was also linked to concern for the morality of those who were poor and their attitude to life and labour. Support was thus often accompanied by individual advice and moral pressure to conform to particular middle-class models of 'respectable' family life. In the latter part of the century it was also structured and coordinated by a national umbrella body, the Charity Organisation Society (COS) (Humphries, 1995).

By the end of the nineteenth century, therefore, state support through the Poor Law was operating alongside privately organised self-help and voluntary charitable aid to people in poverty. Provision of both was patchy, however, and, as the research of Booth and Rowntree discussed in Chapter 1 graphically revealed, it had not removed or prevented poverty. Moreover this revelation was accompanied by the growing political and economic strength of the organised working class in the trade unions and the newly formed Labour Party, and by a fear of unrest from the less-organised groups experiencing poverty and deprivation. There was thus increasing pressure on the government to do more to extend and coordinate state support.

By that time, too, Bismarck had introduced social security reforms in Germany, where work-based insurance protection had been set up on a national basis, coordinated and administered by the state, with the intention of relieving working-class needs and political pressure. The existence of this example and the privately organised insurance of the British Friendly Societies combined in the early twentieth century to create the precedents for the introduction of state-based insurance in Britain. As we discussed in Chapter 11, the first of the new benefits introduced (the old-age pension of 1908) was not in fact a contributory insurance benefit. In 1911, however, insurance-based benefits for sickness and unemployment, based loosely on the Bismarck model, were introduced into some industries, where benefits were paid during temporary absence from the labour market in return for contributions made whilst in work.

The intention was that this state insurance support would be actuarially sound and self-financing, there was thus, for instance, a lower rate of benefit for women, who were assumed to be a greater insurance risk because they were more likely to be outside the labour market. After the First World War the scheme was extended to include pensions and a wider range of workers and potential beneficiaries; but as unemployment rose dramatically during the depression of the 1920s and 1930s this became more difficult to sustain. There was pressure on the government to restrict entitlement and cut benefits, leading eventually to the defeat of the then Labour government. Restricted entitlement and increasing unemployment also meant that a growing number of people were forced to continue to rely on the inadequate and unpopular Poor Law.

Despite the critical recommendations of both the Majority and Minority Reports of the Royal Commission on the Poor Law of 1909 (see Thane, 1996, ch. 3), no significant changes had been made to the nineteenth-century scheme in the early twentieth century. It remained in local control and thus subject to local variation. Sometimes this led to relatively generous support, as in the controversial case of the Poor Law Guardians in the London Borough of Poplar (see Hill, 1990, p. 23), but in general provision was meagre. In part because of the controversy over local variation, the Poor Law was converted into a new means-tested Unemployment Assistance scheme in 1934, and later this was in turn converted into the National Assistance scheme in 1940.

Even after these changes, at the beginning of the Second World War social security provision in Britain was a confused mixture of partial insurance schemes and means-tested assistance, with the remnants of the Poor Law underlying the twentieth-century developments. There was need for a radical structural review, and eventually this was provided in the *Report on Social Insurance and Allied Services* by Sir William Beveridge (1942). Beveridge's report was the first thorough review of state support and the role of social security in the alleviation or prevention of poverty, and although it was commissioned by the government, it was in practice largely his own work (Harris, 1977). It also became an international best-seller when it was released in 1942, and remains the only comprehensive official report on social security provision in the UK.

Beveridge's *Report* was based on the general argument that state intervention was needed to tackle the major social problems of British society, and it contained what was in effect a blueprint for the reform of the social security system around the principle that he called *social insurance*. In essence this involved a full state 'nationalisation' of the various insurance schemes developed earlier in the century, some aspects of which had remained under the administration of the Friendly Societies, and the extension of social insurance to provide a comprehensive cover for all circumstances of need arising from non-participation in the labour market. It was a radical proposal, although its aim was to build on the successes of past policy development; and it was very much a product of its time and of Beveridge's own views about the role of social security protection (see Baldwin and Falkingham, 1994; Hills *et al.*, 1994).

The intention of the Beveridge plan was that nearly full employment, sustained by government policy, would provide support based on the labour market for most breadwinners. Their contributions into the scheme during employment could then be used to provide for the payment of benefits during times of sickness, retirement or temporary unemployment. As we saw in Chapter 9, however, Beveridge's plan was based on clear assumptions about family structure and gender roles. Married women, who had duties other than employment, were expected to receive support through their husbands' wages or benefits, and thus even when they were in employment they would be excluded from full participation in the insurance scheme (Lister, 1994).

Beveridge's aim was that through its link to the labour market and family structure the social insurance scheme would provide comprehensive protection for all. This link was central – social insurance was based on support for the labour market, and not simply an attempt to nationalise private self-protection (Atkinson, 1992). There was thus the potential problem of some poor people being excluded from both the labour market and the social insurance scheme, and for them Beveridge recommended the retention of a means-tested social assistance scheme, although he expected that this would have a declining, safety-net role.

After the end of the Second World War the Labour government introduced most of the changes recommended in the Beveridge plan and completely reformed benefit provision – although the scheme was retitled National Insurance (NI) and some adjustments were made to the benefit rates proposed by Beveridge. In order to avoid a situation in which currently retiring pensioners would be excluded from protection because they had not contributed to the scheme, all pensioners were automatically entitled to the new NI pension. This meant that current contributions had to be used to fund these benefits, rather than being invested to meet future benefit liabilities in the way a strict insurance scheme would operate. Thus from the outset the NI scheme was administered on a 'pay-as-you-go' basis, with the current benefit demand being met from current contribution payments; and, as we shall see, this created problems for the long-term viability of the social insurance plan.

Nevertheless, the basic structures of the Beveridge plan dominated postwar British social security provision. There have been reforms within the structure, and in effect a departure from Beveridge's vision of comprehensive insurance protection; but the broad labour-market insurance principle, supplemented by a means-tested safety net, remained the basis of entitlement to most social security benefits, and the main means of alleviating or preventing poverty, throughout the rest of the last century. In practice, however, the comprehensiveness of the insurance scheme was never realised, and the role of means-tested protection rose to become the principle feature of state support (Alcock, 1999) – an issue to which we shall return shortly.

Social insurance

The Beveridge social insurance plan was in part based on the Bismarckian tradition of social reform to support existing social structures. Insurance protection has thus always been closely tied to support for labour market participation and has operated to provide support only in times of labour-market failure (Baldwin and Falkingham, 1994). Beveridge's report was also heavily influenced by Rowntree's research on poverty and in particular his notion of life-cycle poverty within families. If protection could be provided in such periods of high risk of poverty, therefore, social security could operate not just to alleviate poverty, but to prevent it.

Thus the aim of the social insurance scheme was to utilise contributions made through participation in the labour market to build an entitlement to benefit support in times of need. Social security would provide for the horizontal distribution of resources through the state over the life-cycle of its citizens, or rather its workers. This would operate on a collective basis in the NI scheme, but it would be based on individual contributions and individual entitlement. Indeed it was this individual investment in social security that Beveridge felt was its great popular appeal: 'The capacity and desire of British people to contribute for security are among the most certain and impressive social facts of today' (Beveridge, 1942, p. 119).

Despite the appeal of self-protection through contribution, however, the British NI scheme has never operated as a strict form of individual insurance protection. As explained above, in order to prevent existing pensioners from being excluded, since the start of the scheme contributions have been used to fund benefit payments on a pay-as-you-go basis. Thus although all individual contributions, together with a supplement from general taxation, are paid into a separate NI fund to meet benefit expenditure, and to make a small contribution towards the funding of the National Health Service, the resources in the fund are expended each year on current benefit payments, leaving future contributors to fund future benefit entitlement.

This may in practice, and in principle, be a reasonable way of financing benefit expenditure, in effect utilising NI contributions as a form of hypothecated tax for social security. However, it is not what is generally understood as an insurance scheme and it does not mean that each individual's contributions will be available in the future in the form of guaranteed benefit entitlement, as many contributors may believe to be the case. Although since the payment of contributions by employees and employers is compulsory the consequences of this may not be so significant.

However, although NI contributions are not invested to meet future benefit payments, there is nevertheless a link within the scheme between individual contribution and benefit entitlement. In order to sustain the fiction that benefits are paid in return for contributions, and to limit the number of potential claimants on the NI fund, all NI benefits are subject to contribution tests that restrict entitlement to those who have paid the requisite number of contributions during the requisite period of employment. In practice these tests are complex and extremely difficult to understand and administer. They do include special rules for contributions to be credited during periods of unemployment, and for people caring for dependent children or adults to be made exempt from some of the contribution conditions; but in general the contribution rules make entitlement to NI benefits conditional on payment into the fund during long periods of labour-market participation. They thus retain the logic of the labour-market support discussed by Atkinson (1992) and exclude from NI protection those who have not been able to maintain their contributions through paid employment. As levels of long-term unemployment grew in the latter decades of the twentieth century, the size of these excluded groups increased, and the comprehensive appeal of NI further declined (Alcock, 1996).

Beveridge's recommendation, which was incorporated into the original NI scheme, was that flat-rate benefits would be paid in return for flat-rate contributions. All would be treated equally within the state scheme, and those who wanted additional protection could seek it separately through private insurance. He saw no contradiction between the principle of state protection for all and private protection for some, and in practice the development of private provision for pensions and some other elements of social security support have led to the development of a partnership between public and private social security protection, which is now openly promoted by government.

The flat-rate basis for NI benefits was challenged for a while in the latter part of the twentieth century, however, through the introduction of earnings-related supplements to provide higher levels of benefit support for some claimants, linked to the earnings which they had been receiving whilst in employment. These were first applied to short-term unemployment benefit in the 1960s and 1970s, paying a higher rate for the first six months of unemployment based on NI contribution records. This scheme was abolished by the Conservative government in 1980. In 1978 a similar supplement was introduced into pension protection in the State Earnings-Related Pension Scheme (SERPS). This only gave additional payments to pensioners retiring after 1978, however, and did not reach its full potential until 1998. By this time the concerns about the overall costs of state pensions, discussed in Chapter 11, had begun to dominate policy planning and in the early years of the new century SERPS was removed and replaced by an expectation that most future pensioners would take out private provision to supplement their flat-rate state pensions, with a small additional scheme (the Second State Pensions, SSP) retained only for those on low pay and unable to take out such protection. NI provision has thus largely returned to a flat-rate basis.

The changes to NI provision since the 1940s demonstrate most clearly that, whatever Beveridge's intentions or hopes may have been, the insurance scheme has never been independent of other aspects of social security provision or indeed social policy more generally. Although the appearance of a separate NI fund remains, contributions are now collected and managed by the Inland Revenue alongside other forms of tax collection. Given that payment of contributions is both compulsory and automatic it is unlikely that most contributors do separately identify (or identify with) this particular element of direct taxation and its link to benefit entitlement. This was exposed most starkly by the rise in NI contributions introduced by the Labour government in 2001 to pay for increased public expenditure on the National Health Service. Though welcomed by many, this expenditure did not provide for benefits within the NI scheme and the increase in NI contributions was chosen primarily because the government had made an election pledge not to increase income tax and believed that the NI increase would not involve a breach of this.

In practice, therefore, NI is simply one part of a complex social security system, providing benefits without means tests for some claimants in some circumstances. For those who do benefit, avoidance of the means test is a significant advantage, but the low level of benefits and the large number of people excluded from protection mean that NI claimants alone now make up the minority of social security beneficiaries.

Social assistance

Beveridge recommended the retention of a social assistance scheme, actually called National Assistance (NA), alongside the new NI scheme because he recognised there may be some people with an inadequate income who would not be entitled to insurance benefit because they could not meet the contribution conditions, for instance because they had never been able to secure regular employment. He saw assistance operating as a safety net below the basic state provision, and his expectation was that demand for it would be low and would decline as NI expanded.

The basis for entitlement to assistance was the means test. Only those who could prove they had no other source of adequate support would be able to receive state support under it. The means test was to be administered by the National Assistance Board (NAB) and was based on the assumption that married or cohabiting men and women and their children would support each other, although the broader expectation that other family members would provide support in times of need, which had operated in the inter war scheme, was dropped (see Deacon and Bradshaw, 1983, ch. 2).

Unlike the Poor Law Guardians the NAB operated on a national basis, but in many other respects NA introduced in 1948 was a continuation of the Poor Law, which in effect it replaced. Benefit rates were fixed at a minimum subsistence level to avoid these being viewed as an attractive form of support, and in most cases receipt was conditional on submission to tests of labour market potential – adult claimants of working age were expected to be seeking employment. The principle of less eligibility thus continued into the assistance scheme, and with it went the negative imagery associated with dependence on state support for those unable to provide for themselves. Beveridge expected that stigma would accompany dependence on means testing; indeed this was indirectly a desirable feature for it would underline the attractions of the non-stigmatising NI scheme under which claimants had made provision for their support and thus had a *right* to claim benefit.

Assistance benefits were financed out of direct taxation rather than through individual contributions. They transferred resources vertically from those who were (relatively) rich to those who were poor. It was because of this, however, that stringent eligibility criteria had to be included to ensure that only those who were really poor (and deserving) were able to benefit from them. The process of claiming means-tested benefits thus involved intrusive questioning into the circumstances and opportunities of potential claimants in a climate of suspicion that not all who presented themselves for support might necessarily be in need. This legacy has come to create serious problems for assistance claimants as the number of these has grown significantly over the last fifty years.

The stigma associated with dependency on means-tested benefits might have been a more manageable problem had such dependency remained, as Beveridge predicted, at a minor and declining level. This has not been the case however. Although the NA benefits were initially fixed at a minimum subsistence level, below that of NI benefits, they included separate provision for the cost of rent, which NI did not. This was because rent levels fluctuated widely and yet were an unavoidable cost for those with no adequate support; but it meant that even those who were entitled to NI benefits might also be able to claim NA to pay for their rent. There was thus, as we have seen, an inevitable overlap built into the two schemes.

In addition to the overlap between NI and NA there was the problem of those who had not established an entitlement to NI benefits. For such people dependence on assistance was the only means of surviving in poverty, and contrary to Beveridge's expectations the number of claimants needing such means-tested support because of the inadequacies of the NI scheme grew rather than declined in the 1950s. In their research on poverty in the early 1960s Abel Smith and Townsend (1965) found that over one million people had incomes on or below the NA scale.

In the 1960s many of those depending on NA were pensioners; and both Conservative and Labour Governments during this period promised to improve pension provision to prevent the problem of high levels of means-test dependence in old age. For different reasons, however, neither succeeded in doing this; and in 1966 Labour decided instead to reform the still relatively unpopular NA scheme. It was retitled Supplementary Benefit (SB) and put under the administration of a new government body – the Supplementary Benefit Commission (SBC). In practice not much changed, although the SB scheme did include a fixed basic weekly rate that those with an income below this level would now have a right to claim, with extra payments available on a discretionary basis for extra needs.

The idea of the right to benefit was an attempt to overcome one of the major problems identified with means-tested benefits as a source of state support. Payment of them was not automatic, they had to be claimed; and the claiming of means-tested support involved an intrusive and uncomfortable process of questioning. Many were therefore deterred from claiming because of fear of the process, thus reducing the take-up of such benefits by those who needed them. The idea was that creating a right to the basic weekly rate would help to overcome this. After some initial improvement, however, there is little evidence that this was a successful move (see Deacon and Bradshaw, 1983, p. 107).

In the 1960s and 1970s dependence on the reformed SB scheme continued to increase, in particular as unemployment grew and those unemployed for long periods of time exhausted their entitlement to NI support. By the end of the 1970s the number dependent on SB had grown to four million. However, there was also an extension in the scope of means-tested benefits to provide new forms of state support, including Family Income Supplement (FIS), rent and rate rebates, and a range of other specific benefits in areas such as health and education, for instance free prescriptions for drugs, and free school meals for the children of low-income parents.

What these new benefits did was extend the receipt of means-tested support to those within the labour market on low wages. The reasoning behind this was to make paid work more attractive and so combat the problem of the 'unemployment trap' which, as we shall return to discuss below, was caused when income from benefits for the unemployed exceeded the income which could be earned in low-waged employment in the labour market. However, the effect of this extension in means-testing was to broaden significantly the scope of social security protection beyond support only for the unemployed or those otherwise outside the labour market.

Benefit payments for those outside the labour market are in effect a *substitute* for wages, replacing these as a source of income, and potentially competing with wages, as the unemployment trap problem reveals. Paying benefits to those on low pay within the labour market means that these benefits are acting instead as a wage *subsidy*. This is a different role for benefits and leads to a different relationship between social security support and labour market participation. It also leads to a different range of problems flowing from the relationship between wage levels and benefit support, in particular the 'poverty trap' which we shall also return to shortly. This extension of means-tested support has been carried much further since the 1970s, however. As early as 1976 the National Consumer Council was reporting that forty-five different means-tested benefits were operating in Britain (NCC, 1976); and by the mid-1980s over eight million people were dependent on SB assistance. In 1985 the Conservative government introduced a review of much social security provision, including in particular assistance payments.

The review, published initially as a Green Paper in 1985, did not suggest any fundamental reform of social security, but it did underline the central role that means-testing was by then playing in the delivery of benefit protection; and the reforms that followed in 1988 aimed to simplify the structure and administration of all the major means-tested benefits in order to encourage take-up and reduce administrative costs. As in the 1960s this involved some changing of names. SB was retitled Income Support (IS) and FIS became Family Credit (FC), and rent rebates, which had been renamed Housing Benefit (HB) a few years earlier, kept this new title. Critics at the time argued that the restructuring was motivated largely by a desire to cut costs, and that many claimants would lose out as a result of the changes (Berthoud, 1985, 1986; CPAG, 1985). This seemed to be borne out by later research, which showed that in practice the changes involved only a degree of redistribution between claimants, whereby some lost out, rather than a more general increase in the targeting of resources onto those in poverty (Evans *et al.*, 1994).

The main effect of the 1988 changes, however, was to confirm the central role that means-tested support now had within the benefit system; and since then dependence on such benefits has continued to expand. In the 1990s over a third of the population were in receipt of some form of means-tested support, with around ten million claiming IS (Field, 1995); and since then such selectivity has been extended further through the new mechanism of tax credits.

Tax credits

The payment of means-tested support to those in work inevitably raises questions about the relationship between such benefits and the tax liabilities of workers. Given that income tax and NI contributions are paid by those in work, at least when people earn sufficient to cross over the minimum threshold for tax liability, then there may be an overlap between the benefits that they are entitled to receive and the taxes that they have to pay. It is this overlap which is a major cause of the poverty trap, discussed below. It can also lead to complexity and confusion over tax and benefit entitlement and liability amongst potential claimants – and amongst those administering these provisions.

Such complexity and confusion might be solved if the tax and benefits systems were merged into one scheme administered from one government department, which collected tax from those earning enough to be liable and paid back tax to those earning so little that they qualified for support. This has been referred to in the past as moving towards tax credits as a basis for social security. Such a tax-credit approach was considered by the Conservative government of the early 1970s, and in the 1980s was promoted by organisations such as the Institute for Fiscal Studies (Dilnot *et al.*, 1984) and the Adam Smith Institute (ASI, 1984, 1989). At that time, however, such a radical organisational change was felt to be too costly, or too disruptive, to introduce.

Since 1997, however, the Labour government has introduced a range of tax-credit payments, which have taken us some way towards such a re-structuring of social security support. These new tax credits are in fact a replacement for, and extension of, some of the in-work means-tested benefits introduced in the 1970s and 1980s. These benefits, administered then by the Benefits Agency and Department of Social Security, were replaced by tax credits, administered by the Inland Revenue, alongside income tax and NI contributions. This was not a full-blown tax credit reform, as promoted by the ASI and others in the 1980s, however, as both NI and means-tested benefits for those not in paid work remained as separate schemes, administered by the Jobcentres Plus and Pensions Agency, within the DWP. In effect what happened was that support for those in work became tax credits and was placed alongside tax collection in the Inland Revenue, and that benefits for those out of work remained as the separate social security provision it had always been. Much confusion and complexity therefore remained and continued to contribute to some of the problems with benefit administration discussed below.

The pace of development of these new tax credits has also been rapid, and they have come to occupy an increasingly prominent role in providing support for low wages. The main initial reform in 1999 was to replace the old Family Credit with the Working Families Tax Credit (WFTC), which retained the principle of support for families on low wages, but shifted it into the tax system. It also threatened to lead to a change in the recipient of the credit from the child carer (often the mother), who had been the recipient of Family Credit, to the taxpayer (often the father), although in practice families were given a choice over who should receive the credit. However, it was much more extensive than Family Credit, providing support for families up to higher wage thresholds than under Family Credit and so expanding significantly the impact, and the cost, of state support for low pay.

At around the same time the support for disabled people on low wages, the Disability Working Allowance was also converted into a tax credit, the Disabled Persons Tax Credit (DPTC). This was followed by the introduction of a new tax credit to provide support for families who were having to pay child-care costs for young children in order to be able to work, called the Child Care Tax Credit. This new support, together with WFTC, were major elements in the government's strategy for reducing child poverty, discussed in Chapter 11, and have been instrumental in removing significant numbers of children in low-wage families from poverty. They were also central to the government's commitment to promoting moves from 'welfare to work' by making paid employment more attractive – a policy which also involved the introduction of the guaranteed minimum wage and improved support for jobseekers through the 'New Deal' (see Finn, 2001).

In 2003 these tax credits were extended further and were also rationalised into a simpler framework, which replaced all the existing credits with two, with either workers or families with children as the focus for payment. Support for workers became the Working Tax Credit (WTC), paid to all workers over 25 years old working 30 hours a week or more for a period of at least four weeks (a major extension of support), and to all those over 16 years old working over 16 hours a week, who were either disabled or caring for one or more child (in effect replacing WFTC and DPTC). Support for families became the Child Tax Credit (CTC), which was paid at a standard rate to all families up to a minimum wage threshold and then at a gradually declining rate to all those above this up to a maximum level beyond which entitlement tapered out. This maximum level was well above average wages, however, leaving almost a half of families entitled to some support. The support for child-care costs was retained as an additional element to WTC. It provides 70 per cent of costs up to a fixed ceiling; although these are only paid where the child care is being delivered by an approved provider. Child Credits and Child Care Credits are paid to the carer, in an attempt to ensure that this money does reach those with most responsibility for the children and reversing the feared the shift from 'purse to wallet' discussed by Goode et al. (1998). Working Tax Credits are received by employees.

Later in 2003 the government also introduced the Pension Credit, mentioned in Chapter 11. This provided a means-tested supplement to those with private or occupational pensions which excluded them from support under the Minimum Income Guarantee scheme. The credit supplemented private pension income and tapered away at higher levels of income, disappearing entirely above a top threshold. As with WTC it extended means-tested support much further up the income scale for pensioners than had previously been the case.

Since 2003, therefore, a relatively comprehensive system of tax-credit support has been in operation providing a wide range of support to those in the labour market, targeted on supporting low-paid workers, families with children, and pensioners. These credits are far more extensive than the in-work benefits that they replaced, in the case of child-care support extending coverage to large numbers of workers with children. They also provide a significant element of redistribution of resources across the bottom end of the income scale, providing a much greater equalisation of incomes here than would have been the case without their intervention, a point to which we shall return shortly.

However, although the structure of provision and the administration of support through the Inland Revenue have much simplified the tax-credit schemes, the fact that they are still based in effect on a form of means-testing means that many of the operational problems associated with these benefits, which we discuss below, also affect them. What is more, tax-credit provision has not replaced the Housing Benefit or Council Tax Benefit support for these costs, which are administered separately by local government. In-work benefits remain here, therefore, overlapping with entitlement to tax credits for many workers and continuing confusion and administrative complexity – problems that do not apply to benefits provided on a universal basis.

Universal benefits

Universal benefits have sometimes been confused with insurance protection. Although the NI benefit scheme is informed by universal principles, NI benefits are not really universal, because entitlement is dependent on meeting the contribution conditions. Genuine universal benefits should not require qualifying conditions; and the idea of a universal benefit payment has been proposed by some in order to provide a 'Basic Income' for all citizens (Van Parijs, 1992). This has also been described as a 'Citizen's Income'; and a Citizen's Income Trust was set up to promote debate and discussion on it, as can be seen from their website. Providing an income sufficient to meet all individual needs would be a massive undertaking, of course; and more recently the idea of a partial basic income or 'Participation Income', providing only a measure of support to be supplemented by wages or other benefits, has begun to replace these more radical ideas. It was explored by Atkinson (1995b) and was considered by the Social Justice Commission in the 1990s (Borrie, 1994, pp. 264–5), and it was more recently discussed by Harker (2005) in her contribution to a collection of papers on social justice recalling the work of the Borrie Commission.

Beveridge was aware of the basic income principle and, although he rejected it in favour of social insurance for his major benefit proposals, he did propose universal help towards the costs of children through the introduction of Family Allowances. The idea behind Family Allowances was that the state would provide a contribution towards the costs of rearing all children, in part as a recognition of their role as future citizens and workers and to encourage couples to have children, and in part to raise the overall income of families with children and thus reduce the hardship that might otherwise result in households that had low incomes or were dependent on benefits. Because no children had an income and all families experienced similar needs, allowances were paid universally to all. However, the allowance scheme introduced after the Second World War provided only partial support. Allowances were only paid for second and subsequent children and the rate payable was only a contribution towards the weekly needs of a child – a participation, rather than a basic, income for children.

The Family Allowance did introduce a universal benefit into the British social security system, but the level of the benefit fluctuated and it was allowed to fall below its original postwar levels. It was also not the only state support for children; relief against income tax was also available to tax-paying parents. As discussed in Chapter 13, one of the major focuses of CPAG campaigning in the 1960s and 1970s was the growing problem of child poverty in low-paid and claimant families. The CPAG proposed a reform of Family Allowances to tackle this, and after turbulent political debate changes were made with the introduction of Child Benefit (CB) in 1978 (Field, 1982).

CB is a universal benefit paid to the parents of all children, or rather to the nominated carer, usually the mother. It was based on an amalgamation of Family Allowances and the tax relief for children that had been paid under the income tax system, with the latter disappearing; and it also provided support for the first child in all families, massively extending the scope of protection. However, it remained only a contribution towards the cost of rearing children, and the level of this contribution declined further in the 1980s when CB was not uprated in line with inflation as other benefits were. It has remained significantly below the cost of a child as calculated by researchers such as Piachaud (1979). It is also below the weekly rate provided for children in the means-tested assistance schemes, such as Income Support; and those in entitled to such means-tested support have to claim this on top of CB.

In the 1990s levels of CB increased, including a higher level for the first child, although still only acting as contribution to the real costs of children; and at the beginning of the new century tax relief in the form of the Child Tax Credits discussed above was reintroduced. Support for families with children is therefore now, again, a mixture of a basic universal payment (CB) and tax relief, although the latter is targeted on low-income families. This has led to debates amongst policy-makers about the desirability of retaining CB as a universal payment or replacing it with more targeted tax relief. The debate is one of principle as well as practice (not all families are poor, but all children need support and they are a collective investment in our future), and so far the universal basis of support has survived.

Child Benefit is the best-known universal benefit in the UK, but it is not the only one. The benefits for the attendance and mobility costs of people with disabilities discussed in Chapter 12 are also paid on a universal basis, although they affect only a relatively small proportion of the population. What is more, as we have seen, there are problems with both the scope and the operation of these disability benefits. Thus for those who do receive them they play only a relatively minor role in combating poverty amongst disabled people and further add to the complexity of overlapping benefit provisions.

Problems with benefits

Despite its limitations and restrictions, and despite the other goals it often simultaneously pursues, social security remains the main anti-poverty measure in British social policy. In providing state support as either a substitute for or a supplement to income from the labour market, it aims to relieve or prevent poverty by ensuring that claimants and their families have what the government regards as an adequate income. As we have seen, there is much debate and disagreement about whether such an income is indeed adequate to prevent poverty. Benefit levels may not be sufficient to lift many claimants out of poverty, and future anti-poverty policy may need to address this, as Veit Wilson (1998), for instance, has argued. But leaving this to one side, there are nevertheless some serious problems with the implementation of the current benefit system that lead to many people not receiving even the minimum amounts that the system appears to provide – or, even if they are, not benefiting significantly from these.

Many of the problems experienced in implementing benefits flow from the complexity of the social security system itself. As the short summary above reveals, social security support in the UK involves a mix of different types of benefit, aimed at meeting different kinds of income needs and administered by different public agencies – and when private and informal support is included this picture becomes more complex still. Yet these different provisions and processes impact upon the entitlement, and hence the incomes, of individual benefit claimants, many of whom may in practice be receiving a number of these different benefits, administered by different agencies, at the same time. For them the complexity alone is likely to be a major practical problem.

Of course the complexity of benefit systems is in part a product of the different, and even contradictory, aims that social security support is seeking to achieve and the wide range of different people and households it is seeking to support. In this sense it is an intrinsic feature of social security systems. This complexity was the object of an enquiry by the National Audit Office in 2005 and was discussed in a series of articles in the journal *Benefits*, where Spicker (2005) and Millar (2005) in particular argued that much complexity was a product of the policy and structural context of social security. Although as Patterson and Vaux (2005) argued the problem had often been compounded by piecemeal reform and a reactive approach to new challenges to the system, where solving one problem had only served to create another.

All commentators concluded, though, that solving the problem of complexity will not be an easily achievable goal, and 'quick fixes' would only be likely to make it worse. However, the existence of this complexity also gives rise to other problems, which may in practice significantly undermine the ability of social security to achieve whatever goals are set for it, in particular the combating of poverty. For a start, complexity can lead to errors in the calculation of entitlement by benefit administrators. Determining the scale of errors in benefit administration is, of course, difficult to do – how do we know when mistakes have been made? However, official estimates are produced for some means-tested benefits by the DWP. Error rates are likely to be higher for such benefits because of the more complex criteria for entitlement, but nevertheless the figures put the average level of overpayments at 6.4 per cent for Income Support and Jobseeker's Allowance in the period April 2003 to March 2004, a total of around £840 million (DWP, 2004c) – although this was an improvement on the situation in 1997/98 when targets for reductions in errors in processing claims by claimants of working age were set.

Where errors are made in the calculation of benefit entitlement, claimants do have a right of complaint or appeal. In many cases a complaint and request to review the decision, perhaps with additional information, will suffice to change an initial decision. Nevertheless the formal legal right of appeal exists on all entitlement decisions. Appeals initially go to special appeal tribunals, where claimants can present their own case or be assisted by an advisor or advocate, although from these there is the right of further appeal to the courts if legal grounds can be established (see McKay and Rowlingson, 1999, ch. 7). The tribunal service was restructured in the early 2000s and is now run by the quasi-independent Tribunal Appeals Service (TAS), and the implications of the changes are discussed by Dean (2004) and the other contributors to a special issue of *Benefits* focusing on appeals. Social security appeals can contain complex legal questions, however, especially where there is a substantive disagreement over entitlement; and, without the of kind of specialist welfare rights support discussed in Chapter 15, claimants are likely to find it difficult to prosecute their cases successfully.

Most appeals are about underpayments, of course, and estimates of underpayment are not made in the DWP report, although as we shall discuss shortly there is some evidence of benefits not being paid to all of those who might be entitled to them. The estimates of error also include estimates of fraud as a cause of overpayment. Of course benefits, and in particular means-tested benefits, can be the subject of fraudulent claims, but this is itself a complex and even contradictory area. Establishing when and where fraud has taken place is a difficult practical and legal matter. The DWP figures distinguish between fraud and customer error, recognising that in some cases claimants may innocently provide (what proves to be) incorrect information to benefit administrators. This can lead to overpayment, but is not legally actionable because of the lack of intent.

Intentional fraud can also take on a number of different forms. In particular there is a practical distinction between individual claimants lying about their circumstances to receive more benefits and organised criminal conspiracies producing counterfeit girocheques or order books. The latter are arguably much more serious offences, and yet they are not included in the DWP (2004c) estimates of fraud and error mentioned above. For over two decades, however, governments have been concerned about the levels of individual claimant fraud and have set targets for the identification and investigation of fraudulent claims. Here too, of course, the setting of targets and the estimating of levels of fraudulent claiming are in practice only guesses, and distinguishing between incorrect information and criminal intent is not easy, as commentators on the different dimensions of claimant fraud have argued (Dean and Melrose, 1997).

And, despite the relatively high levels of fraud and error identified by the DWP, criminal prosecutions of fraudulent claimants are in fact very rare.

The converse of fraud and overpayment is the problem of underpayment, and from the point of view of poverty relief this is a more serious problem for it is likely to mean that those who are not receiving their full benefit entitlement are living below the state benefit levels and hence at high risk of poverty. Underpayment can arise even when benefits have been claimed due to the errors mentioned above; but more significant is the potential problem of failure to claim, or non-take-up. Only those who identify themselves as poor enough to qualify for benefit, who recognise the potential of benefit entitlement, and who are prepared to undergo the rigorous process of submitting and defending their claim will be assessed for entitlement and receive benefits. Given the complexity of the benefit system in the UK, and the range of means-tested and other benefits available, many may fail to recognise their potential entitlement; and, given the application process and the stigma associated with dependence on means-tested benefits, many may choose not to claim even when they suspect they might benefit. The problem of non-take-up exists with any form of benefit. However, in general, take-up of universal and insurance benefits is high, with Child Benefit, for instance, achieving nearly 100 per cent take-up. Most of the problems of take-up are associated with means-tested benefits, because of the complexity of entitlement and the stigma of dependency. Such non-take-up is also likely to contribute to the risk of poverty, as means-tested benefits are largely targeted directly at those with low (or no) incomes, who without social security support are likely to be poor.

Estimating levels of take-up of benefits, however, is at least as problematic as estimating levels of error and fraud. We cannot know what people who have not claimed might be entitled to. Nevertheless, it is a widely recognised problem with means-tested benefits, which can be found in many benefit administrations – not only in the UK, as the research by Van Oorschot (1995, 1996) has demonstrated. What is more, 'guesstimates' of take-up levels can be made. The DWP also produce estimates of non-take-up for the major means-tested benefits in the UK, using evidence from the Family Resources Survey. In 2002/03 these showed that the levels of take-up of Income Support for non-pensioners were between 85 and 95 per cent by caseload (that is measuring the numbers claiming against the total that might be entitled). For the pensions Minimum Income Guarantee the levels were 63 to 74 per cent, and for income-based Jobseeker's Allowance they were 55 to 70 per cent (DWP, 2005b). These are potentially staggering figures, revealing that in some cases over a third of claimants may not be receiving the means-tested support to which they ought to be entitled; and they suggest some significant short-comings in the anti-poverty role of social security support.

Errors and non-take-up are problems which flow from the failure of the social security system to deliver the benefit support that it is intended to deliver. There is another set of problems, which may also affect the ability of benefits to combat poverty, that flow not from the failings of the system but from some internal contradictory features within it. These problems concern the impact of benefit entitlement, and in particular means-tested benefit entitlement, upon the incentives that claimants are then faced with in any choices that they may have to make between benefit dependency or alternative means of increasing their income. They are discussed in some detail by Walker (2005, ch. 10) under the heading of economic efficiency, and they are usually referred to as the unemployment and poverty traps.

The *unemployment trap* arises, as suggested earlier, when entitlement to means-tested benefits exceeds the wages which an individual or family might expect to get in the labour market. This can happen where wages are low and household needs high, for instance where a wage earner would have to support a spouse and children and pay relatively high housing costs. In such circumstances a claimant may be better-off remaining on benefits than working for a low wage which could lead to a drop in income – sometimes referred to as an insufficient 'replacement ratio' of wages to benefits. Such claimants are trapped in unemployment.

Support for housing costs through means-tested Housing Benefit and in-work benefits for families, such as the Family Credit, were introduced to tackle this problem in the 1970s. By subsidising low wages such support could ensure that even claimants with large families and high housing costs would be better-off in work. This policy was taken much further by the Labour government after 1997 through the more extensive entitlement to tax credits for those on low wages and through the introduction of the statutory minimum wage to raise the floor of low wages for all.

However, this in-work support creates another incentive problem. Payment of means-tested in-work benefits is linked to wage levels, and so such benefits must be withdrawn if wages rise. This means that an increase in wages, for instance due to promotion at work or additional hours, will lead to a loss in means-tested support, reducing the real value of any wage increase. This is what is referred to as the *poverty trap*, because in circumstances where low wages lead to poverty, then people losing means-tested subsidies are likely to be trapped in this poverty.

The poverty trap was first 'discovered' in the early 1970s (Field and Piachaud, 1971) at a time when means-tested benefits for those on low wages were being rapidly extended, and it was discussed in some detail by Deacon and Bradshaw (1983, ch. 8). The means-tested additions to wages then generally provided a proportion of the difference between low wages and the income level fixed in the scheme: in the case of Family Income Support 50 per cent of the difference was paid and in the case of rent rebates up to 29 per cent. If wages rose, these additions were progressively lost, although in the case of FIS the effect was delayed because it was paid for periods of twelve months at a time. In the early 1980s the combined effect of losing 50p of FIS and 29p of rent rebate for each extra pound earned, together with the need to pay income tax, then at 30p in the pound, and NI contributions at 8p, as well as the potential loss of free school meals for children and other benefits, meant that people on low wages faced a 'marginal tax rate' (the amount of income forgone for each extra pound earned) of over 100 per cent. In other words, even if they were able to secure a rise in wages their overall income *fell*.

The reforms to means-tested benefits in 1988 did remove some of the worst aspects of this poverty trap for those on low wages, in particular by removing the problem of marginal tax rates of over 100 per cent. But rates of over 90 per cent remained for some, and the consequence of removing the worst effects for some was to spread the experience of relatively high rates of tax and benefit withdrawal over an even wider range of low wages, creating was became to be called a 'poverty plateau' (Field, 1995). The new tax credit schemes have spread such support over a much wider spectrum of low wages and so extended the impact such high marginal tax rates. As Walker (2005, pp. 208–10) discusses, however, similar patterns can be found in many other welfare capitalist countries; and in practice it is now recognised that such a flattening of real income differentials at the bottom end of the labour market is an inevitable consequence of targeting state support onto low-wage earners – and may even be a desired outcome.

The contradictory disincentive effects of such targeting not only affect those on low wages either. Most means-testing also takes into account the capital holdings of claimants or the interest that accrues on savings above an allowable capital threshold, and entitlement is reduced to take account of the notional income from such holdings. This can affect even those with relatively modest capital investments, and in particular applies to pensioners who have saved up to accumulate capital sums to support them in retirement. Thus there is also a *savings trap* associated with the expanded role of means-tested provision (Walker, 2005, pp. 210–12). The Pensions Credit, introduced in 2003, reduces the sharpest effects of such reductions in support for pensioners, but at the expense of introducing such 'marginal taxation' across a wide range of those with some support from investment incomes.

The problems of error and non-take-up and the unemployment, poverty and savings traps seriously undermine the effectiveness of social security provision in alleviating poverty in a wage-labour economy. They are also a direct consequence of the expanding role of means-testing in the benefits system that has become the dominant feature of social security policy over the last three decades. The apparent attractiveness of linking receipt of benefits to proof of poverty or low income can produce contradictory outcomes in practice because of the failure of many people in need of benefits to recognise or pursue their entitlement to them, and because of the disincentive effects that flow from targeting state support only on those in poverty.

These practical problems, and the confusion over the policy framework for social security from which they result, are major limitations on the ability of social security policy to prevent or relieve poverty; and these limitations have led increasing numbers of commentators and policy-makers to argue that, if combating poverty is to be a policy goal, then other policy initiatives should be pursued that do not rely solely upon the redistribution of cash resources to those who are poor. These arguments are strengthened by the broader, multi-dimensional, approaches to poverty and social exclusion which we discussed in Part II. Anti-poverty policy is therefore about more than just income redistribution and we will examine some of the other approaches now adopted in the next two chapters.

Developing Local Anti-Poverty Action

SUMMARY OF KEY POINTS

- The 'rediscovery of poverty' in the UK in the 1960s led to new central government initiatives to target anti-poverty action onto 'pockets of poverty' in deprived areas.
- Many of these initiatives were modelled on similar developments in the USA, promoted there as part of a 'War on Poverty'.
- These programmes could not do much to reduce poverty levels in local areas and most were discontinued.
- Local anti-poverty action was taken up and developed by local government in the UK in the 1980s and 1990s, sometimes in direct opposition to central government.
- In the 1990s central government support for local action was again introduced, notably through the Single Regeneration Budget.
- Welfare rights work has always been a key feature of local anti-poverty activity, securing significant gains in social security benefits for local people.

Pockets of poverty

For over a century social security provision has been the major plank of anti-poverty policy in Britain. State support through social security is a response to the identification of the structural relationship between poverty, income and the labour market; and the redistribution of resources to substitute for or to subsidise wages from the labour market has been the major policy commitment to prevent or relieve poverty. What is more, in modern welfare capitalist societies social security has become an extensive and expensive policy commitment. At the beginning of the new century social security expenditure in Britain was running at over £100 billion a year, by far the largest item of public expenditure. Without this expenditure it is certain that many people would experience significantly increased deprivation. However, as we saw in Chapter 14, it is debatable whether social security provision has been entirely successful in either preventing or relieving poverty.

The aspiration of Beveridge's (1942) recommendations for the development of social security was that they would remove 'want' from modern British society; and the expectation of policy-makers and researchers was that the postwar reforms which followed from this would achieve such a goal, as Rowntree's final research seemed to confirm (Rowntree and Lavers, 1951). However, as we discussed in Chapter 1, these hopes proved to be misplaced, and poverty, albeit redefined, remained a continuing problem in affluent postwar Britain. Researchers such as Townsend (Abel Smith and Townsend, 1965; Townsend, 1979) 'rediscovered' poverty in affluent Britain in the 1960s; and this led to campaigning and political debate about what should be done about this.

Townsend and others saw improvements in social security protection as one means of responding to the continuation of poverty alongside welfare support. But this was not the only policy option; and in the 1960s major expansion of social security protection was not perceived by many in government as a viable strategy for combating poverty, in particular because of the additional public expenditure costs that such an expansion might incur. Alternative means of responding to the continuing problem of poverty in the midst of affluence, where the reduced resources available might be concentrated more directly on the worst aspects of the poverty problem, thus began to become more attractive to politicians and policy-makers. This also fitted well with other aspects of the rediscovery of poverty in late twentieth-century welfare society.

As we saw in Chapter 2, the academic and political debates about the rediscovery of poverty were also associated with a renewed emphasis on the problem of poverty as a pathological phenomenon in advanced industrial societies, drawing on the 'culture of poverty' thesis developed by Lewis (1965, 1968). Led by politicians such as the Conservative Minister, Keith Joseph (1972), policy-making began to focus on the role of agency and pathology in the creation and recreation of poverty alongside affluence, suggesting that this might be the product of individual apathy and inadequate upbringing – a 'cycle of deprivation' rather than a policy failure (see Denham and Garnett, 2001).

Such a 'blaming the victim' approach, as we saw in Chapter 2, has serious shortcomings; and yet it has been taken up by right-wing commentators such as Murray (1984; Lister 1996) to suggest that public support for poor people should be withdrawn altogether. However, in the 1960s it did begin to provide a framework for the development of a rather different approach towards state policy to combat poverty, which was being developed in Britain and in a number of advanced industrial societies, and which became much more widespread in the latter part of the last century. As the quote from Ryan in Chapter 2 put it, 'define the difference [of those in poverty] as the cause of the problem. Finally, of course, assign a government bureaucrat to invent a humanitarian action programme to correct the difference' (Ryan, 1971, p. 8).

Implicit in this framework is a perception that poverty is caused not so much by the failings of social and economic policy planning, but rather by the inability of people living in poverty to take advantage of the opportunities that such planning already offers. The action programme that is required, therefore, is not an extension of social security support and the further redistribution of resources to those in need, but rather the identifying of people as poor and the use of state support to employ humanitarian professionals to work with them to encourage them to overcome the cultural and economic barriers that are trapping them in poverty. Resources focused on people who are poor should thus be used not to relieve their poverty but to help them escape from it.

This new approach to the focusing, or targeting, of resources was also a response to another dimension of research and policy debate about the continuing problem of poverty in modern society. The new research of Townsend (1979) and others on the experience of deprivation had revealed that income poverty was only a partial feature of the problems which people in poverty experienced. As we discussed in Chapter 8, these broader aspects of social exclusion are now widely identified and debated within academic and policy debate, and they lead to the inevitable conclusion that anti-poverty policies which concentrate only on income redistribution and support are unlikely to be able to address the broader dimensions of deprivation and exclusion.

As we also saw in Chapter 8, there is evidence that these broader problems of deprivation and exclusion are not distributed equally across the geography of modern social structures, but rather have a distinct, and debilitating, spatial dimension. This was also a feature of the rediscovery of poverty research in the 1960s. Deprived environments were identified in particular with run-down inner-city areas in many of Britain's decaying industrial conurbations. Commentators began to refer to the concentrations of poverty and deprivation in such inner cities areas as the problem of 'pockets of poverty', and policy-making began to respond to this spatial dimension by developing new forms of anti-poverty activity.

If limited state resources were to be focused on people in poverty to help them overcome their deprivation and take advantage of the opportunities of modern society, therefore, then the run-down inner-city areas identified by the poverty researchers provided the obvious target for these resources. In pockets of urban poverty the cultural problems of transmitted deprivation across generations were likely to be greatest, but at the same time the opportunities for escape would be close at hand. Professionals working in such concentrations of deprivation could thus influence a relatively large number of people within relatively limited overall costs, and so provide a model for self-help and upward mobility that could then be applied to other poor areas. Geographical targeting thus coincided with pathological perceptions of the problem of poverty to create a climate for a new approach to anti-poverty policy in advanced industrial societies, which was taken up by governments in Britain and elsewhere from the 1960s onwards, and has become the major feature of a wide range of anti-poverty action at the beginning of the twenty-first century, as we shall see in Chapter 16.

The US War on Poverty

It is interesting that the first major anti-poverty programmes of the twentieth century to adopt a spatial focus were to be found in the affluent United States of the early 1960s. In the USA, too, they were the product of the recognition of the continued problem of poverty amidst affluence, pointed out here by social scientists such as Harrington (1962); and the targeted anti-poverty strategies later developed in Britain were influenced significantly by these US initiatives. Indeed, direct attempts were made to learn from and build on the American experiences – for instance, an Anglo-American Conference on policy development was organised by the UK government at Ditchley Park in 1969 (Higgins, 1978). Although, perhaps typically, the initiatives in the United States were rather grander than their later British counterparts; they were presented as part of a broader federal government commitment to the elimination of poverty in modern America.

In 1964, at more or less the same time as the United States was beginning to step up its involvement in the Vietnam War, President Johnson announced the establishment of a 'National War on Poverty', with the objective of 'total victory' in ensuring that every citizen shared 'all the opportunities of society' (James, 1970, p. 65). What this war on poverty represented in practice was federal government funding for locally targeted initiatives in which professionals would work in deprived areas to help people who were poor to take advantage of the opportunities of affluent American society.

The funding for this was not extensive, only $350 million was allocated to the initial programme in 1964 (Piven and Cloward, 1972, p. 257). But it was channelled through a new government agency called, appropriately, the Office of Economic Opportunity (OEO), and it was linked to a new approach towards anti-poverty action captured neatly in the notion of the provision of a 'hand-up' rather than a 'hand-out'. To use some other jargon of the time, the support provided was intended to provide a 'doors, not floors' approach to combating poverty – an emphasis on education and job programmes to encourage mobility through self-help (*doors* out of the cellar of poverty) rather than the provision of additional resources to people in poverty themselves (a raising of the *floors* on which they stood) (see Higgins, 1978, pp. 108 *et seq.*).

This notion of self-help – 'helping the poor to help themselves' in another popular phrase – was closely linked to pathological explanations of the causes of a transmitted culture of poverty and to the geographical targeting of resources on poor urban areas. In the United States this was furthermore overlain with perceptions of the racial dimension of the problem of urban poverty, which was at its worst in inner-city areas with large black populations and high levels of urban unrest. This had been exposed in a high-profile publication on the problem of 'The Negro Family' by Moynihan (1965), a senior official in the Johnson government, which argued that there were close links between 'race' and 'place' in the inner-city ghettos. Part of the not-so-hidden agenda of the OEO programme of anti-poverty work, therefore, was avoidance or control of racial violence and urban protest; and at the time this was criticised for its racism and pathology by contemporary commentators on the US policy debate (see Rainwater and Yancy, 1967).

Most of the resources of the OEO thus went on a range of community action programmes in poor urban areas. They were designed to improve educational provision and job opportunities and to encourage local people in poverty to take advantage of these. Many of the programmes, such as Head Start and the Neighbourhood Youth Corps, focused particularly on children and youth as the logical point at which to seek to break the 'chain' of transmitted deprivation.

There is little doubt that many youngsters in poor American inner-city areas did benefit from some of these community action initiatives. However, there is also little doubt that the initiatives did not succeed in providing 'total victory' over urban poverty. In an extensive overview of the War on Poverty and related US policy initiatives, Marris and Rein (1974) pointed out that the community agencies which were established in the poor ghettos had little power to challenge the local and central power structures within which urban poverty was located; and, what is more, their role in identifying the problems of urban poverty often brought these local agencies into conflict with broader entrenched social and economic interests. Such a conflict, of course, was inevitable – but it was one local activists could not hope to win.

Piven and Cloward (1972), in another commentary on US anti-poverty policy, were even more critical. They argued that, in channelling anti-poverty activity into limited initiatives to provide for the 'urban poor' within existing welfare programmes, the War on Poverty had in practice diverted attention away from any broader structural approaches to welfare problems, and had thus been a diversion from the need for more fundamental social and economic reform. Targeted anti-poverty policy could not, they asserted, operate independently of the more general context of social and economic development, a point to which we shall return in Chapter 16. To some extent in recognition of these inherent limitations, the War on Poverty in the USA was run down and eventually abandoned in the 1970s without any belief that it had been successful in removing poverty from affluent American society. Nevertheless, policy development in the UK in the late twentieth century drew heavily on these American ideals of community action to combat urban deprivation and provide upward mobility out of the cellar of poverty (Alcock, 2005).

Central government initiatives

In Britain in the 1960s the rediscovery of pockets of poverty and the fears of economic constraints on new policy initiatives provided a climate in which government policies to combat continuing poverty began to follow closely the targeting approaches of the American War on Poverty. The first example of such an approach emerged from the recommendations of the 1967 Plowden Report on the transition to secondary education, which proposed the targeting of additional resources to improve schooling in a number of identified priority areas (see Halsey, 1972).

As a result of these proposals the first government initiative on targeting was introduced in the form of the Educational Priority Area (EPA) programme in 1968. Drawing on similar programmes in the USA, the EPA scheme involved the provision of extra resources for primary schools in a small number of poor areas to ensure that educational disadvantage did not reinforce the cycle of poverty for children in these areas. The scheme was run on a small scale in a small number of areas and it lasted for only a few years, but it was subject to high-profile research analysis (Halsey, 1972) and provided a model of targeted government support that was to be taken much further in a range of later initiatives with much wider horizons.

The most extensive and long-lasting of these broader initiatives was the Urban Aid programme, also launched in 1968 and which lasted until the mid-1990s. This, too, involved extra government resources being channelled into poor urban areas in order to help break the cycle of transmitted deprivation. However, Urban Aid money was not restricted to resources for schools, grants could be obtained for any appropriate scheme aimed at neighbourhood-based action to work with local people to combat poverty. The idea was that local authorities and voluntary agencies would propose projects such as community centres, play schemes or remedial education, which would then receive Urban Aid funding and be run on a partnership basis by the authority and representatives of the local community.

Some local authorities were understandably sceptical of the political motivation behind tying additional local funding to designated action programmes; it suggested to the authorities that they were not trusted to use their own resources to support such community initiatives. But the attraction of extra cash for projects in run-down areas was more than most could resist, and Urban Aid grew rapidly to become a major source of support for a range of community-based activities in urban areas. And in the mid-1970s the idea of additional local resources for designated partnership schemes between central and local government and the voluntary sector was extended with the inner-cities partnership programme. This was part of a more comprehensive attempt to harness neighbourhood-based activities in a selected number of city areas (see Berthoud *et al.*, 1981, pp. 273–4).

However, both politically and symbolically, the most important of the central government anti-poverty initiatives of the 1960s and 1970s was the Community Development Project (CDP), which was based very closely on the American Community Action Programme and ran from 1968 to 1978. Indeed, as I mentioned above, the 1969 Ditchley Park conference, to which a number of American commentators such as Marris and Rein were invited, was specifically intended by the senior civil servant in the Home Office behind the CDPs, Derek Morrell, as a forum for importing US policy ideas into the formulation of the UK strategy (see Higgins, 1978, and Alcock, 2005). What is more the CDPs were explicitly intended to operate as a pilot experiment in the utilisation of government funding for community-based action; and, although they were fairly limited in scope and number, they received a great deal of attention from academics and politicians (see Lees and Smith, 1975; Loney, 1983).

The CDPs were a response to a range of overlapping pressures. These included arguments for a more community-based focus in social work; pressure on the government to act on the problem of urban poverty; fears of racial violence and unrest stemming from immigration-law changes and the West Midlands MP, Enoch Powell's, well-publicised attacks on Britain's black population; and acceptance that any new government measures must contain only minimal public spending commitments. Over their ten-year life the CDPs cost little more than £5 million. They consisted of twelve projects in small areas of high unemployment, the largest being Canning Town in London with a population of 42,000, and they were administered directly by the Home Office. Each project comprised professionals recruited to engage in community development work in the area, and a research team linked to a higher education establishment to assess and analyse the success of the project. The research focus emphasised the experimental nature of the projects and they were given a budget to publish their findings. This helped to raise the profile of the CDPs, but it also contributed to their downfall.

As in the American Community Action Programme the thinking that informed the CDPs was the concept of transmitted poverty. As one of the senior researchers put it:

> Poverty and deprivation and consequent multi-problem families and individuals were conceptualised as the problems of a marginal minority who had slipped through the net of welfare, whether through personal or cultural inadequacy or through the services' own lack of co-ordination or administrative failures. (Mayo, quoted in Loney, 1983, p. 49)

The idea was that highly specialised and focused community development could help overcome this marginalisation and restore the residents of the deprived areas concerned to active social and economic citizenship – but the idea backfired.

The newly recruited action and research teams in the CDPs were quickly made aware of the poverty and deprivation in the areas in which they were based. At the same time, however, they also quickly realised that much of this was the product not of individual inadequacy or service malfunctioning, but of wider social and economic policies leading to industrial decline, rising unemployment and deprived local environments (Corkey and Craig, 1978). A handful of professionals with a few resources to support local activities could do little or nothing to counteract these wider forces. Indeed as one of the most famous of the CDP's numerous published reports, the aptly titled *Gilding the Ghetto* (CDP, 1977), pointed out, the mere existence of the project in the area could actually make things worse by confirming its reputation with potential investors as a neighbourhood in serious economic and social decline.

With their research back-up and high-profile publishing strategy the CDPs became a focus of debate on the theoretical and practical contradictions of utilising small-scale targeted resources to challenge large-scale urban poverty. The workers knew that the experiments were doomed to fail, and they said so. After ten years, during which time economic recession meant that in most of the areas the problem had become worse rather than better, an embarrassed government accepted the inevitable and terminated the project.

As with the US War on Poverty, the CDPs were bound to be a temporary experiment – high-profile, targeted activity cannot be sustained for long. What is more, as with the American experiment they were bound to fail to eliminate poverty and social exclusion; these are not simply the product of pathological inadequacy concentrated into a few run-down neighbourhoods. There are therefore inescapable contradictions to be faced when using targeted resources to combat poverty, as we discuss in Chapter 16. However, it would be short-sighted and unjust to conclude from this that the CDPs, and the other targeted initiatives, could achieve nothing in the struggle against poverty.

The CDP action teams included some highly motivated and innovative community development workers. During the ten years of the projects they developed some interesting and original community-based activities, some of which went a significant way towards tackling some of the problems of deprivation faced by local residents. For instance, community workers collaborated with local residents in the establishment of pressure groups, such as tenants' associations that could challenge local housing departments to improve council housing and other amenities in the area. CDP workers in Batley, Coventry and elsewhere worked to develop a welfare rights service with local residents, providing advice and advocacy to ensure that poor people were at least getting the basic state benefits to which they were entitled (Bradshaw, 1975), as we shall return to discuss shortly. What is more, many of these practice initiatives survived the demise of central support for the CDPs and other national targeted anti-poverty programmes, and became key elements in the shift of emphasis in local anti-poverty activity towards local government.

Local anti-poverty strategies

With the closure of the EPAs and the CDPs and cutbacks in other programmes such as Urban Aid, central government support for targeted anti-poverty activity declined significantly in the late 1970s and the 1980s. However, the local focus of programmes such as Urban Aid had also led to the involvement of local government in the development and delivery of targeted anti-poverty action, and this began to develop further as central government involvement waned. When the CDPs were closed, for instance, a number of the neighbourhood centres that they had established were taken over and supported by the local authorities in which they were based.

By the 1980s a Conservative government under Margaret Thatcher with no commitment to anti-poverty action had come to power. Yet at the same time many of the larger urban local authorities had come under the control of left-wing Labour councils who had a very different view of the problems of modern society and the role of public policy in responding to these. What some of these Labour councils wanted to do was to use local authorities as examples to the Thatcher government of the role that public services could play in tackling what they saw as the continuing problems of local poverty and deprivation. Some high-profile councils, such as the Greater London Council, Sheffield and South Yorkshire, even presented this as a form of 'local socialism' and saw it as a direct political challenge to the Conservative central government (see Boddy and Fudge, 1984; Stoker, 1991).

For political as well as policy reasons, therefore, the 1980s saw the beginning of a shift towards local government as the leading supporters and innovators in targeted anti-poverty policy in the UK. In 1984 the CPAG devoted a special issue of its journal *Poverty* to the role local authorities might play in combating local poverty (CPAG, 1984). A range of local welfare rights and take-up initiatives were summarised; and, in a more general discussion of a possible role for local authorities, it has been argued that there were a number of other areas of local services, such as housing, education and transport, where a focus on anti-poverty initiatives might lead to new means of maximising income and improving services for those in poverty.

These new initiatives were not just informed by political commitment, however. In many cases local authorities were keen to discover the range and scale of poverty and deprivation in their local area and to use research evidence on this as a basis for policy development. Many thus commissioned researchers to draw up a poverty audit or a poverty profile for the local area which could inform anti-poverty action. These profiles generally employed a range of indicators similar to the multi-dimensional definitions of poverty and exclusion discussed in Chapter 5 and more recently taken up by central government in their measurement and monitoring of anti-poverty policy. They played a key role in the development of links between local measurement of poverty and exclusion and the implementation of targeted responses to the problems identified. Although, as these poverty profiles were developed locally, there was much variation in the methods employed and the indicators adopted – and hence in the anti-poverty initiatives which followed (Alcock and Craig, 2000).

Overall, however, local authorities did tend to adopt a wide-ranging approach to the problems of local poverty, which embraced indicators of social circumstances and economic opportunities as well as monetary incomes, and often included a strategic approach to the fostering of economic and social regeneration of their local areas. By the end of the 1980s many local authorities had begun to appoint economic development officers and to enter into plans for the redevelopment of the local area in partnership with other agents, such as representatives of private industry and the voluntary sector. In the 1990s this was given further impetus by the shift within local government from a narrow service provider role to a strategic responsibility for 'enabling' the development and coordination of local service provision across a range of sectors (Clarke and Stewart, 1988; Cochrane, 1993).

Towards the end of the century, therefore, local anti-poverty strategies were a core policy commitment in a growing number of local authorities, and were no longer restricted to the left-wing urban centres of the 1980s. At the end of the 1980s Balloch and Jones (1990) conducted a review of local authority anti-poverty initiatives for the Association of Metropolitan Authorities and found that a range of different activities were being undertaken by a small number of authorities. By the mid-1990s this commitment to local anti-poverty initiatives had expanded significantly, with over 140 authorities reporting an involvement in such work, almost half of which had formally adopted local anti-poverty strategies as part of a corporate commitment to combating local poverty (Alcock et al., 1999).

The local anti-poverty strategies of the 1990s include a wide range of local initiatives and activities, such as the welfare rights and benefit take-up work discussed below, policies to reduce or rebate fees and charges for services for those in poverty, assistance for debt support and the development of credit unions lending money at low interest, moves to decentralise and democratise services into poor areas, community development initiatives with local disadvantaged groups, and economic development work to increase local job opportunities. These strategic commitments were also supported by a national agency, the Local Government Anti-Poverty Unit, funded by the Local Government Association, and examples of good practice were reported in a dedicated magazine called *Anti-poverty Matters* (see Alcock et al., 1995; and Alcock et al., 1999).

Towards the end of the 1990s, however, the pattern of political alignments and policy development began to change. The Conservative government under John Major in the early 1990s introduced a shift in the nature of central government support for local economic and social development. This included in particular the City Challenge and Single Regeneration Budget programmes, which provided targeted support for economic and social regeneration in local areas based on partnerships between local government, private industry and local voluntary-sector agencies, and began to displace local authority-led anti-poverty action. And after 1997 the election of the new Labour government led to a significant acceleration in the range and scale of central government support for such local activity.

We shall return to discuss these new local policy initiatives in Chapter 16. Throughout all of the development of central and local anti-poverty action, however, welfare rights work to provide support for citizens to pursue their entitlement to social security and other benefits has remained a key feature of all targeted anti-poverty activity, acquiring a profile and a momentum which has taken it beyond the particular local projects in which it may have been based.

Welfare rights

Welfare rights work started as something of an experiment in some of the CDPs as a way of working with local people within the existing social and economic policy constraints to minimise their deprivation by ensuring that, at the least, residents were getting the basic state benefits to which they entitled. It drew to some extent on similar initiatives in some of the War on Poverty community action projects in the USA. Given the limits of social security support this was not a transformatory achievement, of course, but it did lead to significant gains in the weekly income of some local people. Furthermore it provided an advice and advocacy service that neither the social security offices nor the local legal services had been willing or able to offer.

When the CDPs were closed down in the mid to late 1970s some of the workers carried on this local advisory service from within revamped community-based agencies, often supported then by local government, as we saw above. In the 1980s and 1990s the number of these new advice and advocacy agencies began to grow, in some places building on the national Citizens' Advice Bureau (CAB) network, which had provided local information and advice on a voluntary basis since the Second World War. With local government funding, or with some central government support for the CABs, these local agencies could employ workers as well as volunteers and so could provide a basis for the development of skills and experience in working within the benefits system.

Welfare rights workers thus became specialists in social security law and practice, in most cases better informed and more experienced than lawyers, or than the benefits administrative staff themselves. Such benefits support was also supplemented in many places by the development of specialist agencies concentrating on particular aspects of welfare rights work, such as tribunal appeals, housing cases or immigration law, and sometimes operating on cases referred from local advice centres. These included housing aid centres (McDonnell, 1982) and especially law centres (Stephens, 1990).

Of course one of the reasons for the rapid growth of community-based welfare rights work was the speedily growing problem of low take-up of means-tested benefits discussed in Chapter 14. Wherever agencies were set up they quickly attracted a large number of local enquiries about benefit rights, and they were often able to secure improved take-up, and thus additional resources, for local people. As a form of anti-poverty activity, welfare rights work thus rapidly acquired a momentum of its own, albeit as a result of the twin failures of economic policy and social security delivery. A study carried out by the PSI revealed a rapid growth in welfare rights work and a wide range of activities developed by workers (Berthoud et al., 1986).

The growing number of poor people and the growing dependency on means-tested benefits in the latter decades of the twentieth century also began to be recognised as a contributory factor to the problems experienced by many clients of social service departments (see Hill and Laing, 1979). Recognition that social services, too, may have a role to play in combating poverty by improving benefit take-up began in 1972 when the Manchester City Council appointed a welfare rights worker to its social services department. The idea was that such a worker could provide specialist advice and support in helping social workers to maximise their clients' incomes by improving their benefit take-up. The appointment in Manchester was quickly followed by other welfare rights workers being recruited to other social service departments, and by the development of welfare rights work as a part of the repertoire of social work tasks (Cohen and Rushton, 1982; Fimister, 1986).

In addition to the increasing number of locally based welfare rights workers, there was also a growth in the range of national organisations providing support for local workers and a central focus for the development and dissemination of welfare rights initiatives. These included the NACAB, which rapidly expanded its role in providing local advice agencies with information and training, and the Citizens' Rights Office of the CPAG, which provided specialist support for welfare rights work and annually published comprehensive guides to benefit rights, which were used by all welfare rights workers. There were also specialist bodies providing support for work with particular groups of claimants, such as the Disability Alliance and the Campaign for the Homeless and Rootless (CHAR).

Welfare rights workers were able to secure significant increases in benefits for the many claimants with whom they worked by encouraging them to make detailed claims for items of need specified in the various regulations. However, providing such advice and encouragement to claimants on an individual basis was time-consuming and costly, and so some welfare rights workers began to experiment with ways of providing such information on a broader and more cost effective basis. The first attempt to do this was carried out in 1980 by Strathclyde Regional Council, then the largest local authority in Britain, which mailed to all local residents a card advising them of benefit entitlements under the regulations and inviting them to make a claim by returning the card to the local social security office. The idea was that a large number of people would thus make claims that they would not otherwise have made, which social security offices would then be required to process and, when appropriate, meet – thus massively increasing local take-up. 'Take-up campaigning', as this form of collective provision of welfare rights advice came to be called, was expanded and developed by many other local authorities following this, generally employing more sophisticated and more effective approaches than the blanket mailing approach used in Strathclyde (Alcock and Shepherd, 1987)

Take-up campaigns, like the welfare rights work from which they sprang, were relatively successful in increasing local benefit take-up, and thus combating local poverty. However they were of course only securing for people the relatively limited benefits that the social security system was failing to deliver to them. This was an important gain for those who benefited from it, but it was also in one sense merely a transfer of benefit delivery work from central to local government. This transfer was also extremely patchy in its operation, since although many local authorities did develop benefit take-up initiatives, many did not; and in such areas a large number of people no doubt remained in more serious deprivation. This is a limitation of local anti-poverty action which can only be overcome by broader central government initiatives to combat poverty through strategic intervention. To some extent this is what has been attempted by the Labour government in the UK since 1997. However, as we shall see in Chapter 16, there are still some significant limitations, and even contradictions, within targeted approaches to anti-poverty action, even where these do have the support and coordination of central government.

Area-Based
Initiatives

16

SUMMARY OF KEY POINTS

- Spatial targeting of anti-poverty activity has again become a major feature of central government policy in the UK at the beginning of the twenty-first century.
- This has led to the development of a range of new area-based anti-poverty programmes targeting additional resources onto deprived areas for limited periods of time.
- Political and policy coordination of these initiatives is provided by the Social Exclusion Unit.
- These area-based programmes aim to promote *partnership* working by local agencies and *participation* of local citizens and communities.
- There are inevitable problems in drawing boundaries around areas targeted for anti-poverty action and distinguishing between 'people poverty' and 'place poverty'.
- Setting performance targets for local action can produce perverse effects in particular the pressures for 'early hits' and 'picking winners'.
- Area-based anti-poverty action can lead to a pathological approach that suggests that the local experience of poverty can only be addressed by the actions of local agents, thus underplaying the importance of more generic national and international social and economic forces.

Spatial targeting of anti-poverty action

It is now widely recognised that poverty and social exclusion are not distributed equally across the UK in geographical terms. We discussed in Chapter 8 the increasing focus in recent years on this spatial dimension of deprivation, referred to by the editor of the CPAG book on the subject as the 'social geography of poverty' (Philo, 1995). As we saw in Chapter 15, however, academic and policy concern with the spatial distribution of poverty and the need to develop policy responses to this is not all that new. The identification of 'pockets of poverty' as a basis for central government targeting of anti-poverty activity began in the 1960s and 1970s (see Herbert and Smith, 1979), and the twenty-first century initiatives discussed in this chapter to a large extent can be seen as a continuation of these themes.

Nevertheless, at the beginning of the new century the spatial inequalities which are still being experienced across the UK, and indeed in most other advanced welfare capitalist nations, have become a more significant focus for policy concern, and for policy action within central government. A report published by the Social Exclusion Unit (SEU) in 1998 found that, according to the government's own measure of the spatial distribution of poverty, the then 1998 Index of Local Deprivation, 85 per cent of the most deprived electoral wards in England could be found in just 44 local authority districts (SEU, 1998, p. 16). And in the National Action Plan for Neighbourhood Renewal which followed in 2001, the 88 most deprived local authority districts were identified as targets for specific support from a new Neighbourhood Renewal Fund (SEU, 2001). We shall return to discuss both the Social Exclusion Unit and the Neighbourhood Renewal Fund in some more detail shortly, for they have now become elements in what is in practice a much broader and wider ranging emphasis in policy practice on the spatial targeting of government anti-poverty activity, now generally referred to as *area-based initiatives*.

Part of the basis for these programmes is the improved and extended availability of official spatial measurement of the distribution of poverty and exclusion now provided by the Indices of Deprivation. As we saw in Chapter 8, these now provide evidence of the distribution of deprivation across a wide range of indicators including employment, health and education (DETR, 2000a) and, more recently, crime and environment (ODPM, 2004); and they are the basis on which a more sophisticated targeting of local anti-poverty action can play a major role in informing new policy action.

However, the wide range of targeted anti-poverty activity which has been developed over the last decade or so, and in particular by the Labour govern-ment since 1997, covers a more diverse set of concerns even than this and in practice has not always been based on such robust and detailed analysis of the identification of variations in local needs. To some extent this is because these initiatives themselves have been built on the earlier area-based programmes developed by the previous Conservative central administration, and by both local government and supra-national agencies in the European Commission.

Throughout much of the 1980s, area-based policy action in the UK was focused primarily upon support for economic development through infra structural investment to increase the competitiveness of local industry, in particular in the inner urban areas most affected by the reduction in manufacturing which had been such a stark feature of the economic decline of the late twentieth century (see Deakin and Edwards, 1993). Perhaps the most high-profile of these schemes (literally) was the redevelopment of the docklands area of East London to provide new office blocks for the information technology and communications industries. This did provide an economic boost to East London, but it was not targeted on the inhabitants of the docklands area itself, and in practice most local residents did not benefit from it.

In the early 1990s, however, the focus of Conservative urban policy began to shift away from physical investment to social and economic regeneration within local communities. In 1992 the government introduced a new framework for support for local regeneration through the *City Challenge* programme. Although this did not really provide new resources for local investment it did gear support for urban areas more closely to specific development activities which were required to provide opportunities for local disadvantaged residents and to link such residents into mainstream economic activity (Blackman, 1995, pp. 50–5). What is more, City Challenge funding was allocated after a bidding round in which local projects had to demonstrate what they were planning to achieve for local residents, and then report on success in meeting these goals.

This competitive bidding framework and external monitoring of outputs and outcomes were carried forward into the much larger local regeneration programme which replaced City Challenge, the Single Regeneration Budget (SRB). The aim behind this was to seek to ensure coordination of targeted funding for development activity into specific local projects with time-limited funding over a number of years, tied to agreed activities and outcomes aimed at securing social and economic regeneration for the residents of disadvantaged areas. SRB funding was much more extensive than City Challenge. Its remit extended beyond inner urban areas (although most funding remained concentrated here), and it provided support for a wide range of local projects many of which provided for investment in education, housing or environmental improvement in poor local communities (Mawson *et al.*, 1995). The SRB was evidence of a significant break from the infrastructural and entrepreneurial investment programmes of the 1980s, and it was initially taken up and developed by the Labour administration after 1997.

The Labour government did not just maintain the SRB, however. They were also influenced by the local government anti-poverty initiatives of the 1980s and 1990s which we discussed in Chapter 15, and by the EU-funded programmes for local regeneration and anti-poverty action which we discussed in Chapter 4, in particular the 'Poverty Programmes' and the Observatory on Social Exclusion (see Room *et al.*, 1993; and Robbins *et al.*, 1994). Since the Lisbon Conference in 2000, all EU member nations have formally committed themselves to drawing up and regularly reviewing National Action Plans on Social Inclusion, and this formal commitment as well as the practical policy initiatives which have flowed from it have been significant factors in shaping Labour's approach to the targeting of anti-poverty and social inclusion activity.

Area-based programmes

As a result of all of these influences area-based programmes have now become a major element of UK government anti-poverty activity. On taking power in 1997 Labour confirmed that they would continue with the support being provided to the existing local projects agreed under the SRB. Following this they further developed the programme, extending the annual round of applications, expanding the range of projects supported, and removing the competitive bidding basis for project approval. By the beginning of the new century the SRB had become a £5.6 billion programme supporting around 900 local schemes across England. The devolution of powers to Scotland, Wales and Northern Ireland meant that support for such programmes in these countries was now determined outside Westminster, but in practice all the devolved administrations have continued with such programmes on a similar basis to those in England, although in some cases taking these further with new forms of anti-poverty action. Within England, too, management of the SRB programme was later devolved to Regional Development Agencies, and it has since then been phased out and replaced by regionally determined support for local regeneration activity.

The government also introduced a range of other targeted development programmes soon after taking office. Within the first year they established three separate *Action Zone* programmes for Education, Employment and Health. The policy focus of each of these was different, as were the funding arrangements and organisational frameworks, with some operating on a relatively small neighbourhood basis and others crossing a number of local authority districts. But the basic principles were much the same; additional resources were provided for an agreed set of activities within a defined geographical area. The purpose of the activities was to combat the higher levels of deprivation and exclusion known to be experienced by residents there, in particular by 'bending' mainstream services to meet better the needs of residents who were poor. This involved developing new forms of partnership working between existing services agencies and improving participation in service development and delivery by local people – referred to as 'joined-up' policy action.

The Action Zones, and the other area-based programmes which followed, were all subject to policy evaluation by academic researchers; and the expectation was that this would help to provide evidence of how to promote local social inclusion and reform public services, which could then be taken up and applied more generally across the country – echoing to some extent the evaluation research linked to the CDPs in the 1970s. There was an expectation in government that policy development could, and should, be based upon evidence of how existing policies were actually operating in practice – referred to as a concern to establish 'what works'. Although, as we shall discuss shortly, the research evidence, both from the 1970s and from the new area-based programmes, has been far from unequivocal in its assessment of the successes of the geographical targeting of anti-poverty activity.

The Action Zone programmes were also established as time-limited interventions. In part this was a matter of resources; the government was not prepared to commit additional funding to such diverse and uncertain activities on a permanent basis. But in part it was also a product of the experimental nature of the initiatives. Over a period of years it was hoped that the partnerships and participation developed would lead to improvements in the development and delivery of mainstream services, in particular in combating poverty and social exclusion, so that the earmarking of additional resources for extra activities would no longer be necessary. Again, as we shall see shortly, concerns have been expressed both by commentators and by participants over the ability of such initiatives to achieve such radical change over relatively short periods of time. Yet in practice some of the programmes did indeed have relatively short lives, with the Health Action Zones, for instance, being wound up after only four years and the resources involved transferred to the service budgets of mainstream NHS agencies (Barnes *et al.*, 2005).

Nevertheless the Action Zones were followed by other area-based programmes also focusing on different aspects of the broader dimensions of social exclusion as now perceived by government. The most popular and successful of these was *Sure Start*. This provided resources for the development of a range of activities with preschool children and their parents in areas where levels of deprivation and low educational achievement were known to exist. The principle behind the programme was that disadvantage at the beginning of people's lives could have a long-term debilitating impact on their prospects and that investment in improved support for very young children could be critical in combating future social exclusion.

Sure Start was popular with parents and children in part because of its scale. By 2004 there were 524 local schemes affecting 400,000 children and benefiting around 30 per cent of those under 4 living in poverty (SEU, 2004, p. 43). It was also providing services valued by users, which largely did not exist before, such as play schemes and toy libraries; and, as a result of this, the Sure Start services are now planned to be expanded to a much wider range of local areas. This will extend services, but it will also spread resources more thinly and will be a significant move away from the targeted approach on which Sure Start was founded, another dilemma in the area-based approach to which we shall return a little later.

Following on from Sure Start a similar programme was developed focusing on school-age children, the Children's Fund, which also adopted the additional funding, time-limited and area-based approach to policy intervention, but which did not last as long as Sure Start. To these can be added the New Deal for Communities (NDC) and the Neighbourhood Renewal Funds (NRF) which we will discuss below. Together with other smaller targeted programmes focusing on issues such as community safety, crime prevention and environmental improvement, these now make up a considerable policy commitment to area-based action from central government.

This commitment, and the broad policy principles which lie behind it, are now formally recognised by government, who have established a Regional Coordination Unit (RCU) within the Office of the Deputy Prime Minister to provide political overview of, and policy guidance upon, area-based action. There is also a website dedicated to these area-based initiatives (ABIs), as they have come to be called, maintained by the RCU, which lists around fifty different programmes and other initiatives. However, the rapid expansion of such a wide range of area-based programmes has itself led to operational problems. Inevitably, given the principles behind the targeting of initiatives on areas of relatively high deprivation, the result has been than these local areas often have projects supported by several different programmes all operating at the same time, drawing on the same partners, and affecting the same citizens. In a review of local partnership working in public services Sullivan and Skelcher (2002, p. 225) commented that 'congestion' of initiatives was being experienced by both citizens and service providers.

This led the government to initiate a review of ABIs in 2000 (RCU, 2002), which recognised the plethora of different schemes in operation in some areas and recommended the closure of some (for instance the Health Action Zones) and the merger of others. Nevertheless, most have remained in operation and now play a major role in the broader commitment to combating poverty and promoting social inclusion through spatial targeting. Critical within this renewed commitment to local anti-poverty has been the Social Exclusion Unit, established by the government within a year of coming to power in 1997.

The Social Exclusion Unit (SEU)

The SEU was established at the beginning of 1998 as a result of the direct initiative of the Prime Minister himself. It took the form of a new inter-departmental unit working directly to the Cabinet Office, as we saw in Chapter 8. This ensured that it had both high political profile and the influence to bring other government departments into collaboration, although since then it has been transferred to the Office of the Deputy Prime Minister and now is part of the coordinating work of the RCU. As with most of the agencies and programmes discussed in this chapter its remit was restricted to England, with the devolved administrations in Scotland, Wales and Northern Ireland now free to pursue their own policies in this area – although in practice similar and in some cases further reaching approaches to area-based action and inter-departmental collaboration have been developed in these other administrations too.

The purpose of the SEU, according to the statements on its website, were 'to co-ordinate and improve government action' and 'to focus on areas where it can add value and address long term causes' – or, to coin the Prime Minister's words at its launch, to develop joined-up solutions to the joined-up problems facing the country's poorest communities. But its remit was specifically one of collaboration and additionality; it was not intended to focus on issues which were of interest to single government departments or to duplicate work being done elsewhere. It thus had a small budget and a skeleton staff, drawn from public servants transferred from other departments and public agencies.

What is more, given the wide-ranging and multi-dimensional nature of the problem of social exclusion, as we discussed in Chapter 8, the SEU had an almost limitless scope for promoting activity. Thus it was decided to focus its concern onto a series of specific social problems, identified as priorities by government. These have included amongst others rough sleepers, truancy and school exclusions, teenage pregnancies and young runaways. Most significantly, however, one of their earliest priorities was the problem of the 'worst estates', those neighbourhoods where problems of deprivation and social exclusion were most acute.

Their report on this spatial concentration of exclusion was published in 1998, appropriately entitled *Bringing Britain Together* (SEU, 1998); and, in a review of the 44 local authority districts with the highest concentrations of deprivation, it concluded that, whatever measures of deprivation were employed, there were poor neighbourhoods, and that over the past decade or so these had been getting poorer. There was a problem of the spatial concentration of social exclusion, therefore, and something ought to be done to address this through specific initiatives to promote regeneration in these neighbourhoods.

As a result of this the government established a new programme to target regeneration resources onto deprived neighbourhoods, called the New Deal for Communities (NDC), echoing the title of the New Deal for the unemployed which had also recently been established. The NDC was a relatively long term programme, with £2 billion committed over a total of ten years. It was focused closely on relatively small geographical areas, some comprising only a few thousand people, with high levels of deprivation. It was also a relatively small-scale programme with only 39 project areas selected (17 in the first round and a further 22 a year later). And, like the other ABIs it was subject to an ongoing evaluation run by academic researchers.

In many respects, therefore, the NDCs were similar in scale and scope to the Community Development Projects of the 1970s, which we discussed in Chapter 15. It may be that the policy activists and the academic evaluators can learn some valuable lessons about the achievements and the limitations of neighbourhood-based action from studying the outcomes of and the commentaries on these earlier programmes (Alcock, 2005). However, as we shall see shortly, one of the key messages of these earlier programmes was that achieving any significant improvement through regeneration and social inclusion in these areas would take time. This is recognised in the ten-year period of support for the NDCs, but it means that so far the official (and indeed unofficial) response to questions about the effectiveness of the NDCs is that it is too early to say.

Neighbourhood renewal

These concerns over the long-term scale of local anti-poverty action have not prevented the development of other initiatives to target resources onto neighbourhood-based regeneration in the early years of the twenty-first century, however. Following on from their initial report in 1998, the SEU produced two papers outlining the need for a broader strategic plan for neighbourhood renewal in England (SEU, 2000 and 2001). These led to the development of a further commitment of resources for targeted social action through the Neighbourhood Renewal Fund (NRF), which involved the allocation of around £900 million to the 88 most deprived local authority districts over a three-year period from 2002, to be spent on designated local action projects designed and developed within the local area and overseen by the RCU within the Office of the Deputy Prime Minister.

The range of activities that could be supported by the NRF was thus a wide and varied one, and one of the key roles played by the RCU was in publicising the different initiatives supported and reporting on good practice in project design and development, including through a regular glossy newsletter called *Inclusion*. The RCU also provide advice and guidance on the establishment and management of area-based action more generally. Central to this advice is the importance of the 'joining-up' of local agencies in *partnerships* to promote and support local action. This was given a structure and a formality through the requirement on the 88 NRF districts to establish Local Strategic Partnerships (LSPs) to coordinate and monitor renewal activity in their area (DETR, 2000b). Other local districts were also encouraged to establish LSPs to coordinate local regeneration activity. Many did so, and support for this has been taken further in the promotion of single local management centres as a forum for coordinating area-based action in all localities.

Partnership is therefore a key theme in central government guidance on and support for local anti-poverty and social inclusion activity, and public service provision more generally (Hudson *et al.*, 1999). Partnership working covers a wide range of different forms of communication, coordination and collaboration, however, and includes a wide range of different partners such as local authority departments, health trusts, voluntary organisations, and even private commercial firms. Some partnership working is long-term and strategic, for instance in the health and social-care field. But much of the partnership working linked to the NRF and other ABIs is short-term and instrumental, linked to meeting programme specifications to access support for local project work; and it is far from clear that policy-makers and practitioners have thought through the complex contextual problems of turning the high ideals of partnership into good practice in the real world, in particular given the plethora of such initiatives now affecting these local areas mentioned above (see Sullivan and Skelcher, 2002).

Alongside partnership in neighbourhood renewal is the requirement, too, to seek *participation* of local residents and communities in the development and delivery of local anti-poverty action. This has also become a central theme of ABI action. Early guidance to the NDCs stressed the importance of including residents and community groups (DETR, 1999, p. 7), and the guidance on LSPs pointed out that 'attention should be given at an early stage to ensuring that all sections of the community have the opportunity to participate' (DETR, 2000b, para. 2.20).

The importance of participation flows in general from the shifting balance between structure and agency within anti-poverty action more generally, as we discussed in Chapter 3. Involving local citizens in local action both addresses the need to promote social inclusion through activating local agents and ensures that the local projects that are established are those most likely to meet the needs and priorities of local people. However, the implementation of participation itself is also far from a simple matter of energising and activating citizens to take a voice and a share in local policy-making.

For a start there is the question of deciding which citizens and what communities should be participating in local action. All citizens cannot get involved in everything, and clearly some citizens are more likely to get involved in some activities than others. The policy-makers do appear to recognise the need to avoid participation by 'the usual suspects' (DETR, 2000b, para. 2.20), but quite how the most marginalised and excluded individuals are to be included and empowered, at the expense in practice of the more articulate and concerned, is not a simple problem to resolve.

What such participation would certainly require is a commitment to develop the capacity of marginalised citizens and communities to take a more active role in their local social affairs, and indeed to develop the capacity of local officials to work with local citizens in these new ways. However, building such capacity, as with other dimensions of local anti-poverty action, is a long-term challenge; and here the contradictions between immediate action and long-term change are more acute. Participation is required to ensure that local people are included in policy action and yet the long-term aim of the policy action is the social inclusion of marginalized individuals and communities. As Alison West, from the Community Development Foundation, put it in a report on the NDCs in *The Observer* newspaper on 7 July 2002, 'The real problem was that the money came first and then the capacity building was supposed to take place. It was the wrong way round – it was trying to make people run before they could walk'.

The contradiction between long-term investments and short-term activity is only one of a number of structural problems within area-based policy action. The commentators on the anti-poverty programmes of the 1960s and 1970s commented on a number of other contradictory tensions facing local anti-poverty action (Eyles, 1979; and see Alcock, 2005); and many of these problems continue to affect the ABIs developed in the new century, as we shall now discuss.

The limitations of local action

The most obvious difficulty inherent in any area-based approach to anti-poverty action is the problem of where to draw the boundaries around local action. Spatial targeting means that some local areas will receive additional resources and additional activities, and others therefore will not. Whatever the advantages of this in principle, there are likely to be problems in practice in determining where to draw the lines around the geographical scope of local action.

There is a broad political dimension to this. There is the issue of the measures of deprivation that should be used to determine the allocation of additional resources and what, if anything, local areas who would like to benefit from such support can do to seek to access these – sometimes referred to as 'post-code politics'. There is also the more practical question what happens to those just across the boundary line, and to what extent they can, and should, benefit from the resources being targeted onto their neighbours.

More generally still there are the difficulties of drawing comparisons between, and making decisions upon, the comparative merits of different sorts of geographical areas. In particular this has involved a debate about the differing needs and priorities of urban and rural areas in determining the allocation of support for area-based action. Since the earlier initiatives of the 1960s and 1970s, area-based anti-poverty action has tended to be targeted on the urban (and often inner city) areas where experience of deprivation is most heavily concentrated. However, to some extent this concentration is a product simply of the greater density of urban living. Poverty is experienced in rural areas too, but here, inevitably, it is more dispersed and hence less likely to be recorded in spatial measurement of deprivation.

Rural poverty has frequently therefore been overlooked in area-based poverty action. As we discussed in Chapter 8, this is compounded by some of the particular features of rural poverty such as geographical isolation, lack of access to public transport, poor local services (both public and private) and limited employment prospects. These can be important dimensions of social exclusion in rural areas, and yet they are much less likely to be problems in urban areas. Where they do not feature in the criteria for determining and responding to area-based poverty and deprivation, then they are likely to result in rural areas missing out on such targeted activity.

Of course, this raises the more general problem of those people in poverty who do not live within the areas with high concentrations of deprivation. Many people in poverty do live in areas of high deprivation, but most do not – the problem of the 'ecological fallacy' which we discussed in Chapter 8. In targeting anti-poverty activity onto such areas, therefore, area-based programmes will inevitably be 'missing the target' in many cases. For instance, the Sure Start programme, which targets resources onto areas containing 30 per cent of the under-four-year-olds experiencing poverty, is therefore in practice failing to benefit 70 per cent of under-fours who are poor. A more sophisticated analysis of this problem was developed, as we saw in Chapter 8, by Powell *et al.* (2001), who argued that a distinction should be drawn between 'people poverty' and 'place poverty'.

People poverty was the deprivation and exclusion experienced by individuals, such as unemployment, low income, poor health and so on. *Place* poverty was the poor environment, infrastructure and services to be found in certain local areas. These different approaches to the problem lead to different measures of deprivation and different policy responses and to the identification of different areas or targets for policy action – and yet much area-based action in practice confuses or conflates the two. This distinction also reveals that many dimensions of the poverty and exclusion experienced in poor areas are not particularly products of the local area or amenable to improvement within it. Area-based poverty is not always a product of area-based problems; and, as we shall see shortly, this is part of a more general limitation within the targeted approach to anti-poverty policy action.

In addition to these boundary problems there are a number of other contradictory tensions within area-based anti-poverty policy which have also created significant practical problems for the ABI programmes and the projects funded under them. In particular, these are associated with the expectation that targeted investment will lead to real improvements for local people, and the concern to ensure that these improvements are identified and evaluated as part of the more general commitment to discover 'what works' in policy development. These are understandable and laudable goals, but they can have unintended and contradictory effects.

The concern to identify and evaluate the achievements of targeted activity has increasingly begun to take on a formal dimension within ABI programmes through the setting of targets for projects and the development of indicators against which achievement of these targets can be measured. For instance, projects may be established to provide training and work experience for local unemployed people; and for this, targets of the number of training programmes created and the numbers of job placements secured need to be established and indicators agreed for measuring the number of people success-fully completing these. The achievement of some targets may also take some time, since even establishing new training programmes can be lengthy process; and so progress towards targets may also be measured by the setting of 'milestones' to identify and quantify interim goals.

Targets, indicators and milestones have become key features in the manage-ment and administration of many of the new ABI programmes (Alcock, 2004c). In practice they draw on broader shifts within the management of public services towards the measurement and management of performance against agreed criteria, and as such have been broadly welcomed by both academics and practitioners. However, they can have the effect of steering the concern of both managers and practitioners within services towards the meeting of targets and milestones, rather than a more general commitment to service effectiveness and improvement. And this can even operate to restrict, rather than open up, policy practice – when the target of (say) two training programmes each recruiting twenty local people has been achieved then there may be a tendency to say 'job done'!

What is more, there may even be indirect pressure upon programme developers and project managers to be cautious in setting relatively unambi-tious targets, because these are more likely to be met and this would mean that the project is more likely to be seen as a success in meeting its targets – good news for the managers and practitioners. Although in practice not much would have been achieved through the attainment of such 'soft targets' – bad news for local people perhaps. Of course, the use of such soft targets can be challenged and more ambition encouraged; but the structure of performance indicators inevitably provides an incentive towards caution and narrow thinking, which may be counterproductive for area-based policy activity more generally.

Linked to the problem of soft targets is what some commentators have referred to as the pressure for 'early hits'. ABIs are by and large based upon the targeting of additional resources onto deprived areas for a limited period of time in order to combat poverty and promote social inclusion; and they are generally doing this in the context of target-setting and evaluation. Policy-makers and politicians will inevitably, therefore, wish to see evidence that their investments are paying off and that targets are being met. Projects need to produce identifiable results, and what is more they may need to do this quickly to reassure policy-makers and politicians (and ultimately of course taxpayers) that money is being well-spent. These sponsors of local action are thus looking for early hits – evidence that something has been done.

The problem here is that pressure for early hits can contradict with the long-term timetable for achieving social change, which all commentators argue is needed in the deprived areas on which most ABI action is concentrated. In principle many policy-makers and politicians also recognise the need for long-term investment for long-term change, as can be seen in the ten-year commitment to the NDCs. However, they may also feel themselves under pressure to justify investments sooner rather than later, in particular within a democratic structure that includes near-annual local government elections and four or five-yearly general elections. Politicians might want to be patient in principle, but may find this hard in practice, and this can be translated into pressure upon ABI project managers and practitioners to achieve early hits, as the quote above from Alison West in *The Observer* newspaper revealed.

Project managers and practitioners seeking to hit targets and under pressure for early results may also come under another contradictory pressure – the tendency to want to 'pick winners'. If it is likely to take more time, and indeed more resources, to bring about major improvements in the lives and life chances of the most deprived and excluded people within project areas, then it may make sense to target activities on those citizens or communities where change is easier to achieve. This can be compounded furthermore by the pressure to aim for participation in project planning and delivery. Those most likely to participate may be the more articulate and committed local citizens (the 'usual suspects'), and they could have a vested interest in promoting activities from which they, and others like them, are most likely to benefit. Conversely those most deprived and most excluded may never get around the participation table and may not feature in the priority targets and early gains.

Across a number of dimensions, therefore, the political, financial and operational pressures which ABI programmes inevitably face may be likely to reduce their ability to target activity onto the most acute and most intractable problems of local poverty and social exclusion – despite the fact that, in principle, this is exactly what they were initially established to do. This is not to suggest that the soft targets and early hits may not in themselves be significant steps in the combating of poverty and the promotion of social inclusion. Just as in the earlier area-based anti-poverty programmes of the 1970s discussed in Chapter 15, there is much in the way of social and economic improvement that has been, and continues to be, achieved by the many project activities targeted onto deprived districts and neighbour-hoods, as the publicity now found in government websites and newsletters reveals. For instance, welfare-rights activity continues as a key focus of local anti-poverty action and continues to secure real gains for poor local citizens. Early gains are still real gains; but they do not mean more cannot, and should not, be done.

However, there remains a broader underlying tension, or contradiction, at the centre of area-based anti-poverty action, which was pointed out by many of the critics of the earlier twentieth-century programmes and remains as a feature of current ABI activity. In simple terms this is the problem of pathologisation, or 'blaming the victim' as identified by the US commentator Ryan (1971) in the quotation at the end of Chapter 2.

The ABI programmes encourage local citizens and communities to participate in local activities designed to improve local services and regenerate their local areas because this will ensure that future provision reflects local needs, and through the process of empowerment will make local people active agents in their own social improvement. This means that citizens should no longer be the passive recipients of services designed and delivered by others, and through the empowerment which they experience from this their capacity to shape their social world more generally will be enhanced. Within a policy context in which, as we discussed in Chapter 3, the role of agents in changing their social world is recognised to be an important dimension of anti-poverty action, the empowerment of local agents through area-based action appears to be an unqualified good.

However, the expectation that local citizens can be, and should be, the agents of local regeneration can suggest that this is so because it is they who are the authors of their current misfortunes. This can pathologise local poverty as a problem of, and for, local people; and it can direct attention away from the broader structural context of national policy and economic trends, which in practice may be the major factors leading to local poverty and can impose severe constraints on any local attempts, however valiant, to combat this.

This was pointed out rather sharply in one of the best-known publications by the CDP researchers in the 1970s, *Gilding the Ghetto*, published by the inter-project team (CDP, 1977). This took its title from an 'off-the-cuff' remark by a Home Office civil servant in 1969 that the CDPs might in practice operate to provide a diversion from the broader structural problems besetting Britain's areas of deprivation. The paper argued, in similar themes (though more Marxist language) to the work of Ryan (1971) in the USA, that, 'the problem experienced by the working class can no longer be explained as a marginal problem of the inner city and the blame put upon the inadequacies of the people living there' (CDP, p. 63); and that, 'the Poverty Programme ... was not developed in order to solve or alleviate *their* problems, but to help the state to meet its problems in dealing with these people' (*ibid.*, p. 64, emphasis in original). In short, they were there to put some gilt on the ghettos, but no more.

It is unlikely that politicians and policy-makers in the new century would subscribe to such an overtly pathological model of social change. However, in a more covert form it is an ever-present danger in the shift towards agency-based local policy practice. In particular, for instance, the insistence on local solutions to local problems can suggest that all such problems and solutions are locally based, and therefore not the concern or the responsibility of larger national institutions or agents. In the case of broader economic forces (such as those leading to the closure of local employers) or of broader public service shortcomings (such as lack of health or social care places) this is clearly not so. Yet achieving change in private industrial investment or public spending on health and social care is not a solution which is open to local agents, no matter how capable and active they become.

Two of the leading commentators on the US anti-poverty programmes of the 1960s, Clark and Hopkins (1968, p. 256), concluded that:

> deprivation in many areas ... may not be responsive to programmes of amelioration and community action. The problems of poverty cannot be resolved as if they were isolated from the wider economic, social and political patterns of the nation.

This is an obvious criticism, and one which would probably be shared by most of the more recent politicians and policy-makers promoting area-based action in the new century. It is also the case that the UK government's broader approach to the problems of poverty and social exclusion does recognise the need to promote and support changes in national service delivery and effective economic growth and investment.

The area-based policy programmes of the twenty-first century do not operate in isolation from, or even in contradiction to, other more general commitments to combating poverty; and, to this extent, some of the lessons from the earlier initiatives do seem to have been learned. However, the inevitable tendency for local responses to local problems to pathologise the victims of social exclusion and suggest that it is they who must be the authors of local solutions, and the agents who deliver these, remains as an ever-present tension within targeted approaches to social exclusion. And when judgement is finally passed on the achievements of the new ABI programmes in combating poverty and promoting social inclusion in the UK, it will be important to continue to bear these inherent limitations on local action in mind.

Poverty, Inequality and Inclusion

17

SUMMARY OF KEY POINTS

- Policies to combat poverty and social exclusion have been informed by changing discourses on the role of social policy in society.
- The Strategy of Equality is a redistributive discourse focusing upon changes in social structure; but it has never been fully embraced by government in the UK.
- The Strategy of Inequality is a moralistic discourse focusing on people in poverty as the agents of change, and aiming to promote economic growth to reduce poverty; but there is no evidence that it has succeeded in achieving this in the UK.
- The Strategy of Inclusion is an integrationist discourse focusing upon support for those who are excluded, underpinned by improved public services; but without significant support for redistribution it is unlikely to be able to combat poverty in twenty-first-century UK society.

Combating poverty and exclusion

Throughout this book we have argued consistently that poverty is a problem and that academic and political concern with poverty has been predicated upon the assumption that something should be done in response to this problem. Poverty is identified and measured in order to provide a basis for anti-poverty policy; and as we have discussed, the disagreements over both definition and measurement are inextricably intertwined with disagreements over the policies that should or should not flow from these.

Our understanding of poverty therefore involves recognition of the political context of the problem and the links within this between definition and policy. As we have seen, however, understanding poverty also involves understanding the broader context of the inequality and exclusion within which it is situated. Poverty is the unacceptable face of broader inequalities; and although they may not be aimed at producing equality, policies to combat poverty must also seek to change the wider patterns of inequality, even if only minimally. What is more, material poverty is only one aspect of the broader social structures and processes within which some individuals and social groups experience marginalisation, disadvantage and social exclusion; so policies that aim to combat poverty must also aim to challenge the structures and processes that accompany it.

Poverty and anti-poverty policy are thus conceived within the wider context of social and economic trends and political and policy debate. As we have seen throughout this book, there are different ways in which this context has been perceived and hence different policy practices and priorities have flowed from these. To adopt sociological terminology, there are different *discourses* of poverty and anti-poverty policy. In a book on social exclusion policy, Levitas (1998) provided a useful classification of these discourses into three contrasting approaches, which she identified by their acronyms – RED, MUD and SID:

- RED is a redistribution and egalitarian discourse, which focuses on social justice and social rights and promotes the policies based on structural redistribution to reduce inequality within society.
- MUD is a moralistic discourse, which focuses on the problems of the underclass and dependency. It emphasises the role of individual values and behaviour in the creation of poverty and social exclusion and promotes policies based upon encouragement or exhortation of those who are poor as the agents of their own integration.
- SID is a social integrationist discourse, which focuses upon exclusion as the context in which poverty is created and recreated and promotes policies which seek to address this by encouraging and supporting social inclusion, in particular through paid employment.

Levitas summed up the discourses by suggesting that they could be distinguished in particular by what it is they conceive those who are poor as lacking – money in RED, morals in MUD and work in SID. This classification is a crude one, of course, but, as we discussed in Chapter 8, it has been taken up and discussed by a number of other commentators on poverty and social exclusion in recent years, including Lister (2004, pp. 76–8). It also provides a framework within which we might seek to differentiate the broad shifts in the focus of anti-poverty policy within the UK over the last fifty years or so and thus make some sense out of the fluctuations that can be identified in both the aims and the achievements of policy-makers and politicians.

The strategy of equality

The Fabian campaigners, such as Sidney and Beatrice Webb, who sought to promote the politics of poverty in the early twentieth century, were aware that the prevention of poverty and the achievement of social reform required a concerted strategy by government to secure greater equality within British society. Evidence of the problem of poverty was used by Fabians to persuade governments to act to prevent it, but the actions the Fabians championed were intended to produce wide-ranging reform through the extension of state provision of welfare to improve the overall standards for all in society. Their aim was not just the elimination of poverty, but the redistribution of wealth and resources to achieve social justice through public welfare. Theirs was a RED discourse in socialist terms, too, and it was shared by other prominent academics and politicians outside the fairly narrow utilitarian perspective of Fabian politics. These included in particular influential writers such as Tawney (1931) and Marshall (1950).

Tawney was a Christian socialist who saw the struggle against poverty in moral as well as practical terms. He believed that greater equality could be achieved by state action to extend welfare in order to minimise the privileges enjoyed exclusively by the rich and raise the standards of the bulk of the population. He did not think that absolute equality was either achievable or necessarily desirable and he believed that all had a duty to contribute to the welfare of society as well as to benefit from it; but his belief in common values and common standards for all people led him to argue for state welfare as a means of reducing differentials and eliminating deprivation. Although they were not intended to produce an egalitarian social order, therefore, Tawney referred to the development of welfare policies through the state as a 'strategy of equality'.

The main focus of Marshall's work was the development of citizen-ship within society. He argued that as industrial society developed then the rights of citizens within it became more extensive, thus creating greater social cohesion. He argued that *civil* rights of freedom of speech and of property had developed in the eighteenth century, and that *political* rights in the democratisation of public power had developed in the nineteenth century. In the twentieth century, he argued, citizenship should be extended to include *social* rights to welfare, security and economic participation, and this would be achieved by the development of a welfare state granting social rights to all citizens and by reducing social divisions. Marshall saw this as leading to 'an equalisation between the more and the less fortunate at all levels – between the healthy and the sick, the employed and the unemployed, the old and the active, the bachelor and the large family' (Marshall, 1950, p. 56). Thus like Tawney he saw in the achievement of social citizenship a strategy to reduce inequality by guaranteeing minimum standards through state welfare.

Both Tawney and Marshall's ideas were taken up by Beveridge (1942) in his proposals for social security reform in the context of the broader provision of state welfare at the end of the Second World War; and in large part these provided the basis for the reforms implemented after the war by the Labour government under Attlee. The postwar reforms did much to fulfil Marshall's hopes of social citizenship, and they did much to translate Tawney's strategy of equality into a wide-ranging reform of the whole social and economic order. Despite the change to Conservative governments in the 1950s the basic structure of the welfare state was maintained throughout the decades following the war, and politicians from both major parties pledged support for its aims and achievements (see Glennerster, 2000).

What is more, the public welfare measures of the postwar period did achieve a redistribution of resources within British society. In the second half of the last century public spending on welfare services rose significantly and operated to transfer resources towards the less well-off, reducing overall levels of inequality (see Hills, 2004, chs 6 and 8). However, these reforms did not remove inequality or poverty. As we have seen poverty was 'rediscovered' in welfare state Britain in the 1960s, and since then levels of inequality have even increased, in particular following the economic recession and high unemployment of the 1970s and 1980s.

By the 1970s there was a widespread view that, even under Labour governments, the strategy of equality had not succeeded in combating poverty in modern British society (Townsend and Bosanquet, 1972; Bosanquet and Townsend, 1980). However, as Hindess (1987) later pointed out, such criticism was really based upon a misplaced belief that such a strategy had ever really been at the heart of social policy planning in the UK over that time. Equality had not been achieved, he argued, in part at least because it had never been overtly attempted; and this itself was in part the product of a lack of political consensus over the desirability of the redistributive discourse. In the 1980s this lack of consensus became much clearer when government began to champion a very different approach to the problems of poverty and welfare reform.

The strategy of inequality

Criticism of the failings of the welfare reforms of the postwar period did not just come from left-wing Fabian commentators such as Townsend and Bosanquet. There were also voices on the right who, following on from the early arguments of Hayek (1944) that state welfare would inevitably conflict with economic freedom, maintained that welfare reforms could not succeed in removing poverty and raising the living standard of all in society. These criticisms were articulated most widely in Britain by members of the right-wing think-tank, the Institute of Economic Affairs (see Green, 1990); but they were also taken up by some prominent Conservative Party politicians, such as Keith Joseph (Joseph and Sumption, 1979) and Rhodes Boyson (1971).

In general terms the right-wing critics argued that state welfare had an inevitable tendency to push the overall cost of public expenditure beyond the limits a market economy could afford. This was because a wide range of state welfare activity providing services for large sections of the population would naturally become expensive when seeking to meet more and more needs; and yet in the absence of any overall assessment of the broader impact of this, it would continue to receive popular support for such expansion. The problem was, they argued, that such activity could not continually expand without endangering overall economic growth – as was revealed by the economic recession in Britain in the 1970s, as a result of which public welfare expenditure had to be curtailed.

Some critics, such as Murray (1984) in the United States, went further than this, however, arguing that redistributive welfare spending also destroyed the incentives that individuals would otherwise have to provide for themselves and their families, and instead that it provided 'perverse incentives' for them to remain dependent on further state support. This notion of the creation through state welfare of a 'dependency culture' had been central to Rhodes Boyson's earlier criticisms of the welfare state, which 'saps the collective moral fibre of our people as a nation' (Boyson, 1971, p. 385), and to Secretary of State John Moore's speech attacking the poverty lobby and the notion of relative poverty in 1989, quoted in Chapter 1. In these views in particular the key features of Levitas's moral underclass discourse (MUD) can be found.

The conclusions the moral underclass academics and politicians drew from these failings within state welfare were not just that public welfare expenditure needed to be curtailed in times of recession in order to support economic growth, but also that redistributive policies that resulted in increased welfare dependency should be withdrawn, or redrawn, in order to reduce, or at least minimise, the extent of the dependency culture. This led to an increased unwillingness to support state welfare expenditure and to calls for the transfer of welfare services to the private or voluntary sectors leaving only a residuum of those who could not afford self-protection to depend on reduced, and targeted state support. The consequence of these conclusions in policy terms was an attempt to reverse the strategy of equality and the growth of state welfare expenditure in order to support market-led economic growth and to provide incentives for self-protection which would itself, it was argued, encourage further growth.

In Britain in the 1980s the Thatcher governments did attempt such a strategy, at least to some extent. Their aim was to reduce state expenditure by reducing state dependency and encouraging private protection through the market. Of course the cuts in state expenditure that resulted from this and the reduction in tax rates, aimed especially at creating incentives for the rich, resulted in the increased inequality and polarisation discussed in Chapter 2. Nevertheless the government believed that this would lead to greater overall economic growth, and that the benefits of this would 'trickle down' to those in poverty at the bottom. A rising (economic) tide, it was argued, would lift all of the boats.

In practice, however, not much did trickle down to those in poverty in the 1980s and early 1990s. As the government's own figures on the changes in the real value of incomes over this period revealed: whilst average incomes rose by 38 per cent and those of the wealthiest 10 per cent increased by 62 per cent, the incomes of the bottom decile of the population *declined* by 17 per cent (DSS, 1995). Not all of the boats were raised; and what is more the tide was not as high as the free-market proponents of such an approach to economic growth had anticipated. Indeed by the early 1990s Britain was in the grip of another economic recession, with unemployment again passing the three million mark; and yet in contrast other Western European countries, such as Sweden and Germany, had achieved growth rates equal to or better than Britain's without equivalent retrenchment of welfare policy.

Nevertheless it is arguable that the right-wing critics were successful in Britain in the 1980s in persuading the Thatcher governments to attempt such a policy reversal and to institute a 'strategy of inequality', the aim of which was to use economic growth supported by free-market policies, rather than redistributive welfare spending, to raise overall standards – neatly encapsulated by Joseph and Sumption's (1979, p. 22) assertion that, 'You cannot make the poor richer by making the rich poorer'.

In one sense of course Joseph and Sumption were clearly wrong. In the short run at least, redistribution does raise the living standards of those in poverty, whereas the trickle-down policies of the 1980s did reduce them, and contributed to broader problems of exclusion and polarisation. And by the mid-1990s Britain seemed to be experiencing the worst consequences of both economic recession and welfare retrenchment, recording the highest increase in inequality and poverty amongst the developed nations, with the exception of New Zealand (Hills, 1995, p. 65). The strategy of inequality also appeared to have failed, and in 1997 the election of the new Labour government created the opportunity for a further shift in the discourse, and the policies, on poverty in the UK.

The strategy of inclusion

On reflection we may conclude that both the strategy of equality and the strategy of inequality were ill-conceived. They were never really achievable, and in practice were never really pursued – in large part because they were based on an over-simplified view of the complex and multi-dimensional nature of poverty and the interrelationship and interdependence of public welfare and economic development in modern welfare capitalist countries. As we have seen in this book, poverty is a multi-dimensional phenomenon which needs, and has led to, a wide range of different policy responses going beyond redistribution or self-sufficiency. And, as most informed commentators now argue, public welfare is not an alternative to market-based economic growth, nor an impediment to it, but an intrinsic feature of how modern economies can, and do, grow (see Esping Andersen, 1990 and 1996; Goodin *et al.*, 1999).

In a classification of approaches to welfare reform and social justice similar to that developed by Levitas, the Commission on Social Justice (Borrie, 1994, pp. 95–6) established by the former Labour Party leader, John Smith, distinguished three different approaches to the future politics of poverty:

- A *Levellers'* Britain, in which social justice is pursued independently of economic production through the redistribution of wealth and incomes, without attention to increasing opportunities and competing in world markets.
- A *Deregulators'* Britain, in which markets are freed of all regulations and dynamic entrepreneurs open up new businesses and where 'the rich' get richer, but 'the poor' also get poorer as social inequalities inevitably grow.
- An *Investors'* Britain, in which the ethics of community are combined with the dynamics of the market and economic prosperity is pursued through the extension of opportunities and the securing of social justice.

As can be seen, these are rather pejorative descriptions of the three different approaches and leave little doubt as to which the Social Justice Commission saw as most desirable. To some extent they identified the former two with past failings of old Labour governments and the Thatcherite Conservative regimes, and argued that a future Labour government should aim to develop a new and different approach based on their third dimension.

Although there has not been much reference to the Social Justice Commission since the mid-1990s, in fact the Labour governments since 1997 have followed many of their prescriptions for policy reform. In particular they have openly championed a *Third Way* for social and welfare policy. This has been based upon seeking to secure an appropriate balance between the different roles of the state and the market in delivering economic development and social justice (see Powell, 1999 and 2002), and upon promoting a new model of 'progressive universalism' in which improved public services for all are supplemented by targeted support for those identified as being poor or in need.

As we have seen in Part IV of this book in particular, this Third Way has also included both the redefinition of the problem of poverty itself to embrace the broader and multi-dimensional notion of social exclusion, and the development of new policies towards both social security and targeted anti-poverty action, which seek to combine both encouragement and support for agents in improving their life chances as well as structural reforms to redistribute resources and improve public services. The current government have sought to combat poverty by promoting social inclusion, in particular through encouraging and supporting paid employment and through promoting participation and activation of all citizens. They seem, therefore, to have embraced the social inclusion discourse (SID) and to have seen this as the most effective and desirable response to the problem of poverty, which they have accepted continues to blight twenty-first century Britain.

As we saw in Chapter 14, the Labour government's reforms of social security have been focused in particular upon promoting employment and encouraging a mixture of self-reliance and state support to meet the future risks of fluctuating incomes. And, as we discussed in Chapter 16, their development of area-based programmes to combat social exclusion has been based in large part upon the promotion of participation of communities and citizens in the development and delivery of the services that should improve their lives and reduce their risk of future deprivation. In all cases the aim has been to balance both structure and agency and to seek inclusion, rather than equality, as the core goal of policy.

Such a Third Way for welfare and anti-poverty policy has certainly transformed the policy landscape in the UK, although similar developments have been taking place in other welfare capitalist nations both in North America and in Europe. Indeed they have been openly encouraged by the EU in their requirement in 2000 that all member-nations establish and monitor National Action Plans on Social Inclusion, and these may become more influential on policy development, at least within Europe, in the future.

However, it is far from clear that this has, or will, deliver a successful challenge to the poverty and social exclusion that still remains in the UK, and elsewhere, at the beginning of the new century. As we have argued earlier in the book employment can never be a route out of poverty for all those who experience it, and yet there has been less emphasis in recent policy debate on what can, and should, be done for those who are not able to enter the labour market, or remain in it. Furthermore, the agency-based approaches of much targeted anti-poverty action will be likely to leave behind some of the most deprived and marginalised agents who cannot, or do not, embrace the empowerment and participation that is apparently on offer to them.

Perhaps the most significant shortcoming within this social inclusion discourse, at least in the form that it has largely taken so far in anti-poverty policy, is its focus upon those who are poor and excluded as both the victims and the agents of poverty and exclusion. This is understandable; policies to combat poverty must address those in poverty. But, if this is all that they do, then they run the risk of identifying the problem of poverty with people who are poor (as did the pauperism of the nineteenth century), and of focusing concern with social exclusion on the excluded rather than the excluders. Exclusion is a two-way process, and a policy of social inclusion would need to change the context and the practices of the individuals and institutions that exclude some citizens as well as the people who are excluded by them. It may also need to embrace some aspects of the strategy of equality championed almost a hundred years ago by Tawney (1913), in order to continue to recognise that (in his words quoted in the Preface), the problem of poverty is a 'problem of riches' too.

Useful Websites

Government websites

www.dwp.gov.uk Department for Work and Pensions, most government documents and statistics relating to social security and anti-poverty policy centrally can be found here under publications.

www.rcu.gov.uk Regional Co-ordination Unit, the government unit based in ODPM which co-ordinates local and regional policy including ABI and contains policy documents relating to these.

www.rcu.gov.uk/abi A specific section of the RCU webpages focusing on area-based initiatives.

www.socialexclusion.gov.uk Social Exclusion Unit, summaries the work of the Unit and policy documents and government research reports on carried out within its remit.

www.statistics.gov.uk The website for the Office of National Statistics, the government national statistical service, contains all official statistics and survey reports, including the decennial Census.

www.scotland.gov.uk The website for the Scottish Executive, the devolved government for Scotland, gives access to different Departments through a topic guide.

www.scottish.parliament.uk The website for the elected Parliament in Scotland with details of recent business and debates.

www.wales.gov.uk The website for the National Assembly for Wales, gives access through an index to the activities of different Departments and national policy initiatives.

www.nics.gov.uk The Northern Ireland Assembly and Executive is suspended at the time of publication; but this website gives access to the Government Departments operating in the Province.

International agencies

www.oecd.org Office for Economic Co-operation and Development, statistics and other research on comparative social and economic trends across the member countries in the developed world.

www.crop.org Comparative Research Programme on Poverty established by the International Social Science Council.

www.globalpolicy.org/socecon Global Policy Forum, A UN observatory with an extensive archive of comparative social policy materials.

Independent research and policy agencies

www.citizensincome.org The Citizens' Income Trust, promoting debate on social security reform and in particular the proposals for the introduction of a Citizens' Income in the UK.

www.cpag.org.uk Child Poverty Action Group, reporting on campaigning and welfare rights activity and poverty research, policy briefings and summaries of new statistics.

www.ifs.org.uk Institute for Fiscal Studies, copies of recent research and briefing papers on equality, tax and other social issues.

www.ippr.org.uk Institute for Public Policy Research, left-leaning think tank, containing policy papers and briefings on topical issues.

www.jrf.org.uk Joseph Rowntree Foundation, copies of research findings from the extensive range of research projects funded, including many on poverty and anti-poverty policy.

www.npi.org.uk New Policy Institute, copies of recent research and briefing papers on topical policy issues, including annual monitoring of poverty and social exclusion indicators.

www.psi.org.uk Policy Studies Institute, copies of recent research and briefing papers on social and economic policy issues.

www.poverty.org.uk The most up to date general website for statistics on poverty and social exclusion, maintained by the NPI and supported by the JRF.

www.york.ac.uk/res/fbu Family Budget Unit, copies of research and briefing papers from the research programme on budget standards carried out by academics at the University of York.

References

Abel Smith, B. and Townsend, P. 1965, *The Poor and the Poorest*, G. Bell & Sons.

Acheson Report 1998, *Independent Inquiry into Inequalities and Health*, Stationery Office.

Adam Smith Institute (ASI) 1984, *Omega Report: Social Security Policy*, ASI.

Adam Smith Institute (ASI) 1989, *Needs Reform: The Overhaul of Social Security*, ASI.

Adelman, L., Middleton, S. and Ashworth, K. 2003, *Britain's Poorest Children: Severe and Persistent Poverty and Social Exclusion*, Save the Children/Centre for Research on Social Policy.

Ahmad, W. and Atkin, K. (eds) 1996, *'Race' and Community Care*, Open University Press.

Alcock, P. 1996, 'The Advantages and Disadvantages of the Contribution Base in Targeting Benefits: A Social Analysis of the Insurance Scheme in the United Kingdom', *International Social Security Review*, vol. 49, no. 1, Geneva.

Alcock, P. 1999, 'Development of Social Security', in J. Ditch (ed.), *Introduction to Social Security: Policies, Benefits and Poverty*, Routledge.

Alcock, P. 2003, *Social Policy in Britain*, 2nd edn, Palgrave Macmillan.

Alcock, P. 2004a, 'Participation or Pathology: Contradictory Tensions in Area-Based Policy', *Social Policy and Society*, vol. 3 no. 2.

Alcock, P. 2004b, 'The Influence of Dynamic Perspectives on Poverty Analysis and Anti-Poverty Policy in the UK', *Journal of Social Policy*, vol. 33 no. 3.

Alcock, P. 2004c, 'Targets, Indicators and Milestones: What is driving area-based policy in England?', *Public Management Review*, vol. 6 no. 2.

Alcock, P. 2005, ' "Maximum Feasible Understanding" – lessons from previous wars on poverty', *Social Policy and Society*, vol. 4 no. 3.

Alcock, P., Beatty, C., Fothergill, S., Macmillan, R. and Yeandle, S. 2003, *Work to Welfare: How Men become Detached from the Labour Market*, Cambridge UP.

Alcock, P. and Craig, G. 2000, 'Local Poverty Profiles and Local Anti-Poverty Work' in J. Bradshaw and R. Sainsbury (eds), *Experiencing Poverty*, Ashgate.

Alcock, P. *et al.* 1995, *Combating Local Poverty: The Management of Anti-Poverty Strategies by Local Government*, Local Government Management Board.

Alcock, P. *et al.* 1999, *What Counts, What Works? Evaluating Anti-Poverty and Social Inclusion Work in Local Government*, Improvement and Development Agency.

Alcock, P. and Shepherd, J. 1987, 'Take-up Campaigns: Fighting Poverty Through the Post', *Critical Social Policy*, issue 19, Summer.

Amin, K. and Oppenheim, C. 1992, *Poverty in Black and White: Deprivation and Ethnic Minorities*, CPAG/Runnymede Trust.

Atkinson, A. B. 1969, *Poverty in Britain and the Reform of Social Security*, Cambridge University Press.

Atkinson, A. B. 1983, *The Economics of Inequality*, 2nd edn, Oxford UP.

Atkinson, A. B. 1989, *Poverty and Social Security*, Harvester Wheatsheaf.

Atkinson, A. B. 1990, *A National Minimum? A History of Ambiguity in the Determination of Benefit Scales in Britain*, WSP/47, STICERD, LSE.

Atkinson, A. B. 1991, *The Development of State Pensions in the United Kingdom* WSP/58, STICERD, LSE.

Atkinson, A. B. 1992, *Social Insurance*, WSP/65, STICERD, LSE.

Atkinson, A. B 1995a, 'Comparing Poverty Rates Internationally: Recent Studies in OECD Countries', in A.B. Atkinson *Incomes and the Welfare State: Essays on Britain and Europe*, Cambridge UP.

Atkinson, A. B. 1995b, *Public Economics in Action: The Basic Income/Flat Tax Proposal*, Clarendon Press.

Atkinson, A. B. 1998, *Poverty in Europe*, Blackwell.

Atkinson, A. B., Cantillon, B., Marlier, E. and Nolan, B. 2002, *Social Indicators: The EU and Social Exclusion*, Oxford UP.

Atkinson, A. B. and Hills, J. (eds) 1998, *Exclusion, Employment and Opportunity*, CASEpaper 4, STICERD, LSE.

Atkinson, A. B. and Sutherland, H. 1991, *Two Nations in Early Retirement?: The Case of Britain*, WSP/56, STICERD, LSE.

Auletta, K. 1982, *The Underclass*, Random House.

Baldwin, S. and Falkingham, J. (eds) 1994, *Social Security and Social Change: New Challenges to the Beveridge Model*, Harvester/Wheatsheaf.

Balloch, S. and Jones, B. 1990, *Poverty and Anti-Poverty Strategy: the Local Government Response*, Association of Metropolitan Authorities.

Bane, M. and Ellwood, D. 1994, *Welfare Realities. From Rhetoric to Reform*, Harvard UP.

Barclay, Sir P. 1995, JR *Foundation Inquiry into Income and Wealth*, vol. 1, Joseph Rowntree Foundation.

Barnes, H. and Baldwin, S. 1999, 'Social Security, Poverty and Disability', in J. Ditch (ed.), *Introduction to Social Security: Policies, Benefits and Poverty*, Routledge.

Barnes, M., Bauld, L., Benzeval, M., Judge, K., Mackenzie, M. and Sullivan, H. 2005, *Health Action Zones: Partnerships for Health Equity*, Routledge.

Barrett, M. and Macintosh, M. 1982, *The Anti-Social Family*, Verso.

Barry, B. 2002, 'Social Exclusion, Social Isolation, and the Distribution of Income', in J. Hills, J Le Grand and D Piachaud (eds), *Understanding Social Exclusion*, Oxford UP.

Beck, U., 1992, *Risk Society. Towards a New Modernity*, Sage.

Beckerman, W. and Clark, S. 1982, *Poverty and Social Security in Britain Since 1961*, Oxford UP.

Beechey, V. 1987, *Unequal Work*, Verso.

Bennett, F. 2005, *Gender and Benefits*, Working Paper Series No. 30, Equal Opportunities Commission.

Bennett, F. and Roberts, M. 2004, *From Input to Influence: Participatory Approaches to Research and Enquiry*, Joseph Rowntree Foundation.

Beresford, P. and Croft, S. 1995, 'It's our problem too! Challenging the exclusion of poor people from poverty discourse', *Critical Social Policy*, issue 44/45, Autumn.

Beresford, P., Green, D., Lister, R. and Woodard, K. 1999, *Poverty First Hand: Poor People Speak for Themselves*, CPAG.

Berghman, J. 1995, 'Social Exclusion in Europe: Policy Context and Analytical Framework', in G. Room (ed.), *Beyond the Threshold: The Measurement and Analysis of Social Exclusion*, Policy Press.

Berthoud, R. 1985, *The Examination of Social Security*, Policy Studies Institute.

Berthoud, R. 1986, *Selective Social Security: an Analysis of the Government's Plan*, Policy Studies Institute.

Berthoud, R. 1998a, *The Incomes of Ethnic Minorities*, ISER, University of Essex.

Berthoud, R. 1998b, *Disability Benefits: A Review of the Issues and Options for Reform*, Joseph Rowntree Foundation.

Berthoud, R., Benson, S. and Williams, S. 1986, *Standing up for Claimants: Welfare Rights Work in Local Authorities*, PSI.

Berthoud, R., Brown, J. and Cooper, S. 1981, *Poverty and the Development of Anti-Poverty Policy in the UK*, Heinemann EB.

Berthoud, R. and Gershuny, J. (eds) 2000, *Seven Years in the Lives of British Families: Evidence on the Dynamics of Social Change from the British Household Panel Survey*, The Policy Press.

Berthoud, R. and Kempson, E. 1992, *Credit and Debt: The PSI Report*, Policy Studies Institute.

Berthoud, R., Lakey, J. and Mckay, S. 1993, *The Economic Problems of Disabled People*, PSI.

Beveridge, Sir W. 1942, *Report on Social Insurance and Allied Services*, Cmd 6404, HMSO.

Blackman, T. 1995, *Urban Policy in Practice*, Routledge.

Blair, T. 1999, 'Beveridge revisited: a welfare state for the 21st century', in R. Walker (ed.), *Ending Child Poverty: Popular Welfare for the 21st Century*, The Policy Press.

Boddy, M. and Fudge, C. (eds) 1984, *Local Socialism? Labour Councils and New Left Alternatives*, Macmillan.

Boheim, R. and Jenkins, S. 2000, *Do Current Income and Annual Income Provide Different Pictures of Britain's Income Distribution?*, Institute for Social and Economic Research, University of Essex.

Booth, C. (1889) *The Life and Labour of the People*, Williams & Northgate.

Booth, C. (1892) *Pauperism: a Picture of the Endowment of Old Age: an Argument*, Macmillan.

Booth, C. (1894) *The Aged Poor: Condition*, Macmillan.

Borrie, Sir G. 1994, *Social Justice: Strategies for National Renewal The Report of the Commission on Social Justice*, Vintage.

Bosanquet, N. and Townsend, P. 1980, *Labour and Equality*, Heinemann EB.

Bowley, A. L. and Burnett-Hurst, A. R. 1915, *Livelihood and Poverty*, G. Bell & Sons.

Boyson, R. 1971, *Down with the Poor*, Churchill.

Bradshaw, J. 1975, 'Welfare Rights: an experimental approach', in R. Lees and G. Smith (eds.), *Action Research in Community Development*, Routledge & Kegan Paul.

Bradshaw, J. (ed.) 1993a, *Budget Standards for the United Kingdom*, Avebury.

Bradshaw, J. (ed.) 1993b, *Household Budgets and Living Standards*, JR Foundation.

Bradshaw, J. 2001, 'Child Poverty under Labour', in G. Fimister (ed.), *An End in Sight? Tackling Child Poverty in the UK*, CPAG.

Bradshaw, J. *et al.* 2003, *Gender and Poverty in Britain*, Working Papers Series no. 6, Equal Opportunities Commission.

Bradshaw, J. and Holmes, H. 1989, *Living on the Edge: a Study of the Living Standards of Families on Benefit in Tyne and Wear*, Tyneside CPAG.

Bradshaw, J. and Lynes, T. 1995, *Benefit Uprating Policy and Living Standards* Social Policy Reports no. 1, Social Policy Research Unit, University of York.

Bradshaw, J., Mitchell, D. and Morgan, J. 1987, 'Evaluating Adequacy: the Potential of Budget Standards', *Journal of Social Policy*, vol. 16, no. 2.

Bradshaw, J. and Morgan, J. 1987, *Budgeting on Benefit: the Consumption of Families on Social Security*, Family Policy Studies Centre.

Brewer, M. 2004, *Will the Government Hit its Child Poverty Target in 2004/05?*, Briefing Note no. 47, Institute for Fiscal Studies.

Brewer, M., Goodman, A., Shaw, J. and Shephard, A. 2005, *Poverty and Inequality in Britain: 2005*, Commentary No.99, Institute for Fiscal Studies.

Brown, C. 1984, *Black and White Britain: the Third PSI Survey*, Heinemann EB.

Brown, M. and Madge, N. 1982, *Despite the Welfare State*, Heinemann EB.

Burchardt, T. 2000a, *Enduring Economic Exclusion: Disabled People, Income and Work*, Joseph Rowntree Foundation.

Burchardt, T. 2000b, 'The Dynamics of Being Disabled', *Journal of Social Policy*, vol. 29 no. 4.

Burchardt, T. 2003, *Being and Becoming: Social Exclusion and the Onset of Disability*, CASE Report no. 21, STICERD, LSE.

Burchardt, T., Le Grand, J. and Piachaud, D. 2002, 'Degrees of Exclusion: Developing a Dynamic Multidimensional Measure' in J. Hills, J. Le Grand, and Piachaud, D. (eds) *Understanding Social Exclusion*, Oxford UP.

Burgess, S. and Propper, C. 2002, 'The Dynamics of Poverty in Britain', in J. Hills, J. Le Grand and D. Piachaud (eds), *Understanding Social Exclusion*, Oxford UP.

Byrne, D. 1999, *Social Exclusion*, Open University Press.

Bytheway, B. and Johnson J. 1990, 'On Defining Ageism', *Critical Social Policy*, issue 29 (Autumn).

Cemlyn, S. and Clark, C. 2005, 'The social exclusion of Gypsy and Traveller children', in G. Preston (ed.), *At·Greatest Risk: The Children Most Likely to be Poor*, CPAG.

Census 2001, *Census 2001*, ONS.

Child Poverty Action Group (CPAG) 1984, *Poverty*, no. 57, CPAG.

Child Poverty Action Group (CPAG) 1985, *Burying Beveridge: a Detailed Response to the Green Paper – Reform of Social Security*, CPAG.

Clark, K. and Hopkins, J. 1968, *A Relevant War Against Poverty: A Study of Community Action Programmes and Observable Social Change*, Harper and Row.

Clarke, M. and Stewart, J. 1988, *The Enabling Council*, Local Government Training Board.

Coates, D. and Silburn, R. 1970, *Poverty: the Forgotten Englishmen*, Penguin.

Cochrane, A. 1993, *Whatever Happened to Local Government?*, Open University Press.

Cockett, N. 2003, 'Disability Living Allowance: What was the point?', *Benefits*, vol. 11, issue 3.

Cohen, R., Coxall, J., Craig, G. and Sadiq-Sangster, A. 1992, *Hardship Britain: Being Poor in the 1990s*, CPAG.

Cohen, R. and Rushton, A. 1982, *Welfare Rights*, Heinemann EB.

Cohen, R. and Tarpey, M. 1986, 'Are we up on take-up?', *Poverty*, no. 63.

Collard, S., Kempson, E. and Dominy, N. 2003, *Promoting Financial Inclusion: An Assessment of Initiatives Using a Community Select Committee Approach*, The Policy Press.

Collard, S., Kempson, E. and Whyley, C. 2001, *Tackling Financial Exclusion: An Area-based Approach*, The Policy Press.

Commission on Poverty, Participation and Power (CPPP) 2000, *Listen Hear: The Right to be Heard*, The Policy Press and UK Coalition Against Poverty.

Community Development Project (CDP) 1977, *Gilding the Ghetto: the State and the Poverty Experiments*, CDP.

Corkey, D. and Craig, G. 1978, 'CDP: Community Work or Class Politics?', in P. Curno (ed.), *Political Issues in Community Work*, Routledge & Kegan Paul.

Craig, P. and Greenslade, C. 1998, *First Findings from the Disability Follow-up to the Family Resources Survey*, DSS.

Crosland, C. A. R. 1956, *The Future of Socialism*, Jonathon Cape.

Dahrendorf, R. 1987, 'The erosion of citizenship and its consequences for us all', *New Statesman*, 12 June.

Dalley, G. (ed.) 1991, *Disability and Social Policy*, Policy Studies Institute.

Deacon, A. 1976, *In Search of the Scrounger: The Administration of Unemployment Insurance in Britain 1920–31*, G. Bell & Sons.

Deacon, A. 2002a, *Perspectives on Welfare*, Open University Press.

Deacon, A. 2002b, 'Echoes of Sir Keith? New Labour and the cycle of disadvantage', *Benefits*, vol. 10 issue 3.

Deacon, A. and Bradshaw, J. 1983, *Reserved for the Poor: the Means-test in British Social Policy*, Basil Blackwell and Martin Robertson.

Deakin, N. and Edwards, J. 1993, *The Enterprise Culture and the Inner City*, Routledge.

Dean, H. 1991, 'In Search of the Underclass', in P. Brown and R. Scase (eds), *Poor Work: Disadvantage and the Division of Labour*, Open University Press.

Dean, H. 2004, 'Losing appeal? The changing face of redress', *Benefits*, vol. 21 issue 1.

Dean, H. and Melrose, M. 1997, 'Manageable Discord: Fraud and resistance in the social security system', *Social Policy and Administration*, vol. 31 no. 2.

Dean, H. and Melrose, M. 1999, *Poverty, Riches and Social Citizenship*, Macmillan.

Denham, A. and Garnett, M. 2001, *Keith Joseph*, Acumen.

Dennehy, A., Smith, L. and Harker, P. 1997, *Not to be Ignored: Young People, Poverty and Health*, CPAG.

Dennett, J. *et al.* 1982, *Europe against Poverty: The European Poverty Programme 1975–1980*, Bedford Square Press.

Department for Work and Pensions (DWP) 2003, *Measuring Child Poverty*, DWP.

Department for Work and Pensions (DWP) 2004a, *Opportunity for All* Fifth Annual Report, DWP.

Department for Work and Pensions (DWP) 2004b, *Simplicity, Security and Choice: Informed Choices for Working and Saving*, DWP.

Department for Work and Pensions (DWP) 2004c, *Fraud and Error in Income Support and Jobseekers' Allowance from April 2003 to March 2004*, Information and Analysis Directorate, DWP.

Department for Work and Pensions (DWP) 2005a, *Households Below Average Income 1994/95–2003/04*, DWP.

Department for Work and Pensions (DWP) 2005b, *Take-up of Income Related Benefits: Summary of Key Results for 2003/03*, DWP.

Department for Work and Pensions (DWP) 2005c, *Delivery of Services to Ethnic Minority Clients*, HC268, The Stationery Office.

Department of Environment (DOE) 1994, *Index of Local Conditions*, DOE.

Department of Environment, Transport and the Regions (DETR) 1999, *Learning Lessons: Pathfinders' Experiences of NDC Phase 1*, New Deal for Communities Unit, DETR.

Department of Environment, Transport and the Regions (DETR) 2000a, *Indices of Deprivation 2000*, DETR.

Department of Environment, Transport and the Regions (DETR) 2000b, *Local Strategic Partnerships: Consultation Document*, DETR.

Department of Social Security (DSS) 1988, *Low Income Statistics: Report of a Technical Review*, HMSO.

Department of Social Security (DSS) 1995, *Households below Average Income: a Statistical Analysis 1979–1992/3*, HMSO.

Department of Social Security (DSS) 1998, *A New Contract for Welfare: Partnership in Pensions*, Stationery Office.

Desai, M. 1986, 'Drawing the Line: on defining the poverty threshold', in P. Golding (ed.), *Excluding the Poor*, CPAG.

De Tombeur, C. and Ladewig, N. 1994, *LIS Information Guide*, Luxembourg: LIS.

Dewilde, C. 2003, 'A Life-Course Perspective on Social Exclusion and Poverty', *British Journal of Sociology*, vol. 54 no.1.

Dex, S. 1985, *The Sexual Division of Work*, Wheatsheaf.

Dey, I. 1996, *The Poverty of Feminisation*, University of Edinburgh.

Dilnot, A., Kay, J. and Morris, C. 1984, *The Reform of Social Security*, Oxford UP.

Donnison, D. 1982, *The Politics of Poverty*, Martin Robertson.

Dorling, D. and Thomas, B. 2004, *People and Places: A 2001 Census Atlas of the UK*, The Policy Press.

Dornan, P. (ed.) 2004, *Ending Child Poverty by 2020: The First Five Years*, CPAG.

Dowler, E., Turner, S. and Dobson, B. 2001, *Poverty Bites: Food, Health and Poor Families*, CPAG.

Doyal, L. and Gough, I. 1991, *A Theory of Human Need*, Macmillan.

Edgell, S. and Duke, V. 1983, 'Gender and Social Policy: the impact of the public expenditure cuts and reactions to them', *Journal of Social Policy*, vol. 12, no. 3.

Ellwood, D. 1998, 'Dynamic Policy Making: an insider's account of reforming US welfare' in L. Leisering and R. Walker (eds) *The Dynamics of Modern Society. Poverty, Policy and Welfare*, The Policy Press.

Esam, P. and Berthoud, R. 1991, *Independent Benefits for Men and Women*, PSI.

Esping Andersen, G. 1990, *The Three Worlds of Welfare Capitalism*, Polity.

Esping Andersen, G. (ed.) 1996, *Welfare States in Transition: National Adaptations in Global Economies*, Sage.

Esping Andersen, G. 1999, *Social Foundations of Postindustrial Economies*, Oxford UP.

European Commission (EC) 1989, *Medium-term Community Action Programme to Foster the Economic and Social Integration of the Least Privileged Groups*, EC Commission Bulletin, Supplement 4/89.

European Commission (EC) 1990, *The Perception of Poverty in Europe in 1989*, EC.

European Commission (EC) 1991, *Final Report on the Second European Poverty Programme 1985–89*, EC.

European Commission (EC) 1994, *The Perception of Poverty and Social Exclusion in Europe 1994*, EC.

Eurostat 1990, *Poverty in Figures: Europe in the early 1980s*, EC.

Evans, M. and Eyre, J. 2004, *The Opportunities of a Lifetime: Model Lifetime Analysis of Current British Social Policy*, The Policy Press.

Evans, M., *et al.* 2002, *Growing Together or Growing Apart? Geographic Patterns of Change of Income Support and Income Based Jobseekers Allowance Claimants in England Between 1995 and 2000*, The Policy Press.

Evans, M., Piachaud, D and Sutherland, H. 1994, *Designed for the Poor Poorer by Design: The Effects of the 1986 Social Security Act on Family Incomes*, LSE/STICERD, WSP/105.

Evason, E. 1980, *Ends That Won't Meet*, CPAG.

Evason, E. and Spence, L. 2003, 'Women and Pensions: Time for a Rethink', *Social Policy and Administration*, vol. 37, no. 3.

Eyles, J. 1979, 'Area-based Policies for the Inner City: Context, Problems and Prospects', in D. Herbert and D. Smith (eds.) *Social Problems and the City: Geographical Perspectives*, Oxford UP.

Falkingham, J. 1989, 'Dependency and Ageing in Britain: a Re-examination of the Evidence', *Journal of Social Policy*, vol. 18, no. 2.

Falkingham, J. and Hills, J. (eds) 1995, *The Dynamic of Welfare: The Welfare State and the Life Cycle*, Harvester Wheatsheaf.

Ferge, Z. and Millar, S. M.(eds) 1987, *Dynamics of Deprivation*, Gower.

Fiegehen, G. C., Lansley, P. S. and Smith, A. D. 1977, *Poverty and Progress in Britain 1953–73*, Cambridge University Press.

Field, F. 1982, *Poverty and Politics: the Inside Story of the CPAG's Campaigns in the 1970s*, Heinemann EB.

Field, F. 1989, *Losing Out: the Emergence of Britain's Underclass*, Blackwell.

Field, F. 1995, *Making Welfare Work: Reconstructing Welfare for the Millennium*, Institute of Community Studies.

Field, F. and Piachaud, D. 1971, 'The Poverty Trap', *New Statesman*, 3 December.

Field, J. 2003, *Social Capital*, Routledge.

Fimister, G. 1986, *Welfare Rights Work in Social Services*, Macmillan.

Finch, J. and Groves, D. (eds) 1983, *A Labour of Love: Women, Work and Caring*, Routledge & Kegan Paul.

Finch, N. and Bradshaw, J. 2003, 'Core Poverty', *Journal of Social Policy* vol. 32, no. 4.

Finn, D. 2001, 'Welfare to Work? New Labour and the Unemployed', in S. Savage and R. Atkinson (eds), *Public Policy under Blair*, Palgrave.

Fisher Committee 1973, *Report of the Committee on Abuse of Social Security Benefits*, Cmnd 5228, HMSO.

Fitzpatrick, P. 2005, 'Asylum seeker families', in G. Preston (ed.), *At Greatest Risk: The Children Most Likely to be Poor*, CPAG.

Flaherty, J., Veit-Wilson, J. and Dornan, P. 2004, *Poverty: The Facts*, 5th edn., CPAG.

Floyd, M. 1991, 'Overcoming barriers to employment', in G. Dalley (ed.), *Disability and Social Policy*, PSI.

Ford, J. 1991, *Consuming Credit: Debt and Poverty in the UK*, CPAG.

Fraser, D. 2003, *The Evolution of the British Welfare State* 3rd edn., Palgrave.

Frayman, H. 1992, *Breadline Britain 1990s: the Findings of the Television Series*, London Weekend Television.

Gallie, D. 1988, 'Employment, Unemployment and Social Stratification', in D. Gallie (ed.), *Employment in Britain*, Basil Blackwell.

George, V. 1988, *Wealth, Poverty and Starvation: an International Perspective*, Harvester Wheatsheaf.

George, V. and Lawson, R. 1980, *Poverty and Inequality in Common Market Countries*, Routledge & Kegan Paul.

George, V. and Wilding, P. 1994, *Welfare and Ideology*, Harvester/Wheatsheaf.

Geyer, R. 2000, *Exploring European Social Policy*, Polity Press.

Giddens, A., 1991, *Modernity and Self-identity. Self and Society in the Late Modern Age*, Polity Press.

Gittins, D. 1993, *The Family in Question: Changing Households and Familiar Ideologies*, 2nd edn, Macmillan.

Glendinning, C. and Millar, J. (eds) 1987, *Women and Poverty in Britain*, Wheatsheaf.

Glendinning, C. and Millar, J. (eds) 1992, *Women and Poverty in Britain: the 1990s*, Harvester/Wheatsheaf.

Glennerster, H. 2000, *British Social Policy Since 1945*, 2nd edn., Blackwell.

Glennerster, H., Hills, J., Piachaud, D. and Webb, J. 2004, *One Hundred Years of Poverty and Policy*, Joseph Rowntree Foundation.

Golding, P. (ed.) 1986, *Excluding the Poor*, CPAG.

Golding, P. and Middleton, S. 1982, *Images of Welfare: Press and Public Attitudes to Welfare*, Basil Blackwell and Martin Robertson.

Goode, J., Callender, C. and Lister, R. 1998, *Purse or Wallet? Gender Inequalities and Income Distribution within Families on Benefits*, Policy Studies Institute.

Goodin, R. E., Headey, B., Muffels, R. and Dirven, H.-J. 1999, *The Real Worlds of Welfare Capitalism*, Cambridge UP.

Goodman, A. and Shephard, A. 2002, *Inequality and Living Standards in Great Britain: Some Facts*, Briefing Note No. 19, Institute for Fiscal Studies.

Gordon, D. 2002, 'The International Measurement of Poverty and Anti-Poverty Policies', in P. Townsend and D. Gordon (eds), *World Poverty: New policies to defet and old enemy*, The Policy Press.

Gordon, D. *et al.* 2000, *Poverty and Social Exclusion in Britain*, Joseph Rowntree Foundation.

Gordon, D. and Pantazis, C. (eds) 1997, *Breadline Britain in the 1990s*, Ashgate.

Gordon, D. and Spicker, P. (eds) 1999, *The International Glossary on Poverty*, Zed Books.

Gordon, D. and Townsend, P. (eds) 2000, *Breadline Europe: The Measurement of Poverty*, The Policy Press.

Gordon, P. and Newnham, A. 1985, *Passport to Benefits: Racism in Social Security*, CPAG/Runnymede Trust.

Graham, H. 1986, *Caring for the Family*, Research Report no. 1, Health Education Council.

Graham, H. 1987, 'Women's Poverty and Caring', in C. Glendinning and J. Millar (eds), *Women and Poverty in Britain*, Wheatsheaf.

Graham, H. 1992, 'Budgeting for Health: Mothers in Low Income Households', in C. Glendinning and J. Millar (eds), *Women and Poverty in Britain: the 1990s*, Harvester/Wheatsheaf.

Grant, L. 1995, *Disability and Debt: The Experience of Disabled People in Debt*, Sheffield Citizens Advice Bureau.

Green, D. G. 1990, *Equalizing People: Why Social Justice Threatens Liberty*, IEA.

Gregg, P., Harkness, S. and Machin, S. 1999, *Child Development and Family Income*, Joseph Rowntree Foundation.

Groves, D. 1988, 'Poverty, Disability and Social Services', in S. Becker and S. MacPherson (eds), *Public Issues and Private Pain: Poverty, Social Work and Social Policy*, Insight.

Hadjipateras, A. 1992, 'Reforming Social Security Provision for People with Disabilities: Ways to Move Beyond Mere Tinkering', *Benefits*, issue 3.

Halsey, A. H. (ed.) 1972, *Educational Priority: EPA Problems and Policies*, HMSO.

Hamnett, C. 1979, 'Area-based Explanations: A Critical Appraisal', in D. Herbert and D. Smith (eds), *Social Problems and the City: Geographical Perspectives*, Oxford UP.

Hantrais, L. 2000, *Social Policy in the European Union*, 2nd edn., Palgrave.

Harker, L. 2005, 'A 21st Century Welfare State', in N. Pearce and W. Paxton (eds), *Social Justice: Building a Fairer Britain*, Politicos/IPPR.

Harrington, M. 1962, *The Other America: Poverty in the United States*, Macmillan.

Harris, C. C. 1991, 'Recession, Redundancy and Age', in P. Brown and R. Scase (eds), *Poor Work: Disadvantage and the Division of Labour*, Open University Press.

Harris, J. 1977, *William Beveridge: a Biography*, Oxford UP.

Harrison, P. 1983, *Inside the Inner City*, Penguin.

Hayek, F. A. von 1944, *The Road to Serfdom*, Routledge & Kegan Paul.

Henwood, M., Rimmer, L. and Wicks, M. 1987, *Inside the Family: Changing Roles of Men and Women*, Family Policy Studies Centre.

Herbert, D. and Smith, D. (eds) 1979, *Social Problems and the City: Geographical Perspectives*, Oxford UP.

Higgins, J. 1978, *The Poverty Business: Britain and America*, Basil Blackwell and Martin Robertson.

Hill, M. 1990, *Social Security Policy in Britain*, Edward Elgar.

Hill, M. and Laing, P. 1979, *Social Work and Money*, George Allen & Unwin.

Hills, J. 1995, *JR Foundation Inquiry into Income and Wealth*, vol. 2, Joseph Rowntree Foundation.

Hills, J. (ed.) 1996, *New Inequalities: The Changing Distribution of Income and Wealth in the United Kingdom*, Cambridge UP.

Hills, J. 1998, *Income and Wealth: The Latest Evidence*, Joseph Rowntree Foundation.

Hills, J. 2002, 'Does a Focus on 'Social Exclusion' Change the Policy Response?', in J. Hills, J. Le Grand and D Piachaud (eds), *Understanding Social Exclusion*, Oxford UP.

Hills, J. 2004, *Inequality and the State*, Oxford UP.

Hills, J., Ditch, J. and Glennerster, H. (eds) 1994, *Beveridge and Social Security: An International Retrospective*, Clarendon Press.

Hills, J., Le Grand, J. and Piachaud, D. (eds), 2002, *Understanding Social Exclusion*, Oxford UP.

Hills, J. and Stewart, K. (eds) 2005, *A More Equal Society? New Labour, Poverty, Inequality and Exclusion*, The Policy Press.

Hindess, B. 1987, *Freedom, Equality and the Market: Arguments on Social Policy*, Tavistock.

Holman, R. 1978, *Poverty: Explanations of Social Deprivation*, Martin Robertson.

Howard, M. 2001, *Paying the Price: Carers, Poverty and Social Exclusion*, CPAG.

Huby, M., Bradshaw, J and Corden, A. 1999, *A Study of Town Life: Living Standards in the City of York 100 Years after Rowntree*, Joseph Rowntree Foundation.

Hudson, B., Hardy, B., Henwood, M. and Wistow, G. 1999, 'In Pursuit of Inter-Agency Collaboration in the Public Sector: What is The Contribution of Theory and Research?', *Public Management*, vol. 2, no. 3.

Humphries, R. 1995, *Sin, Organised Charity and the Poor Law in Victorian England*, Macmillan.

James, E. 1970, *America Against Poverty*, Routledge & Kegan Paul.

Jenkins, S. and Rigg, J. 2003, *Disability and Disadvantage: Selection, Onset and Duration Effects*, CASE paper 74, STICERD, LSE.

Jennings, J. 1994, *Understanding the Nature of Poverty in Urban America*, Connecticut: Praeger.

Johnson, P. and Webb, S. 1990, *Counting People with Low Incomes: The Impact of Recent Changes in Official Statistics*, Institute for Fiscal Studies.

Jones, C. and Novak, T. 1999, *Poverty, Welfare and the Disciplinary State*, Routledge.

Jordan, B. 1996, *A Theory of Poverty and Social Exclusion*, Polity Press.

Joseph, K. 1972, 'The Cycle of Deprivation', Speech to Pre-School Playgroups Association, 29 June.

Joseph, K. and Sumption, J. 1979, *Equality*, John Murray.

Joshi, H. 1988, *The Cash Opportunity Costs of Childbearing*, Centre for Economic Policy Research, Discussion Paper 208.

Joshi, H. 1992, 'The Cost of Caring', in C. Glendinning and J. Millar (eds), *Women and Poverty in Britain: the 1990s*, Harvester/Wheatsheaf.

Kemp, P., Bradshaw, J., Dornan, P., Finch, N. and Mayhew, E. 2004, *Routes Out of Poverty: A Research Review*, Joseph Rowntree Foudation.

Kempson, E. 1996, *Life on a Low Income*, JR Foundation.

Kempson, E., Bryson, A. and Rowlingson, K. 1994, *Hard Times? How Poor Families Make Ends Meet*, PSI.

Kempson, E. and Whyley, C. 1999, *Kept Out or Opted Out? Understanding and Combating Financial Exclusion*, The Policy Press.

Kiernan, K. 1991, 'Men and Women and Work at Home', in R. Jowell *et al.* (eds), *British Social Attitudes, the 8th Report, 1991/92*, SCPR, Dartmouth.

Kleinman, M. 2002, *A European Welfare State: European Union Social Policy in Context*, Palgrave.

Kuchler, B. and Goebel, J. 2003, 'Incidence and Intensity of Smoothed Income Poverty in European Countries', *Journal of European Social Policy*, vol. 13, no. 4.

Land, H. and Rose, H. 1985, 'Compulsory Altruism for All, or an Altruistic Society for Some?', in P. Bean, J. Ferris and D. Whynes (eds), *In Defence of Welfare*, Tavistock.

Langmore, J. 2000, 'Reducing Poverty: the implications of the 1995 Copenhagen Agreement for research on poverty', in D. Gordon and P. Townsend (eds), *Breadline Europe: The Measurement of Poverty*, The Policy Press.

Law, I. 1996, *Racism, Ethnicity and Social Policy*, Harvester Wheatsheaf.

Law, I. *et al.* 1994, 'The Effect of Ethnicity on Claiming Benefits: Evidence from Chinese and Bangladeshi Communities', *Benefits*, issue 9.

Lee, P. Murie, A. and Gordon, D. 1995, *Area Measures of Deprivation: A Study of Current Methods and Best Practices in the Identification of Poor Areas in Great Britain*, University of Birmingham.

Lees, R. and Smith, G. (eds) 1975, *Action Research in Community Development*, Routledge & Kegan Paul.

Leisering, L., and Leibfried, S. 1999, *Time and Poverty in Western Welfare States. United Germany in Perspective*, Cambridge UP.

Leisering, L. and Walker, R. (eds) 1998, *The Dynamics of Modern society. Poverty, Policy and Welfare*, The Policy Press.

Levitas, R. (ed.) 1986, *The Ideology of the New Right*, Polity.

Levitas, R. 1998, *The Inclusive Society?*, Macmillan.

Lewis, J. (ed.) 1993, *Women and Social Policies in Europe: Work, Family and the State*, Edward Elgar.

Lewis, J. and Piachaud, D. 1992, 'Women and Poverty in the Twentieth Century', in C. Glendinning and J. Millar (eds), *Women and Poverty in Britain: the 1990s*, Harvester/Wheatsheaf.

Lewis, O. 1965, *The Children of Sanchez*, Penguin.

Lewis, O. 1968, *La Vida*, Panther.

Lindqvist, M. 2000, 'Poverty in Finland and Europe', in D. Gordon and P. Townsend (eds), *Breadline Europe: The Measurement of Poverty*, The Policy Press.

Lister, R. 1990, 'Women, Economic Dependency and Citizenship', *Journal of Social Policy*, vol. 19, no. 4.

Lister, R. 1994, ' "She has other duties" – Women, Citizenship and Social Security', in S. Baldwin and J. Falkingham (eds), *Social Security and Social Change: New Challenges to the Beveridge Model*, Harvester/Wheatsheaf.

Lister, R. (ed.) 1996, *Charles Murray and the Underclass: The Developing Debate*, Institute of Economic Affairs.

Lister, R. 2003, *Citizenship: Feminist Perspectives*, 2nd edn, Palgrave.

Lister, R. 2004, *Poverty*, Polity.

Lister, R. and Beresford, P. 1991, *Working Together Against Poverty: Involving Poor People in Action Against Poverty*, Open Services Project/University of Bradford.

Loney, M. 1983, *Community Against Government: the British Community Development Project 1968–78*, Heinemann.

Lonsdale, S. 1992, 'Patterns of Paid Work', in C. Glendinning and J. Millar (eds), *Women and Poverty in Britain: the 1990s*, Harvester/Wheatsheaf.

Lupton, R. 2003, *Poverty Street: The Dynamics of Neighbourhood Decline and Renewal*, The Policy Press.

Lupton, R. and Power, A. 2004, *Minority Ethnic Groups in Britain* Case-Brookings Census Briefs no. 2, STICERD, LSE.

MacGregor, S. 1981, *The Politics of Poverty*, Longman.

Machin, S. and Waldfogel, J. 1994, *The Decline of the Male Breadwinner*, LSE/STICERD, WSP/103.

Mack, J. and Lansley, S. 1985, *Poor Britain*, George Allen & Unwin.

Macnicol, J. 1980, *The Movement for Family Allowances 1918–1945: A Study in Social Policy Development*, Heinemann.

Macnicol, J. 1987, 'In Pursuit of the Underclass', *Journal of Social Policy*, vol. 16, no. 3.

Macpherson, Sir W. 1999, *The Stephen Lawrence Inquiry: Report of the Inquiry by Sir William Macpherson of Cluny*, Stationery Office.

Mann, K. and Anstee, J. 1989, *Growing Fringes: Hypotheses in the Development of Occupational Welfare*, Armley.

Manning, N. and Tikhonova, N. (eds) 2004, *Poverty and Social Exclusion in the New Russia*, Ashgate.

Marris, P. and Rein, M. 1974, *Dilemmas of Social Reform*, Penguin.

Marshall, T. H. 1950, *Citizenship and Social Class*, Cambridge University Press.

Martin, J., Melzer, H. and Elliott, D. 1988, *OPCS Report 1, the Prevalence of Disability among Adults*, HMSO.

Martin, J. and White, A. 1988, *OPCS Report 2, the Financial Circumstances of Disabled Adults Living in Private Households*, HMSO.

Marx, K. 1952, *Wage Labour and Capital*, Progress.

Mawson, J. *et al.* 1995, *The Single Regeneration Budget: the Stocktake*, University of Birmingham.

McCarthy, M. 1986, *Campaigning for the Poor: CPAG and the Politics of Welfare*, Croom Helm.

McClelland, J. (ed.) 1982, *A Little Pride and Dignity: the Importance of Child Benefit*, CPAG.

McDonnell, K. 1982, 'Working in Housing Aid', *Critical Social Policy*, vol. 2, no. 1.

McGlone, F. 1992, *Disability and Dependency in Old Age: A Demographic and Social Audit*, Family Policy Studies Centre.

McKay, S. 2004, 'Poverty or Preference: What Do "Consensual Deprivation Indicators" Really Measure?', *Fiscal Studies*, vol. 25, no. 2.

McKay, S. and Rowlingson, K. 1999, *Social Security in Britain*, Macmillan.

Miller, C. 2004, *Producing Welfare: A Modern Agenda*, Palgrave.

Millar, J. 1989, 'Social Security, Equality and Women in the UK', *Policy and Politics*, vol. 17, no. 4.

Millar, J. 1992, 'Lone Mothers and Poverty', in C. Glendinning and J. Millar (eds), *Women and Poverty in Britain: the 1990s*, Harvester/Wheatsheaf.

Millar, J. 2000, *Keeping Track of Welfare Reform: The New Deal Programme*, Joseph Rowntree Foundation.

Millar, J. 2003, 'Gender, Poverty and Social Exclusion', *Social Policy and Society*, vol. 2, no. 3.

Millar, J. 2005, 'Simplification, Modernisation and Social Security', *Benefits* vol. 13, issue 1.

Millar, J. and Glendinning, C. 1989, 'Gender and Poverty', *Journal of Social Policy*, vol. 18, no. 3.

Mitchell, D. 1991, *Income Transfers in Ten Welfare States*, Avebury.

Modood, T., Berthoud, R. *et al.* 1997, *Ethnic Minorities in Britain: Diversity and Disadvantage*, Policy Studies Institute.

Moore, J. 1989, 'The End of the Line for Poverty', speech to Greater London Area CPC, 11 May.

Moore, R. and Wallace, T. 1975, *Slamming the Door*, Martin Robertson.

Morris, A. E. and Nott, S. M. 1991, *Working Women and the Law: Equality and Discrimination in Theory and Practice*, Routledge.

Morris, L. 1989, *The Workings of the Household*, Polity.

Morris, L. 1991, 'Women's Poor Work', in P. Brown and R. Scase (eds), *Poor Work: Disadvantage and the Division of Labour*, Open University Press.

Morris, L. 1994, *Dangerous Classes: The Underclass and Social Citizenship*, Routledge.

Morris, L. 1995, *Social Divisions: Economic Decline and Social Structural Change*, University College London Press.

Morris, L. and Irwin, S. 1992, 'Employment Histories and the Concept of the Underclass', *Sociology*, vol. 26, pp. 401–20.

Moynihan, D. P. 1965, *The Negro Family: the Case for National Action*, Office of Policy Planning and Research, US Department of Labor.

Muffels, R., Fourage, D. and Dekker, R. 1999, *Longitudinal Poverty and Income Inequality: A Comparative Panel study for the Netherlands, Germany and the UK*, EPAG Working Paper 1, University of Essex.

Mullard, M. and Spicker, P. 1998, *Social Policy in a Changing Society*, Routledge.

Mumford, K. and Power, A. 2003, *Eastenders: Family and Community in East London*, The Policy Press.

Murray, C. 1984, *Losing Ground: American Social Policy 1950–1980*, New York: Basic Books.

Murray, C. 1990, *The Emerging British Underclass*, IEA.

Murray, C. 1994, *Underclass: The Crisis Deepens*, IEA.

National Association of Citizens Advice Bureaux (NACAB) 1991, *Barriers to Benefit: Black Claimants and Social Security*, NACAB.

National Consumer Council (NCC) 1976, *Means-tested Benefits: a Discussion Paper*, NCC.

Noble, M., Cheung, S.Y. and Smith, G. 1998, 'Origins and Destinations – Social Security Claimant Dynamics', *Journal of Social Policy*, vol. 27, no. 3.

Novak, T. 1984, *Poverty and Social Security*, Pluto.

Novak, T. 1988, *Poverty and the State: an Historical Sociology*, Open University Press.

Novak, T. 1995, 'Rethinking Poverty', *Critical Social Policy*, issue 44/45, Autumn.

Office for National Statistics (ONS) 1999, *Tracking People: A Guide to Longitudinal Social Sources*, ONS.

Office for National Statistics (ONS) 2005a, *People and Migration*, ONS.

Office for National Statistics (ONS) 2005b, *UK Snapshot: Ethnicity and Identity*, ONS.

Office of the Deputy Prime Minister (ODPM) 2004, *The English Indices of Deprivation 2004 (revised)*, ODPM.

O'Higgins, M., Bradshaw, J. and Walker, R. 1988, 'Income Distribution over the Life Cycle', in R. Walker and G. Parker (eds), *Money Matters: Income, Wealth and Financial Welfare*, Sage.

Oldfield, N. and Yu, A. 1993, *The Cost of a Child: Living Standards for the 1990s*, CPAG.

Oliver, M. 1990, *The Politics of Disablement: a Sociological Approach*, Macmillan.

Oliver, M. 1991a, 'Speaking Out: disabled people and state welfare', in G. Dalley (ed.), *Disability and Social Policy*, PSI.

Oliver, M. 1991b, 'Disability and Participation in the Labour Market', in P. Brown and R. Scase (eds), *Poor Work: Disadvantage and the Division of Labour*, Open University Press.

Organisation for Economic Co-operation and Development (OECD) 2004, *Income Disparities in China: an OECD Perspective*, OECD Publishing.

Organisation for Economic Co-operation and Development (OECD) 2005, *Society at a Glance: OECD Social Indicators, 2005 Edition*, OECD.

Orshansky, M. 1965, 'Counting the Poor: Another Look at the Poverty Profile', *Social Security Bulletin*, vol. 28.

Orshansky, M. 1969, 'How Poverty is Measured', *Monthly Labour Review*, vol. 92.

Pahl, J. 1989, *Money and Marriage*, Macmillan.

Pahl, J. 1999, *Invisible Money: Families Finances in the Electronic Economy*, The Policy Press)

Palmer, G., Carr, J. and Kenway, P. 2004, *Monitoring Poverty and Social Exclusion in Scotland 2004*, Joseph Rowntree Foundation.

Palmer, G., North, J., Carr, J. and Kenway, P. 2003, *Monitoring Poverty and Social Exclusion 2003*, Joseph Rowntree Foundation.

Parker, G. 1988, 'Indebtedness', in R. Walker and G. Parker (eds), *Money Matters: Income, Wealth and Financial Welfare*, Sage.

Patterson, T. and Vaux, G. 2005, 'It's a snip: simplification or the shedding of administrative responsibility?', *Benefits* vol. 13, issue 1.

Paugam, S. 1991, *La disqualification Sociale: Essai sur la Nouvelle Pauvreté*, Presses Universitaires de France, coll. 'sociologies'.

Paxton, W. and Dixon, M. 2004, *The State of the Nation: An Audit of Injustice in the UK* Institute for Public Policy Research.

Pen, J. 1971, 'A Parade of Dwarfs (and a Few Giants)', in T. S. Preston (ed.), *Income Distribution*, Penguin.

Phillipson, C. 1993, 'Older Workers and Retirement: A Review of Current Trends', *Benefits*, issue 8.

Philo, C. (ed.) 1995, *Off the Map: The Social Geography of Poverty in the UK*, CPAG.

Piachaud, D. 1979, *The Cost of a Child*, CPAG.

Piachaud, D. 1981a, 'Peter Townsend and the Holy Grail', *New Society*, 10 September.

Piachaud, D. 1981b, *Children and Poverty*, CPAG.

Piachaud, D. 1982a, 'Patterns of Income and Expenditure within Families', *Journal of Social Policy*, vol. 11, no. 4.

Piachaud, D. 1982b, *Family Incomes since the War*, Study Commission on the Family.

Piachaud, D. 1984, *Round about 50 Hours a Week: the Time Costs of Children*, CPAG.

Piachaud, D. 1987, 'Problems in the Definition and Measurement of Poverty', *Journal of Social Policy*, vol. 16, no. 2.

Piachaud, D. 1988, 'Poverty in Britain 1899 to 1983', *Journal of Social Policy*, vol. 17, no. 3.

Piachaud, D. and Sutherland, H. 2002, 'Child Poverty', in J. Hills, J. Le Grand and D. Piachaud (eds), *Understanding Social Exclusion*, Oxford UP.

Piachaud, D. and Webb, J. 2004, 'Changes in Poverty', in Glennerster, H., Hills, J., Piachaud, D and Webb, J., *One Hundred Years of Poverty and Policy*, Joseph Rowntree Foundation.

Pilkington, A. 2003, *Racial Disadvantage and Ethnic Diversity in Britain*, Palgrave.

Pillinger, J. 1992, *Feminising the Market: Women's Pay and Employment in the EC*, Macmillan.

Piven, F. and Cloward, R. 1972, *Regulating the Poor: the Functions of Public Welfare*, Tavistock.

Platt, L. 2002, *Parallel Lives? Poverty Among Ethnic Minority Groups in Britain*, CPAG.

Platt, L. 2005, *Discovering Child Poverty: The Creation of a Policy Agenda from 1800 to the Present*, The Policy Press.

Powell, M. (ed.) 1999, *New Labour, New Welfare State? The 'Third Way' in British Social Policy*, The Policy Press.

Powell, M. (ed.) 2002, *Evaluating New Labour's Welfare Reforms*, The Policy Press.

Powell, M., Boyne, R. and Ashworth, R. 2001, 'Towards a Geography of People Poverty and Place Poverty', *Policy and Politics*, vol. 29, no. 3.

Preston, G. (ed.) 2005, *At Greatest Risk: The Children Most Likely to be Poor*, CPAG.

Putnam, R. 1993, *Making Democracy Work: Civic Traditions in Modern Italy*, Princeton University Press.

Putnam, R. 2000, *Bowling Alone: The Collapse and Revival of American Community*, Simon and Schuster.

Rainwater, L. and Yancy, W. 1967, *The Moynihan Report and the Politics of Controversy*, Massachusetts Institute of Technology Press.

Regional Co-Ordination Unit (RCU) 2002, *Review of Area-Based Initiatives: Action Plans*, ODPM.

Rex, J. 1973, *Race, Colonialism and the City*, Routledge & Kegan Paul.

Rex, J. 1979, 'Black Militancy and Class Conflict', in R. Miles and A. Phizaklea (eds), *Racism and Political Action in Britain*, Routledge & Kegan Paul.

Ridge, T. 2002, *Childhood Poverty and Social Exclusion: From a Child's Perspective*, The Policy Press.

Ringen, S. 1988, 'Direct and Indirect Measures of Poverty', *Journal of Social Policy*, vol. 17, no. 3.

Robbins, D. *et al.* 1994, *Observatory on National Policies to Combat Social Exclusion*, Third Annual Report, EC.

Roll, J. 1989, 'Social and Economic Change and Women's Poverty', in H. Graham and J. Popay (eds), *Women and Poverty: Exploring the Research and Policy Agenda*, Thomas Coram Research Unit/University of Warwick.

Room, G. (ed.) 1995, *Beyond the Threshold: The Measurement and Analysis of Social Exclusion*, Policy Press.

Room, G. *et al.* 1990, '*New Poverty', in the European Community*, Macmillan.

Room, G. *et al.* (eds) 1991, *National Policies to Combat Social Exclusion*: First Annual Report of the European Community Observatory, CRESEP, University of Bath.

Room, G. *et al.* 1993, *Anti-Poverty Action Research in Europe*, School of Advanced Urban Studies, University of Bristol.

Room, G., Lawson, R. and Laczko, F. 1989, ' "New Poverty" in the European Community', *Policy and Politics*, vol. 17, no. 2.

Rowlingson, K. and McKay, S. 2002, *Lone Parent Families: Gender, Class and State*, Prentice Hall.

Rowntree, B. S. 1901, *Poverty: a Study of Town Life*, Macmillan.

Rowntree, B. S. 2000, *Poverty: a Study of Town Life: Centennial Edition*, The Policy Press.

Rowntree, B. S. 1941, *Poverty and Progress: a Second Social Survey of York*, Longman.

Rowntree, B. S.and Lavers, G. 1951, *Poverty and the Welfare State*, Longman.

Royal Commission 1980, *An A to Z of Income and Wealth, Royal Commission on the Distribution of Income and Wealth*, HMSO.

Runciman, W. G. 1966, *Relative Deprivation and Social Justice: A Study of Attitudes to Social Inequality in Twentieth-Century England*, Penguin.

Runciman, W. G. 1990, 'How Many Classes are there in British Society?', *Sociology*, vol. 24, pp. 378–96.

Rutter, M. and Madge, N. 1976, *Cycles of Disadvantage*, Heinemann.

Ryan, W. 1971, *Blaming the Victim*, Orbach and Chambers.

Sainsbury, R. 1998, 'Putting Fraud into Perspective' *Benefits*, issue 21.

Saunders, P., Bradshaw, J. and Hirst, M. 2002, 'Using Household Expenditure to Develop an Income Poverty Line', *Social Policy and Administration*, vol. 36, no. 3.

Scharf, T., Phillipson, C., Smith, A. with Kingston, P. 2002, *Older People in Socially Deprived Areas*, Help the Aged.

Seabrook, J. 1984, *Landscapes of Poverty*, Blackwell.

Sen, A. 1983, 'Poor, Relatively Speaking', *Oxford Economic Papers*, vol. 35, no. 1.

Shaw, M., Dorling, D., Gordon, D. and Davey-Smith, G. 1999, *The Widening Gap: Health Inequalities and Policy in Britain*, The Policy Press.

Shucksmith, M. 2000, *Exclusive Countryside? Social Inclusion and Regeneration in Rural Areas*, Joseph Rowntree Foundation.

Sigle-Rushton, W. 2004, *Intergenerational and Life Course Transmission of Social Exclusion in the 1970 British Cohort Study*, CASEpaper 78, STICERD, LSE.

Simpson, R. and Walker, R. 1993, *Europe for Richer for Poorer?*, CPAG.

Skellington, R. and Morris, P. 1992, *'Race' in Britain Today*, Sage.

Smeeding, T., O'Higgins, M. and Rainwater, L. (eds) 1990, *Poverty, Inequality and Income Distribution in Comparative Perspective: the Luxembourg Income Study (LIS)*, Harvester/Wheatsheaf.

Smith, A. (1776) *An Inquiry into the Nature and Causes of the Wealth of Nations*, 1892 edn (Routledge.

Smith, D. (ed.) 1992, *Understanding the Underclass*, PSI.

Smith, D. 2005, *On the Margins of Inclusion: Changing labour Markets and Social Exclusion in London*, The Policy Press.

Smith, N. *et al.* 2004, *Disabled People's Costs of Living: 'More than you would think'*, Joseph Rowntree Foundation.

Smith, R. 1985, 'Who's Fiddling? Fraud and Abuse', in S. Ward (ed.), *DHSS in Crisis: Social Security Under Pressure and Under Review*, CPAG.

Smith, T. and Noble, M. 1995, *Education Divides: Poverty and Schooling in the 1990s*, CPAG.

Social Exclusion Unit (SEU) 1998, *Bringing Britain Together: A National Strategy for Neighbourhood Renewal*, Stationery Office.

Social Exclusion Unit (SEU) 2000, *National Strategy for Neighbourhood Renewal: a Framework for Consultation*, Stationery Office.

Social Exclusion Unit (SEU) 2001, *A New Commitment to Neighbourhood Renewal: National Strategy Action Plan*, Stationery Office.

Social Exclusion Unit (SEU) 2004, *Breaking the Cycle: Taking Stock of Progress and Priorities for the Future*, ODPM.

Social Trends 31 2005, *Social Trends 31*, ONS.

Solomos, J. 2003, *Race and Racism in Britain*, 3rd edn, Palgrave.

Spicker, P. 1990, 'Charles Booth: The Examination of Poverty', *Social Policy and Administration*, vol. 24, no. 1.

Spicker, P. 1993, *Poverty and Social Security*, Routledge.

Spicker, P. 2004, 'Developing Indicators: Issues in the Use of Quantitative Data about Poverty', *Policy and Politics* vol. 32, no. 4.

Spicker, P. 2005, 'Five Types of Complexity', *Benefits*, vol. 13, issue 1.

Squires, P. 1990, *Anti-Social Policy: Welfare, Ideology and the Disciplinary State*, Harvester/Wheatsheaf.

Stedman Jones, G. 1971, *Outcast London*, Oxford University Press.

Stephens, M. 1990, *Community Law Centres: a Critical Appraisal*, Avebury.

Stitt, S. and Grant, D. 1993, *Poverty: Rowntree Revisited*, Avebury.

Stoker, G. 1991, *The Politics of Local Government* 2nd edn, Macmillan.

Such, E. and Walker, R. 2002, 'Falling Behind? Research on Transmitted Deprivation', *Benefits*, vol. 10, issue 3.

Sullivan, H. and Skelcher, C. 2002, *Working across Boundaries: Collaboration in Public Services*, Palgrave.

Sutherland, H., Sefton, T. and Piachaud, D. 2003, *Poverty in Britain: The Impact of Government Policy Since 1997*, Joseph Rowntree Foundation.

Swann Report 1985, *Education for All: the Report of the Committee of Enquiry into the Education of Children from Ethnic Minority Groups*, Cmnd 9453, HMSO.

Tawney, R. H. 1913, 'Inaugural Lecture "Poverty as an Industrial Problem"', reproduced in *Memoranda on the Problems of Poverty*, vol. 2, William Morris Press.

Tawney, R. H. 1931, *Equality*, Allen and Unwin.

Thane, P. 1996, *The Foundations of the Welfare State*, 4th edn, Longman.

Titmuss, R. M. 1958, 'The Social Division of Welfare', in R. M. Titmuss, *Essays on the Welfare State*, Allen & Unwin.

Tomlinson, A. 1986, 'Playing Away from Home: Leisure, Disadvantage and Issues of Income and Access', in P. Golding (ed.), *Excluding the Poor*, CPAG.

Topliss, E. 1979, *Provision for the Disabled*, 2nd edn, Blackwell Scientific with Martin Robertson.

Toporowski, J. 1986, 'Beyond banking: financial institutions and the poor', in P. Golding (ed.), *Excluding the Poor*, CPAG.

Townsend, P. 1954, 'The Meaning of Poverty', *British Journal of Sociology*, June.

Townsend, P. 1979, *Poverty in the United Kingdom: a Survey of Household Resources and Standards of Living*, Penguin.

Townsend, P. 1987, 'Deprivation', *Journal of Social Policy*, vol. 16, no. 2.

Townsend, P. 1993, *The International Analysis of Poverty*, Harvester/Wheatsheaf.

Townsend, P. 1995, *The Rise of International Social Policy*, Policy Press.

Townsend, P. and Bosanquet, N. 1972, *Labour and Inequality*, Fabian Society.

Townsend, P., Corrigan, P. and Kowarzik, U. 1987, *Poverty and Labour in London: Interim Report of a Centenary Survey*, Low Pay Unit.

Townsend, P. and Davidson, N. and Whitehead, M. (eds) 1988, *Inequalities in Health: the Black Report and the Health Divide*, Penguin.

Townsend, P. and Gordon, D. (eds) 2002, *World Poverty: New Policies to Defeat an Old Enemy*, The Policy Press.

Toynbee, P. 2003, *Hard Work:Life in Low-pay Britain*, Bloomsbury.

UNICEF (United Nations Children's Fund) 2005, *Child Poverty in Rich Countries*, United Nations Department of Publications.

United Nations 1995, *The Copenhagen Declaration and Programme of Action: World Summit for Social Development 6–12 March 1995*, United Nations Department of Publications.

Van Oorschot, W. 1995, *Realizing Rights: A Multi-Level Approach to Non-Take-Up of Means-Tested Benefits*, Avebury.

Van Oorschot, W. (ed.) 1996, *New Perspectives on the Non-take-up of Social Security Benefits*, Tilburg University Press.

Van Parijs, P. (ed.) 1992, *Arguing for Basic Income: Ethical Foundations for a Radical Reform*, Verso.

Van Praag, B., Hagenaars, A. and Van Weeren, H. 1982, 'Poverty in Europe', *Review of Income and Wealth*, vol. 28.

Veit-Wilson, J. 1986, 'Paradigms of Poverty: a Rehabilitation of B. S. Rowntree', *Journal of Social Policy*, vol. 15, no. 1.

Veit-Wilson, J. 1987, 'Consensual Approaches to Poverty Lines and Social Security', *Journal of Social Policy*, vol. 16, no. 2.

Veit-Wilson, J. 1998, *Setting Adequacy Standards: How Governments Define Minimum Incomes*, The Policy Press.

Vincent, D. 1991, *Poor Citizens: the State and the Poor in Twentieth Century Britain*, Longman.

Vogler, C. 1994, 'Money in the Household', in M. Anderson, E. Bechhofer and J. Gershuny (eds), *The Social and Political Economy of the Household*, Oxford University Press.

Walker, A. 1980, 'The Social Creation of Poverty and Dependency in Old Age', *Journal of Social Policy*, vol. 9, no. 1.

Walker, A. 1986, 'Pensions and the Production of Poverty in Old Age', in A. Walker and C. Phillipson (eds), *Ageing and Social Policy: a Critical Assessment*, Gower.

Walker, A. 1993, 'Poverty and Inequality in Old Age', in J. Bond, P. Coleman and S. Peace (eds), *Ageing in Society: an Introduction to Social Gerontology*, 2nd edn, Sage.

Walker, A. and Phillipson, C. (eds) 1986, *Ageing and Social Policy: a Critical Assessment*, Gower.

Walker, R. (ed.), 1999, *Ending Child Poverty: Popular Welfare for the 21st Century*, The Policy Press.

Walker, R. 2005, *Social Security and Welfare: Concepts and Comparisons*, Open University Press.

Walker, R., Lawson, R. and Townsend, P. (eds) 1984, *Responses to Poverty: Lessons from Europe*, Heinemann EB.

Walker, R. and Leisering, L. 1998, 'New Tools: towards a dynamic science of modern society', in L. Leisering and R. Walker (eds), *The Dynamics of Modern Society. Poverty, Policy and Welfare*, The Policy Press.

Walker, R. and Parker, G. (eds) 1988, *Money Matters: Income, Wealth and Financial Welfare*, Sage.

Ward, S. 1986, 'Power, Politics and Poverty', in P. Golding (ed.), *Excluding the Poor*, CPAG.

Wasoff, F. 2003, 'Data Sources in the UK: National, Central and Local Government', in P. Alcock, A. Erskine and M. May (eds), *The Student's Companion to Social Policy* 2nd edn., Blackwell.

Webb, J. 2002, 'Always with us? The Evolution of Poverty in Britain, 1886–2002', D.Phil. thesis, University of Oxford.

Welshman, J. 2002, 'The Cycle of Deprivation and the Concept of the Underclass' *Benefits*, vol. 10, issues 3.

Whelan, C., Layte, R. and Maitre, B. 2002, 'Multiple Deprivation and Persistent Poverty in the European Union', *Journal of European Social Policy*, vol. 12, no. 2.

Whelan, C., Layte, R. and Maitre, B. 2003, 'Persistent Income Poverty and Deprivation in the European Union: An Analysis of the First Three Waves of the European Community Household Panel', *Journal of Social Policy*, vol. 32, no. 1.

Whiteley, P. and Winyard, S. 1983, 'Influencing Social Policy: the Effectiveness of the Poverty Lobby in Britain', *Journal of Social Policy*, vol. 12, no. 1.

Williams, S. 1986, 'Exclusion: The Hidden Face of Poverty', in P. Golding (ed.), *Excluding the Poor*, CPAG.

Wilson, R. 1994, 'Sectoral and Occupational Change: Prospects for Women's Employment', in R. Lindley (ed.), *Labour Market Structures and Prospects for Women*, Equal Opportunities Commission.

Wilson, W. J. 1987, *The Truly Disadvantaged: The Inner City, the Underclass and Public Policy*, University of Chicago Press.

Zaidi, A. and Burchardt, T. 2003, *Comparing Incomes when Needs Differ: Equivalisation for the Extra Costs of Disability in the UK*, CASE paper 64, STICERD, LSE.

Name Index

Subject Index

WITHDRAWN

179057